Comprehensive Catalog and Encyclopedia of Morgan and Peace Dollars

PART II: MORGAN SILVER DOLLARS

By

Leroy C. Van Allen

A. George Mallis

(With research and contributions in Chapter Five by Pete R. Bishal)

REVISED EDITION OF
*Comprehensive Catlaogue and Encyclopedia of
U.S. Morgan and Peace Silver Dollars*

Containing

POPULARITY OF COLLECTING & INVESTING
BACKGROUND OF SILVER DOLLAR COINAGE
CONDITION AVAILABILITY
DETAILS OF MINTING PROCESSES
HISTORICAL LETTERS o 2100+ ILLUSTRATIONS
DESCRIPTIONS OF 1800 ERRORS/VARIETIES
GSA SALE OF CARSON CITY DOLLARS
SILVER DOLLAR HOARDS
DETECTING COUNTERFEITS
PRESERVATION & STORAGE
GRADING

Published by

Rare Coin Investments (RCI)
P.O. Box C
Ironia, NJ 07845

Copyright © 2021 by Michael S. Fey, Ph.D.

Authors: Leroy C. Van Allen and A. George Mallis

All rights reserved. No part of this book may be reproduced, by and any means, without written permission, except by a reviewer who wishes to quote brief excerpts in connection with a review or newspaper and acknowledges this publication as a source.

Library of Congress Catalog Number: 2023904390

ISBN 978-0-9653645-4-6

Printed in the United States

THE HISTORY OF THE VAM BOOK

VAM book refers to the joint authorship book by Leroy Catlin Van Allen and A. George Mallis with a rather long title of *Comprehensive Catalog and Encyclopedia of Morgan and Peace Dollars*. The book had its genesis as independent efforts and books by both authors in the late 1950's and early 1960's. The following story briefly traces the development of these initial independent books and the later joint efforts to produce the various editions of the VAM book.

EARLY INDEPENDENT EFFORTS

In the mid-1950's, Mallis' collecting interests turned to Morgan dollars, since they were relatively inexpensive to collect and were in need of being catalogued. Beginning late 1958 as CEO of an architect firm, he made weekly trips to a job site at Bailey's Cross Roads in Alexandria, VA. Before returning home in Massachusetts, he would purchase a thousand dollar bag of silver dollars from the Treasury Department sales counter in Washington DC. Each bag was subsequently checked and recorded for dates, mint marks, and varieties. When the Treasury Department stopped issuing silver dollars in 1964, Mallis had examined some THIRTY-FIVE THOUSAND of them. When the Treasury released the scarce New Orleans Morgan dollars late in 1962, Van Allen became interested in them. From early 1963 through 1964, he examined some ten-thousand silver dollars from the Treasury Department in Washington, DC and the Baltimore Federal Reserve.

Mallis began preparing a pamphlet in 1962 of his recordings on the silver dollars he had examined. In mid-1963, Francis Kleas published a pamphlet entitled *Die Varieties of Morgan Silver Dollars*. This was a real eye opener with large clear photos of some major varieties. It was Klaes' pamphlet that started Van Allen writing an independent manuscript on Morgan varieties in late 1963. He thought Klaes' listings and photographs could be expanded with additional varieties.

Van Allen's first manuscript was sent to Neil Shafer of Whitman Publishing early in 1964. Shafer advised him that it was NOT READY for publication and that he needed to consult the mint records to explain the WHY of the varieties (as he had in several articles). Van Allen then spent a good deal of the spring of 1964 at the National Archives and Library of Congress in Washington, DC gathering material and studying additional coins.

In the spring of 1964, Mallis approached Klaes about collaborating on a revised list of Morgan dollar die varieties, but this partnership never developed. Mallis then continued his research alone. In October 1964, this effort was completed with his distribution of 50 free copies of a pamphlet entitled *List of Die Varieties of Morgan*

Head Silver Dollars. The pamphlets were distributed to interested numismatists and libraries.

By September 1964, Van Allen sent a completely revised manuscript of the Morgan dollar series varieties to Charles "Shotgun" Slade III (a prominent silver dollar dealer who owned a printing shop). Slade thought the manuscript was of interest but that a SHORTER pamphlet would be more suitable for him to publish. In October 1964, Van Allen submitted a new manuscript on the 1878 Morgan varieties to Slade. He then suggested a DIE CLASSIFICATION SYSTEM was needed and that Sheldon's *Penny Whimsy* should be studied. Taking his suggestion, Van Allen rewrote the 1878 dollar manuscript and resubmitted it to him late in November 1964. This book was not printed as scheduled in February 1965 and the manuscript was again revised and forwarded to Slade in March 1965.

After some negotiations in early 1965, Walter Breen agreed to act as consulting or collaborating author with Mallis on a new book, *United States Silver Dollars, Morgan Type*. Unfortunately, Breen suffered a lengthy illness and was unable to assist in the manuscript preparation. Mallis pressed on alone and copyrighted the complete manuscript in June 1965. He worked with Whitman Publishing in 1965 to prepare the book for publication, but the project was abandoned early in 1966 because of the efforts with Van Allen. Only THREE copies of this manuscript exist - one in the Library of Congress, one with Mallis and one with Van Allen (extensively marked up as a basis for the later collaboration effort).

At this point, Van Allen decided to publish his own book entitled *Morgan and Peace Dollar Varieties*. His wife, Ruth, typed the camera ready copy and 5,000 softbound and 100 hardbound copies were printed by December 1965. Izzy Fishman of Ace Coin Exchange in Baltimore, Maryland distributed the books which were sold out within about a year at a retail price of $2.50.

VAN ALLEN AND MALLIS JOINT EFFORTS

In January 1966, Mallis suggested to Van Allen that their two works and Shafer's efforts should be combined into ONE reference work. Mallis and Van Allen first met at Mallis' home in Massachusetts in April 1966 to discuss a joint book venture. Jim Johnson of Coin World's Collectors' Clearinghouse was very much in favor of such a project and endorsed it several times in Coin World in 1965. Walter Breen had also recommended the collaboration in his November 1964 column in Coin world.

In June 1966, Whitman Publishing was contacted concerning the publication of their joint book on silver dollar varieties. Whitman Publishing would not accept the project since it was not one hundred percent ready with each variety of silver dollar verified. The manuscript was completely ready in mid 1986. Then began a long string of publisher rejection notices! Twelve publishers declined offers to print the book.

Meanwhile, new varieties of silver dollars were pointed out to the authors by various coin collectors. This kept increasing the size of the manuscript.

In February 1971, the authors decided to finance the publication of the book and Van Allen's wife, Ruth, again typed the final text. Van Allen pasted the camera ready copy. By December 1971, 2,610 softbound and 205 hardbound copies were received from the printer with the title of *Guide to Morgan and Peace Dollars*. Frank and Louise Katen of Katen Coins in Silver Springs Maryland distributed the book. These books were sold in about a year and a half. By 1975, the book had become hard to find and the going price for a copy was two to three times its original price.

Collectors continued to point out new varieties to the authors. By mid 1975, enough new material had accumulated that it was time to revise the VAM book as it had become known. A publishing agreement was made with First Coinnvestors of Long Island, New York and Arco Publishing delivered 5,500 hardbound books in October 1976 followed by 2,800 hardbound and 50 leather bound books were delivered in December 1976. Minor changes were incorporated in the second printing of 4,500 hardbound books delivered in March 1977. The retail price of the initial printing of the book was $19.95 and the title was *Comprehensive Catalogue and Encyclopedia of U.S. Morgan and Peace Silver Dollars*. This second edition had four printings with the last one in 1981. There were more than 20,000 hardbound copies printed. In 1977, it received the Book of the Year award from the Numismatic Literary Guild.

A great many new varieties were reported by collectors after the 1976 book release and new material on silver dollars accumulated during the coin market boom of the late 1970's and early 1980's. The authors intended to publish a revised edition of the VAM book in the mid 1980's and the manuscript was ready by early 1986. Meanwhile, Arco Publishing had been sold and was no longer interested in publishing the book and First Coinvestors had moved and lost most of the negatives. The book had to be typeset again and Van Allen had to reprint the majority of the book photos from his old film negatives.

From 1986 through 1991, the authors were unable to find a publisher for the VAM book. In 1991, DLRC Press of Virginia Beach, Virginia agreed to republish the book. Further additions and revisions were made and the third edition was released in September 1992 at $49.95 retail with 4,400 softbound and 600 hardbound copies printed. The VAM book again received the Book of the Year award from the Numismatic Literary Guild in 1993, and had the title of *Comprehensive Catalog and Encyclopedia of Morgan and Peace Dollars*.

Leroy Van Allen

Glossary of Abbreviations

MINT MARKS:

P	Philadelphia
O	New Orleans
S	San Francisco
CC	Carson City
D	Denver

OTHERS:

Obv.	Obverse
Rev.	Reverse
TF	Tail Feathers
PAF	Parallel Arrow Feathers
SAF	Slanted Arrow Feathers
I...IV	Type of Mint Mark or Obverse Design
A...D	Type of Reverse Design
O/O	O Repunched Over O
O/S	O Repunched Over S
O/CC	O Repunched Over CC
II/I Obv.	Second Design Obverse Over First Design Obverse
7/8TF	Seven Over Eight Tail Feathers
BU	Brilliant Uncirculated

RARITY SCALE:

R-1	Common (Tens of Millions)
R-2	Not so Common (Several Millions)
R-3	Scarce (Hundreds of Thousands)
R-4	Very Scarce (Tens of Thousands)
R-5	Rare (Several Thousands)
R-6	Very Rare (Several Hundred)
R-7	Extremely Rare (Few Tens)
R-8	Unique or Nearly Unique (Several)

INTEREST FACTOR:

I-1 Normal die variety with little interest to variety collectors.
I-2 Minor die variety with some interest to variety collectors.
I-3 Significant die variety with general interest to variety collectors.
I-4 Major die variety with universal interest to variety collectors.
I-5 Outstanding die variety with prime interest to variety collectors.

AMPLIFYING DESCRIPTIONS:

I-1 Normal die variety with no unusual die states. Can have hairline die cracks, small die chips, or minor clash marks which are normal as die wears or portions of the design may be weak due to polishing of the die.

I-2 Minor variations from normal die such as slight shifts in date or mint mark placement and orientation; micro doubling of date or mint mark; and slight abnormalities in die state such as fairly large die cracks or die chips (i.e., spiked dates). Such die variations may not be of interest to all collectors but they are identifiable using a medium power magnifying glass.

I-3 Significant variations from normal die such as changes in mint mark or date digit sizes; small die design changes; large shifts in date or mint mark placement and orientation; major doubling of date or mint mark; slight doubling of die design; small modifications of individual dies (touch ups, polishing, and weak overdates and over mint marks), and large abnormalities in die state such as big die cracks or gouges. These die variations are of general interest to many variety collectors and are usually noticeable with a low power magnifying glass.

I-4 Major variations from normal die such as large die design changes; unusually large doubling of date or mint mark; large doubled die design; and strong individual die modifications of date or mint mark (i.e., over dates and over mint marks). Most of these die variations are visible to the naked eye and are of universal interest to variety collectors.

I-5 An outstanding major die variation representing the best example of its type.

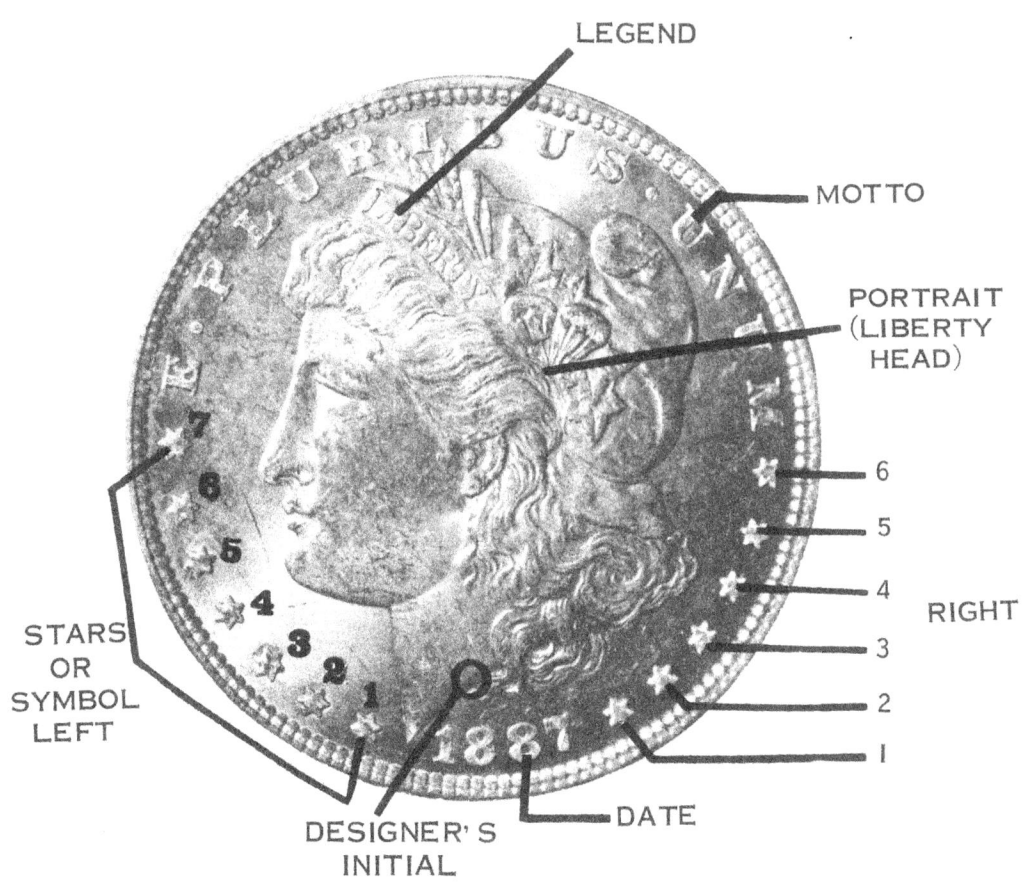
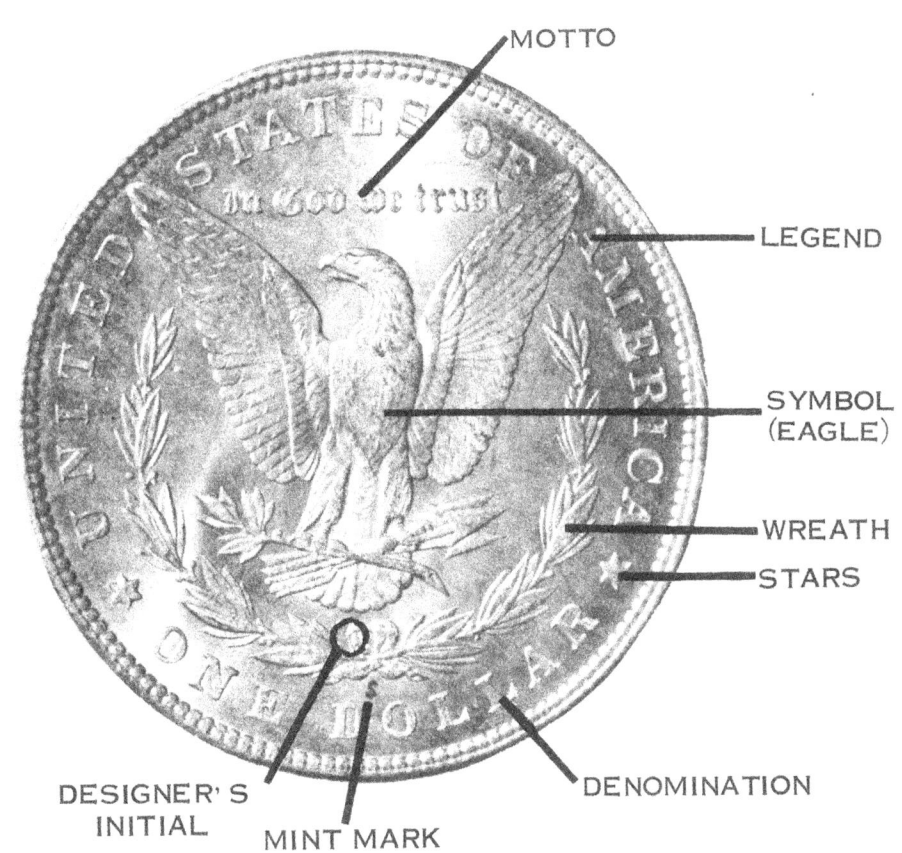

ix

Part II

Table of Contents

Page

Chapter Eight...
CONDITION ANALYSIS and
LIST OF DIE VARIETIES 142
    Key To Classification
    Die Descriptions

Chapter Nine...
GSA SALE OF CARSON CITY
DOLLARS 397
    Background of the Sales
    Transfer of Dollars
    Initial Sorting
    GSA Holdings of Silver Dollars
    Packaging The Coins
    GSA Sales

Chapter Ten...
REDFIELD and
CONTINENTAL-ILLINOIS BANK
HOARDS 403
    Redfield Hoard
    Continental-Illinois Bank Hoard

1878-P 8 Tail Feathers

This design type was the first to be struck for the Morgan silver dollars. Pete Bishal first, correctly identified the first pair of Morgan dollar dies used, the VAM 9. Twelve proof presentation pieces were struck at the initial striking of the Morgan dollar on March 11, 1878 and given to various dignitaries. (The first Morgan struck was given to President Hayes.) These same dies of VAM 9 were used to strike business coins. However, only about four proof and four business strike VAM 9 specimens are currently known making the coins struck from the first pair of dies very rare.

Eight tail feather proofs are also known in the VAM 14-3 and 14-8 varieties with VAM 14-3 being the most common. According to the coiner's daily delivery records, 300 Morgan proofs were delivered during the time the 8 tail feather design was struck. This is fewer than the usual quoted figure of 500. All 8 tail feather proofs exhibit only moderate cameo contrast.

Many of the 8 tail feather varieties exhibit strong doubling of parts of the obverse and/or reverse design. This was due to problems experienced in preparing the new design dies. These coins are generally fully struck. Many exhibit only one sided proof-like because of the frequent changing of dies to maintain production with the short lived dies.

1878-P 7/8 Tail Feathers

A number of reverse dies were modified by impressing the newer seven eagle's tail feather design over the original eight tail feather design. This was done to save die preparation time, but many of these die varieties show some of the original eight tail feathers tips below the seven tail feathers. Only those varieties with four to seven tips showing command the price premium of the 7/8 tail feathers (TF) with VAM 41 being the most prominent one. VAM's 31 and 43 with doubled legs command a modest premium. The scarcest 7/8 TF variety is VAM 44 with only about a twenty specimens known. It commands a substantial premium. VAM's 32 and 45 are also fairly scarce.

The 7/8 TF are also generally fully struck. Fully proof-like specimens usually have only moderate cameo contrast and some of the 7/8 TF are only one sided proof-like.

1878-P 7 Tail Feathers (Flat Breast)

Numerous varieties of the seven tail feathers B reverse with flat eagle's breast and parallel arrow feathers exist. Most of these are minor with the II/I obverse although a few show large design doubling. VAM's 117 and 141 show some strongly tripled stars. None of these 7 TF varieties command a significant premium, however, because there are so many.

Only 200 7 TF flat breast proofs were struck according to the coiner's daily delivery records. All of these are the VAM 131 variety with normal dies that did not have the doubling so common with this design type. Generally these proofs have only moderate contrast and are scarce.

Some business coins show strike weakness in the eagle's talon and in the arrow shafts and olive branch. But usually they are well struck. Fully two-sided proof-likes exist but most exhibit only moderate contrast.

1878-P 7 Tail Feathers (Round Breast)

This design type uses the seven tail feather C reverse with round eagle's breast and slanted arrow feathers that was used on later years from 1879 to 1904. A few die varieties exist but none are very significant or scarce. The exceptions are VAM 220 which is rare, VAM 203 which is fairly scarce and VAM 222 – some of which have the unusually low edge reeding count of 168 (lowest of any Morgan except 1921-P Infrequent Reeding which has 157).

Only about half a dozen 1878 proofs with the round breast reverse are known. From Treasury Department records, 50 proof Morgan dollars were delivered on November 8, 1878. These would have been the round breast reverse type since the Philadelphia Mint had been using this reverse type since June of that year. It is the rarest of the Philadelphia Mint proof Morgan dollars from 1878-1904. All are VAM 215 variety. These proofs exhibit the deep mirrors and white cameos characteristic of early Morgan dollar proofs.

Business strikes with this round breast C reverse are usually fully struck. Proof-like specimens are scarcer than for the 8 TF and 7 TF flat breast type because the die life was much longer for this design type. Some proof-likes with the C reverse show very deep mirrors and excellent cameo contrast.

1878-P
(Listed in Order of Reverse Type)

1 **I²1 • A¹a (Doubled E)** (188) I-2 R-4
   Obverse I²1 – Slightly doubled bottom letters in E PLURIBUS UNUM. First star on right doubled on left side. First five stars on left doubled slightly on right side. 187 in date slightly doubled. 1 is doubled at top of bottom crossbar. First 8 is doubled at bottom inside of lower loop. 7 doubled on left side of vertical shaft.
   Reverse A¹a – First 8 TF design type used, with raised beak, small feathers between eagle's legs and bottom wings, I of IN touching top of eagle's wing. This die variety has inside of E of ONE, R of DOLLAR and last A of AMERICA strongly doubled. Letters of legend frequently have machine doubling. Two small feathers added on eagle's right side and three on eagle's left side between leg and bottom of wing.

2 **I²2 • A¹b (Doubled Reverse)** (189) I-2 R-4
   Obverse I²2 – Doubled bottoms of E PLURIBUS and both sides of first U in UNUM. Left side of all left stars slightly doubled. Doubled 87 in date. First 8 doubled slightly at top of inside of lower loop. 7 doubled on left side and tripled on right side of vertical shaft.
   Reverse A¹b – Doubled reverse mostly apparent in lower left of wreath and in lettering of UNITED, AMERICA, and ONE DOLLAR. Three small feathers added on eagle's right and two on eagle's left side between leg and bottom of wing.

3 **I¹1 • A¹c (Doubled Reverse)** (189) I-2 R-4
   Obverse I¹1 – Slightly doubled tops of E and P of E PLURIBUS. Doubled bottom of last star on left. Doubled 87 in date. First 8 doubled slightly at bottom right outside. 7 doubled slightly on right side of vertical shaft.
   Reverse A¹c – Letters in UNITED doubled strongly on top and bottom. STATES OF AMERICA letters doubled at bottom. ONE DOLLAR letters doubled at top. Left wreath strongly doubled. Three small feathers added on eagle's right and two on eagle's left side between leg and bottom of wing.

4 **I²3 • A¹c (Doubled Date)** (189) I-3 R-4
   Obverse I²3 – Shallow doubled lower obverse, including all of date, all left and right stars, E, PLURIB and UNUM. The stars have a regular shift indicating a rotation of hub and die between blows.

5 **I²4 • A¹c (Doubled Motto)** (189) I-3 R-4
   Obverse I²4 – Doubled motto with R, I, and B having large shifts at bottom. All stars on left slightly doubled. 78 in date slightly doubled on right outside.

6 **I²5 • A¹d (Doubled Motto)** (189/193) I-2 R-4
   Obverse I²5 – Slightly doubled motto at bottom and all left stars on right side. Doubled date with 1 at lower left, both 8's at bottom inside of lower loop and top of both loops and 7 on left side of vertical shaft.
   Reverse A¹d – Doubled reverse especially evident in left side of wreath, end leaves in the branch held in eagle's talons, stars and legend letters on side away from rim. Two small feathers added on eagle's right and three on eagle's left side between leg and bottom of wing.

7 **I²6 • A¹d (Spiked A)** (189) I-2 R-4
   Obverse I²6 – Doubled left stars, E, PLURIBUS U, and 187 in date. A slight rotation of hub and die between blows.
   Reverse A¹d – Die shows evidence of wearing out, with a scratch in the die causing spikes at the side of A in STATES and filled center of E in ONE.

8 **I²7 • A¹g (Doubled Reverse)** (180) I-2 R-4
   Obverse I²7 – Doubled E PLUR of the motto on the left side and top of the letters. All stars on left doubled. Slightly doubled 87 in date with 8 doubled at bottom inside of lower loop and 7 doubled on left side of vertical shaft.
   Reverse A¹g – Doubled left side, top and bottom including legend, wreath, star and wing tip. Top of UNITED tripled. Wreath to left of ribbon bow heavily polished with parts of leaves missing. Two small feathers added on eagle's right and one long one on eagle's left side between leg and bottom of wing.

9 **I¹2 • A¹h (Doubled Reverse)** (Some Presentation Proof pieces also) (193) I-2 R-7
   Obverse I¹2 – Doubled E PLUR-BU and-UM of the motto at the top of the bottom serifs. First four stars on left and all of the stars on right slightly doubled on out side. First 8 doubled at top inside of upper loop. 7 in date doubled slightly on right side. First obverse die used.
   Reverse A¹h – All of legend and motto doubled. Left wreath and olive leaves slightly doubled. Three small feathers added on eagle's right and two one eagle's left side between leg and bottom of wing. First reverse die used.

10 **I²8 • A¹e (Doubled Motto)** (180) I-3 R-4
   Obverse I²8 – First six stars on left doubled on left and right sides. E PLURIB doubled on left side and at bottom. Doubled date with 1 doubled at top left, above bottom cross bar and on right side of vertical shaft. First 8 doubled at bottom left inside of lower loop and right outside of both loops. 7 doubled on right side of vertical shaft and top left serif. Second 8 doubled slightly at bottom inside and upper left outside of lower loop.
   Reverse A¹e – Doubled left side including legend, wreath, and wing tip. Two small feathers added on eagle's right and left side between leg and bottom of wing. Slightly concave reverse.

1878-P

11   I²6 • A¹f (Doubled Reverse)   I-2   R-7
Reverse A¹f – Doubled lower and left wreath, all of legend, and stars. Three small feathers added on eagle's right and two on eagle's left side between leg and bottom of wing. Eagle's right leg and right wing doubled on outside. Olive branch leaves are doubled on outside.

12   I²9 • A¹f (Doubled Motto)   (179)   I-3   R-4
Obverse I²9 – Doubled bottoms of E, PL-RIB-S. First four stars on left doubled on left and right sides. Five to seven stars on left doubled on right side only. First star on right doubled on left side only. Both 8's in date doubled at top inside of upper and lower loops. 7 doubled at top right of vertical shaft.

13   I²1 • A¹i (Concave Field)   I-3   R-4
Reverse A¹i – Slight doubling of UNTED, TTES, and MERICA on bottom of letters toward coin rim and of ONE DOLLAR on tops of letters toward coin rim. Right star is doubled on right side. Slight doubling on outside of wreath. Three small feathers added on eagle's right and two on eagle's left side between leg and bottom of wing. Field has more curvature than any other Morgan dollar and is especially concave near rim.

1 O I²1   1 O I²1   

2 O I²2

      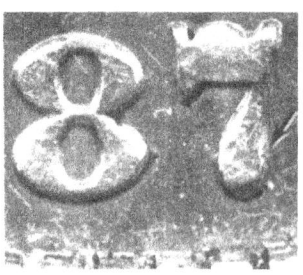

1 R A¹a   2 R A¹b   3 O I¹1

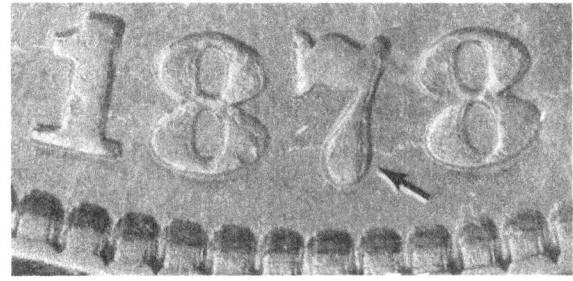   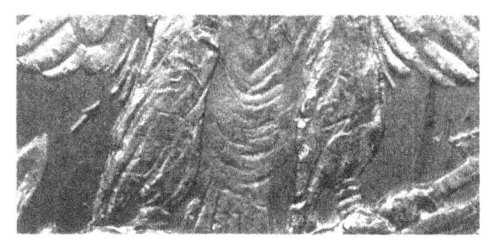

4 O I²3   3 R A¹c

5 O I²4   6 O I²5

1878-P

6 O I⁵5

6 R A¹d

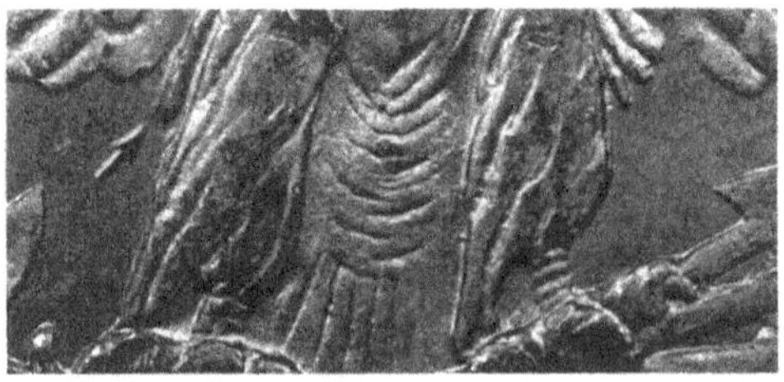

6 R A¹d

7 O I⁶6

8 O I⁷7

8 R A¹g

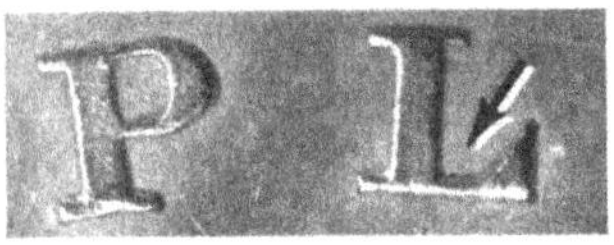

9 O I⁷2

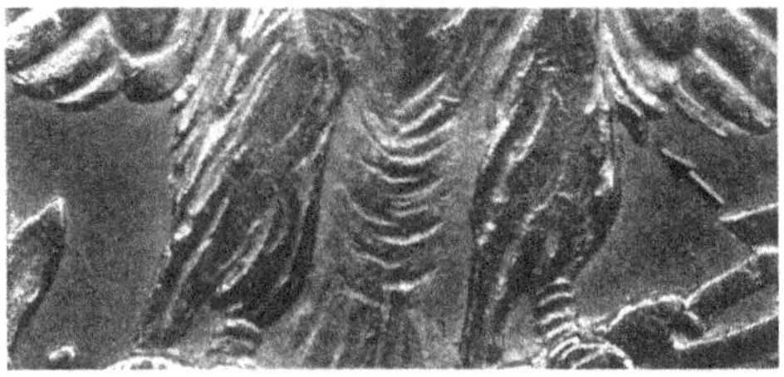

9 R A¹h

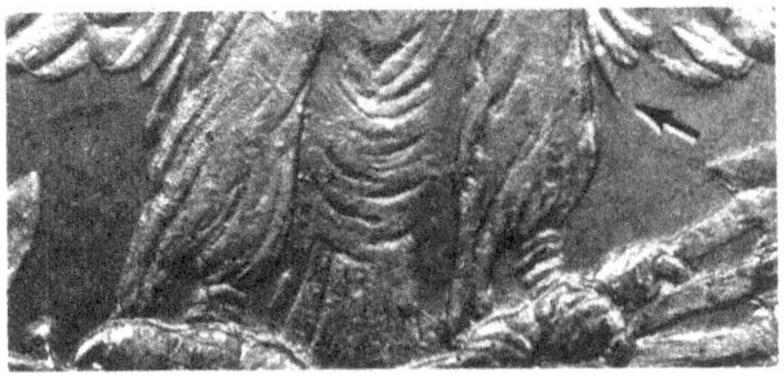

10 R A¹e

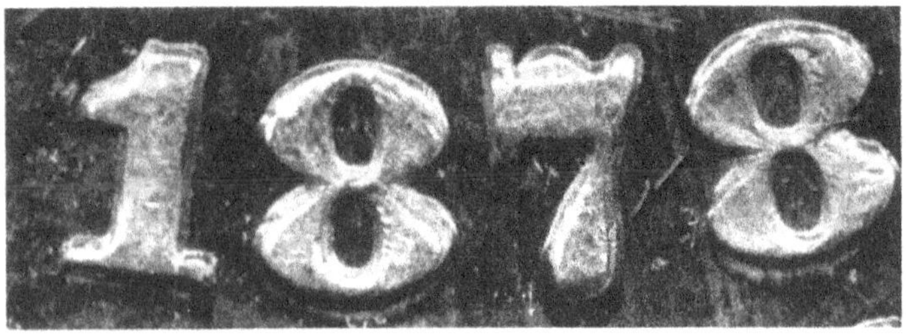

10 O I⁸8

11 R A¹f

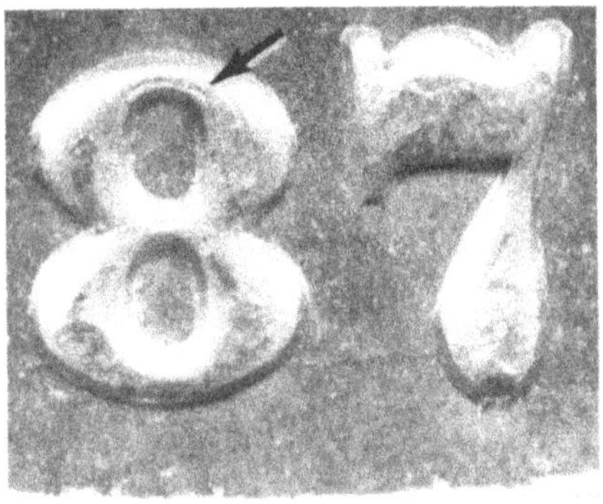

12 O I⁹9

12 O I⁹9

13 R A¹i

1878-P

14 $I^1 2 \cdot A^1 j$ (Doubled Motto)   (193)   I-2   R-4

Reverse $A^1 j$ – Strong doubling of ONE, UNITED, STATES, OF and IN GOD WE TRUST. Slight doubling of M, E, I and A in AMERICA, D, O, and R in DOLLAR, right star and wreath. Two small feathers added on eagle's right and one small and one long on eagle's left side between leg and bottom of wing.

14-1 $I^1 3 \cdot A^1 k$ (Normal Obverse)   (188)   I-2   R-4

Obverse $I^1 3$ – Normal Type I obverse with no apparent die breaks or doubling except for slight doubling to top of P in PLURIBUS.

Reverse $A^1 k$ – Slight doubling of lower and left side of wreath, olive leaves and bottom of eagle's right wing. Slightly doubled bottom of UNITED STATE and top of ONE. Three small feathers added on eagle's right and two on eagle's left side between leg and bottom of wing.

14-2 $I^1 4 \cdot A^1 l$ (Polished Ear)   (193)   I-2   R-4

Obverse $I^1 4$ – Normal I die that has been overpolished so that stars and date are shallow. Hair lines to right of ear are shallow. Inside of ear is flat with shortened inner ear fill.

Reverse $A^1 l$ – Slightly doubled bottom of AMERICA, AR in DOLLAR and right star. One long and two short feathers added on eagle's right and two on eagle's left side between leg and bottom of wing. Heavy vertical die polishing scratch above extra feathers on eagle's left wing.

14-3 $I^1 5 \cdot A^1 m$ (Doubled Reverse)   (Some Proofs)   (188)   I-2   R-4

Obverse $I^1 5$ – All stars on right and first four stars on left doubled on lower right side. Date slightly doubled with 1 doubled below upper crossbar. First 8 doubled at top inside and lower left outside of both loops. 7 doubled at top right and below crossbar. Second 8 doubled at top inside of both loops and lower left outside of upper loop.

Reverse $A^1 m$ – Doubled UNITED STATES OF ONE DOLLAR near rim and AMERICA away from rim. Both stars and outside of wreath doubled. Three small feathers added on eagle's right and two on eagle's left side between leg and bottom of wing similar to $A^1 b$ but wings have not been polished as much.

14-4 $I^2 2 \cdot A^1 i$ (Concave Field)   (180)   I-3   R-4

14-5 $I^1 10 \cdot A^1 d$ (Spiked A)   (189)   I-2   R-4

Obverse $I^1 10$ – Slightly doubled motto letters R-US, UNU, all left stars on left side, and all right stars toward rim. All digits in date doubled with 1 doubled at top of lower crossbar; both 8's doubled at lower inside of lower loop, and 7 doubled on left side of vertical stem. Die overpolished with weak nostril and lower hairlines.

Reverse $A^1 d$ – Die scratch causing spikes at sides of A in STATES.

14-6 $I^1 6 \cdot A^1 c$ (Dot on Ear)   (189)   I-3   R-5

Obverse $I^1 6$ – Slightly doubled first three right stars and first six left stars towards rim. E doubled at bottom, and U-UNU doubled at bottom inside towards rim. Both 8's doubled slightly at top inside of both loops and 7 is doubled slightly on right side of vertical shaft. Ear is over polished with dot die break in middle of lower earlobe. Some specimens show a large radial crack next to fourth right star.

14-7 $I^1 7 \cdot A^1 c$ (Dot Next to Ear)   (189)   I-2   R-4

Obverse $I^1 7$ – Doubled first five stars on right and first four on left towards rim. Slightly doubled below upper crossbar towards rim. Slightly doubled date with 1 doubled below upper bar, both 8's doubled at top inside of both loops, and 7 doubled below crossbar and on right side of vertical shaft. Die flake next to ear at top right outside. Radial die crack on right side of 1.

14-8 $I^1 8 \cdot A^1 d$ (Doubled Eyelid)   (189)   I-2   Proof

Obverse $I^1 8$ – Slightly doubled top of P in PLURIBUS. Eyelid doubled in front of eye about one third down from top. All left and right stars quadrupled towards rim. Entire date doubled with 1 doubled below upper crossbar, both 8's at top inside and lower left outside of upper loop and 7 below upper crossbar and right side of vertical shaft.

14-9 $I^1 9 \cdot A^1 n$ (Tripled Eyelid)   (189)   I-2   R-5

Obverse $I^1 9$ – Eyelid tripled in front of eye just below front of eyelid. First three stars on left slightly doubled towards rim. First three stars on right slightly tripled towards rim. Entire data doubled with 1 doubled slightly below upper crossbar, both 8's at top inside of upper loop, and 7 below crossbar and on upper right of vertical shaft.

Reverse $A^1 n$ – All legend letters and wreath leaves doubled towards rim. Bottom of eagle's right wing doubled. Two small isolated feathers added on eagle's right and two on eagle's left side between leg and bottom of wing.

14-10 $I^1 10 \cdot A^1 k$ (Doubled Hair)   (188)   I-2   R-4

Obverse $I^1 10$ – All stars on right tripled and quadripled on lower right side. First four stars on left doubled on lower right side. Date doubled with 1 doubled below upper crossbar. First 8 doubled at bottom outside, top inside of both loops and lower left outside of upper loop. 7 doubled at top right and below crossbar. Second 8 doubled slightly at top inside of both loops and lower left outside of upper loop. Doubled nose, lip, chin and lower hair.

1878-P

14 R A¹j

14-1 R A¹k

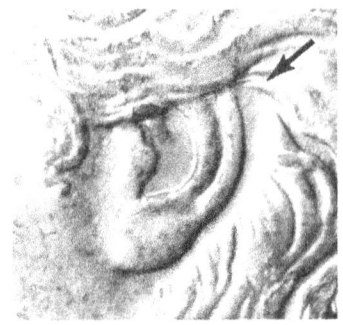
14-2 O I¹4

14-2 R A¹l

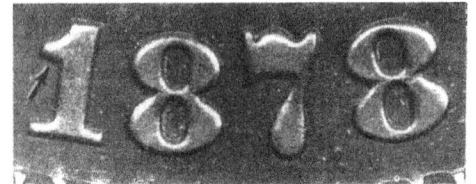
14-8 O I¹8

14-8 O I¹8

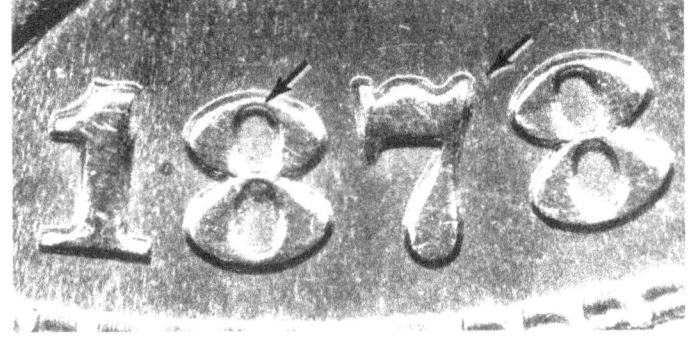
14-3 O I¹5

14-3 R A¹m

14-6 O I¹6

14-9 O I¹9

14-5 O I²10

14-7 O I¹7

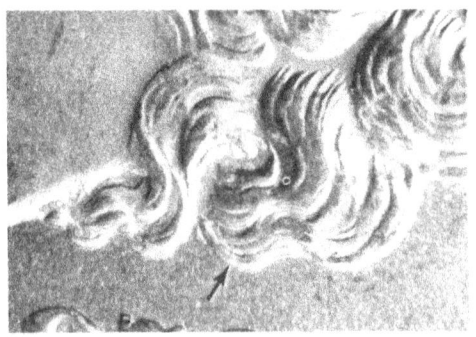
14-10 O I¹10
(Photo courtesy Jeff Oxman)

14-9 R A¹n

147

1878-P

15   II/I 1 • A¹e (Doubled LIBERTY)   (180)   I-3   R-4
       Obverse II/I 1 – Second obverse design type, II, reimpressed over first type, I. Doubled LIBERTY with large shift to left. Doubled R in PLURIBUS. All left and right stars are doubled. First 8 and 7 doubled at top.

16   II/I 4 • A¹f (Doubled LIBERTY)   (179)   I-3   R-4
       Obverse II/I 4 – Doubled LIBERTY shifted left. First four stars on left tripled with rest of stars on left and right doubled, some with large shifts. 1 and 7 in date doubled with 1 doubled on both sides of shaft and 7 doubled at top and left side of crossbar. Some specimens have a spike of metal between loops of first 8 in left side.

17   II/I 5 • A¹f (Doubled Reverse)   (179)   I-2   R-4
       Obverse II/I 5 – Slightly doubled LIBERTY shifted left. All stars on right and left doubled. Die chips in lower loop of first 8; first 8 doubled slightly at top outside and right outside of upper loop and top inside of lower loop. 7 doubled at top right and left side of upper serif.

18   II/I 2 • A²/A¹a (Doubled Date)   (180)   I-4   R-4
       Obverse II/I 2 – Doubled LIBERTY shifted up and left. Doubled E, P, L, U, R, S, and M in motto with large shift in date and all stars on right. All left stars tripled.
       Reverse A²/A¹a – Second 8 TF design type, A², with hooked beak and I of IN away from top of eagle's right wing reimpressed over first 8 TF design type, A¹. Doubled inside of wreath, NE of ONE and AR of DOLLAR. Two extra small feathers added on eagle's right and partial one on left side between leg and bottom of wing. Top of left wreath overpolished so that tip of leaf appears to be an extra berry on the left side but shadow of leaf remains on field of coin. (See page 149). Eagle's lower beak and tongue are doubled. Doubled strike on tops of letters on some coins. Top arrow head and shaft doubled.

19   II/I 2 • A²/A¹b (Doubled Date)   (180)   I-4   R-4
       Reverse A²/A¹b – Doubled inside of wreath, N of ONE, DOLLAR, and right star with AR tripled at bottom. Partial small feather added on eagle's right side between leg and bottom of wing. Top of wreath overpolished so that tip of leaf appears to be an extra berry on the left side. Eagle's lower and upper beak are doubled. Top arrow head and shaft doubled.

20   II/I 2 • A²/A¹c (Doubled Date)   (189)   I-3   R-4
       Reverse A²/A¹c – Doubled left lower wreath, olive branch leaves, arrow tips and bottom of eagle's wings. ON of ONE, lower parts of LLAR in DOLLAR, and U, N, and T of UNITED strongly doubled with most of other letters faintly doubled. Thin small feather added on eagle's right side between leg and bottom of wing. Top arrow head and shaft doubled.

21   II/I 3 • A²/A¹d (Doubled B)   (180)   I-3   R-4
       Obverse II/I 3 – Slightly doubled LIBERTY shifted left. Doubled P, U, R, and B in PLURIBUS and 1 and 2 stars on right. Nostril missing from overpolished die. First 8 doubled at top inside of upper loop and second 8 doubled at bottom outside of lower loop.
       Reverse A²/A¹d – Doubled wreath, N of ONE tripled. L, A and R of DOLLAR doubled, and bottom of UNITED doubled. Thin small feather added on eagle's right side between leg and bottom of wing. Eagle's lower beak slightly doubled on inside. Top arrow head and shaft doubled.

22   II/I 6 • A²/A¹e (Doubled ERTY)   (180)   I-3   R-4
       Obverse II/I 6 – Doubled last four letters of LIBERTY, shifted down. First three letters have polishing marks. Slightly doubled E PLURIBUS UNUM at left top serifs, doubled 2 and 3 stars on left, and doubled 3 and 4 stars on right. Doubled tops of wheat leaves and grains, cotton leaves and blossoms.
       Reverse A²/A¹e – Doubled A and R of DOLLAR, ERICA of AMERICA, N of ONE, and both stars, two small feathers added on eagle's right and two fine lines on eagle's left side between leg and bottom of wing. Eagle's top and lower beak slightly doubled. Top arrow head and middle arrow shaft doubled.

15 O   II/I 1

16 O   II/I 4

17 O   II/I 5

18 O   II/I 2

1878-P

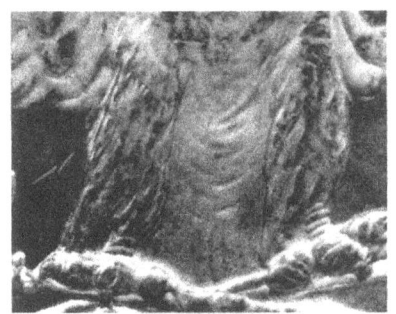
18 R A²/A¹a

18 R A²/A¹a

19 R A²/A¹b

19 R A²/A¹b

20 R A²/A¹c

20 R A²/A¹c

21 R A²/A¹d

21 R A²/A¹d

18 and 19 R
A²/A¹a and A²/A¹b
Extra Berries

20-22 R
A²/A¹c-e
Normal Berries

21 O II/I 3

22 O II/I 6

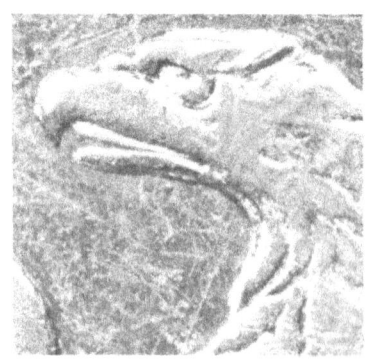
22 R A²/A¹e

1878-P

23   I²11 • A²/A¹b (Doubled Eagle's Beak)   (180)   I-3   R-4

Obverse I²11 – Doubled motto letters at top with E-P showing very thin tops of letters. All stars left and right are doubled slightly near rim. Date doubled slightly at bottom with 7 doubled also on right side. Nose, lips and chin slightly doubled. LIBERTY doubled left and up and also slightly to right.

30   II/I 7 • B/Aa (Extra Talons)   (180)   I-3   R-4

Obverse II/I 7 – Type II LIBERTY; doubled E, P, and R; doubled 187 in date with 1 doubled on left at shaft, 8 on top surface and 7 on left of top serif; all stars on left and first three stars on right doubled. Area around nose and lips overpolished. Fine diagonal polishing line through R in LIBERTY.

Reverse B/Aa – Four talons on left and right; extra one shifted to left by width of one toe. Tail feather lines to left of eagle's right leg.

31   II/I 8 • B/Ab (Doubled Legs)   (177)   I-5   R-4

Obverse II/I 8 – Type II LIBERTY; doubled P on left and tripled S at top right; partially broken bottom serifs of N and M in UNUM. Doubled 2, 3, 6 and 7 stars on left, and 1, 3, 4 and 5 stars on right. 1 and 7 in date doubled at top right.

Reverse B/Ab – Extra set of legs and talons on the right; design remains in leaves of branch and above branch on right; polishing scratches across arrow feathers and eagle's right talon, and also across bow in wreath. Possible faint tail feathers between 1 and 2 TF. Die chips around R in TRUST.

32   II 2 • B/Ac (3 TF)   (179)   I-3   R-6

Obverse II 2 – Normal type II obverse with broken point off number 4 star on right and 7 in date doubled on right side (hub defect).

Reverse B/Ac – Three tail feather ends showing under 2, 3 and 4 TF. Design remains in leaves of branch and in bow of wreath. Die chips in IN GOD WE TRUST; doubled O, D, and W.

33   II/I 7 • B/Ad (3TF)   (180)   I-3   R-4

Obverse II/I 7 – Some coins show die chip at left between loops of first 8.

Reverse B/Ad – Three tail feather ends showing; a strong one under 4 TF and two faint ones between 4 and 5 TF and 5 and 6 TF. Sometimes a very faint tail feather shows under 6 TF on early strike specimens. Eagle's legs are one and a half times normal width, with the talons doubled (double set of claws). Design remains in leaves of branch and below branch on left; also some in center of wreath bow. Diagonal polishing line from 1 TF down through 4 TF.

34   II 2 • B/Ae (4 TF)   (179)   I-3   R-5

Reverse B/Ae – Four tail feather ends showing; one between 2 and 3 TF and one under each 3, 4, and 5 TF. Design remains in leaves of branch and below branch on left, also around wreath bow. Doubled O, D, W, and E of IN GOD WE TRUST.

35   Former VAM 35 now VAM 41 A; B/Af was polished down B/Ak.

36   II 1 • B/Ag (4 TF)   (179)   I-4   R-4

Obverse II 1 – Normal type II obverse with no apparent die breaks or doubling except for 7 in date slightly doubled on right side (hub defect).

Reverse B/Ag – Four tail feather ends showing; between 2 and 3 TF and under 3, 4, and 5 TF. Design remains in leaves of branch, below branch on left, and around wreath bow. Die chips around D, W, E, and U of IN GOD WE TRUST.

37   II 2 • B/Ag (4 TF)   (179)   I-4   R-4

Obverse II 2 – E and P have bulges at top right and B is doubled at right inside and bottom of outside of lower loop.

38   II/I 9 • B/Ah (5 TF)   (180)   I-4   R-4

Obverse I/II 9 – Doubled LIBERTY with shift to left; largest shift of this kind known. All letters in E PLURIBUS UNUM and all left and right stars doubled. Doubled date with 1 doubled on both sides of shaft, first 8 doubled at top outside and inside right of upper loop, 7 doubled on right, second 8 doubled on inside right of upper loop.

Reverse B/Ah – Five tail feather ends showing; between 2 and 3, 3 and 4, 4 and 5, and under 5 and 6 TF. Design remains in leaves of branch, below branch on left, and around wreath bow. Eagle's right wing separated from leg due to over polishing.

22 R A²/A¹e

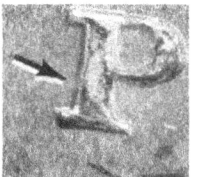

30 O II/I 7

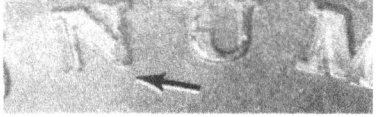

31 O II/I 8

32 O II 2

1878-P

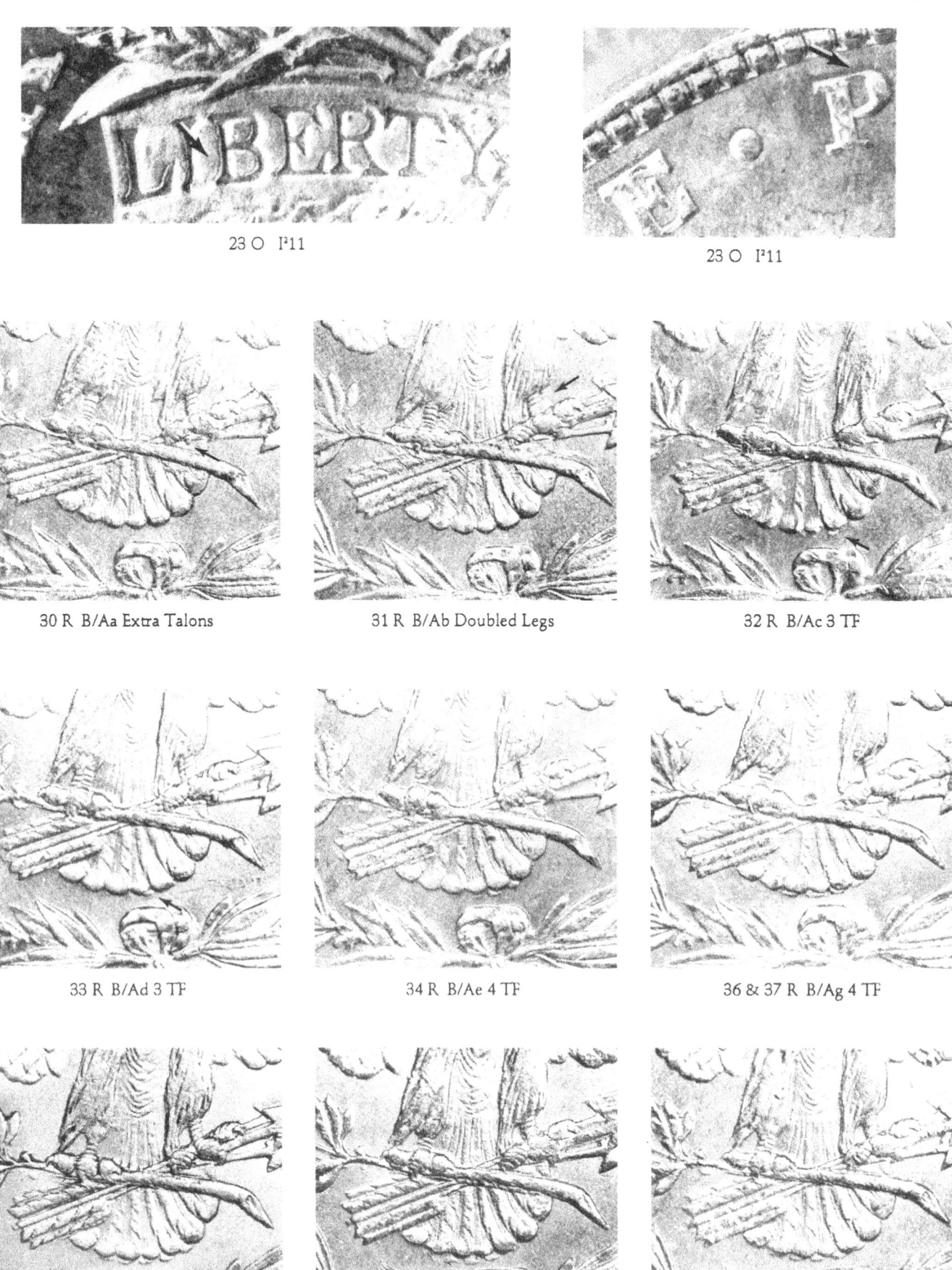

23 O I²11

23 O I²11

30 R B/Aa Extra Talons

31 R B/Ab Doubled Legs

32 R B/Ac 3 TF

33 R B/Ad 3 TF

34 R B/Ae 4 TF

36 & 37 R B/Ag 4 TF

38 R B/Ah 5 TF

39 R B/Ai 5 TF

40 R B/Aj 5 TF

1878-P

38 O II/I 9

39	**II 2 • B/Ai (5 TF)**	(179)	I-4	R-5

Reverse B/Ai – Five tail feather ends showing; between 2 and 3, 3 and 4, 4 and 5, 5 and 6 and under 6 TF. Design remains in leaves of branch, below branch on left, and inside wreath bow. Die chips around R in TRUST.

40	**II/I 8 • B/Aj (5 TF)**	(180)	I-4	R-5

Reverse B/Aj – Five tail feather ends showing; between 2 and 3, 3 and 4, 4 and 5 and under 5 and 6. Design remains in leaves of branch, below branch on left, and inside left outside of wreath bow. Die chips around R and U in TRUST on some coins.

41	**II 2 • B/Ak (7 TF)**	(180)	I-5	R-5

Obverse II 2 – Fourth star on right has just part of point broken off.
Reverse B/Ak – Seven tail feather ends showing; under 2, between 2 and 3, under 3, 4, 5, 6, and faintly between 6 and 7 TF (one of the best examples of the 7/8 TF, with the ends extending halfway between the 7 TF ends and the top of the bows). Design remains in leaves of branch, below branch on left, and around wreath bow. Faint outline of arrow shafts below crossover of branch and arrow shafts. Extra feather below eagle's head. Die chips around R in TRUST. Doubled right leg and talons on eagle.

41A	**II 2 • B/Ak (4 TF)**	(179)	I-3	R-4

Reverse B/Ak – Four tail feather ends showing; partial end between 2 and 3 TF, thin line between 3 and 4 TF, full end below 5 TF, and partial end between 5 and 6 TF. Some early strikes show a broken line below 4 TF. Design remains in leaves of branch, below branch on left, and around wreath bow. Doubled right leg and talons. Polished down version of B/Ak.

42	**II/I 5 • B/Al (7 TF)**	(180)	I-4	R-5

Reverse B/Al – Seven tail feather ends showing; between 1 and 2 (weak), between 2 and 3, under 3, 4, 5, and 6, and between 6 and 7 (weak). Some of the extra tail feather ends show a doubled appearance. Design remains in leaves of branch, below branch on left, and around wreath bow. Portion of extra arrow head below middle one. Die chips around E, T, R, and U in WE TRUST. Top of U in UNITED missing, polishing marks on lower half, and doubled D in GOD and T in TRUST.

43	**II/I 3 • B/Am (Doubled Legs)**	(180)	I-5	R-5

Reverse B/Am – Doubled legs and talons on the left; design remains in leaves of branch, at end of arrow feathers and around wreath bow. Three tail feather ends showing, faint ones between 4 and 5 TF, 5 and 6 TF and 6 and 7 TF. Die chips in IN GOD WE TRUST.

44	**II/I 37 • B/Ad (3 TF)**	(179)	I-5	R-7

Obverse II/I 37 – LIBERTY doubled slightly with BER showing faint shadows on right side. First star on right and number seven on left doubled. Cotton blossoms and leaves are tripled on right side.

45	**II 2 • B/An (Doubled Talons)**	(179)	I-3	R-6

Reverse B/An – Left leg is doubled with one and one-half normal width. Middle talon is doubled on left foot and outside talon is doubled on right foot. Olive branch is doubled above tail feathers. Die has been overpolished in eagle's wings and tail feathers. Diagonal polishing marks are in tail feathers.

70	**I²12 • B¹a (Doubled Letters)**	(180)	I-2	R-4

Obverse I²12 – Doubled motto with R, I and B having large shifts at bottom and UM tripled on right side. All stars on right tripled at bottom. 878 in date doubled. First 8 doubled at top inside of both loops and at bottom outside of lower loop. 7 doubled below upper crossbar and at bottom left and upper right of vertical shaft. Second 8 doubled at top inside and bottom outside of lower loop and tripled at lower left outside of upper loop. Nostril slightly overpolished.
Reverse B¹a – Earlier type B reverse; 7 TF parallel arrow feather, with long center arrow shaft. Die overpolished with last three leaves disconnected from olive branch and part of eagle's lower right wing missing.

79	**II/I 35 • B¹a (Missing Nostril)**	(180)	I-2	R-4

Obverse II/I 35 – Slightly doubled LIBERTY shifted left. Doubled 2 through 7 stars on left and first three stars on right. Lower part of Liberty head nose missing because of overpolished die.

80	**II/I 6 • B¹b (Disconnected Leaves)**	(180)	I-2	R-4

Reverse B¹b – Die overpolished with last three leaves disconnected from olive branch. Diagonal polishing lines below tail feathers. Small die chip on eagle's right wing at top next to body.

81	**II/I 7 • B¹c (Spiked P)**	(180)	I-2	R-4

Reverse B¹c – Die overpolished with last three leaves disconnected from olive branch and blank spots in middle of both eagle's wings. Die chip on eagle's right wing in middle next to body.

1878-P

41 R B/Ak 7 TF

41A R B/Ak (Polished) 4 TF

42 R B/Al 7 TF

43 R B/Am Doubled Legs

44 O II/I 37

45 R B/An Doubled Talons

70 O I²12

70 O I²12

81 R B¹c

70 R B¹a

79 O II/I 35

80 R B¹b

1878-P

82	**II/I 10 • B¹c (Doubled LIBERTY)**	(180)	I-3	R-4

Obverse II/I 10 – Doubled LIBERTY shifted up. Doubled E, P, R, B, S, U, and N in motto. Doubled 1, 2, 3 and 5 stars on right with first one very strong; doubled 1, 2, 4, and 5 on left. Doubled 1 on right side, both 8's doubled over center of top loop.

83	**II/I 11 • B¹d (High 1)**	(180)	I-3	R-4

Obverse II/I 11 – Doubled LIBERTY shifted left; all letters in E PLURIBUS UNUM doubled. Doubled 1, 2, 5 and 6 stars on left and 1, 2, 3, and 4 stars on right. 1 in date doubled on right side and set high. First 8 doubled at top right outside and left outside of upper loop and bottom inside of lower loop. 7 doubled slightly on left side of left top serif and right side on left lower serif.

Reverse B¹d – B¹ type reverse with no apparent defects except for slight overpolishing in middle of eagle's wing.

84	**II/I 12 • B¹e (Washed-out L)**	(180)	I-2	R-4

Obverse II/I 12 – Slightly doubled LIBERTY shifted left, with surface around L flat and detail not brought out. Missing nostril. Doubled E, P, L, U, R, B and S in E PLURIBUS. Doubled 1, 2, 3, 4, 6, and 7 stars on left and all stars on right. Slanted dash below first 8 and die chip at top left inside of first 8 upper loop.

Reverse B¹e – D of DOLLAR broken at bottom with just two lines remaining. Die chip on eagle's right wing, 6th feather down and also next to body. Die overpolished with blank areas in eagle's left wing and tail feathers. Clash marks with faint remains of E of LIBERTY below tail feathers.

100	**I¹10 • B²a (Doubled Letters)**	(180)	I-2	R-4

Obverse I¹10 – Doubled top of E PLURIBUS UNUM and some stars toward rim.

Reverse B²a – Later type B reverse, with shorter center arrow shaft and die chips around R and U of TRUST. The eagle's wings show at least 6 different states of overpolishing where the field shows through.

110	**II/I 8 • B²a (Broken N and M)**	(180)	1-3	R-4
111	**II/I 13 • B2a (Dropped R)**	(193)	I-2	R-4

Obverse II/I 13 – Slightly doubled LIBERTY (L, I, and B only). Doubled U and R in PLURIBUS, with the R dropped down. Doubled 7 star on left and 1 star on right.

112	**II/I 14 • B2a (Line in B)**	(194)	I-2	R-4

Obverse II/I 14 – Type II LIBERTY. Extra vertical line in top loop and extra horizontal lines in bottom loop of B of PLURIBUS. Doubled 2 and 3 stars on left and 1 and 3 stars on right. 1 in date doubled at top right.

113	**II/I 15 • B²a (Flake on Cheek)**	(194)	I-2	R-4

Obverse II/I 15 – Type II LIBERTY; doubled N, U, M in UNUM; doubled 2 star on left and 1, 2 and 5 stars on right. Both 8's in date doubled. Die break through center ear, and large die flake on cheek.

114	**II/I 16 • B²a (Doubled R)**	(178)	I-2	R-4

Obverse II/I 16 – Slightly doubled LIBERTY. Doubled P, R and B in PLURIBUS. Doubled first six stars on left and first four on right. Die overpolished in hair above date on some specimens.

Reverse B²a – Die slightly overpolished with flat spot in middle of eagle's left wing and right wing slightly separated from the leg.

115	**II/I 17 • B²a (Doubled Date)**	(194)	I-3	R-4

Obverse II/I 17 – Doubled I, B, E, R, T, and Y in LIBERTY, shifted left with R, T, and Y having large shifts. Doubled N, U, and M in UNUM and doubled date. All stars on right and left doubled, some with large shifts.

116	**II/I 18 • B²a (Doubled P)**	(180, 179)	I-2	R-4

Obverse II/I 18 – Type II LIBERTY; doubled P, L, R, and B in PLURIBUS and doubled 1, 3 and 4 stars on left and 1, 2, 3 and 4 on right. 1 in date doubled on top right. Lower part of nostril missing. Die flake near hairline behind eye with die crack leading to hair.

117	**II/I 19 • B²a (Tripled Star)**	(194)	I-4	R-4

Obverse II/I 9 – Doubled LIBERTY shifted right; doubled E, P and R in E PLURIBUS. Doubled 2, 3, and 4 stars on left and doubled 1 – 5 stars on right (number 2 is tripled and is one of the best examples of a tripled star). 1 in date is doubled on left side of stem. Incomplete band in cap.

82 O II/I 10

83 O II/I 11

1878-P

83 O II/I 11

84 O Dash Below First 8

100 O I'10

84 O II/I 12

111 O II/I 13

112 O II/I 14

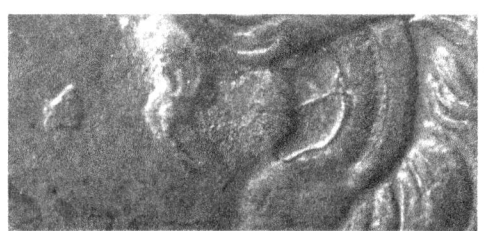

113 O II/I 15

114 O II/I 16

115 O II/I 17

116 O II/I 18

117 O II/I 19

118 O II/I 20

1878-P

118	II/I 20 • B²a (Shifted P)		(194)	I-2	R-4

Obverse II/I 20 – Type II LIBERTY. Doubled bottom serif of P; metal on top of serif in U of PLURIBUS. Doubled 3, 4, and 7 stars on left; doubled 1 and 2 stars on right.

119	II/I 21 • B²a (Shifted E)	(193)	I-2	R-4

Obverse II/I 20 – Slightly doubled LIBERTY, shifted left and up. E in motto doubled on top and bottom right outside. All left stars are doubled. Ear is doubled on the inside.

120	II/I 31 • B²a (Doubled P)		I-2	R-4

Obverse II/I 31 – Type II LIBERTY. Doubled bottom serifs of P and metal on R of PLURIBUS. Metal on right side of U in UNUM. All stars on left and first three on right doubled.

121	II/I 38 • B²a (Doubled Motto)		I-3	R-4

Obverse II/I 38 – LIBERT in LIBERTY doubled slightly on left side. Strongly doubled 1 and 3 stars on right. E, P, U and R in E PLURIBUS strongly doubled.

122	II/I 36 • B²a (Doubled Motto)	(194)	I-3	R-4

Obverse II/I 36 – Type I LIBERTY doubled slightly to left. Type II ear. Motto letters all doubled with PLURI particularly strong. All left stars doubled slightly on left side. Doubled 1, 4, 5 and 6 stars on right with number one having a large shift.

130	II 1. B²a (Normal)		(194)	I-1	R-2
131	II 2 • B²a (Normal)	(Some Proofs)	(179, 180, 194)	I-1	R-2

Obverse II 2 – Some specimens show die chip on hair below LIBERTY, or diagonal die scratch through B or through R and top of T in LIBERTY.

132	II 3 • B²a (Missing Nostril)	(179, 180)	I-2	R-4

Obverse II 3 – Same as II 2 but die has been overpolished so that nostril is missing.

133	II 4 • B²a (Doubled)	(193)	I-2	R-4

Obverse II 4 – Same as II 2, but with slightly doubled LIBERTY, doubled letters in E PLURIBUS UNUM, and metal in P.

140	II/I 18 • B²b (Partially Open O)	(180, 189)	I-2	R-4

Reverse B²b – Same as B²a, but with hub break fill which leaves open the upper part of O in GOD (this example is only partially open).

141	II/ 19 • B²b (Tripled Star)	(194)	I-4	R-4
142	II/I 22 • B²b (Doubled 878)	(179)	I-3	R-4

Obverse II/I 22 – Doubled LIBERTY shifted left; doubled P, R, U, U, and M in PLURIBUS UNUM; doubled top of 878 in date and right side of 7 vertical shaft. All left and right stars slightly doubled.

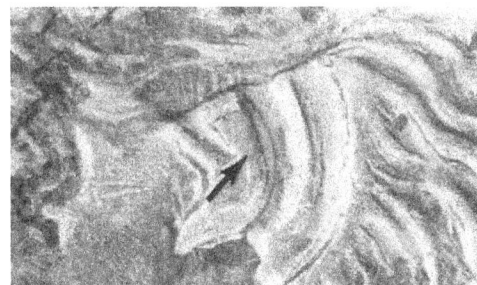

119 O Doubled Ear

119 O II/I 21

120 O II/I 31

121 O II/I 38

1878-P

121 O II/I 38

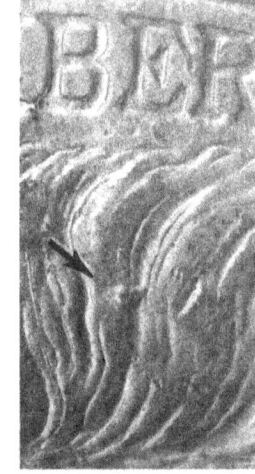
131 O II 2

131 O II 2

131 O II 2

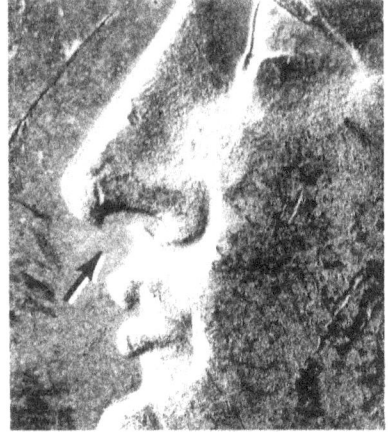
132 O II 3

133 O II 4

142 O II/I 22

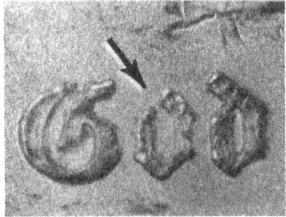
140 R B²b

143 O II/I 23

143   II/I 23 • B²b (Doubled 8)   (180)   I-2   R-4
    Obverse II/I 23 – Doubled LIBERTY shifted left; doubled R in PLURIBUS. Doubled 2, 6, and 7 stars on left. Doubled top of first 8 in date.

144   II/I 24 • B²b (Doubled LIBERTY)   (180)   I-2   R-4
    Obverse II/I 24 – All letters slightly doubled in LIBERTY with shift to left. Metal at top right of E; slightly doubled R.

145   II/I 25 • B²b (Broken N and M)   (180)   I-2   R-4
    Obverse II/I 25 – Type II LIBERTY, doubled U and R in PLURIBUS; broken bottom serifs of N and M, with bottom right serif of M completely gone. Doubled 3 star on left and 5 star on right. 1 and 7 in date doubled on right side with 1 slanted to left.

146   II 2 • B²b (Line in E, R, Y)   (194)   I-2   R-3
    Obverse II 2 – Same as II 2, but with diagonal die gouge through bottom of E, two through top of R and one through middle of Y in LIBERTY.

1878-P

144 O II/I 24

146 O II 2
Line in E, R, Y

145 O II/I 25

160	II/I 20 • B²c (Shifted P)	(194)	I-2	R-4

Reverse B²c – Same as B²a, but with die fill on the arm of R in TRUST which results in TIUST. This is a break in the hub, since the variety appears on many dies (some of the 1878-P 7 TF, 1878-S, and 1879-S).

161	II/I 21 • B²c (Shifted E)	(194)	I-2	R-4
162	II/I 25 • B²c (Broken N and M)	(180)	I-2	R-4
163	II/I 26 • B²c (Shifted U)	(194)	I-3	R-4

Obverse II/I 26 – Slightly doubled LIBERTY (L, I, B, and T only) shifted to left. Doubled E, U, R, and M in E PLURIBUS UNUM (U and M are particularly large shifts). Doubled 7 star on left. Doubled 18 in date.

164	II/I 27 • B²c (Broken R)	(180)	I-2	R-4

Obverse II/I 27 – Slightly doubled LIBERTY (I, B, and T only) shifted to left. Metal on P, and broken upper part of R in PLURIBUS. Doubled 1, 3, and 4 stars on right.

165	II/I 28 • B²c (Spiked P)	(180)	I-2	R-4

Obverse II/I 28 – Type II LIBERTY. Metal on E, P, L, U, R, and S in E PLURIBUS UNUM. Doubled 2, 3, and 5 stars on left and 1, 3, and 5 stars on right.

166	II/I 29 • B²c (Spiked P)	(193)	I-2	R-4

Obverse II/I 29 – Type II LIBERTY. Metal on E, P, U, and R of E PLURIBUS. All stars on left and first star on right doubled.

167	II/I 30 • B²c Spiked P)	(194)	I-2	R-4

Obverse II/I 30 – Type II LIBERTY. Metal bottom left side of P; shifted U and doubled bottom of R in PLURIBUS. Slightly doubled right side of 7 in date.

168	II/I 31 • B²c (Doubled P)	(193)	I-2	R-4
169	II/I 32 • B²c (Quadrupled Stars)	(193)	I-3	R-4

Obverse II/I 32 – Doubled LIBERTY shifted to left, E, PLUR-R doubled on left side, S doubled at bottom; UNUM doubled at top. First five stars on left quadrupled with 2-4 having very large shifts. 6 and 7 stars on left tripled. 1-3 nd 5 stars on right doubled 4 tripled. Doubled date with 1 doubled at top right and 878 doubled on surface at bottom of loops and crossbar.

170	II/I 33 • B²c (Doubled Date)	(193)	I-3	R-4

Obverse II/I 33 – Doubled LIBERTY shifted slightly to left; doubled P, U, and R. All stars on left slightly doubled; all stars on right doubled. Date doubled, with tops of 1878 showing the greatest shift.

171	II/I 34 • B²c (Tripled R)	(193)	I-3	R-4

Obverse II/I 34 – Doubled LIBERTY with no shift (good example of perfect register with thicker type II LIBERTY letters). Doubled P and U, tripled R in PLURIBUS. Doubled 1 and 3 stars on left and 1, 3 and 4 stars on right.

185	II 1 • B²c (Broken R)	(193	I-2	R-3
186	II 2 • B²c (Broken R)	(193)	I-2	R-3

Reverse B²c – (Some also with open O and some with overpolished reverse.)

1878-P

160 R B²c

163 O II/I 26

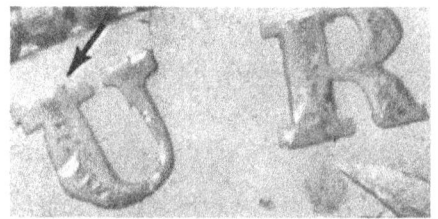
163 O II/I 26

164 O II/I 27

165 O II/I 28

166 O II/I 29

167 O II/I 30

169 O II/I 32

170 O II/I 33

171 O II/I 34

187 O II 5

188 O II 6

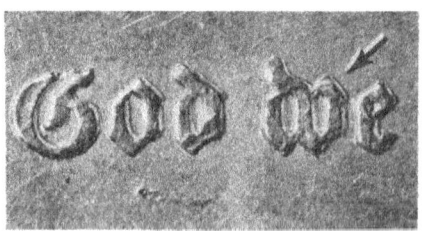
190 O B²d

1878-P

187	II 5 • B²c (Doubled R)	(193)		I-2	R-4

Obverse II 5 – Same as II 1, except letters L, U, R, and B in PLURIBUS and UN in UNUM are doubled. R is doubled strongly at top, middle and lower right side. Bottom serif of U is doubled strongly at top left.

188	II 6 • B²c (Washed Out L)	(193)		I-2	R-4

Obverse II 6 – Same as II 1, except that die is polished down so that L of LIBERTY is weak and wheat leaf above L is shortened.

190	II 3 • B²d (Doubled Motto)	(179)		I-2	R-4

Reverse B²d – Same as reverse B²a but with doubled GOD and WE to right, eagle's left wing feathers at top and top edge of eagle's right. Wings are overpolished in center.

195	II 2 • B²e (Broken D)	(179)		I-2	R-3

Obverse II 2 – Diagonal line through B in LIBERTY.
Reverse B²e – Bottom of D of DOLLAR completely broken.

195A	II 2 • B²e (Broken D)	(179)		I-2	R-3

Obverse II 2 – Diagonal line through R and top of T in LIBERTY.
Reverse B²e – Same as reverse B²a, but with partially broken bottom of D of DOLLAR.

196	II/I 22 • B²f (Doubled 878)	(179)		I-3	R-4

Reverse B²f – Die overpolished with part of eagle's lower right wing missing next to leg.

197	II 2 • B²f (Missing Feathers)	(180, 194)		I-2	R-4
198	II/I 2 • B²f (Doubled Date)	(194)		I-3	R-4
199	II/I 27 • B²f (Broken) R)	(180)		I-2	R-4
200	II/I 39 • C¹a (Broken N and M)	(179, 194)		I-2	R-6

Obverse II/I 39 – Serifs of N and M in UNUM broken similar to II/I 25. Type II LIBERTY. First six stars on left and first three stars on right doubled. 1 doubled at top right.
Reverse C¹a – Serif of A of AMERICA almost touches eagle's wing, with bottom of letter serifs slanting down and to left. Inner side of right serif of A is cut off square. Bottom feather of eagle's right wing next to leg is rounded and not connected to wing on left. Leaves of right wreath doubled on outside and inside of legend letters doubled towards rim.

201	II/I 35 • C¹a (Thick Letters)	(179)		I-2	R-6
202	III¹ 1 • C¹a (Lines in Wheat Leaves)	(180)		I-3	R-5

Obverse III¹ 1 – Lines in all wheat leaves, with more detail in cotton blossom tops than type II obverse. Thin letters in LIBERTY. Complete line at bottom of cap. Date slightly doubled at top inside of upper and lower loops of 8's and left sides of 1 and 7 shafts; all left and right stars doubled.

203	III¹ 2 • C¹a (Short Wheat Leaf)	(179)		I-2	R-6

Obverse III¹ 2 – Same as III1 1, but with heavy die polishing at top. Wheat leaf below R is short, well below the R, and contains lines. Wheat grains are well separated, with a long wheat leaf between the stalks. Bottom serifs are thin in motto. Bottom of E and R run together in LIBERTY.

210	II 2 • C²a (Extra Feather)	(194)		I-2	R-4

Reverse C²a – Same as C¹a, except that inner serif of A is thinner. Bottom feather of eagle's right wing extends to junction of next two feathers, and a thin line is present between eagle's leg and first feather.

210A	II 2 • C²a (Line Through R)	(179)		I-2	R-5

Obverse II 2 – Diagonal line through R and top of T in LIBERTY.

210B	II 2 • C²a (Line Through IB)	(194)		I-2	R-5

Obverse II 2 – Diagonal line through the middle of I and lower part of B in LIBERTY and curving downwards from B into hair and extending up from I across wheat leaf.

215	III¹1 • C²a (Extra Feather)			I-2	Proof
220	II/I 34 • C³a (Triple R)	(176)		I-3	R-7

Reverse C³a – Left serif of A is cut down so it is not flat on top and is away from wing. Bottom of serif is not slanting. Bottom feather of eagle's right wing is squared off and raised. This is normal reverse design used for most of the Morgan silver dollar series.

221	II 1 • C³a (Cut Down A)	(193)		I-1	R-3
222	II 2 • C³a (Cut Down A)	(168, 178, 193, 194)		I-1	R-2

1878-P / 1878-CC

| 223 | II 6 • C³a (Washed Out L) | (194) | I-2 | R-6 |
| 230 | III²1 • C³a (Normal) | (193, 194) | I-1 | R-2 |

Obverse III²1 – Long wheat leaf below R, close to R, with weak lines. Short wheat leaf between wheat stalks. Thicker bottom serifs in motto letters. LIBERTY letters are thinner, with shorter serifs on B and R. This is the normal obverse design for most of the Morgan silver dollar series.

195 R B²e

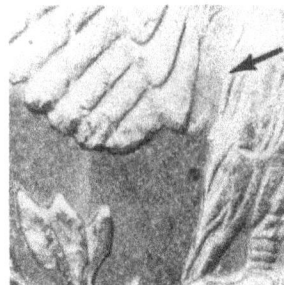

196 R B²f

202 O III²1

203 O III¹2

210B O Lines in IB

221 O II 1

1878-CC

All 1878-CC have the B reverse with flat breast eagle and parallel arrow feathers. The minor design types B¹ with long center arrow shaft and B² with short center arrow shaft are about equally available. VAM's 6, 18 and 24 have doubled cotton leaves and bolls and are worth a modest price premium. VAM's 11 and 14 have heavy die polishing lines in the eagle's wing and while interesting, bring only a slight premium. The CC mint marks vary in position and spacing since they were punched in by hand into each die.

Although the center portions of the design are well struck on 1878-CC, the B reverse did cause weak strike problems. On the obverse, occasionally planchet striations will show on the jaw along with a creamy color of the original planchet surface. Planchet striations are caused by rough edges of the draw benches used to obtain the final thickness of the silver strips. Weakly struck coins did not smooth out these planchet striations where planchet contact against the die was weak. On the reverse, weakly struck 1878-CC will show on the eagle's legs and talons and on the arrows.

Proof-like surfaces are available although not as high a proportion as for later lower mintage years of 1879-1885-CC. The dies were used longer for the 1878-CC to achieve the higher mintage thus resulting in a lower percentage of early strike proof-like specimens. Extremely deep mirror white cameos are available but quite scarce. The average 1878-CC proof-like has fairly good contrast.

1878-CC

1   **II 1 • B¹a (Normal Die)**   I-1   R-3
     Obverse II 1 – Normal die of 1878-P type II with the 7 in date doubled slightly on right side (a hub defect).
     Reverse B¹a – Normal die of 1878-P type B¹ with a long center arrow shaft. Medium spaced small mint marks, II CC, at medium height.

1A   **II 1 • B¹a (Line in Eye)**   (179)   I-2   R-4
     Obverse II 1 – Same as Obverse II 1 except a die scratch which shows as a thin line through the bottom of the R in LIBERTY, a thick line extending down from the middle of the eye lash, a thin line in the bottom corner of the eye, and a thick line at the rear of the nostril.

1B   **II 1 • B¹a (Line in IB)**   I-2   R-3
     Obverse II 1 – Slanted die gouge in top of I and bottom of B in LIBERTY. Date is doubled.

2   **II 2 • B¹ a (Doubled LIBERTY)**   I-2   R-3
     Obverse II 2 – LIBERTY slightly doubled shifted left. Some specimens show die chip on nostril. Some also show die chip on front of forehead and top of eyelid or between loops of 8 on left.
     Reverse B¹a – Normal die of type B¹ with medium mint marks, II CC, at medium height with die chips in the center of both C's.

3   **II 1 • B¹b (Very Wide CC)**   I-3   R-3
     Obverse II 1 – Line in eye variety.
     Reverse B¹b – Normal die of type B¹ with very widely spaced mint marks, IV CC, set high and touching wreath.

4   **II 3 • B¹c (Close CC)**   (177)   I-2   R-3
     Obverse II 3 – Normal die of 1878-P type II with broken point off number 4 star on right (a hub chip).
     Reverse B¹c – Normal die of type B¹ with closely spaced mint marks, I CC, at medium height. Die chips show in center of both C's.

5   **II 3 • B¹d (Wide CC)**   I-2   R-3
     Reverse B¹d – Normal die of type B¹ with widely spaced mint marks, III CC, at medium height.

6   **II 4 • B¹b (Doubled Obverse)**   (178)   I-3   R-4
     Obverse II 4 – Doubled ear and cotton blossom leaves on the right edges, date, all stars on right and left on bottom edges.

7   **II 1 • B²a (Medium CC)**   (177)   I-2   R-3
     Reverse B² a – Normal die of 1878-P type B² with a short center arrow shaft. Medium spaced mint mark, II CC, at medium height.

8   **II 1 • B²b (Wide CC)**   (177)   I-2   R-3
     Reverse B²b – Normal die of type B² with widely paced mint marks, II CC, at medium height tilted slightly to right. Some specimens show die polishing lines in eagle's left wing and across breast.

9   **II 3 • B²c (CC Tilted Right)**   (177)   I-2   R-3
     Reverse B² c – Normal die of type B² with widely spaced mint marks, III CC, set high and slanted right.

10   **II 3 • B²d (Wide CC)**   I-2   R-3
     Reverse B² d – Normal die of type B² with widely spaced mint marks, III CC, at medium height.

11   **II 3 • B²b (Lines in Eagle)**   I-3   R-5
     Reverse B²b – Die polishing marks strongly evident as heavy lines at the bottom of the eagle's right wing and in the middle left wing. III CC mint mark at medium height and tilted slightly to right.

12   **II 3 • B²e (Very Wide CC)**   (177)   I-2   R-3
     Reverse B²e – Normal die of type B² with very widely spaced mint marks, IV CC, at medium height.

1 O Doubled 7

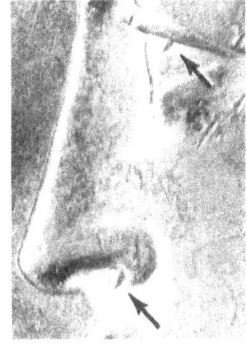

1A O Line in Eye

1B O Line in IB

1878-CC

| 13 | II 5 • B²a (Doubled Date) | | I-3 | R-4 |

Obverse II 5 – Same as II 4 obverse except cotton blossom leaves are not doubled.

| 14 | II 2 • B²b (Doubled LIBERTY) | (178) | I-2 | R-3 |

| 15 | II 3 • B²f (Spiked Lip) | | I-2 | R-4 |

Obverse II 3 – Vertical die gouge from lower lip to chin and die gouge running through IB of LIBERTY up to wheat leaf.
Reverse B²f – Normal die of type B² with widely spaced mint marks, III CC, at medium height. Left C is doubled at left inside and right C has diagonal spike at left inside.

| 16 | II 1 • B¹e (Doubled CC) | | I-3 | R-4 |

Reverse B¹e – Normal die of type B¹ with very widely spaced mint marks, IV CC, set high with right one touching wreath and doubled inside at top.

| 17 | II 1 • B¹e (Doubled CC) | (179) | I-3 | R-4 |

Obverse II 1 – Line in Eye variety.

| 18 | II 4 • B¹c (Doubled Obverse) | | I-3 | R-4 |

| 19 | II 1 • B¹f (Wide CC With Dot) | (179) | I-2 | R-3 |

Reverse B¹f – Normal die of B¹ with widely spaced mint marks, III CC at medium height. Left mint mark C has die chip in center and is punched deeper in die than right C.

| 20 | II 1 • B¹g (Medium CC with Dot) | | I-2 | R-3 |

Obverse II 1 – Line in eye variety.
Reverse B¹g – Normal die of type B¹ with medium spaced mint marks, II CC at medium height. Left mint mark C has die chip in center.

| 21 | II 4 • B²a (Doubled Obverse) | (179) | I-3 | R-4 |

Obverse II 4 – Late die state with die cracks in date, stars, and letters.

| 22 | II 3 • B¹a (Die Chips in CC) | (177) | I-2 | R-3 |

Reverse B¹a – Closed II CC's with die chip inside.

| 23 | II 1 • B¹c (Close CC) | (177) | I-2 | R-3 |

| 24 | II 6 • B¹f (Doubled Cotton Leaves) | (179) | I-3 | R-4 |

Obverse II 6 – Doubled cotton leaves and bolls on right side. Eyelash doubled at top.

2 O Doubled LIBERTY

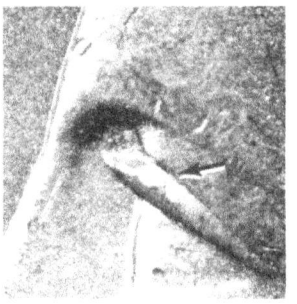

2 O Die Chips

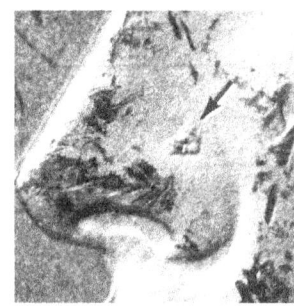

2 O Die Chip

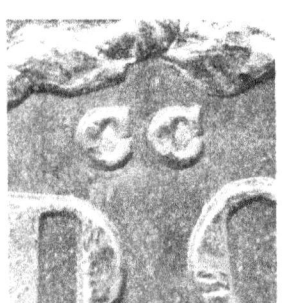

2 R Die chips in C's

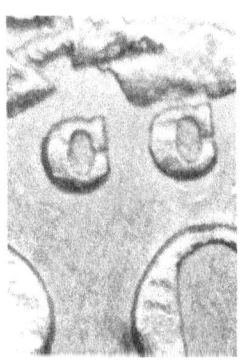

3 R CC Set High

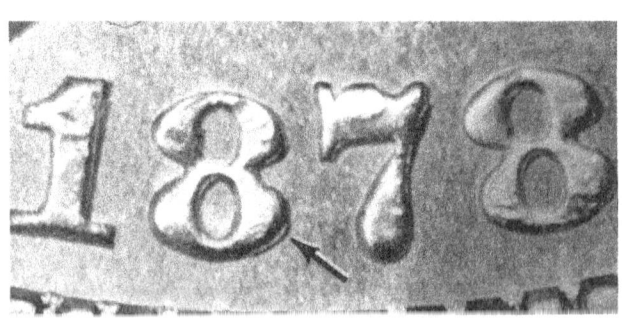

6 O Doubled Date

1878-CC / 1878-S

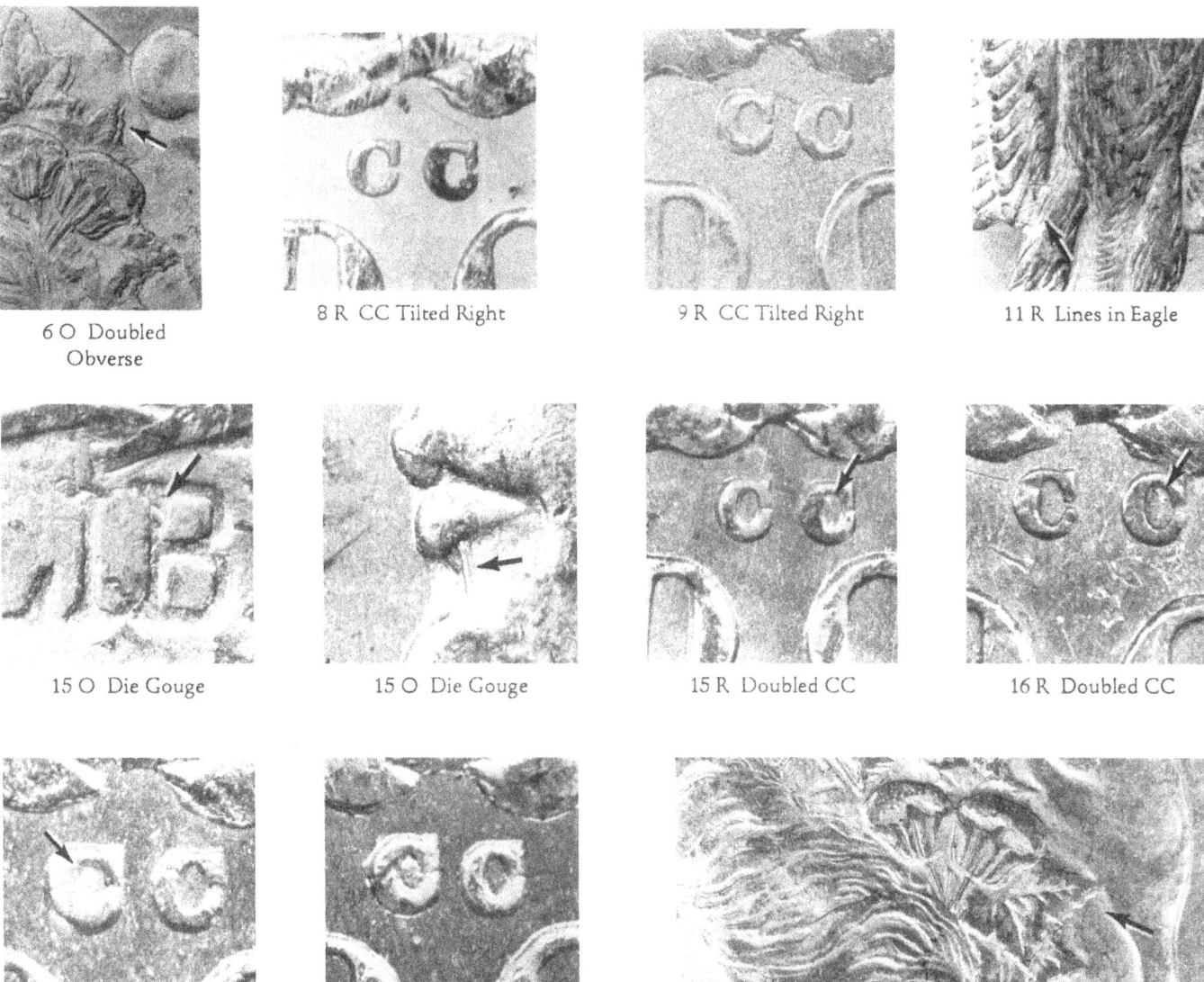

6 O Doubled Obverse
8 R CC Tilted Right
9 R CC Tilted Right
11 R Lines in Eagle
15 O Die Gouge
15 O Die Gouge
15 R Doubled CC
16 R Doubled CC
19 R Wide CC With Dot
20 R Die Chip in CC
24 O Doubled Cotton Leaves

1878-S

The 1878-S also comes in only the B reverse with flat breast and parallel arrow feathers. However, practically all are the B^2 reverse with short center arrow shaft. About a dozen B^1 reverse with long center arrow shaft are known and they are all circulated. VAM's 26 and 27 with B^1 reverse command substantial premiums and were from the first dies used at that mint. Many of the 1878-S reverse dies were individually touched up at that mint to add feathers between the eagle's right wing and leg. This area tended to be overpolished by the die basining. Although these touched up dies by the branch mint are unique in the Morgan series (along with some 1879-S flat breast), the many touched up dies makes them common with no price premium. There are also many slightly doubled design dies for the 1878-S but they command only modest price premiums to collectors.

As with the 1878-CC, the 1878-S had some striking problems because of the B reverse. Planchet striations on the jaw occasionally show as well as weak eagle's legs and talons and arrows. Unless very noticeable and distracting they will not lower the coin's value significantly.

Proof-like 1878-S are fairly common but most have brilliant devices with low contrast. There are a lot of one-sided proof-like 1878-S due to the frequent changing of dies during this first year of striking and use of the B reverse. Buyers of this date should always check to see that proof-likes purchased are reflective on both sides because the excellent luster of this year can be deceptive. Some extraordinary deep mirror white cameo exist for this date but are quite rare.

1878-S

1 II 1 • B² a (Normal Die) (184) I-1 R-2
Obverse II 1 – Normal die of 1878-P type II with broken point off number 4 star on right and 7 in date doubled slightly on right side (a hub defect). Some specimens show a die gouge through IB of LIBERTY
Reverse B² a – Normal die of 1878-P type B² with small III S mint mark. Some specimens show diagonal polishing marks in eagle's tail feathers and through first top berry in left wreath or long horizontal polishing lines through neck and eagle's right wing.

1A II 1 • B² a (Die Scratch on Wing) I-2 R-4
Reverse B² a – Vertical die scratch through lower part of eagle's right wing with a die chip in the middle of eagle's breast similar to VAM 16.

1B II 1 • B²a (Pitted Tail Feathers) (184) I-2 R-4
Reverse B²a – Pitted die from rust in eagle's tail feathers and lower right wreath. Two dies chips in lower part of eagle's right wing.

2 II 1 • B² b (Broken R) (184) I-2 R-2
Reverse B² b – Same as B² a, but with die fill on the arm of R in TRUST which results in TIUST. (A hub break since it also appears on some 1878-P 7 TF and 1879-S.) Some specimens show a die fill on the top of G in GOD separating the loop from the stem. Some specimens show a die break through the berry and leaf in wreath under N in UNITED.

3 II 2 • B² a (Doubled LIBERTY Right) I-2 R-3
Obverse II 2 – LIBERTY slightly doubled to right.

4 II 3 • B² a (Doubled Date) (184) I-2 R-4
Obverse II 3 – Date doubled at bottom. In addition, both 8's are doubled at the top left inside the upper loop. The 7 is doubled at the top and upper right side. Broken 4 star on right. All letters of LIBERTY slightly doubled on right side. Nostril and eyelid are slightly doubled.

1 R Line in Tail Feathers

1 R Die Break in Wreath

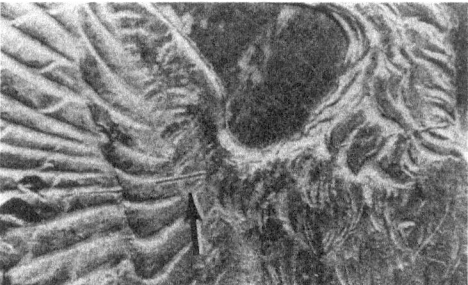
1 R Die Gouge in Eagle

1 O Die Gouge through B

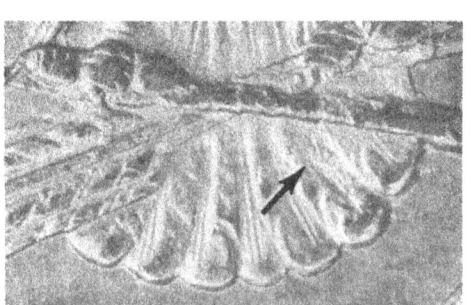
1B R Pitted Tail Feathers

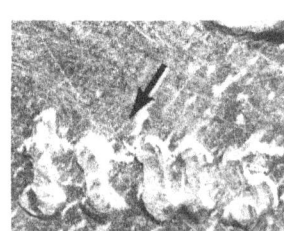
2 R Broken R

2 R Open G

3 O Doubled LIBERTY Right

1878-S

5   **II 4 • B² i (Doubled 878)**   I-2   R-4
      Obverse II 4 – Both 8's are doubled on the right side of the upper loop opening. Crossbar of the 7 is doubled at top and right side. S of PLURIBUS and UNU of UNUM slightly doubled right side. All letters of LIBERTY doubled with shift down. Lower hair slightly doubled. Nostril, lips and chin doubled.
      Reverse B² i – Feather engraved between eagle's right wing and leg. R in TRUST broken.

6   **II 5 • B² j (Doubled Motto)**   (184)   I-2   R-3
      Obverse II 5 – Motto letters doubled on top surface. Doubled 6 and 7 stars on left and 4, 5, and 6 stars on right. Doubled LIBERTY shifted left and up. Point on number 4 star on right is not broken off.
      Reverse B² j – Feather engraved between eagle's right wing and leg. R in TRUST broken.

7   **II 6 • B² i (Doubled LIBERTY Down)**   (184)   I-3   R-3
      Obverse II 6 – All letters of LIBERTY doubled with shift down. Point on number 4 star on right is broken off. Both 8's in date doubled at top right of upper loop opening and 7 is doubled on right and at top. Doubled nose, lips, chin, and neck.

8   **II 7 • B² k (Doubled LIBERTY Left)**   (184)   I-2   R-3
      Obverse II 7 – LIBERTY slightly doubled to left and also right on IB-R-Y. Point on number 4 star on right is broken.
      Reverse B² k – Feather engraved between eagle's right wing and leg. R in TRUST not broken.

9   **II 7 • B² l (Doubled LIBERTY Left)**   I-2   R-3
      Reverse B² l – Feather engraved between eagle's right wing and leg. R in TRUST broken.

10   **II 8 • B² b (Doubled Motto)**   I-2   R-3
      Obverse II 8 – LURIB of PLURIBUS doubled with LU doubled at top and RIB doubled at bottom.

11   **II 9 • B² b (Doubled Motto)**   I-3   R-3
      Obverse II 9 – All motto letters doubled strongly. All left stars doubled on left side with 6 and 7 also doubled on right. Doubled 1, 2, 4, 5, and 6 right stars. 1 and 7 in date doubled at top right. First 8 doubled on lower left outside of upper loop. Second 8 tripled at left inside of upper loop.

12   **II 10 • B² b (Doubled Motto)**   I-2   R-4
      Obverse II 10 – Motto letters doubled slightly on lower portion of top surface. Broken 4 star on right.

13   **II 7 • B² c (Doubled LIBERTY Left)**   I-2   R-3
      Reverse B² c – Small III S mint mark set slightly high and to right.

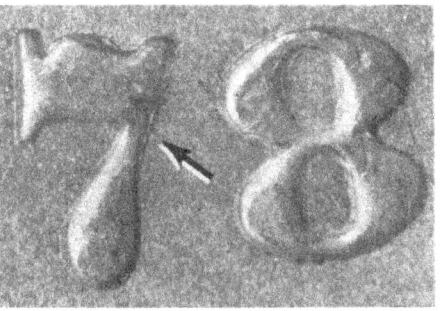

4 O Doubled Date

5 O Doubled 878

5 and 7 R Engraved Feather

6 R Engraved Feather

6 R Doubled Motto

7 O Doubled LIBERTY

1878-S

8 R Engraved Feather

8 O Doubled LIBERTY

11 O Doubled Motto

9 R Engraved Feather

10 O Doubled Motto

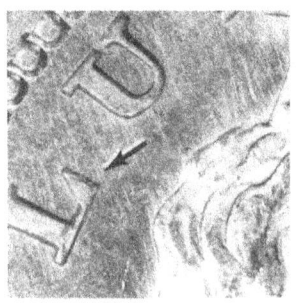

12 O Doubled Motto

13 R S Set High

14 R Engraved Feather

14 O Doubled LIBERTY

14 O Doubled P-R

14 O Doubled P-R

15 R Engraved Feather

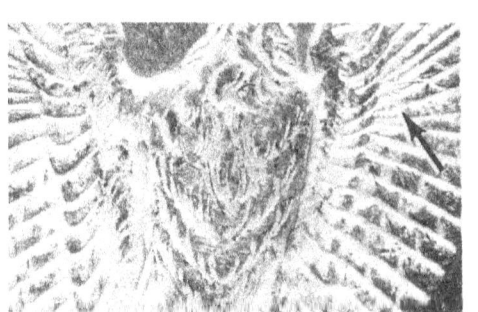

15 R Lines in Eagle

167

1878-S

14   II 11 – B² m (Doubled LIBERTY Left)   (181)   I-2   R-3
   Reverse B²m – Portions of eagle's wings over polished in middle. Feather engraved between eagle's right wing and leg. R in TRUST not broken.

15   II 11 • B² n (Lines in Eagle)   I-2   R-3
   Obverse II 11 – LIBERTY slightly doubled to left. P in PLURIBUS has bulge at top right outside, R is doubled slightly on left side and bottom crossbar of B is thin. 7 in date doubled at top and right side.
   Reverse B²n – Die polishing marks are strongly evident as heavy lines in middle of both wings and two diagonal lines between eagle's legs. Feathers engraved between eagle's right wing and leg. R in TRUST partially broken.

16   II 12 • B² o (Die Scratch on Wing)   (184)   I-2   R-4
   Obverse II 12 – E PLURIB letters in motto doubled on right side and some on bottom. 18-8 in date doubled slightly on bottom. Number 3 stars doubled on right and left. LIBERTY doubled slightly to left.
   Reverse B²o – Vertical die scratch through lower part of eagle's right wing. Some specimens show a die chip in middle of eagle's breast. Feather engraved between eagle's right wing and leg. R in TRUST not broken.

17   II 13 • B² d (Doubled D)   (184)   I-2   R-4
   Obverse II 13 – Bottom of die overpolished with shallow date and missing portions of lower hairline. First 8 in date has small die chip on right side between loops. 7 has raised slanted dash at very bottom on some specimens.
   Reverse B²d – D in DOLLAR doubled at left top outside and at left and right bottom outside. R in TRUST not broken.

18   II 1 • B² e (Extra Wing in Feathers)   (184)   I-3   R-4
   Obverse II 1 – Point of number four star on right only partially broken.
   Reverse B²e – Fine engraving lines in middle of both eagle's wings where die was overpolished due to incorrect basining.

19   II 14 • B² b (Doubled Motto, Die Gouge)   (181)   I-3   R-4
   Obverse II 14 – LIBERTY slightly doubled with shift up. Point on number 4 star on right is broken off. Nostril and eyelid doubled. Letters of E PL-R-BUS and U of motto doubled. Thick broad horizontal die gouge across wheat leaves and top cotton leaf. Field is slightly concave.
   Reverse B²b – Arm of R completely missing in TRUST with open G in God. Die extremely overpolished with letters of UNITED STATES very shallow and a number of leaves disconnected in the wreath. Small dots of metal all over eagle.

20   II 15 • B² o (Concave Obverse)   (184)   I-2   R-3
   Obverse II 15 – Field slightly concave, especially near the rim. Point of number 4 star on right broken off. Die chips on surface of E.

21   II 16 • B²f (Concave Obverse, Doubled Reverse)   I-3   R-3
   Obverse II 16 – Field slightly concave, especially near the rim. Point of number 4 star on right broken off. LIBERTY doubled slightly to left. E, P and B in E PLURIBUS slightly doubled at top with B also doubled and broken at bottom.
   Reverse B²f – Left wreath and lower part of right wreath doubled towards rim. UNITED STATES, ONE DOLLAR and left star doubled towards rim. Feather engraved between eagles right wing and leg.

22   II 19 • B²g (Doubled Motto, S Set Left)   I-3   R-3
   Reverse B²g – Small III S mint mark set left and slightly high. R in TRUST not broken.

23   II 1 • B²h (S/S Left)   I-3   R-3
   Reverse B²h – III S mint mark doubled with short diagonal line at top middle inside of upper loop and curved line within lower loop. R of TRUST is partially broken. Eagle's left wing slightly overpolished in center.

24   II 6 • B²a (Doubled LIBERTY Down)   (185)   I-3   R-3
   Reverse B²a – Portions of eagle's left wing overpolished in middle.

16, 20, and 28 R
Engraved Feather

16 R Line in Eagle's
Wing

16 R Die Chip

1878-S

16 O Doubled Motto

17 O Dash 7, Overpolished Die

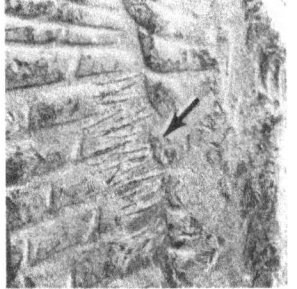 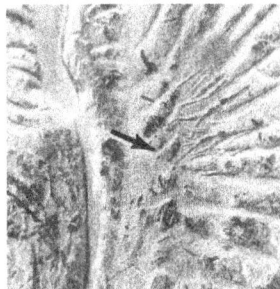

18 R Extra Wing Feathers   18 R Extra Wing Feathers

17 R Doubled D   20 O Die Chips on E

19 R Shallow Letters

19 O Die Gouge

19 O Doubled Motto

21 O Doubled B

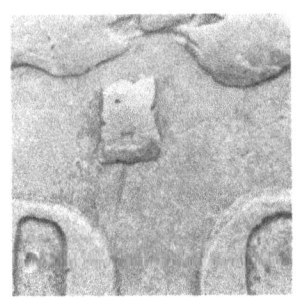 

22 R S Set Left   23 R S/S Left

21 R Engraved Feather

1878-S

25	II 1 • B²e (S Set High and Right)	(184)	I-2	R-3
26	II 1 • B¹a (Long Center Arrow Shaft)	(186)	I-3	R-7

Reverse B¹a – Normal die of 1878-P type B¹ with long center arrow shaft. Small III S mint mark set slightly to right with slight tilt to left.

27	II 1 • B¹b (Long Center Arrow Shaft)	(185)	I-3	R-7

Reverse B¹b – Small III S mint mark centered and upright.

28	II 1 • B²o (Die Scratch on Wing)	(184)	I-2	R-4
29	II 17 • B²q Tripled LIBERTY)	(184)	I-2	R-4

Obverse II 17 – LIBERTY tripled with images to left and right. Doubled eyelid and nostril.
Reverse B²q – Feather engraved between eagle's right wing and leg. R in TRUST not broken.

30	II 18 • B²r (Quadrupled LIBERTY)	(185)	I-2	R-3

Obverse II 18 – LIBERTY quadrupled with images to left, right and above.
Reverse B² r – Feather engraved between eagle's right wing and leg. R in TRUST not broken. Portions of eagle's left wing overpolished in middle.

31	II 1 • B²s (Engraved Wing Feather)	(184)	I-2	R-3

Reverse B²s – Feather engraved between eagle's right wing and leg. R in TRUST not broken.

32	II 1 • B²t (Engraved Wing Feather)	(184)	I-2	R-3

Reverse B²t – Feather engraved between eagle's right wing and leg. R in TRUST not broken.

33	II 1 • B²u (Engraved Wing Feather)	(184)	I-2	R-3

Reverse B²u – Feather engraved between eagle's right wing and leg. R in TRUST not broken.

34	II 1 • B²v (Engraved Wing Feather)	(184)	I-2	R-3

Reverse B²v – Feather engraved between eagle's right wing and leg. R in TRUST not broken. UNITED STATES OF doubled slightly towards rim.

35	II 1 • B²w (Engraved Wing Feather)	(181)	I-2	R-3

Reverse B²w – Feather engraved between eagle's right wing and leg. R in TRUST broken.

26 R B¹ Reverse, Tilted S

27 R B¹ Reverse

29 R Engraved Feather

29 O Doubled LIBERTY

30 O Doubled LIBERTY

1878-S

30 R Engraved Feather

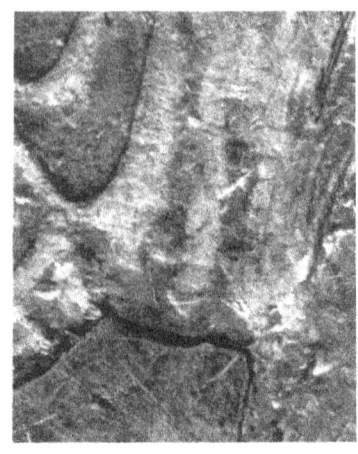
31 R Engraved Feather

32 R Engraved Feather

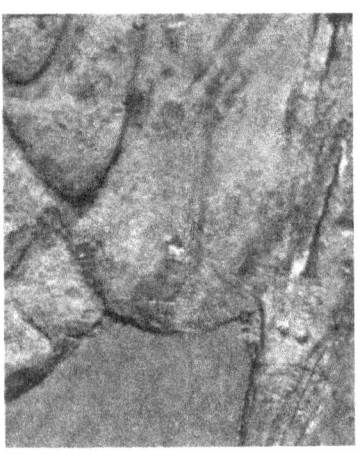
33 R Engraved Feather

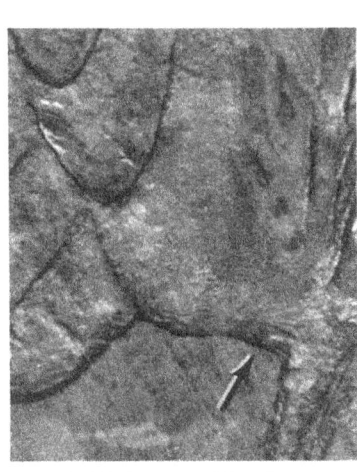
34 R Engraved Feather

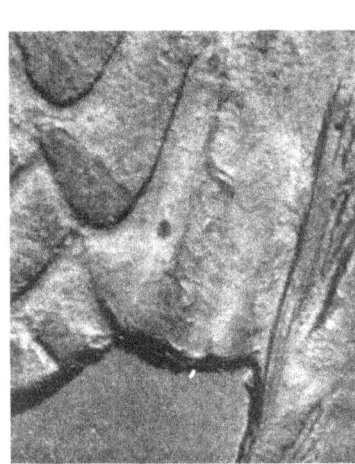
35 R Engraved Feather

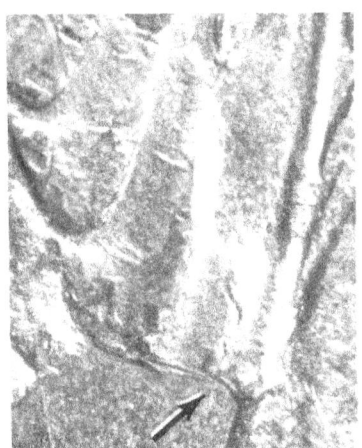
36 R Engraved Feather

36 R Engraved Feathers
Left Wing

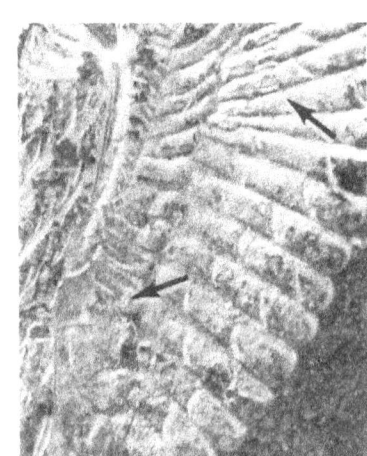
36 R Engraved Feathers
Right Wing

1878-S

36	II 1 • B²x (Engraved Wing Feathers)	(184)	I-2	R-3

Reverse B²x – Feather engraved between eagle's right wing and leg plus portions of feathers engraved in center of wings and next to body on eagle's left wing. R in TRUST broken.

37   II 1 • B²y (Engraved Wing Feather)   (184)   I-2   R-3
Reverse B²y – Feather engraved between eagle's right wing and leg. R in TRUST broken.

38   II 1 • B²z (Engraved Wing Feather)   (184)   I-2   R-3
Reverse B²z – Feather engraved between eagle's right wing and leg. R in TRUST broken.

39   II 1 • B²aa (Engraved Wing Feather)   (181)   I-2   R-3
Reverse B²aa – Feather engraved between eagle's right wing and leg. R in TRUST broken.

40   II 1 • B²ab (Engraved Wing Feather)   (184)   I-2   R-3
Reverse B²ab – Feather engraved between eagle's right wing and leg. R in TRUST broken.

41   II 19 • B²a (Doubled LIBERTY Up)   (184)   I-2   R-3
Obverse II 19 – LIBERTY doubled up.
Reverse B²a – Heavy vertical polishing lines in eagle's right wing.

42   II 20 • B²ac (Engraved Wing Feather)   (184)   I-2   R-3
Obverse II 20 – Doubled L-R-B U in Motto. Broken 4 star on right.
Reverse B²ac – Feather engraved between eagle's right wing and leg. R in TRUST not broken.

43   II 1 • B²r (Engraved Wing feather)   (185)   I-2   R-3

44   II 1 • B²j (Engraved Wing Feather)   (184)   I-2   R-3

45   II 1 • B²ad (Engraved Wing Feather)   (184)   I-2   R-3
Obverse II 1 – Small die chips below eyelid, on nose, behind eye and on cheek.
Reverse B²ad – Feather engraved between eagle's right wing and leg. R in TRUST slightly broken.

46   II 1 • B²i (Engraved Wing Feather)   (184)   I-2   R-3

47   II 1 • B²ae (Engraved Wing Feather)   (184)   I-2   R-3
Reverse B²ae – Feather engraved between eagle's right wing and leg. R in TRUST broken. Slightly doubled bottom inside of ITED STATES F and tops of IN GOD W.

48   II 1 • B²af (Engraved Wing Feather, S Tilted Right)   (184)   I-2   R-3
Obverse II 1 – Slight doubling of B in PLURIBUS.
Reverse B²af – Feather engraved between eagle's right wing and leg. R in TRUST partially broken. III S mint mark set slightly high with tilt to right.

49   II 1 • B²ag (Engraved Wing Feather)   (184)   I-2   R-3
Reverse B²ag – Feather engraved between eagle's right wing and leg and extending up towards body.

50   II 21 • B²ah (Tripled Eyelid, Engraved Wing Feather)   (184)   I-2   R-3
Obverse II 21 – Eyelid tripled in front of eye just below front of eyelid. 7 doubled on right side of vertical shaft. Broken 4th star on right.
Reverse B²ah – Feather engraved between eagle's right wing and leg extending upwards to top of wing with dots on surface.

37 R Engraved Feather   38 R Engraved Feather   39 R Engraved Feather

1878-S

40 R Engraved Feather

41 R Gouges in Wing

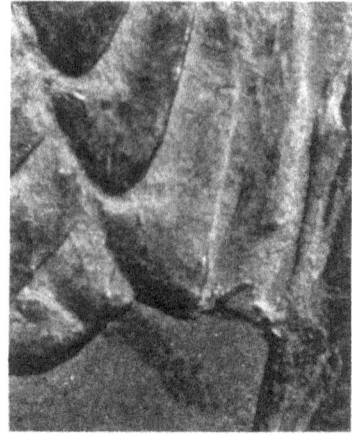
42 R Engraved Feather

41 O Doubled LIBERTY

42 O Doubled B

45 R Engraved Feather

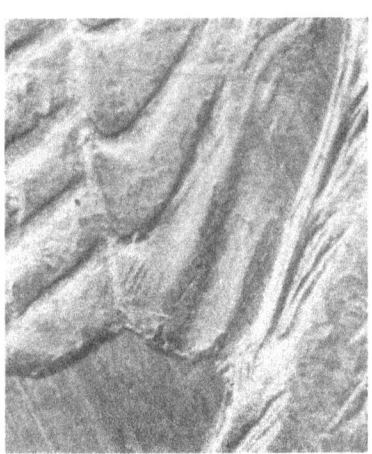
47 R Engraved Feather

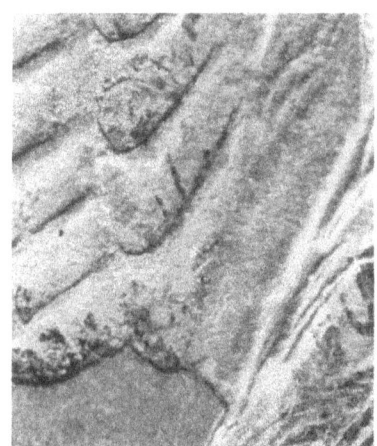
48 R Engraved Feather

48 R S Tilted Right

51	II 1 • B²ai (Engraved Wing Feather)		(184)	I-2	R-3
	Reverse B²ai – Feather engraved between eagle's right wing and leg.				
52	II 1 • B²aj (Engraved Wing Feather)		(184)	I-2	R-3
	Reverse B²aj – Feather engraved between eagle's right wing and leg. R in TRUST broken.				
53	II 1 • B²ak (Engraved Wing Feather)		(184)	I-2	R-3
	Reverse B²ak – Feather engraved between eagle's right wing and leg. R in TRUST not broken.				

1878-S

54   **II 22 • B²a (Doubled Profile)**   (181)   I-2   R-3
  Obverse II 22 – Liberty head profile doubled on nose, lips and chin. First four stars on left doubled towards rim. LIBERTY doubled slightly on left.

55   **II 1 • B²aj (Engraved Wing Feather)**   (181)   I-2   R-3
  Reverse B²aj – Feather engraved between eagle's right wing and leg. R in TRUST not broken.

56   **III 1 • B¹c (Long Center Arrow Shaft)**   (184)   I-3   R-7
  Reverse B¹c – Small III S mint mark set high, slightly to left and upright.

49 R Engraved Feather

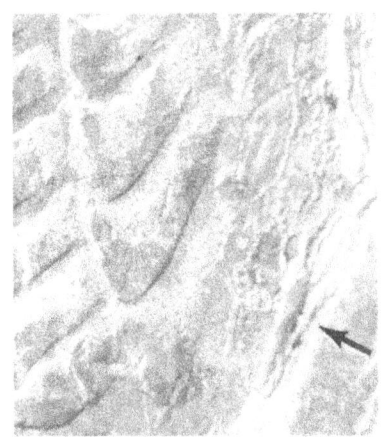

50 R Engraved Feather

51 R Engraved Feather

52 R Engraved Feather

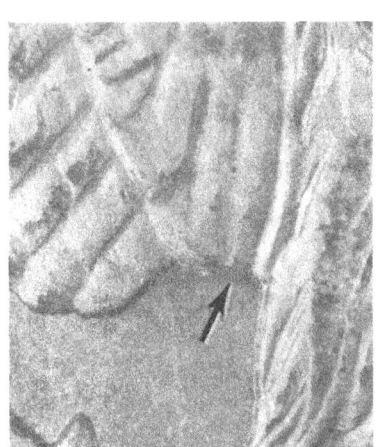

53 R Engraved Feather

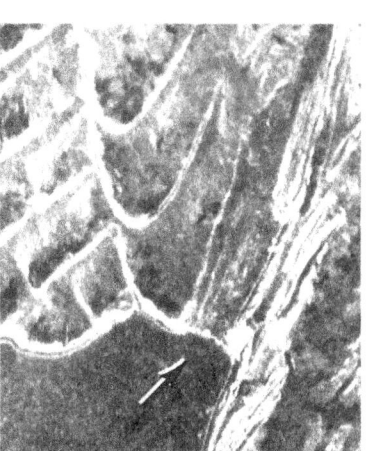

55 R Engraved Feather

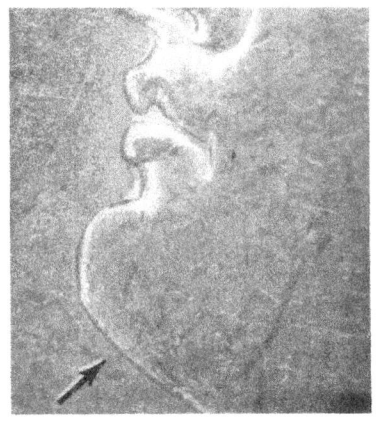

54 O Doubled Profile

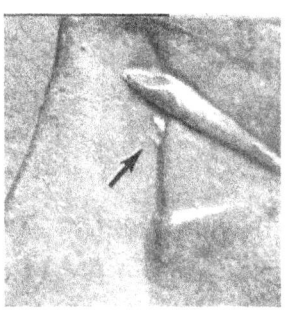

50 O Tripled Eyelid

174

1879-P

This was the first year that the C³ reverse with round breast and slanted arrow feathers was used exclusively. Usually this date is fully struck. Luster is average because of long use of dies to achieve high mintage. Quite a number of minor die varieties exist but none command significant premiums.

Fully proof-like specimens are fairly scarce for this date and the later 1880-1884-P mints. Deep mirror cameos exist for some of the proof-likes. Proofs are usually much better than the 1878-P proofs with deep mirrors and excellent contrast.

1	III² 1 • C³ a (Closed 9)		I-1	R-1

Obverse III² 1 – Normal die of III² type with closed 9 in date. Knob of 9 touches body.
Reverse C³ a – Normal die of C³ type.

1A	III²1 • C³ a (Pitted Reverse)	(180)	I-2	R-3

Reverse C³ a – Pitted die to right of wreath bow and on right side of eagle's tail feathers.

2	III²2 • C³ a (Open 9)		I-1	R-2

Obverse III²2 – Normal die with open 9 in date. Knob of 9 does not touch body.

3	III²3 • C³ a (Doubled 879)	(181)	I-2	R-4

Obverse III²3 – Doubled 879 in date. Slight doubling on right outside of both loops of 8. 7 doubled on lower right side and at top with dash below shaft. Both loops of 9 doubled on outside left. Closed and open 9 varieties.

4	III²4 • C³ a (Doubled 187)	(180)	I-2	R-4

Obverse III²4 – Doubled 187 in date. 1 is doubled strongly at bottom right and on right side of lower crossbar. 8 is doubled slightly at top right outside of both loops. 7 is doubled on right side and at top right. Open 9.

5	III²5 • C³ a (Doubled Date)		I-2	R-4

Obverse III² 5 – Date doubled at top with all numbers doubled at top outside. Open 9 variety.

6	III²6 • C³ a (Doubled 79)		I-2	R-4

Obverse III² 6 – Doubled 79 in date. Seven is doubled to the left with two points at the lower left of the top crossbar and a doubled stem. The 9 is doubled outside and inside at ten o'clock. Open 9 variety. Some specimens show a die chip between the loops of the 8 on the left side.

7	III²7 • C³ a (Doubled 9)	(179)	I-2	R-3

Obverse III²7 – Upper left outside of 9 is doubled. Some specimens show a die chip between the loops of the 8 on the left side. Open 9 variety.

1A R Pitted Wreath

3 O Doubled 879

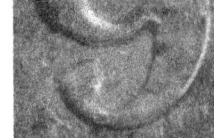

7 O Doubled 9

4 O Doubled 187

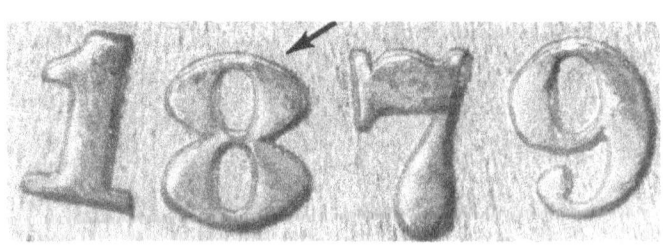

5 O Doubled Date

1879-P

8   III²8 • C³a (Doubled 1-79)   (179)   I-2   R-3
       Obverse III²8 – Doubled 1-79 in date. The right side of stem of the 1 and 7 are doubled. The lower left side of upper loop of the 9 is doubled.

9   III²9 • C¹a (Doubled 8-9)   I-2   R-3
       Obverse III²9 – Doubled 8-9 in date. 8 is doubled slightly on lower left outside of upper loop and bottom right outside of lower loop. 9 doubled strongly on left side of upper loop. Closed 9.

10   III²10 • C³a (Doubled 1)   I-2   R-3
       Obverse III²10 – 1 in date is doubled at top left of upper serif and on top left and right of bottom crossbar. Open 9 variety.

11   III²11 • C³a (Doubled 7)   I-2   R-3
       Obverse III²11 – 7 is doubled on left side of upper left serif and on right side of lower left serif. Closed 9.

12   III²12 • C³a (Doubled Date, Tripled 1)   I-2   R-4
       Obverse III²12 – Entire date doubled. 1 doubled on right and left sides of vertical shaft, on lower surface of top crossbar and is tripled on middle and right bottom of lower crossbar. 8 doubled on surface of right side of lower loop and top left of lower loop opening. 7 doubled strongly on lower right side of vertical shaft. Lower left outside of upper loop of 9 is doubled. Open 9 variety.

13   III²13 • C³a (Doubled 18-9)   (179)   I-2   R-3
       Obverse III²13 – Doubled 18-9 in date. 1 is doubled slightly at top left point, on surface of top crossbar and strongly at top left and right of bottom crossbar. The arc shows at top inside of lower loop of 8. 9 is doubled slightly at left outside of upper loop. Closed 9 variety.

14   III²14 • C³a (Doubled 879)   I-2   R-3
       Obverse III²14 – Doubled 879 in date. 8 is doubled at top inside of lower loop. 7 is doubled on right side of lower serif. 9 is doubled on left outside of upper loop. Closed 9 variety.

15   III²15 • C³a (Doubled Date)   (180)   I-2   R-3
       Obverse III²15 – All digits in the date are doubled. 1 is doubled slightly on the lower surface of the upper crossbar. 8 doubled at bottom right outside of lower loop. 7 doubled slightly at right of lower serif and strongly at bottom right of shaft. 9 doubled on left outside of both loops. Open 9 variety.

16   III²16 • C³a (Doubled Date)   (180)   I-2   R-3
       Obverse III²16 – All digits in date are doubled. 1 is doubled at upper left as vertical step on side of serif. 8 is slightly doubled on lower left outside of upper loop with die chip between loops on left side. Right side of 7 lower serif is doubled with bottom of crossbar slightly doubled. Loops of 9 are both slightly doubled on left outside. Open 9 variety.

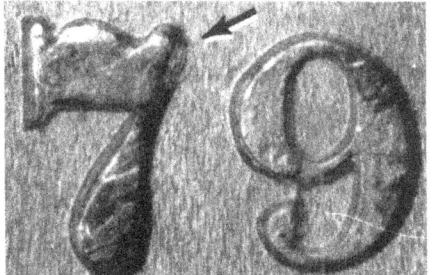
6 O Doubled 79

10 O Doubled 1

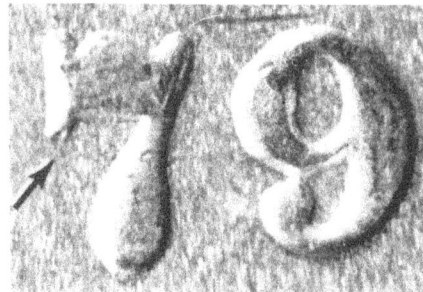
11 O Doubled 7

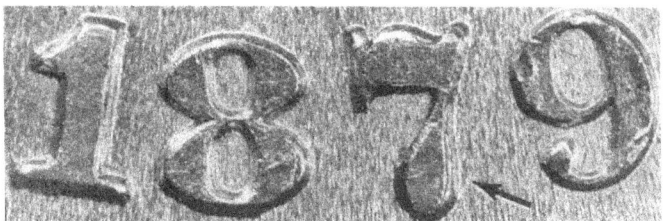
8 O Doubled 1-79

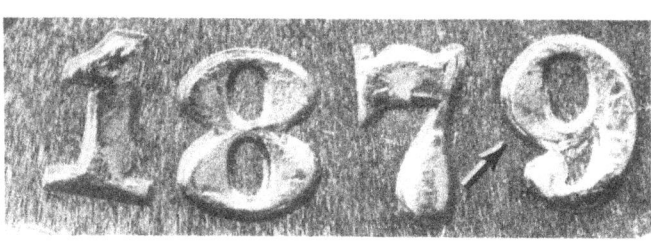
9 O Doubled 8-9

17   III²17 • C³b (Doubled Date)   (179)   I-3   R-4

Obverse III²17 – Entire date is strongly doubled at 10 o'clock. 1 is doubled at top left and on left side of vertical shaft. 8 is doubled at left outside and right inside of both loops with slight doubling at bottom right outside of lower loop. 7 doubled at very top, on left side of crossbar, at top left vertical shaft and faintly at bottom right. 9 doubled at left outside and right inside of both loops.

Reverse C³b – Centers of both eagle's wings overpolished with fine diagonal polishing lines on eagle's left wing.

12 O Tripled 1, Doubled Date

13 O Doubled 18-9

14 O Doubled 8-9

15 O Doubled Date

16 O Doubled Date

17 O Doubled Date

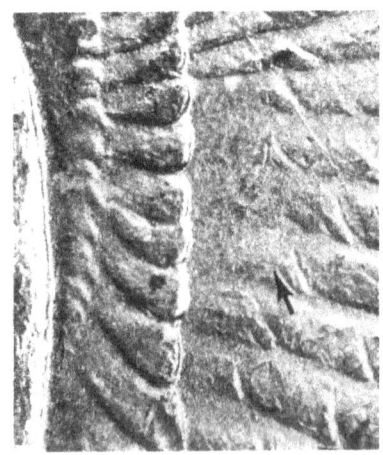
17 R Overpolished Wing

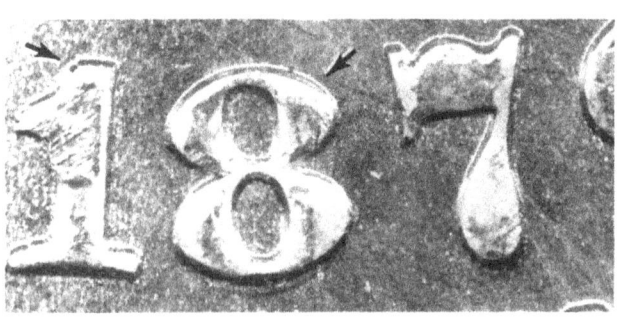
18 O Doubled 187

1879-P

18   III² 18 • C³ a (Doubled 187)   (180)   I-2   R-3
     Obverse III² 18 – Doubled 187 in date at top. 1 doubled at top and left corners as two steps. 8 doubled at top outside and bottom inside of upper loop. 7 doubled slightly on right side of top serif. Open 9 variety.

19   III² 19 • C³ a (Doubled Date)   (180)   I-2   R-3
     Obverse III² 19 – All digits in date are doubled. 1 is doubled above lower crossbar and slightly at top of upper crossbar. 8 doubled slightly at bottom left outside of lower loop. 7 doubled all across very top of crossbar. 9 doubled slightly at bottom left outside of lower loop. Heavy vertical polishing lines inside of ear and in hair.

20   III² 20 • C³ a (Doubled Date)   (179)   I-3   R-4
     Obverse III² 20 – Entire date strongly doubled. 1 doubled at very top, on top right of vertical shaft and at top on both sides of bottom crossbar. 8 doubled at top and lower left outside of upper loop and at right inside of both loops. 7 doubled at very top, on left side of crossbar and at top left on right side of vertical shaft. 9 doubled on left outside of both loops and at right inside of lower loop. First three stars on left doubled towards rim.

21   III² 21 • C³ a (Doubled Date)   (178)   I-2   R-3
     Obverse III² 21 – Entire date slightly doubled. 1 doubled at lower right side of vertical shaft and at bottom and right side of lower crossbar. 8 doubled slightly at left inside and lower right outside of lower loop. 7 doubled across very top and right side of vertical shaft. 9 doubled at left outside of both loops.

22   III² 22 • C³ a (Doubled Date)   (179)   I-2   R-3
     Obverse III² 22 – Entire date is slightly doubled. 1 doubled at top and left corner as two steps. 8 doubled at lower left outside of upper loop and bottom right outside of lower loop. 7 doubled at top left and right. 9 doubled at left outside of both loops.

23   III² 23 • C³ b (Doubled Date and Olive Leaves)   (181)   I-2   R-3
     Obverse III² 23 – Entire date is doubled. 1 doubled slightly at lower left of base. 8 doubled at left inside and right outside of both loops. 7 doubled slightly at top outside and strongly at lower right side of vertical shaft. 9 doubled at left outside of both loops.
     Reverse C³ b – Top olive leaves are doubled on left side as thin lines.

24   III² 24 • C³ a (Doubled 1-9)   (179)   I-2   R-3
     Obverse III² 24 – Doubled 1-9 in date. 1 doubled slightly below bottom of crossbar. 9 doubled at left outside of both loops. Open 9 variety. Number 4 – 7 left stars doubled slightly towards rim.

25   III² 25 • C³ a (Doubled Date)   (180)   I-2   R-3
     Obverse III² 25 – Entire date is doubled. 1 doubled slightly below upper crossbar. 8 doubled strongly on lower right outside of lower loop. 7 doubled at right of lower serif and strongly on lower right of vertical shaft. 9 doubled at left outside of both loops.

19 O Doubled Date

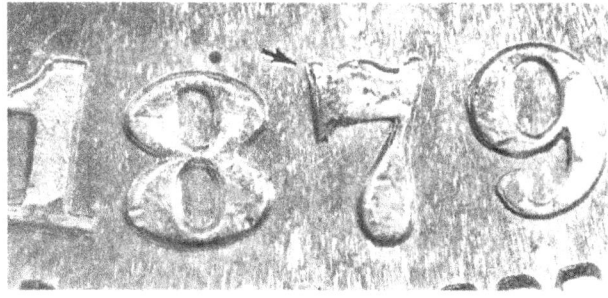

20 O Doubled Date

21 O Doubled Date

22 O Doubled Date

1879-P

23 O Doubled Date

23 R Doubled Olive Leaves

24 O Doubled 1-9

25 O Doubled Date

26   **III²26 • C³a (Doubled Date)**   (181)   I-2   R-3
Obverse III²26 – Entire date is doubled. 1 doubled slightly at top right of vertical shaft. 8 is doubled strongly at right outside of lower loop. 7 doubled on left side of crossbar and strongly on lower right of vertical shaft with dash below shaft. 9 doubled slightly on left outside of upper loop.

27   **III²27 • C³a (Doubled 879)**   (179)   I-2   R-3
Obverse III²27 – Doubled 878 in date. 8 doubled slightly at left inside and lower right outside of lower loop. 7 doubled at lower right of vertical shaft. 9 doubled at left outside of lower loop.

28   **III²28 • C³a (Doubled 8-9)**   (180)   I-2   R-3
Obverse III²28 – Doubled 8-9 in date. 8 doubled slightly at bottom right outside of lower loop. 9 doubled at left outside of both loops.

29   **III²23 • C³a (Doubled Date)**   (179)   I-2   R-3
Obverse III²23 – Die has been lightly polished with some missing lower hair detail.
Reverse C³a – Die has been lightly polished with some disconnected wreath leaves.

30   **III²29 • C³a (Doubled 879)**   (179)   I-2   R-3
Obverse III²29 – Double 879 in date. 8 doubled slightly at left inside and both loops. 7 doubled on right side of vertical shaft on surface. 9 doubled on left outside of both loops.

31   **III²1 • C³c (Double Reverse)**   (179)   I-2   Proof
Reverse C³c – Doubled UNIT, ES OF, AMERICA, and ONE DOLLAR toward rim. TED, O, ERICA, ONE DOLL also doubled on side toward coin center, left and right wreaths doubled at top outside.

32   **III²30 • C³a (Doubled 1-79)**   (179)   I-2   R-3
Obverse III²30 – 1-79 in date. 1 doubled below upper crossbar as a notch, on lower right side of vertical shaft and below lower crossbar as notch on left side and notch on right end. 7 doubled slightly on lower right side of vertical shaft. 9 doubled on left outside of upper loop.

33   **III²31 • C³a (Doubled 8-9, Pitted Left Wreath)**   (179)   I-2   R-3
Obverse III²31 – Doubled 8-9 in date. 8 doubled on left inside of upper loop. 9 doubled on left outside of both loops.
Reverse C³a – Pitted die from rust in lower left wreath and above D of DOLLAR.

34   **III²7 • C³d (Doubled 9 and Reverse Lettering)**   (179)   I-2   R-3
Reverse C³d – Doubled UNITED STATES OF AMERICA, ONE DOLLAR, stars and IN GOD WE TRUST on sides and top outside of left wreath.

1879-P

26 O Doubled Date

27 O Doubled 879

28 O Doubled 8-9

30 O Doubled 879

Proof 31 R Doubled Legend

32 O Doubled 1-79

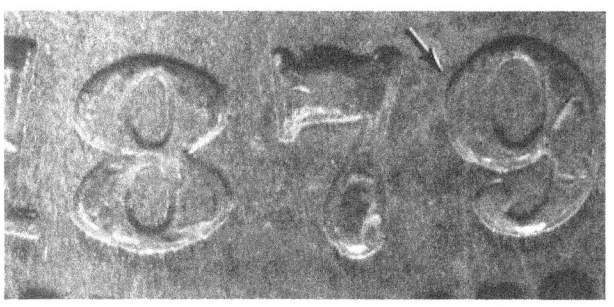
33 O Doubled 8-9

33 R Pitted Wreath

34 R Doubled Reverse Lettering

35   III²32 • C³a (Doubled Date and Stars)   (179)   I-3   R-3

Obverse III²32 – Entire date is doubled. 1 doubled below top and bottom crossbar. 8 doubled at lower left outside of upper loop and right inside and bottom outside of lower. 7 doubled slightly at bottom of stem. 9 doubled at left outside of upper loop. All left and right stars doubled towards rim. Liberty head profile of forehead, nose, lips and chin slightly doubled.

35 O Doubled Date

1879-CC

This is the first of the more expensive key date Morgan dollars. Not many die varieties are known for this date. The most prominent is VAM 3 with a large CC over small CC, the so-called capped CC variety. This is the only major die variety in the Morgan series that is price discounted. Apparently the large CC was punched over the small CC of the type used for the 1878-CC and attempts were made to obliterate the small CC remains with engraving tools. The result is a messy looking CC which in the past was mistaken for a counterfeit CC.

Generally this issue is strongly struck although some slightly weak strikes exist. Although scarce in uncirculated condition, a fairly large percentage of these are full proof-like with average to good contrast. But deep mirror cameos are quite rare.

1   III²1 • C³a (Closed 9)   I-1   R-3
Obverse III²1 – Normal die of III² type with closed 9 in date.
Reverse C³a – Normal die of C³ type with V CC mint mark shifted to the left.

2   III²2 • C³b (Open 9)   (177)   I-1   R-3
Obverse III²2 – Normal die with open 9 in date.
Reverse C³b – Normal die with V CC mint mark shifted slightly and tilted to the left. Bottom of G in GOD partially filled.

3   III²3 • C³c (Large Over Small CC)   I-3   R-3
Obverse III²3 – 18 in date doubled strongly at top. Open 9 doubled slightly at bottom.
Reverse C³c – Metal above and within the CC mint mark, a large over small mint mark. G in GOD filled on some specimens.

4   III²1 • C³d (Doubled C)   (178)   I-2   R-3
Obverse III²1 – Die chip on the left between the loops of the first 8 in date. Closed 9 variety.
Reverse C³d – V CC mint mark shifted to left with large spacing between C's. Right C is doubled on left inside.

 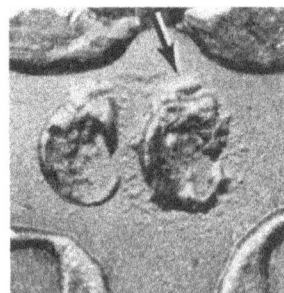  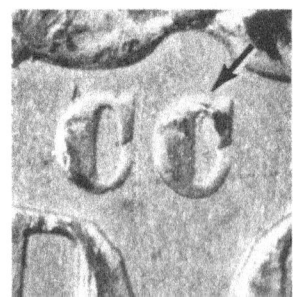

3 O Doubled 18

2 R CC Tilted Left   3 R Large Over Small CC   4 R Doubled C

1879-O

1879-O

The first issue for the New Orleans Morgan dollar is usually characterized by a strong strike and good luster. Some soft strikes with slightly weak hair over the ear and breast feathers exist, however. Although a number of minor varieties exist the only major one for this date is VAM 4 O/O horizontal which is possibly a tripled O. The remains of a horizontal O shows within the normal O mint mark and it brings some price premium. There are also two size mint marks but both are common and do not bring any premium.

Proof-likes are fairly scarce for this issue but some deep mirror cameos exist. Many coins of this issue were lightly circulated and then put back into storage vaults. Always carefully examine purported uncirculated specimens for gray areas and traces of wear.

Twelve branch mint proofs were struck for this date to commemorate the reopening of the New Orleans Mint. Four proofs are known to have survived and two of these are very deep mirror cameos.

1   III²1 • C³a (Closed 9)   (176)   I-1   R-2
Obverse III²1 – Normal die of III² type with closed 9. Some specimens show die chip between loops of 8 on left side.
Reverse C³ a – Normal die of C³ type with tall, oval medium mint mark centered and upright.

2   III²2 • C³a (Open 9)   (176)   I-1   R-2
Obverse III²2 – Normal die of III² type with open 9 in date.

3   III²3 • C³b (Large O)   (176)   I-1   R-2
Obverse III²3 – The loop of the 9 is doubled to the left. Closed and open 9 varieties.
Reverse C³ b – Normal die of C³ type with large, IV O centered mint mark.

4   III²4 • C³c (O/O horizontal)   (176)   I-3   R-5
Obverse III²4 – 9 in date has the upper loop strongly doubled to the left. Open 9 variety.
Reverse C³ c – Medium II O centered mint mark over horizontal O. The horizontal O shows as lines at the top and bottom of the opening. Possibly triple O with first two punches high and low.

5   III²5 • C³a (Doubled 9)   (176)   I-2   R-3
Obverse III²5 – 9 in date is doubled at bottom lower left. Open 9 variety.

6   III²5 • C³d (O Tilted Right)   (176)   I-2   R-3
Reverse C³ d – Centered II O mint mark tilted right.

7   III²2 • C³e (O Tilted Left)   (176)   I-2   R-3
Reverse C³ e – Centered II O mint mark tilted slightly left.

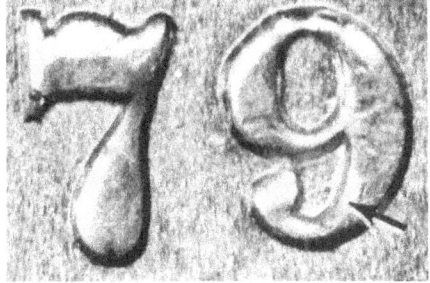
1A O Die Chips in Date

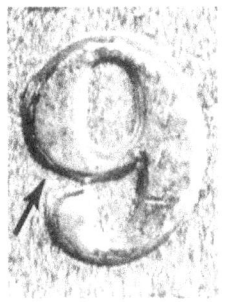
3 O Doubled 9

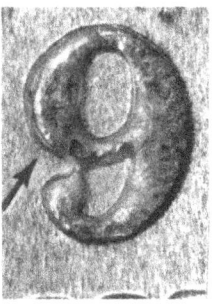
4 O Doubled 9

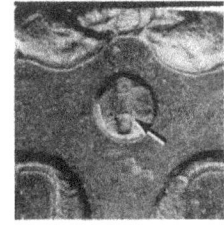
4 R O/O Horizontal

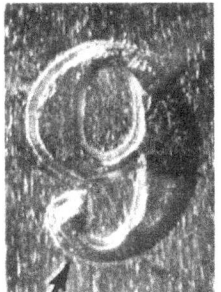
5 O Doubled 9

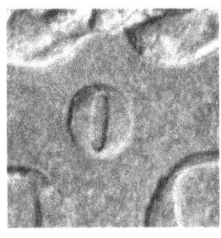
6 R O Tilted Right

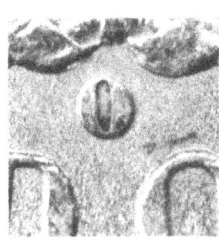
7 R O Tilted Left

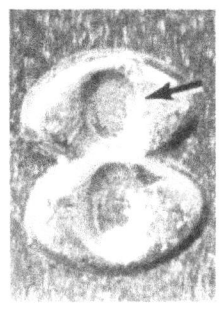
8A O Die Chips in 8

11 R O Set Left

1879-O

8	III²2 • C³b (Large O)	(176)	I-1	R-2
8A	III²2 • C³b (Die Chips in 8)	(176)	I-1	R-3

Obverse III²2 – Die chips with horizontal polishing marks inside upper loop of 8 and at top and bottom inside of lower loop.

9	III²5 • C³b (Doubled 9)	(176)	I-2	R-3
10	III²6 • C³b (Doubled 8-9)	(176)	I-2	R-3

Obverse III²6 – Doubled 8-9 in date. 8 doubled at left and top inside of lower loop with polishing marks inside of lower loop and lower right inside of upper loop. 9 doubled on top surface of left outside of lower loop.

11	III²6 • C³f (Doubled 8-9)	(176)	I-2	R-3

Reverse C³f – IV O mint mark set left and tilted slightly right.

12	III²7 • C³b (Doubled 87)	(176)	I-2	R-4

Obverse III²7 – Doubled 87 in date. 8 doubled slightly on lower outside of lower loop and slightly at top inside of upper loop. 7 doubled on right side and slightly at bottom of crossbar.

13	III²8 • C³e (Doubled Date)	(176)	I-2	R-3

Obverse III²8 – Entire date is doubled. 1 doubled at very top. 8 doubled slightly at very top and right outside of upper loop and very slightly on right outside of lower loop. 7 doubled slightly on right side of left serif, top outside of crossbar and right outside of vertical stem. 9 doubled on left outside of upper loop.

14	III²9 • C³b (Doubled 879)	(176)	I-2	R-3

Obverse III²9 – Doubled 879 in date. 8 doubled at top right inside of lower loop. 7 doubled at right side below crossbar and as a short spike on right side of lower serif. 9 doubled slightly on surface at left outside of both loops.

15	III²10 • C³b (Doubled Date)	(176)	I-2	R-3

Obverse III²10 – Entire date doubled slightly on top surface. 1 doubled at very top and half of loop at left side of bottom crossbar. Right outside of upper loop of 8 is slightly doubled. Bottom of 7 crossbar is doubled. Upper and lower loops of 9 are doubled on left outside.

10 O Doubled 8-9

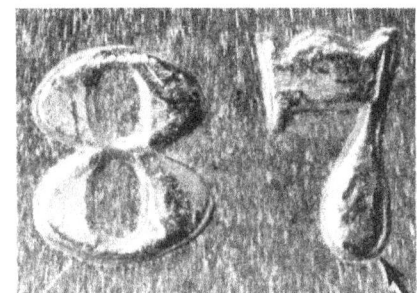

12 O Doubled 87

13 O Doubled Date

14 O Doubled 879

15 O Doubled Date

16 R Low O

1879-O

16	III²3 • C³g (Doubled 9, Low O Set Right)	(176)	I-2	R-3

Reverse C³g – IV O mint mark set low, upright and slightly to the right.

17	III²11 • C³a (Doubled 87)	(176)	I-2	R-4

Obverse III²11 – Doubled 87 in date. 8 doubled slightly at the top outside and left inside of lower loop. 7 doubled on right side of vertical stem.

18	III²12 • C³h (Doubled 8-9, Low O)	(176)	I-2	R-3

Obverse III²12 – Doubled 8-9 in date. 8 doubled at bottom of lower loop. 9 doubled at left outside of both loops. Open 9 variety.
Reverse C³h – IV O mint mark set low, upright and centered.

19	III²13 • C³a (Doubled 87)	(176)	I-2	R-3

Obverse III²13 – Doubled 87 in date. 8 doubled slightly at bottom left outside of both loops. 7 doubled below crossbar. Open 9 variety.

20	III²7 • C³a (Doubled 87)	(176)	I-2	R-4
21	III²14 • C³a (Doubled 187)	(176)	I-2	R-3

Obverse III²14 – Doubled 187 in date. 1 slightly doubled below both crossbars. 8 doubled at lower left outside of upper loop and at bottom outside of lower loop. 7 doubled slightly below upper crossbar.

22	III²15 • C³a (Doubled 8-9)	(176)	I-2	R-3

Obverse III²15 – Doubled 8-9 in date. 8 doubled slightly at top outside of upper loop. 9 doubled on left outside of both loops.

23	III²16 • C³a (Tripled 8, Doubled 9)	(176)	I-2	R-3

Obverse III²16 – 8 tripled at left inside of upper loop. 9 doubled slightly on left outside of upper loop.

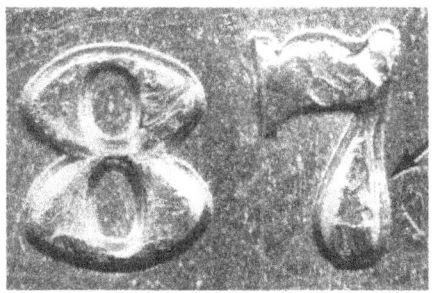
17 O Doubled 87

18 O Doubled 8-9

18 R O Set Low

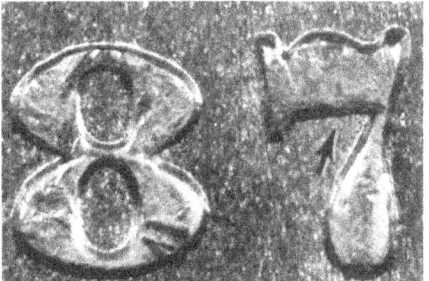
19 O Doubled 87

21 O Doubled 187

22 O Doubled 8-9

23 O Tripled 8, Doubled 9

1879-O / 1879-S

24   III²17 • C³h (Doubled Date, Low O)   (176)   I-2   R-3
    Obverse III²17 – All digits in date are slightly doubled. 1 doubled at very bottom of base. 8 doubled at bottom outside of lower loop. 7 doubled on lower right of vertical shaft. 9 doubled on left outside of both loops. Open 9 variety.

25   III²18 • C³b (Doubled Date)   (176)   I-2   R-3
    Obverse III²18 – All digits slightly doubled in date. 1 doubled slightly on right side of vertical shaft. 8 doubled slightly at top outside of upper loop and top right inside of lower loop. 7 doubled at very top and slightly on lower right side of vertical shaft. 9 doubled at left outside of both loops.

26   III²3 • C²a (Doubled 9, Die Chips in Date)   (176)   I-2   R-3
    Obverse III²3 – Both loops of 9 are doubled on left outside. Die chips with polishing marks in upper part of lower loop of 8 and 9. Closed 9 variety.

27   III²19 • C³a (Doubled 18)   (176)   I-2   R-3
    Obverse III²19 – Doubled 18 in date. 1 doubled at top left and at top left and right of bottom crossbar. First 8 doubled at top outside of upper loop.

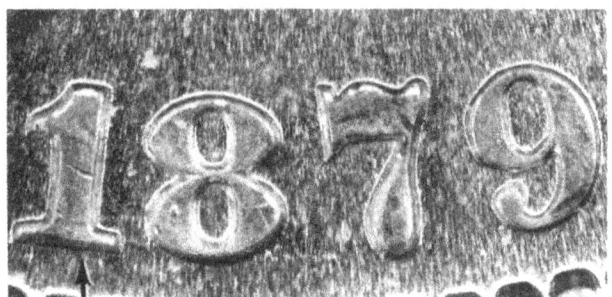
24 O Doubled Date

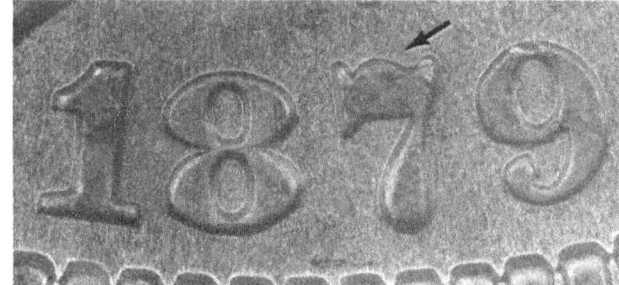
25 O Doubled Date

26 O Doubled 9

27 O Doubled 18

1879-S

This issue is usually fully struck as are most of the other common date S mints from 1880 to 1882. Occasionally a slightly weak strike will surface, however. A number of minor die varieties exist that do not command any premium. The one major variety is the B reverse with flat eagle's breast and it commands a substantial premium in all grades. Most of these flat breast reverse of 1879 have engraved wing feathers like the 1878-S. Although a number of the dies were engraved at the San Francisco Mint they do not bring any additional premium over the usual flat breast variety.

Proof-like 1879-S are available although somewhat scarcer than those of 1880-S and 1881-S. A few exhibit deep mirror cameo on both sides. Some 1879-S are only one sided proof-like and command only a slight premium over a non proof-like. Proof-like 1879-S flat breast reverse of 1878 are very scarce for the high uncirculated grades.

1   III²1 • C³a (Closed 9)   (183)   I-1   R-2
    Obverse III²1 – Normal die of the III² type with closed 9.
    Reverse C³a – Normal die of C³ type with medium IV S mint mark centered and upright.

1A   III²1 • C³a (Polished 8)   I-1   R-3
    Obverse III²1 – 8 in date has polishing lines within loops. There are also polishing lines in lower hair.

1879-S

1B   III²1 • C²a (Hair Ribbon)   (185)   I-2   R-3
Obverse III²1 – Horizontal die gauge through lower hair.

2   III²2 • C³a (Open 9)   (185)   I-1   R-2
Obverse III²2 – Normal die of III² type with open 9.

3   III²3 • C³b (Doubled 9)   (185)   I-2   R-3
Obverse III²3 – 9 in date doubled on left side. On some specimens 8 has spike of metal on left side between loops. Open 9 variety.
Reverse C³b – Centered IV S mint mark tilted to left.

4   III²2 • B²a (PAF Reverse)   (184)   I-4   R-5
Reverse B²a – PAF reverse of B² type with small III S mint mark. R in TRUST not broken.

5   III²1 • B²b (Broken R)   (184)   I-4   R-4
Reverse B²b – PAF reverse of B² type with small III S mint mark. Broken R in TRUST with upper serif partially missing

6   III²2 • B²c (TIUST)   (184)   I-4   R-4
Reverse B²c – PAF reverse of B² type with small III S mint mark tilted slightly to the left. Broken R in TRUST to form TIUST with upper serif completely missing. Feather engraved between eagles right wing and leg.

7   III²1 • B²d (S/S Up)   I-4   R-4
Reverse B²d – Small III S mint mark doubled at bottom. PAF reverse of B² type with R in TRUST not broken.

7A   III²1 • B²d (S/S Up)   (184)   I-4   R-4
Reverse B²d – R in TRUST partially broken.

8   III²4 • B²e (Doubled 9)   I-4   R-4
Obverse III²4 – 9 in date doubled in left inside and left outside of both loops.
Reverse B²e – Feather engraved between eagle's right wing and leg. R in TRUST is partially broken.

9   III²5 • B²e (Doubled 9)   (184)   I-4   R-4
Obverse III²5 – Closed 9 in date doubled on left outside of lower loop.

10   III²6 • B²b (Doubled 79)   I-4   R-4
Obverse III²6 – 7 in date doubled at bottom of upper crossbar. Closed 9 with some showing a die flake at top left outside showing as a short arc.

11   III²1 • C³c (S/S Left)   (182)   I-3   R-3
Reverse C³c – IV S mint mark doubled with a short vertical line within the upper loop on right inside and curved line on right inside of lower loop.

12   III²7 • C³c (S/S Left)   (182)   I-3   R-3
Obverse III²7 – 7 in date slightly doubled on surface on right side of vertical shaft and on right side of bottom serif.

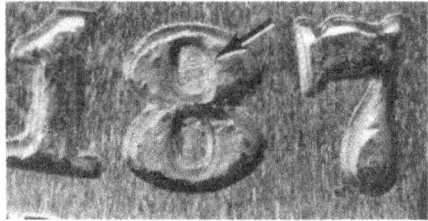

1A O Polished 8

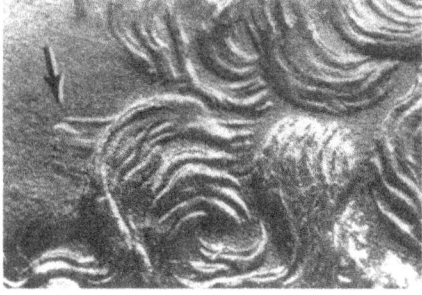

1B O Hair Ribbon, Die Gouge

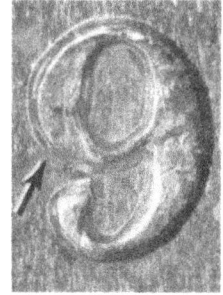

3 O Doubled 9

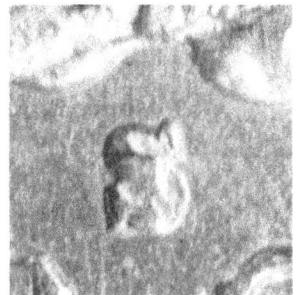

3 R S Tilted Left

5 R Broken r

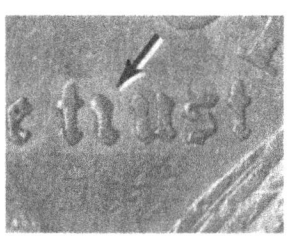

6 R TIUST

1879-S

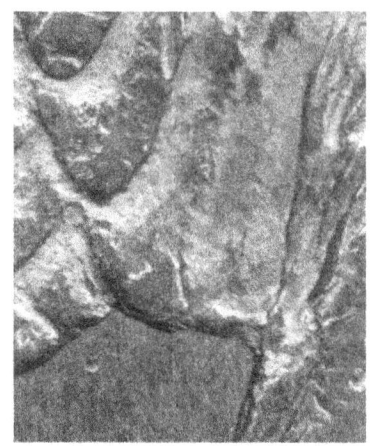
6 R Engraved Feather

7 R S/S Up

8 O Doubled 9

9 O Doubled 9

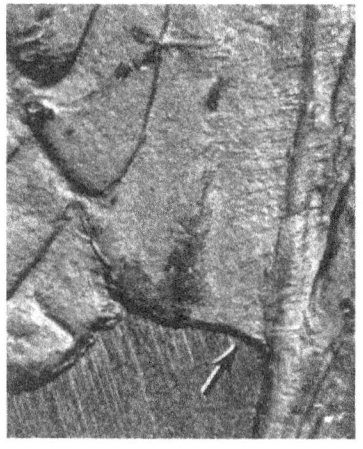
9 R Engraved Feather

10 O Doubled 79

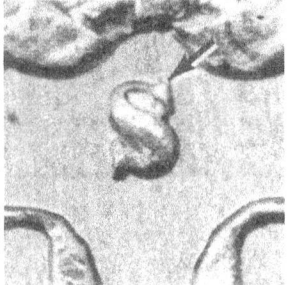
11 R S/S Left

12 O Doubled 7

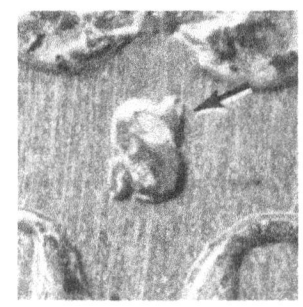
13 R S/S Right

13	III²2 • C³d (S/S Right)		(184)	I-2	R-3

Reverse C³d – IV S mint mark doubled on all of right side of upper serif.

14	III²3 • C³e (S/S Middle)		(184)	I-2	R-3

Reverse C³e – IV S mint mark doubled at bottom of upper loop opening as thick slanted bar and in middle of lower loop opening as a curved line.

15	III²8 • C³f (Doubled 18 and S/S)		(185)	I-2	R-3

Obverse III²8 – 1 in date doubled at top left and right of lower crossbar. First 8 doubled at top right inside of lower loop. Open 9 variety.
Reverse C³f – Filled IV S mint mark with top serif doubled on lower right side and slightly at very bottom.

16	III²3 • C³a (Doubled 9)		(182)	I-2	R-3
16A	III²3 • C³a (Doubled 9, Gouge in Bow)			I-2	R-4

Reverse C³a – Triangular die gouge from lower right end towards mint mark.

17	III²9 • C³f (Doubled Date)		(185)	I-2	R-3

1879-S

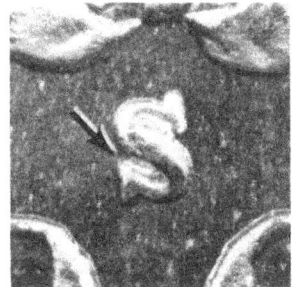
14 R S/S Middle

15 O Doubled 1

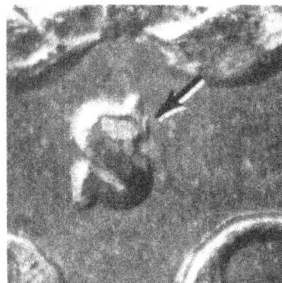
15 R Doubled S

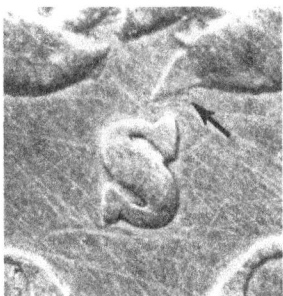
16A R Gouge in Bow

18 O Doubled Date

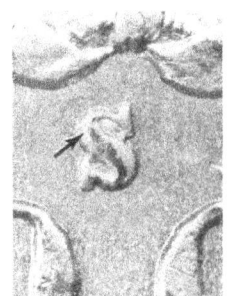
19 R S/S Tilted Left

| 18 | III²9 • C³b (Doubled Date) | | I-2 | R-3 |

Obverse III²9 – Entire date slightly doubled on surface. 1 doubled at top right. 8 doubled at bottom right outside. 7 doubled on bottom of upper serif and right side of shaft plus very bottom. 9 is doubled at left outside of both loops.

| 19 | III²1 • C³g (S/S Tilted Left) | (184) | I-2 | R-3 |

Obverse III²1 – With polishing lines in 8.
Reverse C³g – IV S mint mark doubled on left side of top loop with tilt to left.

| 20 | III²8 • C³a (Doubled 1) | (185) | I-2 | R-3 |

| 21 | III²10 • C³h (Doubled Date, S/S High) | (184) | I-3 | R-3 |

Obverse III²10 – Entire date is doubled. 1 is doubled at bottom of lower crossbar in middle. 8 doubled slightly at left inside and right outside of lower loop. 7 doubled strongly at very top and slightly on right side of vertical shaft. 9 doubled slightly at left outside of both loops.
Reverse C³h – IV S mint mark doubled with curved diagonal line in middle of upper loop opening and a diagonal line at top of lower loop opening.

| 22 | III²11 • C³b (Doubled Date) | (183) | I-2 | R-3 |

Obverse III²11 – Entire date is doubled. 1 is doubled at very top and top right of vertical shaft. 8 is doubled at top outside of upper loop and bottom right outside of lower loop. 7 is doubled below crossbar and on right side of vertical shaft. 9 is doubled on left outside of both loops.

23	III²4 • B²a (PAF Reverse, Doubled 9)		I-4	R-4
24	III²5 • B²a (PAF Reverse, Doubled 9)		I-4	R-4
25	III²6 • B²a (PAF Reverse, Doubled 7)	(184)	I-4	R-4

Obverse III²6 – Top of 9 not broken away to form arc. Some specimens show raised dots on feathers from rusted die.

| 26 | III²12 • C³a (Doubled 879) | (184) | I-2 | R-3 |

Obverse III²12 – Doubled 879 in date. 8 doubled slightly at lower left outside of upper loop and top inside of lower loop with spike of metal between loops on left of some specimens. 7 doubled in middle at top and on lower right side of shaft. 9 doubled strongly on left outside and slightly on inside of upper loop and slightly on left outside of lower loop.

| 27 | III²13 • C³b (Doubled Date) | (185) | I-2 | R-3 |

Obverse III²13 – Entire date is doubled. 1 is doubled below upper crossbar. 8 doubled at top inside of lower loop, doubled slightly at lower left outside of upper loop, and has a notch on the left outside of the upper loop. 7 doubled below upper crossbar and at very bottom of stem. 9 doubled slightly at lower left outside of both loops.

1879-S

28   III² 14 • C³a (Doubled 1-9)   (185)   I-2   R-3
Obverse III² 14 – Doubled 1-9 in date. 1 doubled below upper crossbar. 9 doubled slightly on left outside of both loops.

29   III² 15 • C³a (Doubled 9 and Right Obverse)   (185)   I-3   R-4
Obverse III² 15 – 9 in date doubled at left outside of upper loop. Right side doubled towards rim on wheat grain, top leaf, back of Liberty cap, BUS UNUM and 3 to 6 stars on right. Long diagonal die gouge in hair above eye.

30   III² 1 • C³i (S/S Far Left)   (182)   I-3   R-3
Reverse C³i – IV S mint mark doubled with short vertical spike at top middle of upper loop opening and curved line in middle of lower loop opening. S mint mark set slightly to right with slight tilt to left.

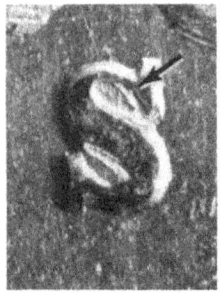
21 R   S/S High

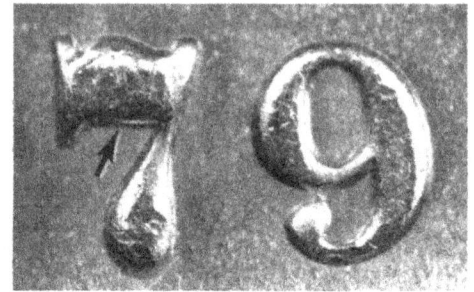
21 O   Doubled Date   25 O   Doubled 7

22 O   Doubled Date

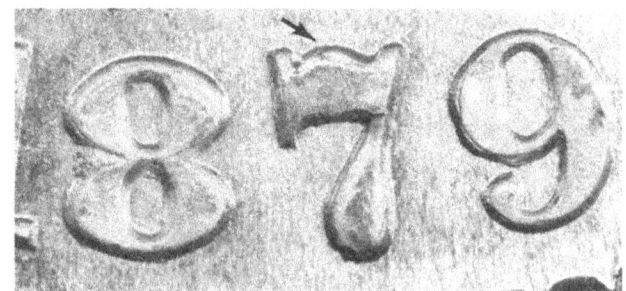
26 O   Doubled 879

27 O   Doubled Date

28 O   Doubled 1-9

29 O   Die Gouge

29 O   Doubled Obverse

30 R   S/S Far Left

1879-S

31 III²16 • C³j (Doubled 879, S Set Left) (182) I-2 R-3
Obverse III² 16 – Doubled 879 in date. 8 tripled at bottom right outside of lower loop. 7 doubled slightly below crossbar. 9 doubled at left outside of upper loop.
Reverse C³j – Medium IV S mint mark set to left and upright.

32 III²5 • C³a (Doubled 9) (184) I-2 R-3

33 III²17 • C³k (Doubled 18-9, S Set Right) (181) I-2 R-3
Obverse III² 17 – Doubled 18-9 in date. 1 doubled at below lower crossbar. 8 doubled at lower outside of lower loop. 9 doubled slightly at left outside of lower loop.
Reverse C³k – Medium IV S mint mark upright and set to right.

34 III²5 • B²f (PAF, Engraved Wing Feather) (181) I-4 R-4
Reverse B²f – Feather engraved between eagle's right wing and leg. R in TRUST broken with upper serif almost completely missing.

35 III²5 • B²g (PAF, Engraved Wing feather) (181) I-4 R-4
Reverse B²g – Feather engraved between eagle's right wing and leg. R in TRUST partially broken.

36 III²1 • C³b (Polished 8, S Tilted Left) (184) I-2 R-3
Obverse III² 1 – Polishing lines within loops of 8.

37 III²1 • C³l (S/S Line) (184) I-2 R-3
Reverse C³l – Medium IV S mint mark doubled with a long thin line on right side of upper loop opening and a curved line on right side of lower loop opening. S mint mark centered and upright.

38 III²18 • C³a (Doubled 879) (185) I-2 R-3
Obverse III² 18 – Doubled 879 in date. 8 doubled at top right outside and lower left outside of upper loop. 7 doubled at top of crossbar and lower right of vertical shaft. 9 doubled on left outside of both loops.
Reverse C³a – Polishing lines in upper loop of IV S mint mark.

39 III²1 • B²g (PAF, Engraved Wing Feather) (183) I-4 R-4

40 III²19 • C³a (Doubled 18-9) (185) I-2 R-3
Obverse III² 19 – Doubled 18-9 in date. 1 doubled in middle of lower crossbar on ends. 8 doubled at top right outside of upper loop. 9 doubled outside of both loops.

41 III²20 • C³a (Doubled Stars and Date) (185) I-2 R-3
Obverse III² 20 – All left and right stars doubled towards rim. All digits in date slightly doubled. 1 is doubled at very bottom. 8 doubled slightly at lower left outside of upper loop. 7 doubled at top outside and below crossbar. 9 doubled slightly at left outside of lower loop.

31 O Doubled 879

33 O Doubled 18-9

31 R S Set Left

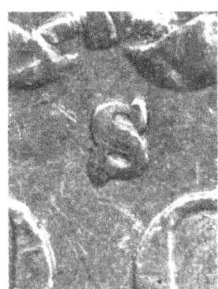

33 R S Set Right

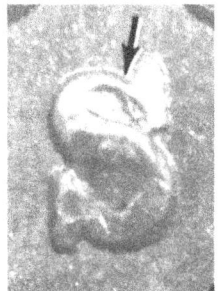

37 R S/S Line

1879-S / 1880-P

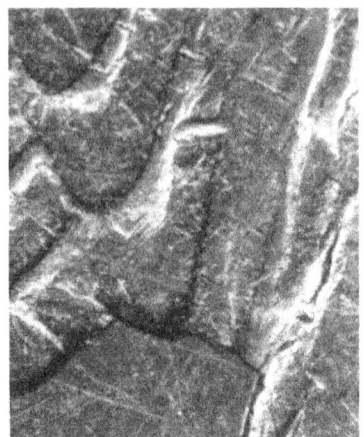

34 R Engraved Feather

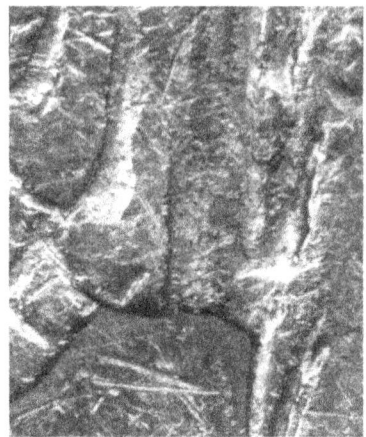

35 R Engraved Feather

38 O Doubled 879

40 O Doubled 18-9

41 O Doubled Date and Stars

1880-P

The strike for 1880-P is average for the series with most fairly well struck. But quite a few show a touch of weakness in the hair over the ear. This date contains its share of slightly doubled dates because of its fairly high mintage. It does have a number of interesting and scarce overdates however. The most prominent are VAM's 6, 7 and 8 with remains of the 7 within and above the 8. These command sizeable premiums in any grade. Only a few uncirculated specimens of VAM 7 and 8 are known, they are rare in all grades, however, and they are worth large premiums. VAM's 2, 9, 10, 11, 16, 25 and 29 are weaker overdates and not as scarce so they command little premium. VAM 23 shows the remains of the 79 on top of the 80 digits. It is quite scarce and brings a substantial premium.

Proof-like coins as with most early P mints are fairly scarce. Some deep mirror cameos do exist. The proof issue is one of the most available and generally has excellent contrast.

1   **III² 1 • C³ a (Normal Die)**   I-1   R-1
       Obverse III² 1 – Normal die of III² type.
       Reverse C³ a – Normal die of C³ type.

1880-P

1A III²1 • C³a (Broken 8)   I-2   R-5
Obverse III²1 – First 8 has a vertical die crack on the right side showing as a line below and a large knob of metal at top with line continuing up into hair and neck.

1B III¹1 • C³a (Lines in 8)   I-2   R-4
Obverse III¹1 – Second 8 has diagonal polishing lines at top right inside of lower loop.

2 III²2 • C³a (Doubled 0, 8/7)   I-3   R-4
Obverse III²2 – 0 in date doubled at top inside showing as a thin arc with a dot on right side below arc. Remains of 7 shows on surface of left side of upper loop of second 8 in form of check mark.

3 III²12 • C³a (Doubled 80 and Dash)   (180)   I-2   R-4
Obverse III²12 – 80 in date is doubled. The second 8 is doubled slightly at the very bottom, on lower left outside of upper loop and at the top on the left and right sides. It also has a faint long dash well below the bottom. The 0 is strongly doubled at top left and right outside and inside of lower left.

4 III²3 • C³3 (Doubled 0 and Dash)   I-2   R-3
Obverse III²3 – 0 in date is strongly doubled at top left and right bottom inside left side. A dash appears below the 8 in the date.

5 III²4 • C³a (Doubled Date)   (180)   I-2   R-3
Obverse III²4 – Entire date doubled. 1 doubled on right side of vertical shaft and below bottom of crossbar. First 8 doubled slightly on left inside of loops and bottom right outside of lower loop. Second 8 is doubled on lower left side of upper loop. The 0 is doubled on top left and right and on left inside. Some specimens show a large vertical die crack through 0 extending from hair down to the rim.

6 III²5 • C³a (8/7 Spikes)   (180)   I-5   R-5
Obverse III²5 – 8 repunched over 7 in date. Two serifs of 7 are clearly visible above second 8 as two short spikes and crossbar of 7 is visible inside the upper loop of the 8. There is a slight bulge on left side of the 0 where original 9 was punched. 1 is tripled at the very bottom. First 8 is doubled slightly at bottom outside of lower loop. Second 8 is doubled slightly at lower left outside of upper loop. 0 is doubled at left inside. Fine die chips show on right inside of first 8 lower loop.

7 III²6 • C³ (8/7 Crossbar)   I-5   R-7
Obverse III²6 – 8 repunched over 7 in date different than III²5 obverse. There are no ears above the 8 but the crossbar of the 7 is clearly visible in the upper loop with a straight lower edge. In the lower loop of the 8 remains the shaft of the 7 shows as two short lines. The 9 does not show in the 0. 1 doubled at very bottom left.

8 III²7 • C³a (8/7 Ears)   (179)   I-4   R-6
Obverse III²7 – Second 8 has two short ears at top. A small piece of metal is on the right side of the upper loop opening. The 9 does not show in 0.

1A O Broken 8

1B O Lines in 8

2 O Doubled 0

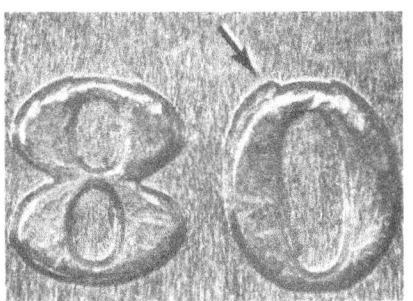
3 O Doubled 80 and Dash

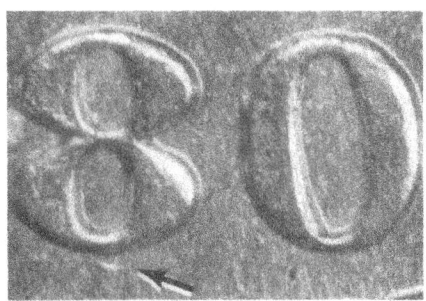
4 O Doubled 0 and Dash

1880-P

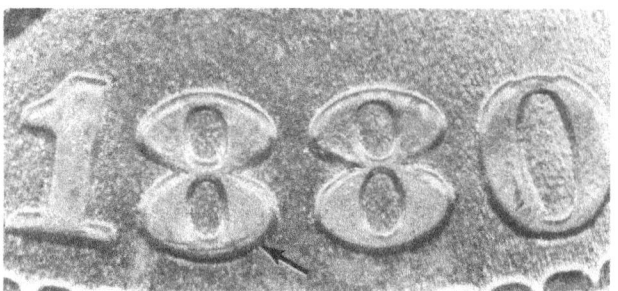

5 O Doubled Date

6 O 8/7 Spikes, Doubled Date

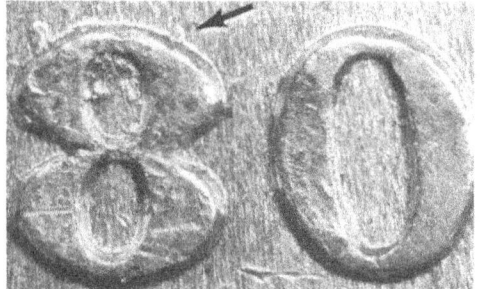

6 O 8/7 Spikes

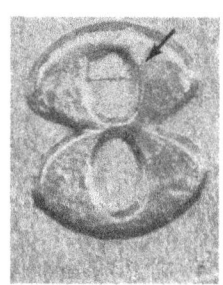

7 O 8/7 Crossbar

8 O 8/7 Ears

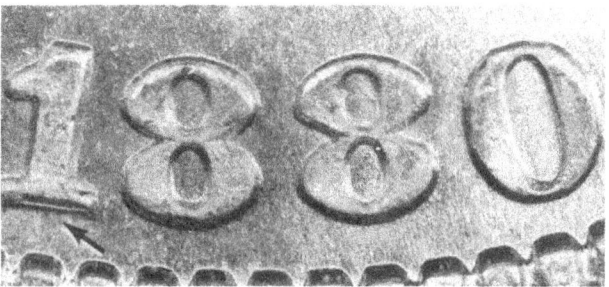

9 O 8/7 Stem

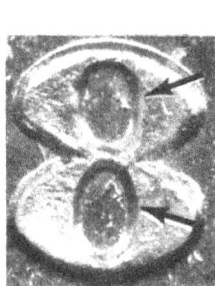

9 O 8/7 Stem

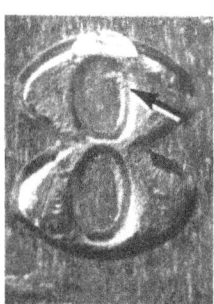

10 O 8/7 Bit

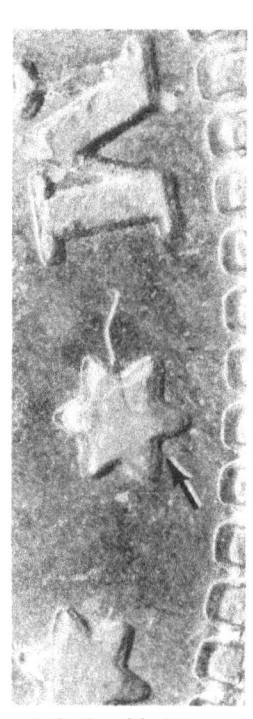

9 O Doubled Stars

9   III²8 • C³a (8/7 Stem)   (179)   I-3   R-5

Obverse III²8 – Second 8 has small piece of metal on right side of upper loop. Bottom loop has stem of 7 showing as a faint outline and metal inside. The 9 does not show in 0 but a bulge shows at 10 o'clock. 1 is doubled at very bottom. First 8 doubled at lower loop left outside of both loops. Second 8 tripled at lower left outside of upper loop. 0 doubled at left and right top outside and lower inside. All left stars and motto letters doubled near rim and all right stars tripled near rim.

10   III²9 • C³a (8/7 Bit)   (180)   I-3   R-4

Obverse III²9 – Second 8 has two spikes on right inside of upper loop and metal on top of right of lower loop. Some specimens have one spike in upper loop. Possible 8/7 but evidence is not conclusive. 0 doubled at top left inside.

1880-P

11   III² 10 • C³ a (Doubled 880, 8/7)   (179)   I-3   R-4
     Obverse III² 10 – Doubled 880 in date. Bottom outside and lower loop and top inside of lower loop of first 8 is doubled. Lower left outside of upper loop on second 8 is doubled. 0 is doubled at top left outside and top inside. Die chip to left between loops of first 8. Remains of 7 shows on surface of the left side of upper loop of second 8 in form of check mark.

12   III² 11 • C³ a (Doubled 1-80)   (181)   I-2   R-4
     Obverse III² 11 – 1-80 in date is doubled. The 1 is doubled above the bottom crossbar. The 0 is doubled on the inside right and is faintly doubled at top left and right outside. Second 8 is doubled at bottom left outside of upper loop.

13   III² 13 • C³ e (Doubled 1)   I-2   Proof
     Obverse III² 13 – 1 in date is doubled at top left of upper crossbar and slightly at top left of bottom crossbar.

14   III² 14 • C³ e (Doubled First 8)   (180)   I-3   R-4
     Obverse III² 14 – First 8 in date doubled strongly at very bottom right outside.

15   III² 15 • C³ a (Doubled Second 8)   (179)   I-2   R-3
     Obverse III² 15 – Second 8 in date doubled at top on right and left outside.

16   III² 16 • C³ a (Doubled 80, 8/7)   (179)   I-3   R-4
     Obverse III² 16 – 80 in date doubled. Second 8 is doubled on lower left outside of upper loop. The 0 is doubled at top left and right outside. Remains of 7 shows on surface of left side of upper loop of second 8 in the form of a check mark.

17   III² 17 • C³ a (Doubled 18-0)   I-3   R-4
     Obverse III² 17 – 18-0 in date doubled. 1 doubled slightly at bottom. First 8 doubled very strongly at bottom outside and is doubled at top inside of both loops and bottom right outside of upper loop. 0 doubled slightly on lower left inside of loop.

18   III² 18 • C³ a (Doubled 1-80)   (178)   I-2   R-3
     Obverse III² 18 – 1-80 in date is doubled. The 1 is doubled below upper crossbar. The second 8 is doubled on the lower left outside of the upper loop and right outside of lower loop. The 0 is doubled at the top left and right outside and on the lower left inside.

19   III² 19 • C³ a (Tripled 8, Doubled 1-80)   I-3   R-4
     Obverse III² 19 – 1 doubled slightly below crossbar. First 8 is tripled at bottom right outside of both loops. Second 8 and 0 are doubled slightly at top left and right outside. 0 is tripled slightly on left inside.

20   III² 20 • C³ a (Doubled Date)   (181)   I-2   R-4
     Obverse III² 20 – Entire date is slightly doubled. 1 is doubled at bottom edge of crossbar. First 8 is doubled on bottom right outside and with a short spike between loops on right. Second 8 is doubled on top left and right and left outside of lower loop with short dash below lower loop. 0 is doubled on top left and right outside.

21   III² 21 • C³ a (Doubled Date)   I-2   R-4
     Obverse III² 21 – Entire date is doubled. 1 is doubled slightly below the upper crossbar and at bottom. First 8 is doubled on bottom outside and with a short spike between loops on right. Second 8 is doubled slightly on lower left outside of upper loop. 0 is doubled on left inside and slightly on right inside of opening. Left and right stars slightly doubled towards rim.

22   III² 22 • C³ a (Doubled Date)   I-3   R-4
     Obverse III² 22 – Entire date is doubled. The 1 is faintly doubled below top crossbar and at left bottom of lower crossbar. First 8 is faintly doubled at top left side of both loops. Second 8 is strongly doubled all across bottom and faintly at top inside of lower loop and bottom outside on right and left sides of upper loop. 0 is tripled at bottom at left and right sides of bottom next to field and at top surface on left.

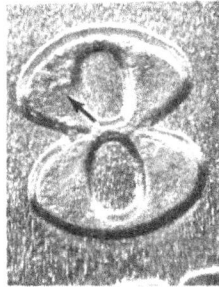
11 O 8/7
Check Mark

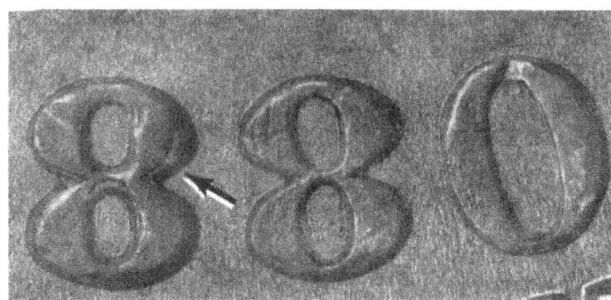
11 O Doubled 880

1880-P

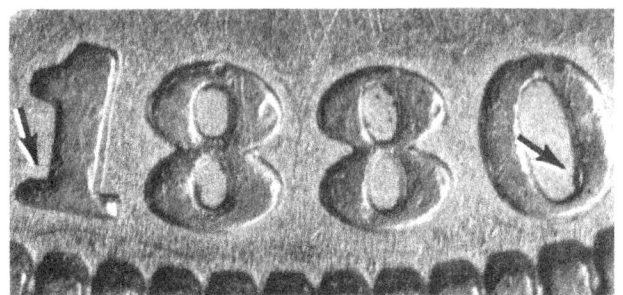

12 O Doubled 1-0

13 O Doubled 1

14 O Doubled First 8

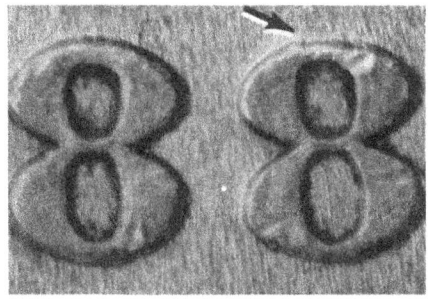

15 O Second 8 Doubled

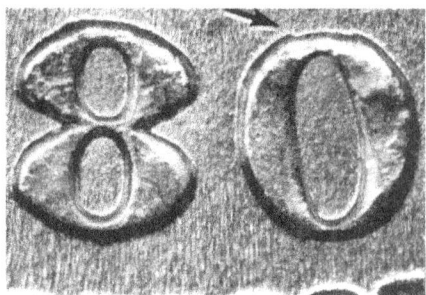

16 O Doubled 80

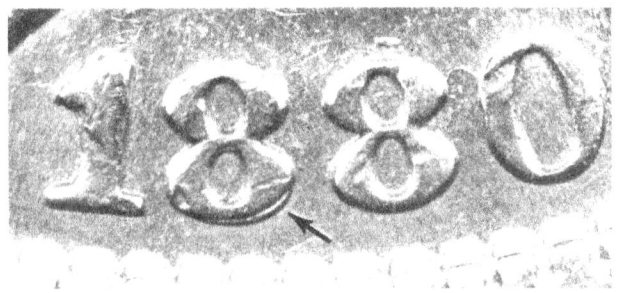

17 O Doubled 18-0

18 O Doubled 1-80

19 O Tripled 8, Doubled 80

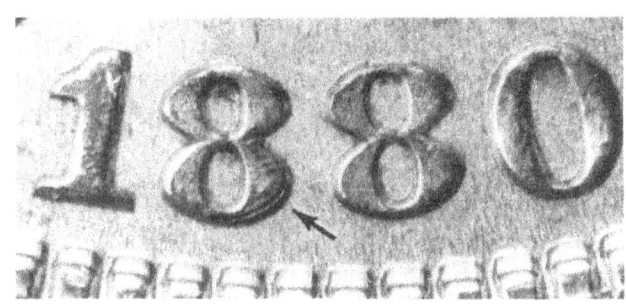

20 O Doubled Date

1880-P

21 O Doubled Date

22 O Doubled Date

23   III² 23 • C³ a (80/79)   I-4   R-6
Obverse III² 23 – 80 repunched over 79 in date. Remains of 7 shows on top of 8 as check mark on left side of upper loop and a vertical line on right side of upper loop extending down to top of lower loop and up to short spike on field at top right outside of upper loop. Remains of 9 shows on top of 0 as raised metal on upper left side ending diagonally at middle left side, dot on lower left that was end of 9 loop, vertical bar on middle right side. 1 doubled below bottom crossbar and slightly below upper crossbar, first 8 doubled slightly on surface of upper loop and outside and tripled below bottom loop.

24   III² 24 • C³ a (Doubled 1-80)   (179)   I-2   R-3
Obverse III² 24 – 1-80 in date doubled. 1 doubled slightly at top left of lower crossbar. Second 8 is doubled on the lower left outside of upper loop. 0 doubled at top left and right outside and slightly on lower left inside. Die chips at top inside at upper loop of second 8 and 0.

25   III² 25 • C³ a (0/9)   (180)   I-3   R-5
Obverse III² 25 – Faint remains of 9 on top of 0 showing as raised metal on lower left side of 0. Lower crossbar of 1 doubled at very bottom. Second 8 doubled slightly at lower left outside of upper loop. Upper inside of loop of 0 doubled strongly.

26   III² 26 • C³ a (Doubled Date, Tripled 8)   I-3   R-4
Obverse III² 26 – Entire date is doubled. 1 is doubled slightly above crossbar and strongly above bottom crossbar on both sides. First 8 is strongly doubled at top left outside and bottom inside of lower loop. Second 8 is tripled at top inside of both loops. 0 is doubled at top left and right outside plus lower right inside.

27   III² 27 • C³ a (Doubled 1-80)   I-2   R-3
Obverse III² 27 – Doubled 1-80 in date. 1 doubled slightly above lower crossbar on left side and at very left bottom. Second 8 doubled at top inside of both loops and at bottom left outside of both loops. 0 doubled slightly at bottom outside and left and right top outside.

28   III² • C³ a (Doubled 1-8, Tripled 0)   (181)   I-2   R-3
Obverse III² 28 – Doubled 1-8 in date. 1 doubled slightly below upper crossbar and on left side of crossbar. Second 8 doubled at left outside and bottom inside of upper loop. 0 tripled at lower left inside and doubled at top inside and left and right top outside.

29   III² 29 • C³ a (Doubled 80, 8/7)   I-3   R-3
Obverse III² 29 – Doubled 80 in date and 8/7 checkmark similar to VAM 16. Second 8 is doubled on the lower left outside of upper loop. The 0 is doubled at the top left and right outside but not as strong as VAM 16. First 8 has die chip on upper left inside of lower loop. Remains of 7 show on surface of left side of upper loop of second 8 in the form of a check mark. Right side of check mark is more curved than VAM 16.

30   III² 30 • C³ a (Doubled 1-80)   (181)   I-2   R-3
Obverse III² 30 – Doubled 1-80 in date. 1 doubled slightly below lower crossbar. Second 8 doubled slightly at bottom left outside of upper loop. 0 doubled slightly at left and right inside. Some specimens show large die flakes around R in date and 7th star on left.

31   III² 31 • C³ a (Doubled Date)   (180)   I-2   R-3
Obverse III² 31 – Entire date doubled slightly. 1 doubled on surface at top of upper crossbar and above bottom crossbar on left side. First 8 doubled slightly at right inside of lower loop. Second 8 doubled slightly at lower left outside of upper loop. 0 doubled slightly at left inside.

32   III² 32 • C³ a (Doubled Date)   (178)   I-2   R-3
Obverse III² 32 – Entire date doubled slightly. 1 doubled slightly above lower crossbar. First 8 doubled at top left inside of both loops and tripled at bottom outside at lower loop. Second 8 doubled at lower left outside of upper loop. 0 doubled slightly at top left and right outside and tripled at lower left inside. Slightly doubled Liberty head profile on lips, chin and nose.

1880-P

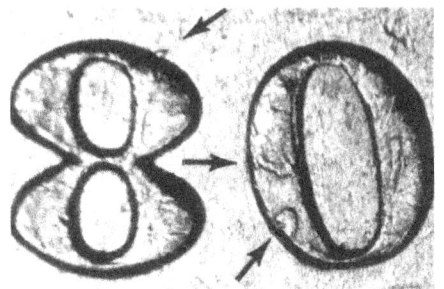
23 O 80/79

24 O Doubled 80

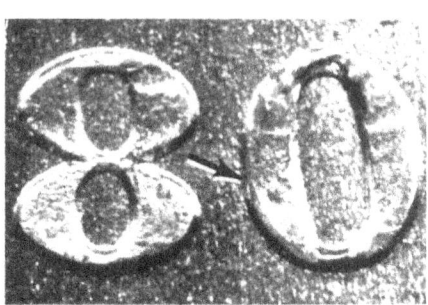
25 O 0/9

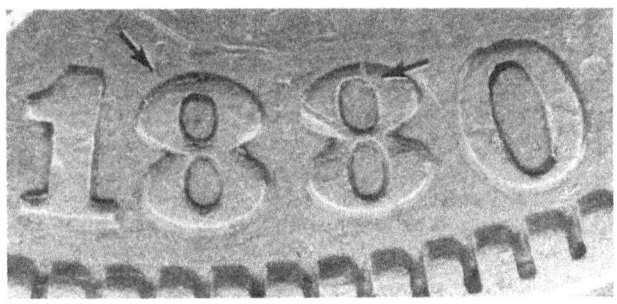
26 O Doubled Date, Tipled 8

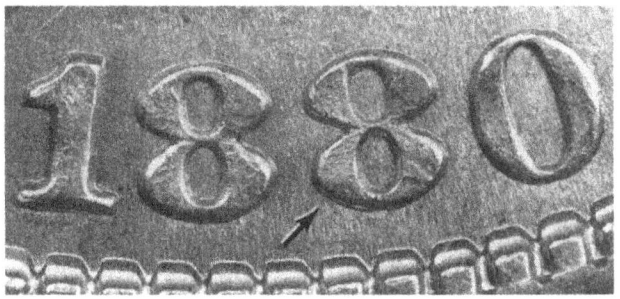
27 O Doubled 1-80

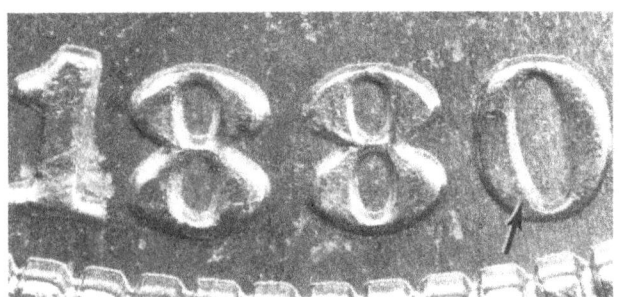
28 O Doubled 1-8, Tripled 0

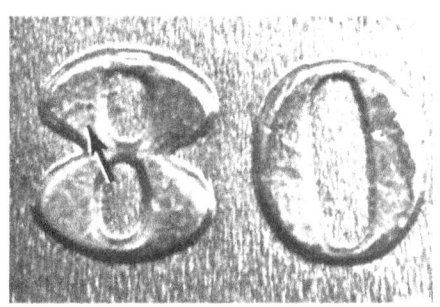
29 O Doubled 80, 8/7 Check mark

30 O Doubled 1-80

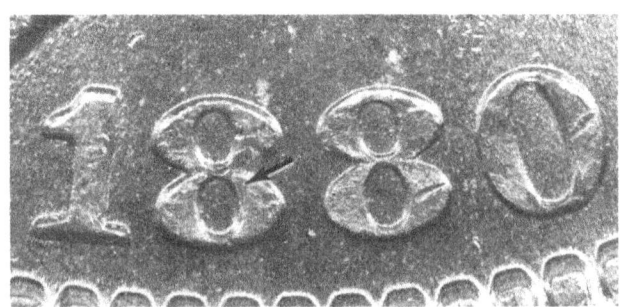
31 O Doubled Date

1880-P

33   III²33 • C³a (Doubled Date)   (180)   1-2   R-3
Obverse III²33 – Entire date doubled. 1 is doubled strongly at top of upper crossbar. First 8 doubled on surface at bottom right outside of lower loop. Second 8 doubled at lower loop, 0 doubled on left and right bottom outside.

34   III²34 • C³a (Doubled 188, Doubled Obverse)   (180)   I-2   R-3
Obverse III²34 – Doubled 188 in date. 1 doubled below upper and lower crossbars. First 8 doubled on bottom left outside of lower loop. Second 8 doubled slightly on lower left outside of upper loop. All stars and legend letters doubled at top towards rim.

35   III²35 • C³a (Doubled 1-80)   (180)   I-2   R-3
Obverse III²35 – Doubled 1-80 in date. 1 doubled slightly below bottom crossbar. Second 8 doubled on lower left outside of upper loop. 0 doubled at upper left and lower right inside. First 8 shows die chips in lower loop on some specimens.

36   III² • C³a (Doubled Date)   (180)   I-2   R-3
Obverse III²36 – Entire date doubled slightly 1 doubled above lower crossbar on left and right. First 8 doubled on surface at right inside of lower loop. Second 8 doubled slightly at lower left outside of upper loop. 0 doubled at lower right inside with die chip at lower left outside.

37   III²37 • C³a (Doubled Date)   (180)   1-2   R-3
Obverse III²37 – Entire date is doubled. 1 doubled at lower right of vertical stem. First 8 doubled on left inside of lower loop. Second 8 doubled on lower left outside of upper loop. 0 doubled at top left and right outside.

38   III²38 • C³a (Doubled Date)   (181)   1-2   R-3
Obverse III² 38 – Entire date is doubled. 1 doubled on left of top and bottom crossbars. First 8 doubled on surface at top and right inside and bottom of lower loop. Second 8 doubled slightly at lower left outside of upper loop. 0 doubled slightly at top left and right outside and lower left outside. 0 set lower than rest of date digits.

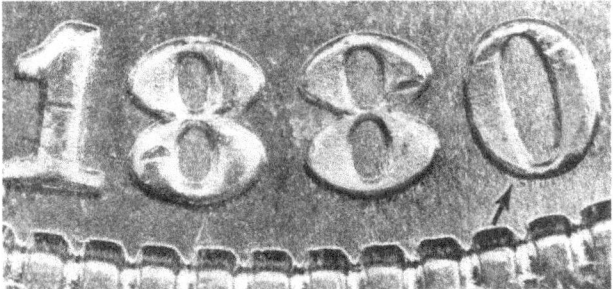

32 O Doubled Date

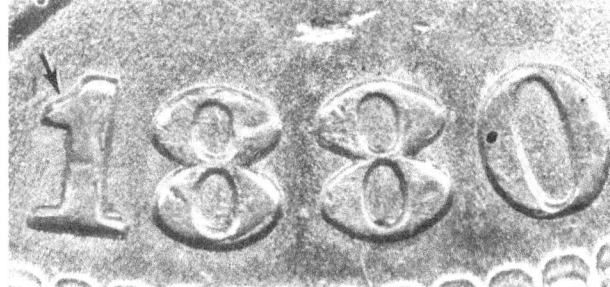

33 O Doubled Date

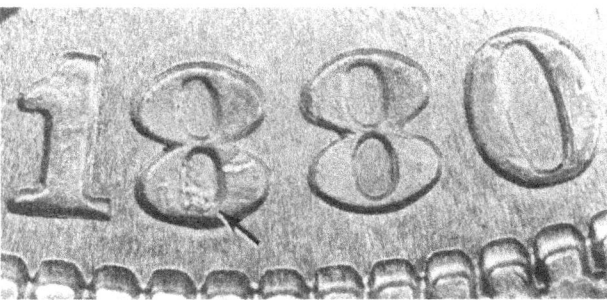

35 O Doubled 18-0

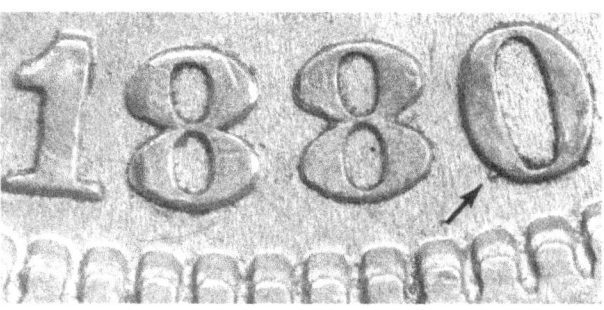

36 O Doubled Date

37 O Doubled Date

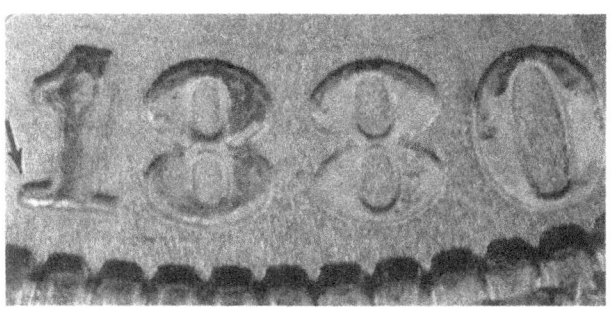

38 O Doubled Date

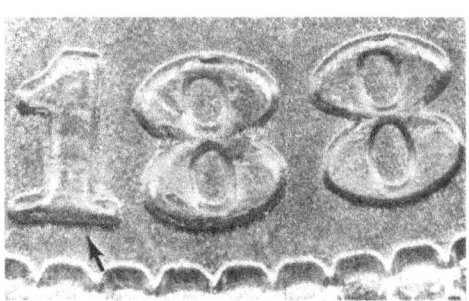

34 O Doubled 188

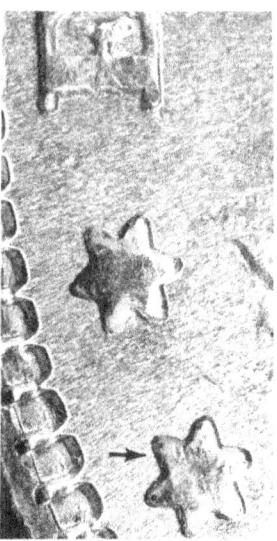

34 O
Doubled Stars and Letters

1880-CC

This issue was beset by numerous problems. To begin with, the Annual Assay Commission discovered early in 1881 that some of the issues were defective with low fineness (less silver content than normal). As a result 96,000 of the 1880-CC dollars were melted in 1881 decreasing the net mintage to 495,000. The strike is quite variable with an even distribution from well struck to quite weak. Many of the coins have cloudy surfaces probably due to storage contamination. Planchet striations sometimes are evident in the hair above the ear and on the eagle's breast feathers. Locating a problem free high grade specimen can be quite a challenge.

Normal dies without varieties do not exist. Some B reverse dies with flat breast were used but they are not scarce for the issue and only bring a modest premium. Most of the varieties are overdates. VAM's 4, 5 and 6 are the most prominent overdates of the entire Morgan series with complete 79 digits showing under the 80. However, they make up a sizeable percentage of this issue as well as a couple other less prominent overdates and do not bring any premium.

Proof-likes make up a good percentage of the issue but it is difficult to locate a problem free specimen with minimal abrasions.

1   III^2 1 • C^3 a (SAF Large CC)   Normal die does not exist
     Obverse III^2 1 – Normal die of III^2 type.
     Reverse C^3 a – Normal die of C^3 type with large V CC mint mark and slanted arrow feathers.

2   III^2 1 • B^2 a (PAF Small CC)   Normal die does not exist
     Reverse B^2 a – Normal die of B^2 type with centered small II CC mint mark and parallel arrow feathers.

3   III^2 2 • C^3 b (Dash Under 8)   I-2   R-3
     Obverse III^2 2 – First 8 is doubled at top inside of lower loop and upper loop has polishing marks. A high set dash appears just below the second 8 with upper loop doubled on left outside. 0 is doubled at the top left and right. First stars on left and right have die chips.
     Reverse C^3 b – Normal die of C^3 type with centered large V CC mint mark. There are die chips at the top inside of the loop of each C of the mint mark and at top left of O in DOLLAR.

4   III^2 3 • B^2 a (80/79)   (178)   I-5   R-4
     Obverse III^2 3 – 80 repunched over the 79 in date. The two serifs of the 7 show above the 8, the bottom of the crossbar shows in the top of the upper loop and the stem show on the right side of the lower loop. The 9 shows within the 0 in the top left and bottom and a bulge shows outside at 10 o'clock. 1 has die chip at top right of shaft. First 8 has vertical polishing marks inside partially filled loops.

1880-CC

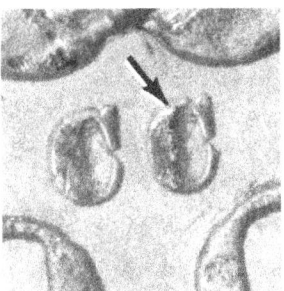

3 R Doubled CC

3 O Dash

4 O 80/79

5   III² 4 • C³ c (8/7 High)   (177)   I-5   R-4
Obverse III² 4 – 8 repunched over the 7 in the date with the original 7 punched high. There are prominent ears above the 8, a crossbar in the upper loop, the stem of the 7 shows on the right side of the lower loop, and the bottom of the 7 stem shows just below the 8.
Reverse C³c – Normal die of C³ type with slanted arrow feathers and small II CC mint mark with slight tilt to right. Vertical die gouge below arrow feathers and olive branch.

6   III2 5 • C³ d (8/7 Low)   (177)   I-5   R-4
Obverse III² 5 – 8 repunched over 7 in date with the original 7 punched low. The ears are faint above the 8 and the crossbar and stem of the 7 show strongly. The bottom of the 7's stem shows well below the 8. A small piece of metal with polishing marks shows at the bottom inside the 0. First 8 has diagonal polishing marks inside partially filled loops.
Reverse C³d – Normal die of C³ type with centered small I CC mint mark and slanted arrow feathers. CC has a dot of metal in center of each C. Die scratch through M of AMERICA, bottom of eagle's right wing and inside of eagle's left wing.

7   III² 6 • B² a (8/7 Dash)   I-3   R-4
Obverse III² 6 – 8 repunched over 7. A short ear shows at the left at top of the second 8. Bottom of stem shows as low dash below 8. Bottom loop of 8 shows two diagonal polishing marks and die chips on the right side and top. The 0 shows no part of the 9 but has a slight bulge on outside at 10 o'clock. First 8 is doubled at top inside of lower loop and has die chips inside upper loop.

8   III2 6 • C³ d (8/7 Dash)   (177)   I-3   R-3
Obverse III² 6 – Same as III² 6 but has been further polished down after receiving heavy clash marks. A vertical polishing mark shows on right outside between loops of second 8.

9   III² 6 • C³ a (8/7 Dash)   I-3   R-5

10   III² 7 • C³ c (8/7 Dash and Doubled 8)   (177)   I-3   R-4
Obverse III² 7 – First 8 has horizontal polishing lines on right side of upper loop and is doubled at top inside of lower loop. Second 8 has a short dash just below bottom and is doubled at lower left outside of upper loop.

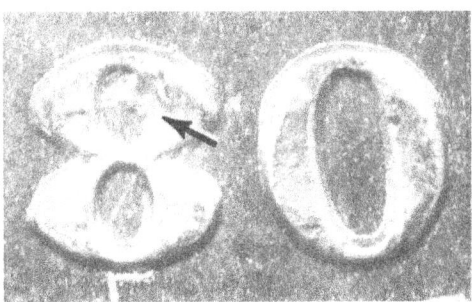
5 O 8/7 High

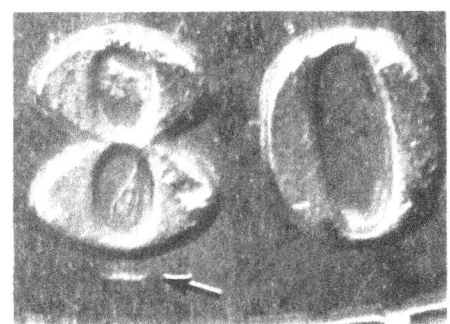
6 O 8/7 Low

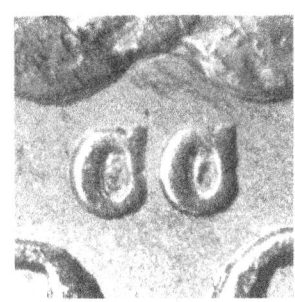
6 R CC Dots

1880-CC / 1880-O

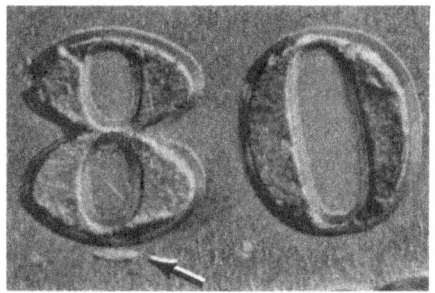
7 O 8/7 Dash

8 O 8/7 Dash

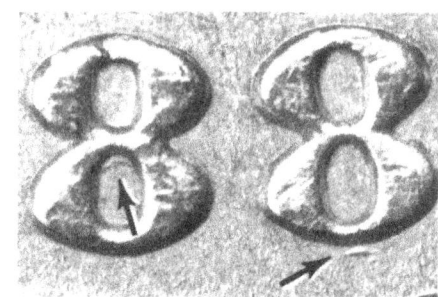
10 O Doubled 8 and 8/7 Dash

1880-O

The 1880-O is similar to the 1879-O with strong strike usual, some soft strikes exist, and many coins exist that have been lightly circulated. Proof-likes are fairly scarce and some deep mirror cameos exist.

This issue has numerous varieties, but most are minor. Two size O mint marks were used but both are readily available and do not bring any premium. Quite a few overdate die varieties exist with VAM's 4 and 5 fairly prominent but commanding only a modest premium because of their availability. The other overdates are less prominent and do not bring much of a premium except for VAM 6B because of its rarity.

1	III²1 • C³a (Small O)	(176)	1-1	R-2

Obverse III²1 – Normal die of III² type.
Reverse C³a – Normal die of C³ type with small, round I O mint mark centered and upright.

1A	III²1 • C³a (Hangnail Eagle)	(176)	1-2	R-5

Reverse C³a – Die gouge through the eagle's left tail feather and lower arrow feather.

2	III²1 • C³b (Medium O)	(176)	I-2	R-2

Reverse C³b – Normal die of C³ type with medium, tall, oval shaped, II O mint mark centered and upright.

2A	III²1 • C³b (Impaled Eagle)	(176)	I-2	R-4

Reverse C³b – Horizontal spike of metal through eagle's neck due to die scratch. II O mint mark.

3	III²2 • C³b (Dash Under 8, Doubled 80)	(176)	I-2	R-3

Obverse III²2 – A thin dash appears well below the second 8. Second 8 also doubled slightly at bottom left outside of upper loop. 0 doubled slightly at bottom left inside and slightly at top left and right outside.

1A R Hangnail Eagle

2A R Impaled Eagle

3 O Dash Under 8, Doubled 80

1880-O

4	III²3 • C³a (80/79)		(176)	I-4	R-4

Obverse III²3 – 80 repunched over 79 in date. Faint ears appear above the 8 and metal is at the top within the upper loop. The 0 has metal inside the upper part of the loop. 1 doubled on right side of vertical shaft. First 8 doubled on left inside and right outside of lower loop. Second 8 doubled at left outside of both loops.

5	III²4 • C³b (8/7 Ear)		(176)	I-4	R-5

Obverse III² 4 – 8 repunched over 7 in date. Metal in top loop of second 8 but different than III²3. Faint ear above 8 on left. No metal in 0.

Reverse C³ b – Die scratch below wreath center, within mint mark opening, below the arrow shaft, and a spike of metal from the right wing to the eagle's neck.

6	III²5 • C³a (8/7 Spike)		(176)	I-4	R-5

Obverse III²5 – 8 repunched over 7 in date. A long spike extends from the top left side of the second 8. Small horizontal spike on right inside of upper loop of second 8. Die clash marks are evident on some specimens.

Reverse C³a – Heavy die clash marks are evident on some specimens.

6A	III²5 • C³a (8/7 Spike)		(176)	I-4	R-5

Reverse C³a – Die gouge on left side of left wreath.

6B	III²5 • C³a (Hangnail Eagle)		(176)	I-4	R-6
7	III²1 • C³c (O/O)		(176)	I-2	R-4

Obverse III²1 – Date has die chips at top and left side of 1, on the right of first 8 upper loop, and below 0.

Reverse C³ c – I O mint mark is doubled on right and left side of top surface.

8	III²1 • C³d (High O)		(176)	I-2	R-3

Reverse C³d – I O mint mark set high.

9	III²6 • C³a (Doubled 0)		(176)	I-2	R-4

Obverse III²6 – 0 in date is doubled strongly at top right and left outside and on lower left of the opening.

10	III²7 • C³b (Doubled 1-8)		(176)	I-2	R-3

Obverse III² 7 – 1-8 doubled in date. 1 doubled slightly below upper crossbar and lower right side of shaft. Second 8 doubled slightly at lower outside of upper loop. 0 has three patches of shallow die chips inside. Lower part of hair has heavy polishing marks.

11	III²8 • C³a (Dash Under 8, Doubled 188)		(176)	I-2	R-3

Obverse III² 1 – A faint dash appears below the second 8 and the upper loop is doubled slightly at bottom left outside. 1 is doubled on top serif surface. First 8 is doubled on lower loop surface at bottom right.

12	III²9 • C³a (Doubled 1-80)		(176)	I-2	R-3

Obverse III²9 – 1-80 doubled in date. 1 doubled on surface at top right of vertical shaft. Second 8 is doubled at lower left outside of upper loop. 0 is doubled at top left and right outside and at top left of opening.

13	III²10 • C³a (Doubled 80)		(176)	I-3	R-4

Obverse III² 10 – Doubled 80 in date. Second 8 is doubled on lower left outside of upper loop. 0 is doubled strongly at top left outside and tripled at top right outside. It is also tripled on lower left inside and doubled almost entirely up the left inside.

14	III²11 • C³a (Doubled 80)		(176)	I-2	R-3

Obverse III²11 – Doubled 80 in date. Second 8 is doubled slightly at outside top left and right. 0 is doubled slightly at top left outside.

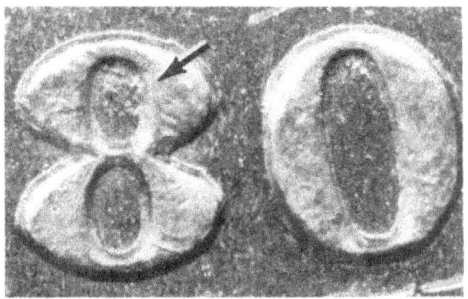
4 O 80/79

5 O 8/7 Ear

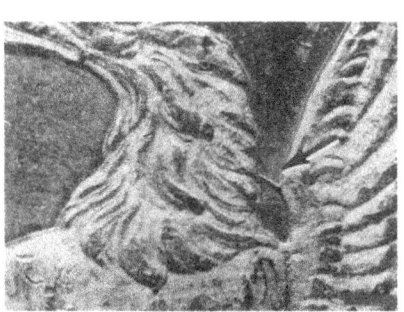
5 R Die Scratches

1880-O

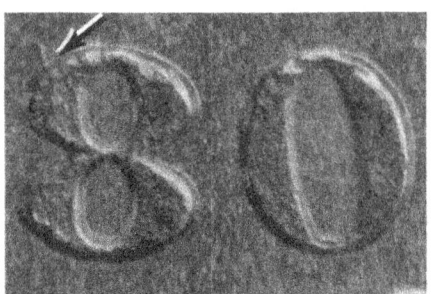
6 O 8/7 Spike

7 O Die Chips

6A R Die Gouge

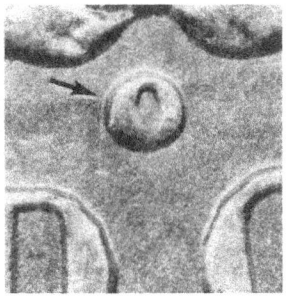
7 R Doubled O

8 R O Set High

9 O Doubled 0

11 O Dash Under 8

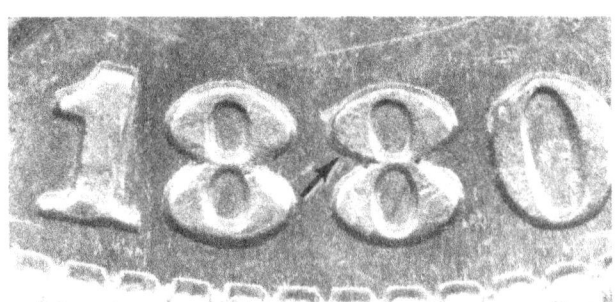
10 O Doubled 1-8

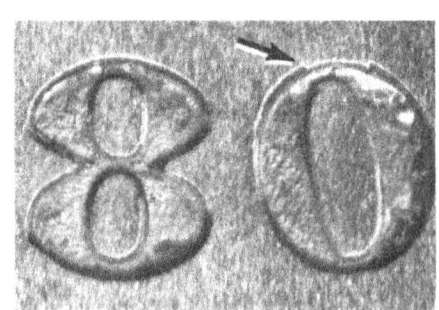
12 O Doubled 80

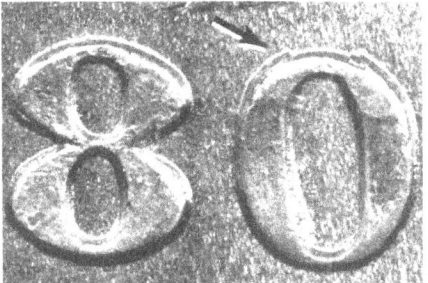
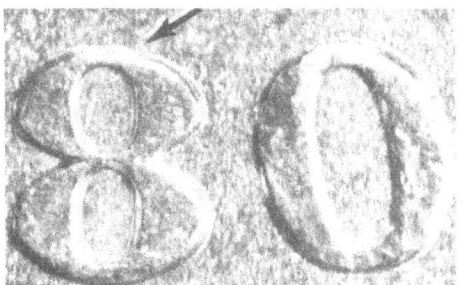
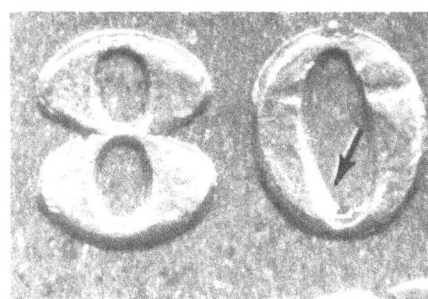

13 O Doubled 80   14 O Doubled 80   15 O Doubled 80

15   **III² 12 • C³ b (Doubled 80)**   (176)   I-2   R-3
Obverse III² 12 – Doubled 80 in date. Second 8 doubled slightly at lower left outside of upper loop. 0 double strongly at lower left inside and lower left outside surface.
Reverse C³ b – Letters of UNITED STATES OF AMERICA have die chips and breaks at top. II O mint mark.

16   **III² 13 • C³ a (8/7 Check Mark)**   I-3   R-5
Obverse III² 13 – 8 repunched over 7 in date. Remains of 7 shows on surface of left side of upper loop of second 8 in the form of a check mark. Short vertical bar on surface at right side of junction of 8 loops extending down into side of top of lower loop opening. Second 8 is doubled on lower left side of upper loop.

17   **III² 13 • C³ b (8/7 Check Mark)**   I-3   R-5

18   **III² 14 • C³ a (Doubled 1-8)**   (176)   I-2   R-3
Obverse III² 14 – 1 tripled on top left outside of upper crossbar and doubled to top left and right and slightly below bottom crossbar. Second 8 doubled slightly at lower left outside of upper loop.

19   **III² 15 • C³ a (Doubled 188)**   I-2   R-3
Obverse III² 15 – 188 in date slightly doubled. 1 doubled above and below and to right of bottom crossbar. Both 8's doubled slightly at bottom inside of loops. Second 8 doubled at lower left outside of upper loop. Some specimens show die chips at lower left outside of lower loop of both 8's.

20   **III² 1 • C³ e (O/O Right)**   I-2   R-4
Reverse C³ e – II O mint mark repunched with original showing as a bar in the middle and top right of opening and ending in a thin line curving to left at bottom of loop opening.

21   **III² 16 • C³ a (8/7 Check Mark, Ear)**   I-3   R-4
Obverse III² 16 – 8 repunched over 7 in date. Remains of 7 shows on surface of the left side of upper loop of second 8 in the form of a faint check mark set high. Vertical line on side of lower loop opening at upper right. Short ear at top right outside of loop. First 8 is doubled at right inside of lower loop. 0 doubled at lower left inside.

22   **III² 17 • C³ f (Doubled 880, O/O Low)**   (176)   I-2   R-3
Obverse III² 17 – Doubled 880 in date. First 8 doubled at top inside of upper loop as a thin curved line. Second 8 doubled slightly at lower left outside of upper loop. 0 doubled on surface at lower right inside.
Reverse C³ f – II O mint mark doubled at lower right outside as a short thin line.

23   **III² 17 • C³ a (Doubled Date)**   (176)   I-2   R-3
Obverse III² 17 – Entire date is doubled. 1 and first 8 doubled slightly at very bottom outside. Second 8 doubled at lower left outside of upper loop. 0 doubled slightly at top left and right outside and at bottom outside on surface.

24   **III² 18 • C³ a (Doubled 880)**   (176)   I-2   R-3
Obverse III² 18 – Doubled 880 in date. First 8 doubled at top and right inside of lower loop. Second 8 doubled at top left and right outside of upper loop. 0 doubled slightly at lower right inside.

25   **III² 5 • C³ g (8/7 Spike, High O Set Right)**   (176)   I-4   R-5
Reverse C³ g – I O mint mark set high and to right.

26   **III² 19 • C³ a (Doubled 80)**   (176)   I-2   R-3
Obverse III² 19 – 80 in date doubled. Second 8 doubled at lower left outside of upper loop. 0 doubled at top left inside on surface.
Reverse C³ a – Die overpolished with surface roughness around wreath, eagles tail feathers, olive leaves and UNIT ONE.

27   **III² 20 – C³ a (Doubled 80)**   (176)   I-2   R-3
Obverse III² 20 – 80 in date slightly doubled. Second 8 doubled at lower left outside of upper loop. 0 doubled at lower left inside and at top right inside.

1880-O

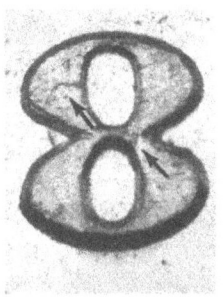

16 O
8/7 Check mark

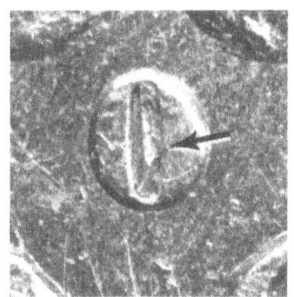

20 R O/O Right

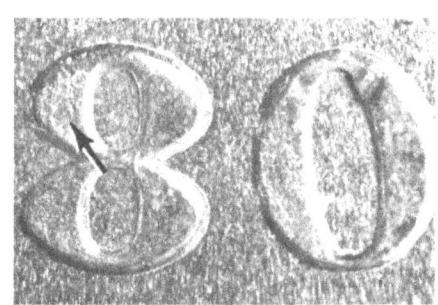

21 R 8/7 Check mark

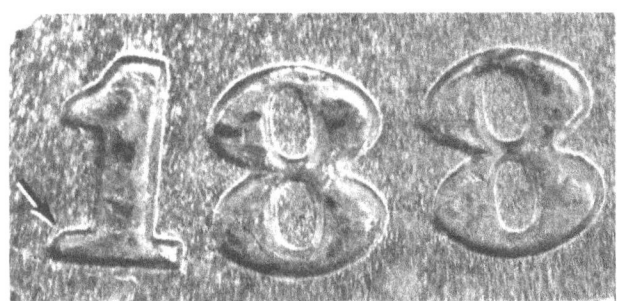

18 O Doubled 1-8

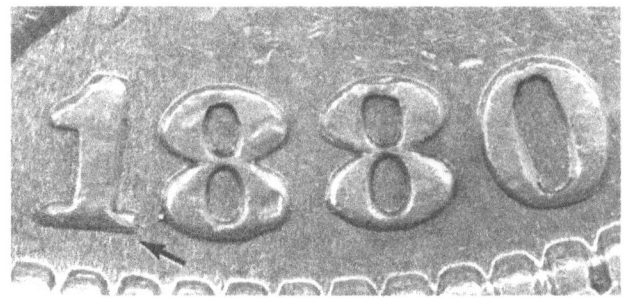

19 O Doubled 188

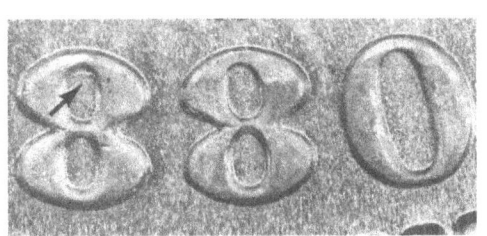

22 O Doubled 880

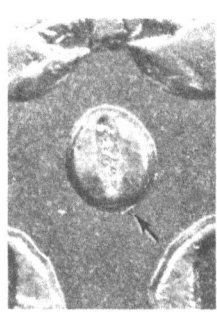

22 R O/O Low

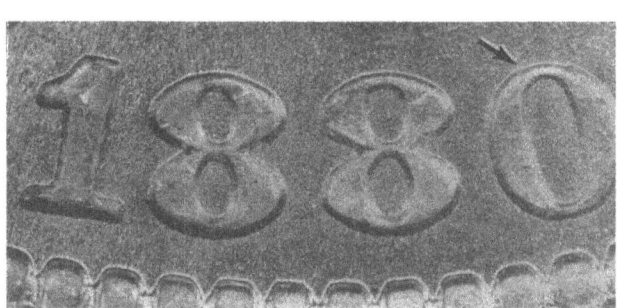

23 O Doubled Date

24 O Doubled 880

26 O Doubled 80

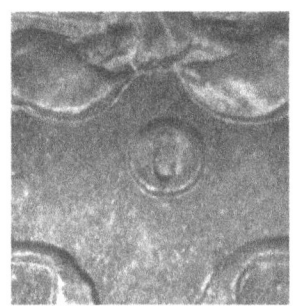

25 R High O

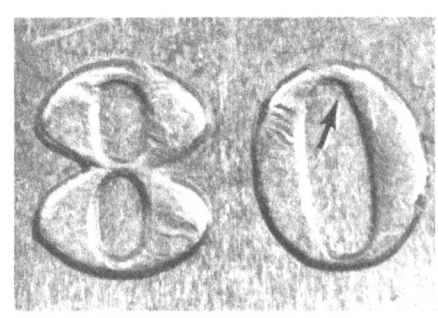

27 O Doubled 80

205

1880-O

28	III² 21 • C³ c (Doubled 188, High O Set Right)	(176)		I-2	R-3
29	III² 21 • C³ c (Doubled 188, O/O)	(176)		I-2	R-3

Obverse III² 21 – 188 in date doubled. 1 doubled slightly at top left. First 8 doubled at left inside of upper loop and right outside of lower loop. Second 8 doubled at lower left outside of upper loop.

30	III² 22 • C³ a (Doubled 880)	(176)		I-2	R-3

Obverse III² 22 – Doubled 880 in date. First 8 doubled at top right inside and bottom outside of lower loop. Second 8 doubled at lower left outside. 0 doubled slightly at top left and right outside.

31	III² 18 • C³ b (Doubled 880)	(176)		I-2	R-3
32	III² 23 • C³ a (Doubled 18-0)	(176)		I-2	R-3

Obverse III² 23 – Doubled 18-0 in date. 1 and first 8 doubled slightly at bottom outside. 0 doubled at lower left inside.

33	III² 24 • C³ a (Doubled 80)	(176)		I-2	R-3

Obverse III² 24 – Doubled 80 in date. Second 8 doubled slightly at top left and right outside. 0 also doubled slightly at top and right outside plus lower left inside.

34	III² 25 • C³ b (Doubled 188)	(176)		I-2	R-3

Obverse III² 25 – Doubled 188 in date. 1 doubled on lower right side of vertical shaft. First 8 doubled on left inside of lower loop. Second 8 doubled slightly on lower left outside of upper loop.

35	III² 21 • C³ b (Doubled 188)	(176)		I-2	R-3
36	III² 26 • C³ b (Doubled 1-80)	(176)		I-2	R-3

Obverse III² 26 – Doubled 1-80 in date. 1 doubled slightly at top right of lower crossbar. Second 8 doubled at lower left outside of upper loop. 0 doubled slightly at lower right inside.

37	III² 2 • C³ a (Dash Under 8, Doubled 80)	(176)		I-2	R-3
38	III² 27 • C³ b (Doubled 18)	(176)		I-2	R-3

Obverse III² 27 – Doubled 18 in date. 1 doubled at top of upper serif. First 8 doubled slightly at top left outside of upper loop and on surface at bottom right outside of lower loop.

39	III² 28 • C³ h (Doubled 1-8, O Tilted Right)	(176)		I-2	R-3

Obverse III² 28 – Doubled 1-8 in date. 1 doubled at top left and right of lower crossbar. Second 8 doubled slightly at lower left outside of upper loop. Ear has die flake in middle.
Reverse C³ h – Small I O mint mark set slightly high and tilted right.

40	III² 29 • C³ a (Doubled 880, Dash Under 8)	(176)		I-2	R-3

Obverse III² 29 – Doubled 880 in date. First 8 doubled slightly at right inside and bottom right outside of lower loop. A very thin horizontal dash appears just below the second 8. 0 tripled at lower left inside and doubled at top right inside.

41	III² 30 • C³ b (Doubled 1-80)	(176)		I-2	R-3

Obverse III² 30 – Doubled 1-80 in date, 1 doubled slightly below upper crossbar. Second 8 doubled slightly at lower left outside of upper loop. 0 tripled at lower left outside surface and doubled at lower left inside.

42	III² 31 • C³ a (Doubled 80)	(176)		I-2	R-3

Obverse III² 31 – Second 8 doubled slightly at lower left outside of upper loop. 0 doubled at lower left inside.

43	III² 32 • C³ i (Doubled Ear, O/O Center)	(176)		I-3	R-3

Obverse III² 32 – Ear doubled on right side of inner ear fill and outside. Hair line above ear slightly doubled as is eyelid and lower cotton leaf edge. Second 8 in date doubled at lower left outside of upper loop.
Reverse C³ i – II O mint mark doubled inside as thin vertical line in middle of opening.

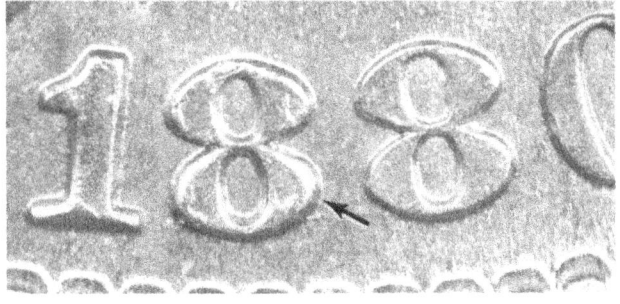

29 O Doubled 188

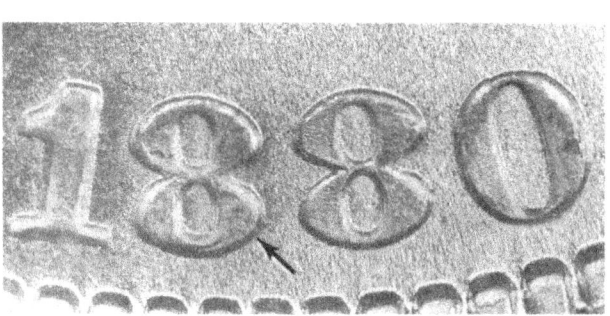

30 O Doubled 880

1880-O

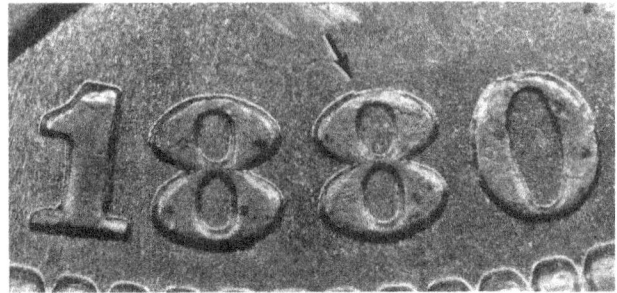
32 O Doubled 18-0

33 O Doubled 80

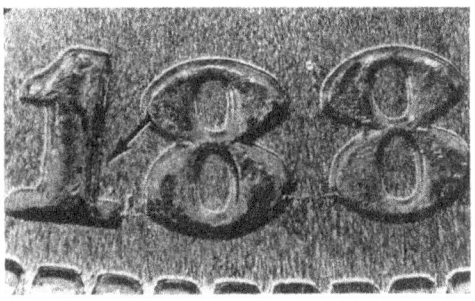
34 O Doubled 188

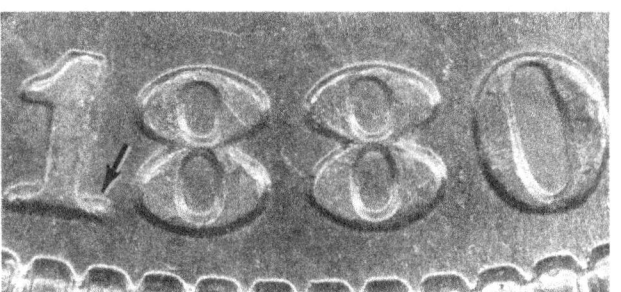
36 O Doubled 1-80

38 O Doubled 18

39 O Doubled 1-8

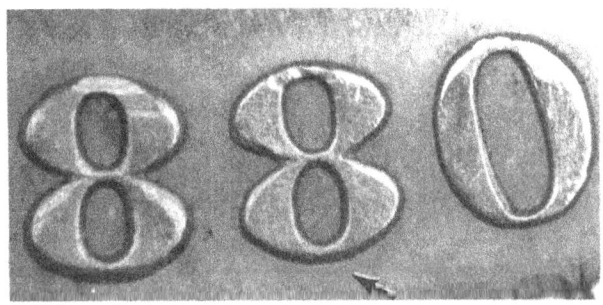
40 O Doubled 880, Dash Under 8

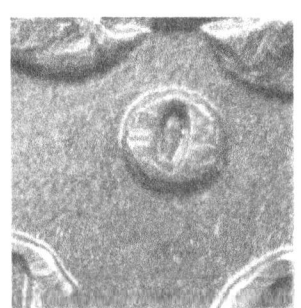
39 R O Tilted Right

207

1880-O / 1880-S

44   III²33 • C³a (Doubled Date)   (176)   I-2   R-3

Obverse III²33 – Entire date is doubled. 1 doubled at top left of top and bottom crossbar. First 8 doubled on surface of right inside of lower loop. Second 8 doubled at top left and right outside of upper loop and slightly at left inside of lower loop. 0 slightly doubled at right and lower left inside.

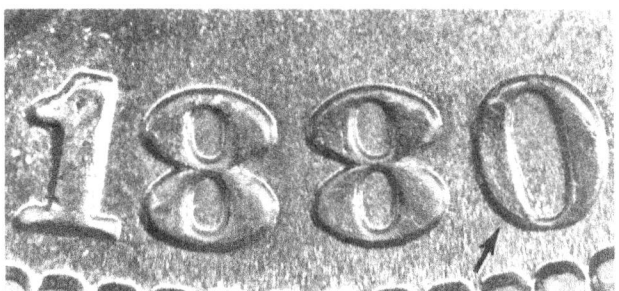
41 O Doubled 1-80

42 O Doubled 80

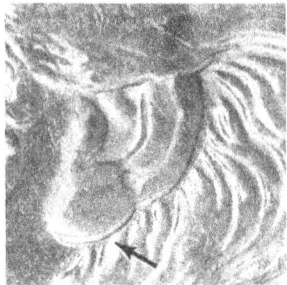
43 O Doubled Ear

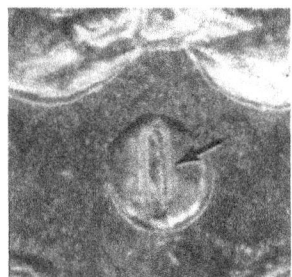
43 R O/O

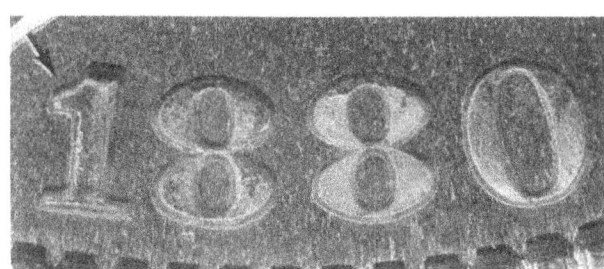
44 O Doubled Date

1880-S

The 1880-S is usually fully struck with good luster. Some slightly weak strikes do exist. It is the most readily available Morgan dollar in proof-like condition with good cameo contrast.

There are a large number of die varieties for the 1880-S but the majority are minor doubled dates and mint marks. Five overdate die varieties are known. VAM 8, 9 80/79 and VAM 11 0/9 bring a modest premium and VAM 10 brings a substantial premium because of its rarity. The other overdate, VAM 12, is not very prominent and fairly common with little price premium. There are two size mint marks but both are common and do not bring any premium.

1   III²1 • C³a (Medium S)   (186)   I-1   R-2
Obverse III²1 – Normal die of III² type.
Reverse C³a – Normal die of C³ type with medium IV S mint mark.

2   III²1 • C³b (Large S)   (186)   I-1   R-2
Reverse C³b – Normal die of C³ type with a very large centered and upright VI S mint mark.

3   III²1 • C³c (S Tilted Left)   I-2   R-3
Reverse C³c – Normal die of C³ type with very large centered mint mark tilted left.

4   III²2 • C³a (Doubled Date)   I-2   R-3
Obverse III²2 – Entire date is doubled. 1 doubled at the bottom. First 8 is doubled on bottom surface of lower loop. Second 8 is doubled on lower left outside of upper loop. 0 is doubled at top left and right outside.

5   III²3 • C³a (Doubled 0)   (185)   I-2   R-3
Obverse III²3 – 0 in date is doubled at top outside at left and right. Some specimens show a die crack through B of Liberty.

6   III²3 • C³c (Doubled 0)   (188)   I-2   R-3

1880-S

7   III²4 • C³d (Doubled Date)   (188)   I-3   R-4
   Obverse III²4 – All digits in date doubled. The 1 is doubled below the top and bottom crossbars The first 8 is doubled at top and bottom outside and on surface at top inside of lower loop. Second 8 is doubled on the lower left outside of the upper loop. The 0 is doubled at the bottom outside and top outside left and right.
   Reverse C³d – Normal die with IV S mint mark tilted left and partially filled.

8   III²5 • C³a (80/79 Ear)   (186)   I-4   R-3
   Obverse III²5 – 80 repunched over 79 in date. Second 8 has metal in upper loop, faint spike at top left and faint line at bottom. The 0 has a small piece of metal at the top right inside.

9   III²5 • C³e (80/79 Ear)   (185)   I-4   R-4
   Reverse C³e – VI S mint mark repunched with original showing as a spike to left top serif.

10   III²6 • C³q – (8/7 Crossbar)   (186)   I-4   R-6
   Obverse III²6 – 8 repunched over 7 in date. Second 8 has a few small dots of metal at top within upper loop. A horizontal line shows at bottom of upper loop curving slightly up on the left side. An additional small amount of metal shows on the right inside of the upper loop. No metal in 0.
   Reverse C³q – All legend letters doubled slightly in radial direction. Motto letter doubled at top. Right and left wreath doubled slightly towards rim. Very large centered VI S mint mark tilted left.

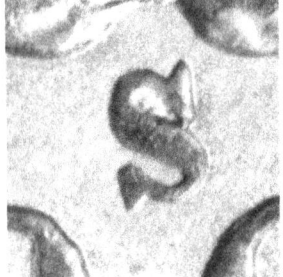
3 R S Tilted Left

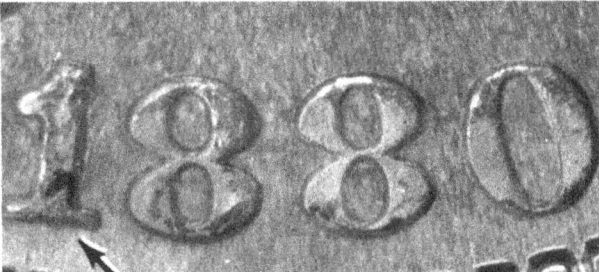
4 O Doubled 1-0

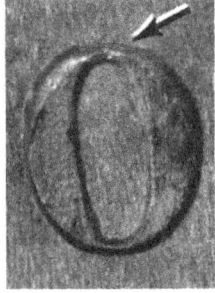
5 O Doubled 0

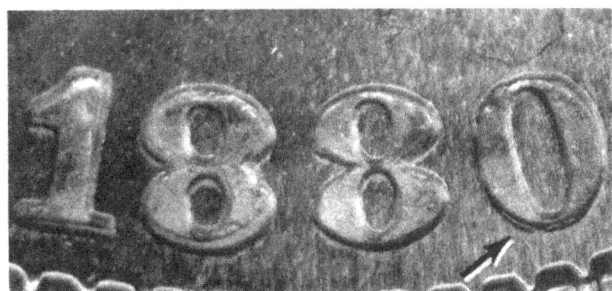
7 O Doubled Date

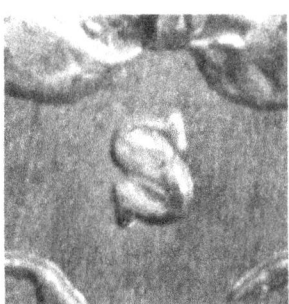
7 R IV S Tilted Left

8 O 80/79

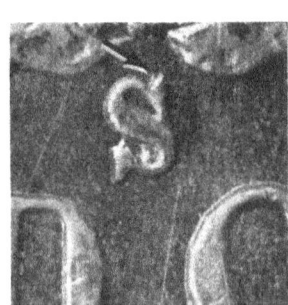
9 R S/S

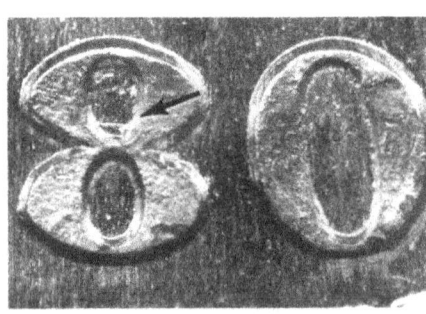
10 O 8/7 Crossbar

1880-S

11   III² 7 • C³ f (0/9)   (184)   I-4   R-3

Obverse III² 7 – Metal with polishing marks in the remains of the 9 within the top of the opening in 0 of the date. There is a bulge on the outside of the 0 at 10 o'clock. The top loop of the second 8 has a few dots of metal on the right outside of lower loop. 1 doubled on right side of shaft and below upper crossbar. Second 8 doubled on lower outside of upper loop.

Reverse C³ f – IV S mint mark set high and repunched with short vertical spike extending downwards from middle of top loop opening and curved line in middle inside of lower loop opening.

12   III² 8 • C³ d (8/7 Spikes, Doubled 188)   (183)   I-4   R-3

Obverse III² 8 – 80 repunched over 79 in date. Second 8 has a check mark on top of left side of upper loop, a thin diagonal line at top left outside, a faint vertical line at top right outside, a slight bulge of metal at top right inside of upper loop, a diagonal pointed dash attached to bottom outside of lower loop and is doubled at bottom left outside of upper loop. 0 has a small piece of metal at top right inside and a slight bulge at top left outside. 1 is doubled slightly on surface at right side. First 8 doubled at top left inside and on right inside on surface of lower loop.

13   III² 9 • C³ a (Dash Under 8, Doubled Date)   I-2   R-4

Obverse III² 9 – A high set and thin dash appears just below the second 8 in date. The second 8 is also slightly doubled at bottom left outside of upper loop. The 0 is doubled on the lower right inside. 1 is doubled at top right of vertical shaft. First 8 doubled on top and right inside of lower loop.

14   III² 10 • C³ a (Dash Under 8)   (185)   I-2   R-4

Obverse III² 10 – A high set and thin dash appears just below and angles slightly down to the right of the second 8. A small dot of metal is at top inside of upper loop of second 8 and upper loop is doubled at lower left outside. 0 is doubled slightly at top and bottom left side of opening.

15   III² 11 • C³ g (S/S Right, Dash Under 8)   (183)   I-3   R-4

Obverse III² 11 – Second 8 in date doubled at bottom left side as a thin curved line; a thin dash is set well below the bottom and the bottom left outside of the upper loop is slightly doubled.

Reverse C³ g – IV S mint mark repunched with original showing as a short vertical line at top right of upper loop opening and as a vertical curved line at very right side of lower loop opening. Mint mark set slightly left.

16   III² 12 • C³ a (Doubled 8)   (188)   I-2   R-3

Obverse III² 12 – Die chip on right between the loops of the first 8 of the date. Second 8 is doubled on left bottom outside of upper loop.

17   III² 12 • C³ c (Doubled 8)   (186)   I-2   R-3

18   III² 3 • C³ h (S/S, Doubled 0)   I-3   R-4

Reverse C³ h – Mint mark repunched with original showing as a curved line centered inside upper loop. IV S mint mark is partially filled.

19   III² 3 • C³ i (S/S Tripled, Doubled 0)   (185)   I-3   R-4

Obverse III² 3 – Doubled 0 same as VAM 5 but with horizontal die gouge in upper loop of first 8 and several die chips at top right of upper loop of second 8.

Reverse C³ i – IV S mint mark tripled with original showing as short and long vertical bars to right of upper serif.

20   III² 13 • C³ h (Tripled 0)   I-2   R-4

Obverse III² 13 – 188 in date is doubled and 0 is tripled. 1 is doubled slightly below upper serif and first 8 is doubled slightly at top of upper loop opening. Second 8 doubled slightly at lower left outside of upper loop. 0 in date is tripled strongly on lower left outside and is raised well above the surface of the original 0. The 0 is also doubled at very bottom left inside of opening.

Reverse C³ h – Eagle's right wing has a die chip near the tip of the wreath in addition to repunched mint mark.

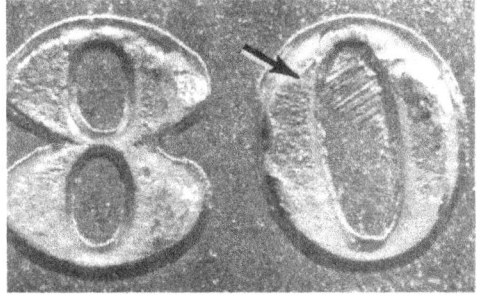   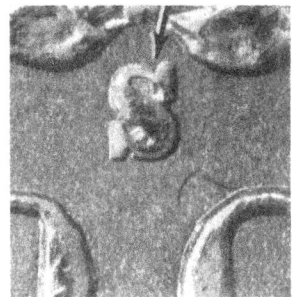   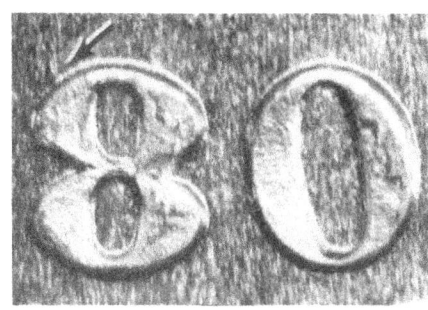

11 O 0/9   11 R S/S   12 O 8/7 Spikes

1880-S

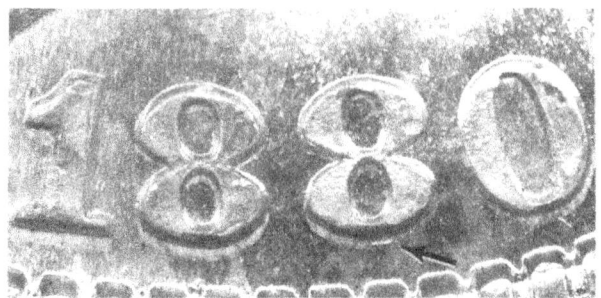
13 O Dash Under 8, Doubled Date

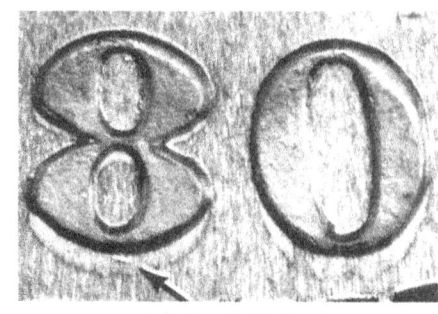
14 O Dash Under 8

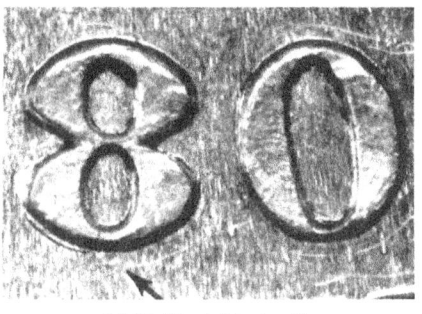
15 O Dash Under 8

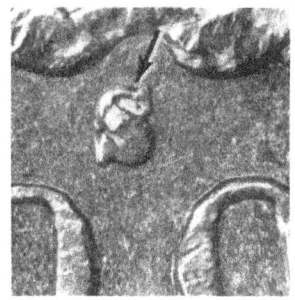
15 R S/S

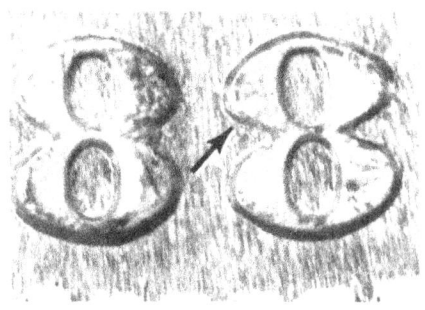
16 O Doubled 8

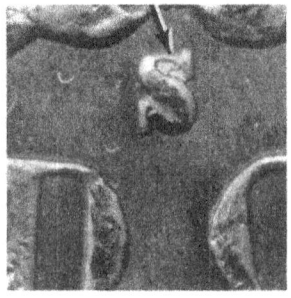
18 R S/S

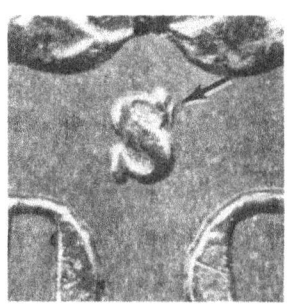
19 R S/S

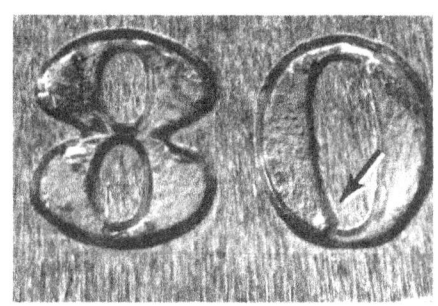
20 O Tripled 0

20 O Doubled 18, Tripled 0

20 R Die Chip

211

1880-S

21	III² 14 • C³ j (Doubled 80)		(185)	I-2	R-3

Obverse III² 14 – 80 doubled in date. Second 8 has top loop doubled on the outside at bottom on both sides and inside as a thin line at top and bottom. Lower loop is doubled as a thin line at the top inside. 0 doubled at top on left and right sides.
Reverse C³ j – IV S mint mark with top loop filled and diagonal shaft doubled inside lower loop.

22	III² 14 • C³ c (Doubled 80)	(188)	I-2	R-3

23	III² 15 • C³ e (S/S Top, Doubled 80)		I-2	R-4

Obverse III² 15 – Doubled 80 in date. Second 8 is doubled on lower left outside of upper loop. 0 is doubled on right inside.

24	III² 16 • C³ k (Doubled 80, Die Chip 8)		I-3	R-3

Obverse III² 16 – 80 in date is slightly doubled. First 8 has a small die chip in top inside of upper loop. Second 8 is doubled slightly on lower left outside of upper loop. 0 is doubled at top left and right outside.
Reverse C³ k – Slight doubling of legend letters in radial direction plus motto and wreath leaves on outside. Very large VI S mint mark tilted left.

25	III² 17 • C³ a (Doubled 880)	(187)	I-2	R-4

Obverse III² 17 – 880 in date is doubled. First 8 is doubled at bottom right outside of lower loop. Second 8 slightly doubled at lower left outside of upper loop. 0 is doubled strongly on lower left side and is raised well above the surface of the original 0. The 0 is also doubled at very bottom left inside of opening similar to III² 13 obverse. Some specimens show die chip on right side of first 8.

26	III² 18 • C³ a (Doubled 880)	(184)	I-2	R-3

Obverse III² 18 – Doubled 880 in date. First 8 is doubled at bottom and has die chip between loops on left side. Second 8 slightly doubled at lower left outside of upper loop. 0 doubled at top left and right outside and slightly at lower left and right outside.

27	III² 18 • C³ j (Doubled 880)		I-2	R-4

28	III² 19 • C³ a (Doubled 880)		I-2	R-3

Obverse III² 19 – Doubled 880 in date. First 8 is doubled on top surface at bottom right outside and top left inside of lower loop. Second 8 doubled at lower left outside of upper loop. 0 doubled slightly at lower left inside.

29	III² 19 • C³ c (Doubled 880)	(187)	I-2	R-3

30	III² 20 • C³ h (S/S and Doubled Date)	(187)	I-3	R-3

Obverse III² 20 – Entire date doubled. 1 doubled faintly on right surface of vertical shaft. First 8 doubled on surface at top inside and right outside of lower loop. Second 8 doubled at left outside of upper loop. 0 doubled faintly on right inside.

31	III² 21 • C³ c (Doubled Date)	(187)	I-2	R-4

Obverse III² 21 – Entire doubled faintly at very bottom right. First 8 doubled strongly on surface at bottom of lower loop. Second 8 doubled at lower left outside of upper loop. 0 doubled on left and right outside at top and bottom.

32	III² 21 • C³ h (S/S and Doubled Date)	(187)	I-3	R-3

Reverse C³ h – No dot on eagle's wing.

33	III² 22 • C³ l (Doubled Date)	(184)	I-2	R-3

Obverse III² 22 – Entire date is doubled. 1 is doubled on left side of vertical shaft. First 8 is doubled on top surface at bottom of lower loop with a die chip between loops on right side. Second 8 is doubled at lower left outside of upper loop. 0 is doubled slightly at lower left inside.
Reverse C³ l – VI S mint mark tilted left and doubled with short diagonal spike on left inside of upper loop and a long diagonal line within lower loop.

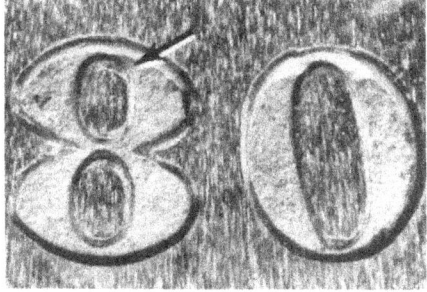

21 O Doubled 80

21 R Doubled S

24 O Doubled 80, Die Chip in 8

1880-S

23 O Doubled 80

25 O Doubled 880

26 O Doubled 880

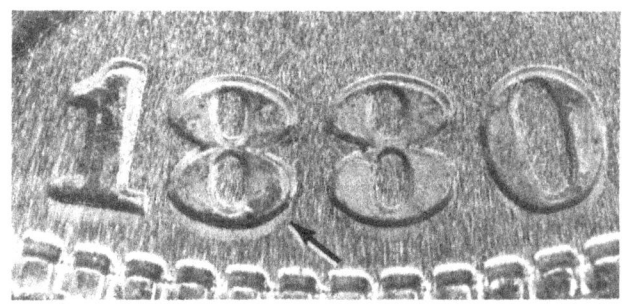
31 O DOubled Date

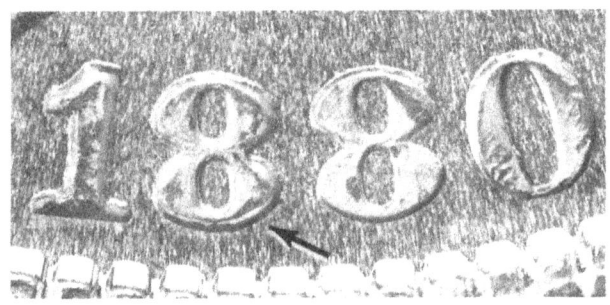
32 O Doubled Date

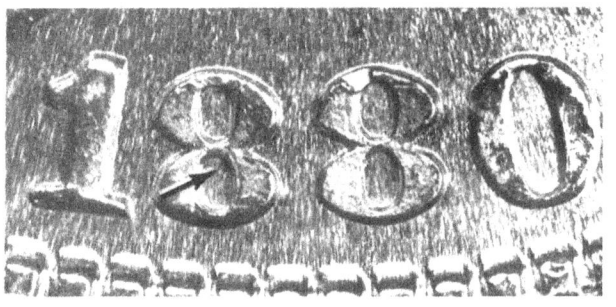
34 O Doubled Date

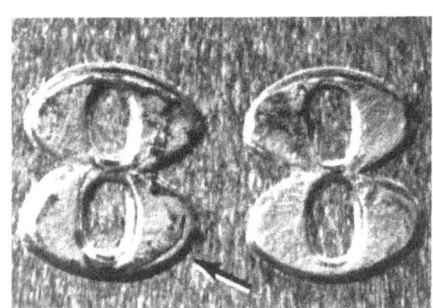
28 O DOubled 800

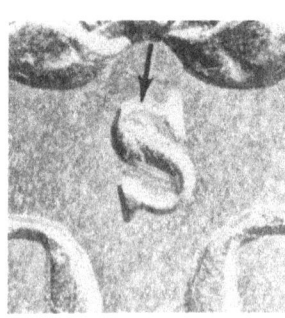
33 R Doubled S

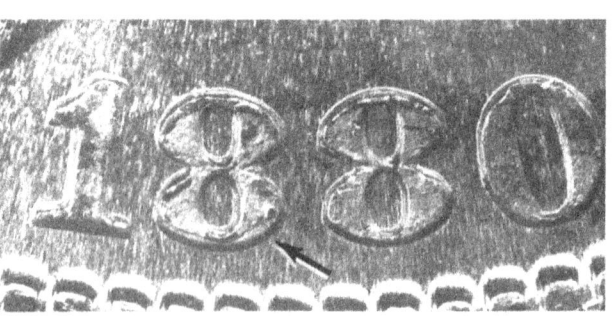
33 O Doubled Date

213

1880-S

34 III²23 • C³m (Doubled Date) I-2 R-3
Obverse III²23 – Entire date is doubled slightly. 1 is doubled faintly below top crossbar and above bottom crossbar. First 8 is doubled on right inside of lower loop and slightly on bottom outside. Second 8 is doubled at bottom left outside of upper loop. 0 is doubled on top surface at left inside and slightly on lower right inside.
Reverse C³m – IV S mint mark set to left.

35 III²24 • C³n (Doubled Date) (188) I-3 R-3
Obverse III²24 – Entire date slightly doubled. 1 is doubled faintly at bottom of top crossbar. First 8 is doubled at top inside of upper loop. Second 8 is doubled at bottom left outside of upper loop. 0 is doubled at top left and right outside and faintly at top right inside.
Reverse C³n – VI S mint mark tilted very far to left.

36 III²4 • C³o of (Doubled Date, S/S Right) (188) I-2 R-4
Reverse C³o – IV S mint mark repunched with the original showing as a curved line at top and left inside of loop, a curved line in middle of lower loop, and a short vertical line to middle right of upper serif.

37 III²25 • C³a (Doubled 80) (188) I-2 R-3
Obverse III²25 – Doubled 80 in date. Second 8 doubled faintly at left bottom outside of upper loop. 0 doubled faintly at left and right outside.

38 III²12 • C³g (Doubled 8, S/S Right) I-2 R-4
Obverse III²12 – No die chip between first 8 loops.

39 III²25 • C³g (Doubled 80, Large S) I-2 R-3

40 III²26 • C³a (Doubled 80, S Tilted Left) I-2 R-3
Obverse III²26 – Doubled 80 in date. Second 8 doubled faintly at left bottom outside of upper loop. 0 doubled faintly at bottom left outside on top surface.

41 III²27 • C³a (Doubled 1-80) I-2 R-3
Obverse III²27 – Doubled 1-80 in date. 1 doubled as a notch at the top left of lower crossbar. Second 8 doubled at left bottom outside of upper loop. 0 doubled at left inside and strongly at top left and right outside.

42 III²21 • C³a (Doubled Date) I-2 R-4
Reverse C³a – Some specimens show a large die chip on wreath leaf opposite NI of UNITED and a smaller die chip on field next to I of UNITED.

43 III²28 • C³p (Doubled 1-80, S/S) I-2 R-3
Obverse III²28 – 1-80 doubled in date. 1 doubled slightly at top of bottom serif on both sides. Second 8 doubled slightly at lower left outside of upper loop. 0 doubled at left and right inside.
Reverse C³p – VI S mint mark doubled with curved line at top inside of upper loop and a thin diagonal line at top inside of lower loop.

44 III²29 • C³a (Doubled Date) (186) I-2 R-3
Obverse III²29 – Entire date is doubled. 1 is doubled on surface at top left of upper crossbar, top left and right of lower crossbar and at lower left of vertical shaft. First 8 doubled on surface at top inside and right outside of lower loop. Second 8 doubled at lower left outside of upper loop. 0 doubled slightly at top left and right outside.

45 III²30 • C³r (Doubled Date, S/S Up) (188) I-2 R-3
Obverse III²30 – Entire date is doubled. 1 is doubled on surface at lower right side of vertical shaft top right of lower crossbar. First 8 doubled on surface at left inside of lower loop. Second 8 doubled at lower left outside of upper loop. 0 doubled at top left and right outside and on surface at lower right inside.
Reverse C³r – IV S mint mark repunched with original showing as a carved bulge at bottom inside of upper loop and a horizontal curved line within middle of lower loop.

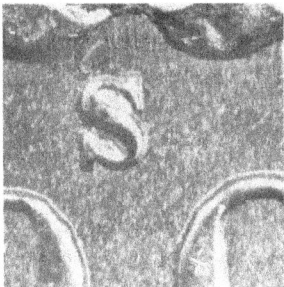 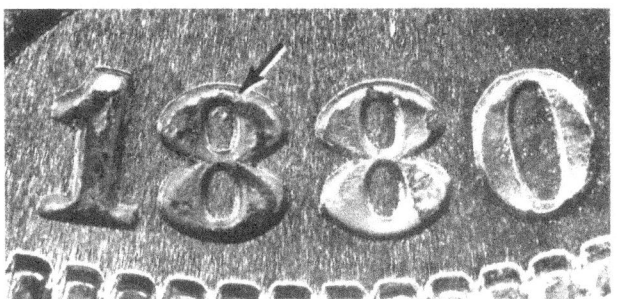 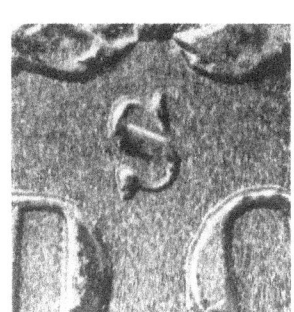

34 R S Set Left   35 O Doubled Date   35 R S Tilted Left

1880-S

36 R S/S Right

37 O Doubled 80

40 O Doubled 80

41 O Doubled 1-80

43 O Doubled 1-80

44 O Doubled Date

45 O Doubled Date

42 R Die Chip in Wreath

43 R S/S

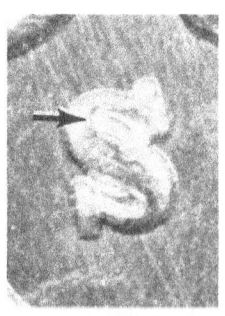
45 R S/S Up

1880-S

46	III²31 • C³b (Dash Under 8, Doubled 80)	(183)		I-2	R-3

Obverse III²31 – A high set and short dash appears just below the second 8. Second 8 is also doubled at lower left outside of upper loop. 0 is doubled at top left and right outside.

47	III²32 • C³a (Doubled Date)	(188)		I-2	R-3

Obverse III²32 – Entire date is doubled. 1 is doubled on surface at lower right side of vertical shaft and top right of lower crossbar. First 8 doubled on surface at left inside of both loops and on right outside of lower loop. Second 8 doubled at lower left outside of upper loop. 0 doubled strongly at top left outside and faintly on top right outside.

48	III²33 • C³c (Doubled Date, S Tilted Left)	(186)		I-2	R-3

Obverse III²33 – Entire date is doubled. 1 is doubled on surface at top left of upper crossbar and at top left and right of lower crossbar. First 8 doubled on surface at lower left outside of upper loop and at bottom outside of lower loop. Second 8 doubled slightly at lower left outside of upper loop. 0 doubled slightly at lower left inside and outside.

49	III²29 • C³r (Doubled Date, S/S Up)	(186)		I-2	R-3
50	III²13 • C³s (Tripled 0, S/S Down)	(185)		I-2	R-3

Reverse C³s – IV S mint mark repunched showing as a horizontal line within the middle of the upper loop opening and a diagonal line at top of lower loop opening.

51	III²18 • C³r (Doubled 880, S/S Up)	(186)		I-2	R-3
52	III²20 • C³a (Doubled Date)	(185)		I-2	R-3
53	III²27 • C³c (Doubled 1-80, S Tilted Left)	(187)		I-2	R-3
54	III²15 • C³a (Doubled 80)			I-2	R-3
55	III²34 • C³a (Doubled 80, Die Chip Wreath)	(189)		1-2	R-3

Obverse III²34 – Doubled 80 in date. Second 8 doubled slightly on lower left outside of upper loop. 0 doubled at left and right outside at top and bottom.

Reverse C³a – Large die chip on wreath leaf opposite NI of UNITED and a smaller die chip in field next to I of UNITED as in VAM 42.

56	III²35 • C³a (Doubled Date)	(188)		I-2	R-3

Obverse III²35 – Entire date doubled. 1 doubled at top right of vertical shaft. First 8 doubled strongly at top inside and bottom outside of lower loop. Second 8 doubled slightly at lower loop. 0 doubled slightly at lower left inside.

57	III²24 • C³c (Doubled Date)	(186)		I-2	R-3
58	III²36 • C³c (Doubled 88, S Tilted Left)	(184)		I-2	R-3

Obverse III²36 – Doubled 88 in date. First 8 doubled at right inside and slightly at bottom outside of lower loop. Second 8 doubled slightly at lower left outside of upper loop.

59	III²36 • C³d (Doubled Date, S Tilted Left)	(182)		I-2	R-3
60	III²33 • C³t (Doubled Date, S/S)	(187)		I-2	R 3

Reverse C³t – IV S mint mark repunched showing as a curved diagonal line in middle of upper loop opening.

61	III²33 • C³d (Doubled Date, S Tilted left)	(187)		I-2	R-3
62	III²12 • C³b (Doubled 8)	(183)		I-2	R-3
63	III²37 • C³b (Doubled Date)	(188)		I-2	R-3

Obverse III²37 – Entire date is doubled. 1 doubled slightly below upper crossbar. First 8 doubled on surface at lower right outside of upper and lower loops and at top right inside of lower loop. Second 8 doubled at lower left of upper loop. 0 doubled at left and right outside at top and bottom.

 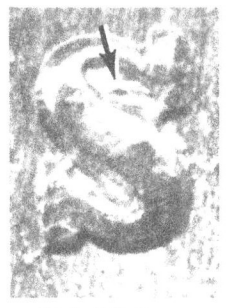 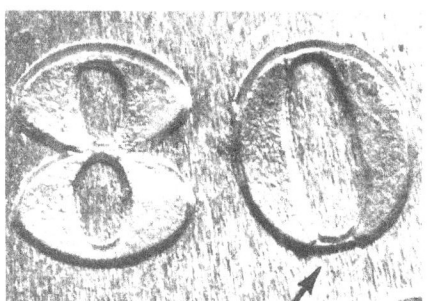

46 O Doubled 80, Dash 8 | 50 R S/S Down | 55 O Doubled 80

1880-S

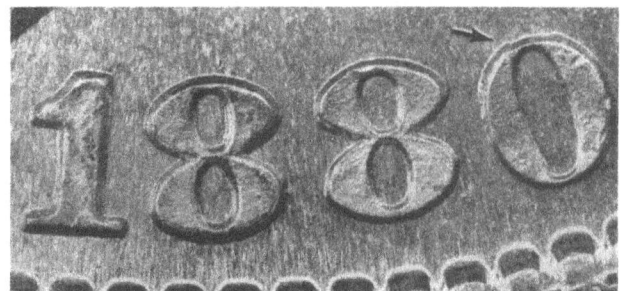
47 O Doubled Date

48 O Doubled Date

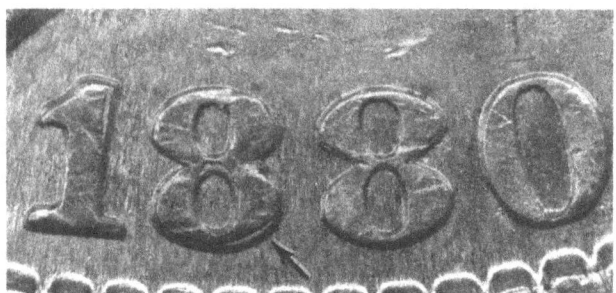
56 O Doubled Date

58 O Doubled 88

60 R S/S

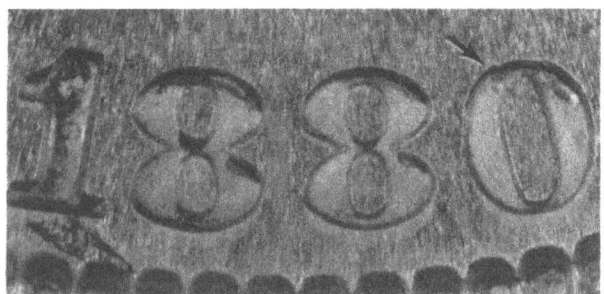
63 O Doubled Date

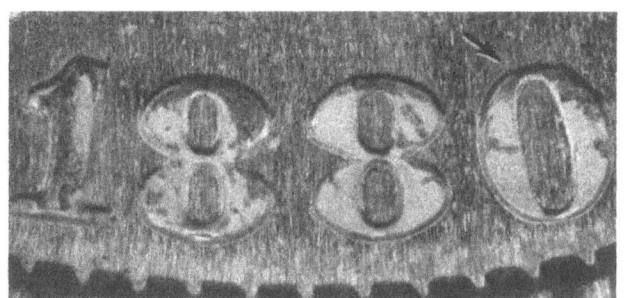
64 O Doubled Date

64	III²38 • C³u (Doubled Date, S/S)	(188)	I-2	R-3

Obverse III²38 – Entire date is doubled. 1 doubled slightly on right side of vertical shaft. First 8 doubled at top inside of lower loop. Second 8 doubled at lower left outside of upper loop. 0 doubled at left and right top outside.

Reverse C³u – IV S mint mark is doubled with diagonal line at top of upper loop opening and a short horizontal line on right inside of lower loop. Mint mark is set slightly left with slight tilt to right.

65	III²30 • C³c (Doubled Date, S Tilted Left)	(188)	I-2	R-3
66	III²24 • C³a (Doubled Date)	(185)	I-2	R-3
67	III²39 • C³a (Doubled Date)	(188)	I-2	R-3

Obverse III²39 – Entire date is doubled. 1 doubled as a notch on left side of lower crossbar. First 8 doubled on surface at left and right of lower loop. Second 8 doubled at lower left outside of upper loop. 0 doubled top left and right outside and lower left inside.

68	III²31 • C³j (Doubled Date, S/S)	(188)	I-2	R-3
69	III²15 • C³v (Doubled 80 and Reverse)	(186)	I-2	R-3

Reverse C³v – Doubled left wreath, UNITED STATES OF AMERICA, and left star towards rim. VI S mint mark centered and tilted slightly left.

70	III²22 • C³b (Doubled Date)	(184)	I-2	R-3

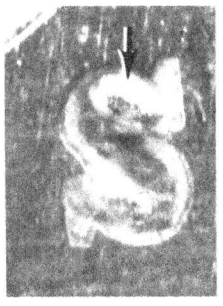  

64 R S/S

67 O Doubled Date

69 R Doubled Wreath and Lettering

1881-P

A full strike is typical for this date but weak strikes do exist. Luster is variable however and many are dull because of the high mintage. A few minor die varieties exist but none are significant enough to command a price premium.

Proof-like coins are fairly scarce and are a little more difficult to find than other early P mints. Proofs tend to have excellent contrast and nice ones are somewhat available.

1   III²1 • C³a (Normal Die)   I-1   R-2
     Obverse III²1 – Normal die of III² type. Some specimens show a die chip between the loops of the first 8 or a small die gouge at bottom of Y in LIBERTY.
     Reverse C³a – Normal die of C³ type.

1A   III²1 • C³a (Die Chips in 8)   (180)   I-2   R-3
     Obverse III²1 – Short die chip at top left inside of upper loop of first 8. In some specimens, second 8 has die chips in middle of both loops. Some specimens show die chip at top inside of both loops.

2   III²2 • C³a (Dash Under 8)   I-2   R-3
     Obverse III²2 – A dash appears below the second 8 in the date.

3   III²3 • C³a (Doubled 1)   I-2   R-3
     Obverse III²3 – Second 1 in date doubled at top.

4   III²4 • C³a (Doubled 1 Left)   I-2   R-3
     Obverse III²4 – Second 1 in date doubled at top on left side only. First 8 has a spike of metal between loops on right.

5   III²5 • C³a (Doubled 8)   (180)   I-2   R-3
     Obverse III²5 – First 8 in date doubled at right inside of upper loop.

6   III²6 • C³a (Tripled 8)   (179)   I-2   R-4
     Obverse III²6 – First 8 in date is tripled strongly at bottom right outside of upper and lower loops and at top left inside of lower loop. Upper loop of first 8 is also doubled at top left inside.

7   III²7 • C³a (Doubled 1, Tripled 8)   (180)   I-2   R-3
     Obverse III²7 – First 1 doubled at bottom of lower crossbar. First 8 tripled at bottom outside of lower loop and doubled at top inside of upper and lower loop with short spike at top left inside of upper loop. All left and right stars doubled faintly towards rim.

8   III²8 • C³a (Doubled 18-1)   (181)   I-2   Proof
     Obverse III²8 – 18-1 in date doubled. First 1 is doubled slightly at top right of vertical shaft. First 8 is doubled on surface at top right inside lower loop. Second 1 is doubled at top left.

1881-P

9   III²9 • C³a (Doubled 18-1)   (180)   I-2   R-4
Obverse III² 9 – 18-1 in date doubled. First 1 doubled slightly above crossbar on right. First 8 is doubled strongly on surface of lower right inside of both loops and at top right outside of upper loop with die chip between loops on right side. Second 1 is doubled at top left.

10   III²10 • C³a (Doubled 18-1)   (181)   I-2   R-4
Obverse III² 10 – 18-1 in date doubled. First 1 is doubled slightly at top right of vertical shaft. First 8 is doubled at top inside of upper loop with die chip at top left inside of upper loop, doubled at top and right inside of lower loop and doubled at bottom outside of lower loop. Second 1 is doubled slightly at top left. Faint dash just under second 8 in some specimens.

1A O Die Chip in 8s

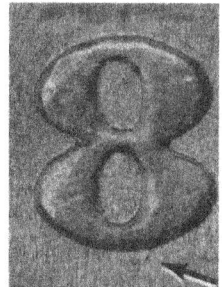
2 O Dash

3 O Doubled 1

5 O Doubled 8

4 O Doubled 1 Left

6 O Tripled 8

7 O Doubled 1, Tripled 8

8 O Doubled 18-1

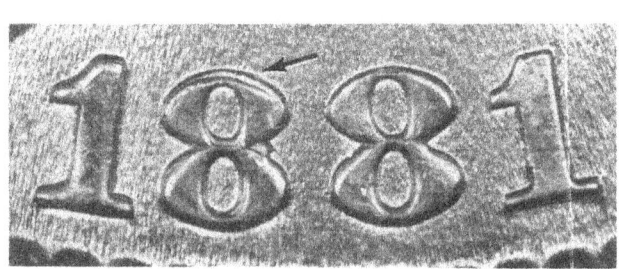
9 O Doubled 18-1

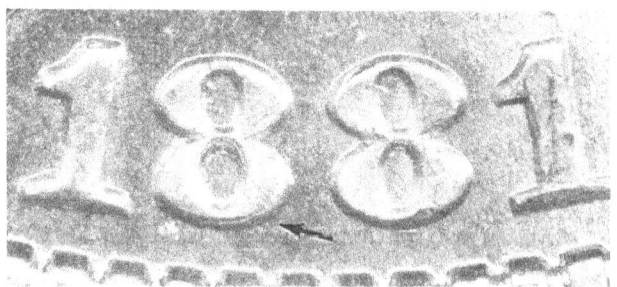
10 O Doubled 18-1

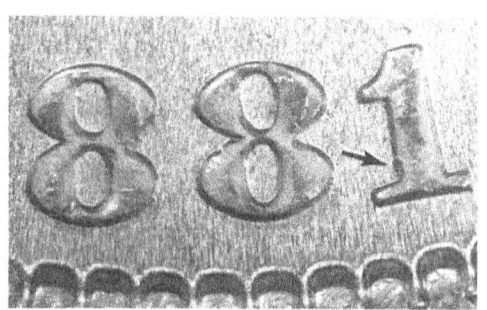
11 O Doubled 8-1

1881-P

11	III² 11 – C³ a (Doubled 8-1)	(180)	I-2	R-3

Obverse III² 11 – Doubled 8-1 in date. First 8 doubled on surface at top outside of upper loop. Second 1 has a notch at lower left of vertical shaft.

12	III² 12 • C³ a (Doubled 1-1)	(179)	I-2	R-3

Obverse III² 12 – Both 1's in date are doubled below upper crossbar. Short die chip at top left inside of first 8.

13	III² 13 • C³ a (Doubled 18)	(181)	I-2	R-3

Obverse III² 13 – 18 doubled on surface at very bottom outside. First 8 has die chip at left inside of upper loop.

14	III² 14 • C³ a (Doubled 18-1)	(180)	I-2	R-3

Obverse III² 14 – Doubled 18-1 in date. First 1 doubled slightly on top right of vertical shaft. First 8 doubled at top right outside and on right outside surface of upper loop. Second 1 doubled all across very top.

15	III² 15 • C³ a (Doubled Second 1)	(181)	1-2	R-3

Obverse III² 15 – Second 1 doubled below upper crossbar. First 8 has short die chip at top left inside of upper loop.

16	III² 16 • C³ a (Doubled 18 and Stars)	(180)	I-3	R-3

Obverse III² 16 – All left and right stars tripled towards rim. First 1 doubled at top inside of both loops and tripled at bottom outside of lower loop plus a short die chip at top left inside of upper loop.

12 O Doubled 1-1

13 O Doubled 18

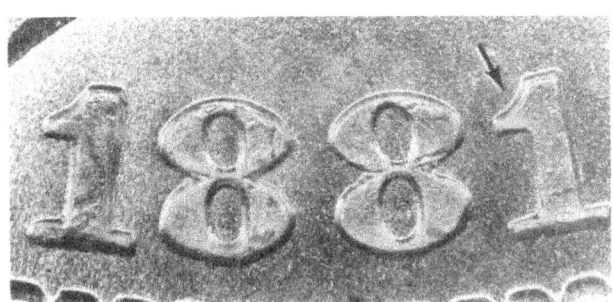

14 O Doubled 18-1

15 O Second 1 Doubled

16 O Doubled 18 and Stars

1881-CC

Half the mintage was released as uncirculated coins during the 1973-74 and 1980 GSA sales, so BU coins are not scarce. The strike is generally full and the luster excellent because of the low number of coins struck by the dies. The overall quality is the highest for the Carson City Mint. No significant die varieties exist.

A considerable percentage of the issue are proof-likes because of the low die mintages. A significant number of these have very deep mirrors with cameo devices.

1   III²1 • C³a (Normal Die)   I-1   R-3
Obverse III²1 – Normal die of III² type.
Reverse C³a – Normal die of C³ type with large V CC mint mark.

2   III²2 • C³a (Doubled 88)   I-2   R-4
Obverse III²2 – Both 8's in date doubled. First 8 has die chip on left inside of top loop and is doubled as a thin line at the top inside of the lower loop. Second 8 has die chips in a band across middle inside of upper loop and is doubled on the right inside of lower loop.
Reverse C³a – Thin line die scratch from olive branch to leaves just above the arrow feathers.

3   III²3 • C³a (Dash Under 8)   (178)   I-2   R-4
Obverse III²3 – The second 8 in the date has a thin dash below the bottom loop. The first 1 is doubled on the surface of the vertical shaft on the right side. The first 8 is doubled on the surface at the top inside and bottom right outside of both inside of upper loops.

4   III²4 • C³a (Doubled 18)   I-2   R-3
Obverse III²4 – Doubled 18 in date. 1 doubled slightly on right side of vertical bar. First 8 doubled on surface on left inside and lower right outside of both loops.

5   III²1 • C³b (CC Tilted Left)   (178)   I-2   R-3
Reverse C³b – V CC mint mark centered and tilted slightly to left.

6   III²3 • C³b (Doubled 18, CC Tilted Left)   (178)   I-2   R-3
Obverse III²3 – There is no dash under the second 8.

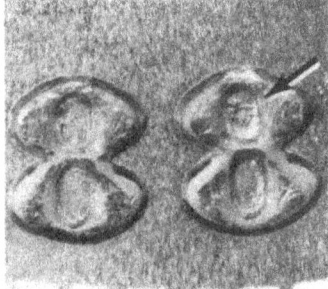
2 O Doubled 88

2 R Die Scratch

3 O Dash 8, Doubled 18

4 O Doubled 18

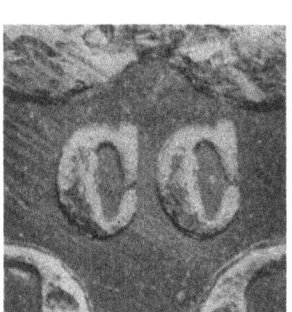
5 R CC Tilted Left

1881-O

Most coins of this date are fully struck but the luster tends to be subdued because of long use of the dies to achieve high mintages. Slider coins are fairly common although not as much as 1879-O and 1880-O. Numerous minor die varieties exist but none are significant.

Proof-likes are not especially scarce but many have little or dull contrast.

1   III²1 • C³a (Normal Die)   (176)   I-1   R-2
Obverse III²1 – Normal die of III² type.
Reverse C³a – Normal die of C³ type with tall oval medium II O mint mark, centered and upright.

1A   III²1 • C³a (Spike in 8)   (176)   I-2   R-3
Obverse III²1 – First 8 had a short die chip at top left inside of upper loop.

2   III²1 • C³b (O/O Low)   (176)   I-2   R-4
Reverse C³b – Mint mark tilted to left and repunched with original showing at bottom of opening.

2A   III²1 • C³b (O/O Low, Spike in 8)   (176)   I-2   R-3
Obverse III²1 – First 8 has a short die chip spike at top left inside of upper loop.

3   III²2 • C³a (Doubled 18)   (176)   I-2   R-3
Obverse III²2 – Doubled 18 in date. The 1 has a doubled vertical bar on the right side. The upper and lower loops of the first 8 are doubled on the left inside.

4   III²3 • C³a (Doubled 1)   (176)   I-2   R-3
Obverse III²3 – Last 1 in date doubled at top and on lower right side of vertical bar.

5   III²3 • C³c (O/O Right, Doubled 1)   (176)   I-2   R-3
Reverse C³c – II O mint mark doubled on right inside with a shallow thin diagonal bar (die gouge) two-thirds way up in opening.

6   III²1 • C³d (O Tilted Left)   (176)   I-2   R-3
Reverse C³d – II O mint mark centered and tilted left.

6A   III²1 • C³d (Spike in 8)   (176)   I-2   R-3

7   III²1 • C³e (O Set High)   (176)   I-2   R-3
Reverse C³e – II O mint mark centered and set high.

8   III²1 • C³f (O Tilted Right)   (176)   I-2   R-3
Reverse C³f – O mint mark centered and tilted slightly to right.

9   III²4 • C³g (Bar O, Doubled 8)   (176)   I-2   R-3
Obverse III²4 – First 8 in date doubled at top inside of upper and lower loops and on surface at bottom outside of lower loop.
Reverse C³g – Short die chip at lower right inside of II O mint mark.

10   III²5 • C³h (O/O Top Right, Tripled 18-1)   (176)   I-3   R-4
Obverse III²5 – Tripled 18-1 in date. First 1 tripled at bottom of top and bottom crossbars. 8 tripled at top inside of both loops, lower left outside of top loop and bottom outside of lower loop. Second 1 is doubled slightly at bottom of crossbar and on right side of vertical bar.
Reverse C³h – II O mint mark doubled on middle and top right side of opening.

11   III²1 • C³i (O/O Left)   (176)   I-3   R-3
Obverse III²1 – Spike in 8 same as 1A.
Reverse C³i – II O mint mark doubled slightly on the left side of opening as a thin vertical line.

   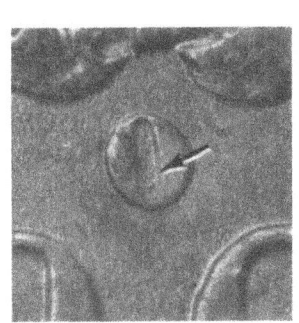   

1A O Spike in 8   2 R O/O Low   3 O Doubled 18

1881-O

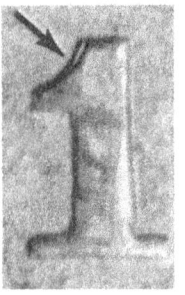
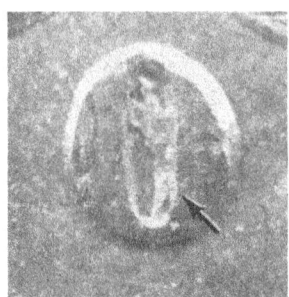

4 O Doubled 1   5 R O/O Right   6 R O Tilted Left   7 R O Set High

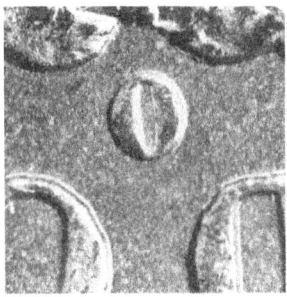

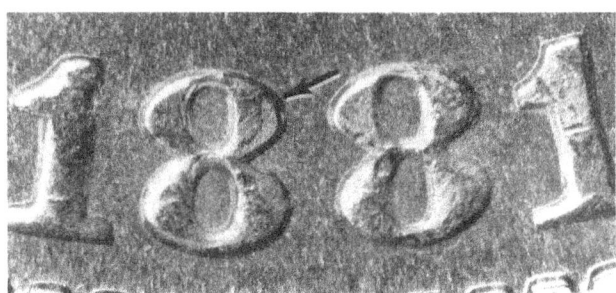

8 R O Titled Right   9 R Bar O   10 O Tripled 18-1

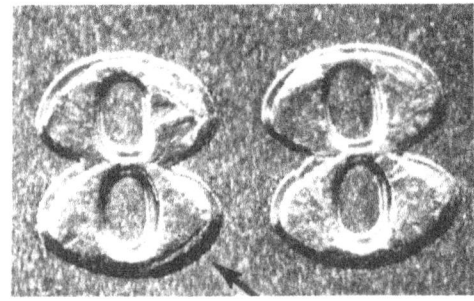

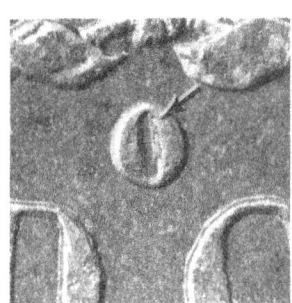

9 O Doubled 8   10 O Tripled 18-1   10 R O/O Top Right

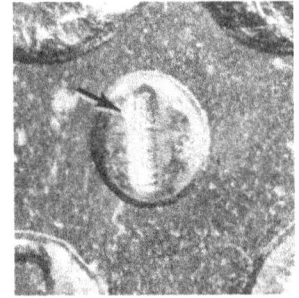

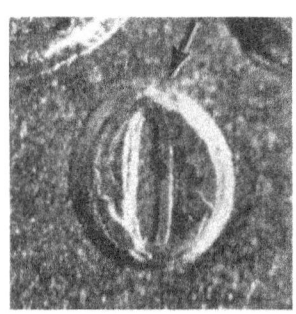

11 R O/O Left   12 R O/O Lower Right   13 R O/O High

223

1881-O

12	III²1 • C³i (O/O Lower Right)	(176)	I-2	R-4

Reverse C³i – Centered II O mint mark doubled right inside of opening as a thin vertical bar curving to left at bottom of opening.

13	III²4 • C³k (Doubled 8, O/O High)	(176)	I-3	R-3

Reverse C³k – II O mint mark doubled strongly at top left and right outside.

14	III²6 • C³a (Doubled First 8, Die Gouge DO)	(176)	I-2	R-3

Obverse III²6 – Spike in first 8 as in 1A. First 8 is doubled on surface at bottom right outside of lower loop.
Reverse C³a – Doubled die gouge through DO in Dollar.

15	III²7 • C³a (Doubled 1)	(176)	I-2	R-3

Obverse III²7 – Second 1 doubled slightly at top left of upper crossbar and as a notch on the lower right side of vertical shaft. Spike in first 8 as in 1A.

16	III²8 • C³a (Doubled 1)	(176)	I-2	R-3

Obverse III²8 – First 1 doubled slightly at bottom of upper crossbar and at top right of vertical shaft. First 8 has a short die chip in top left inside of upper loop.

17	III²9 • C³a (Dash Under 8)	(176)	I-2	R-3

Obverse III²9 – Second 8 in date has a thin dash just below the bottom loop. First 8 has a short die chip in top left inside of upper loop.

18	III²10 • C³a (Doubled 18)	(176)	I-2	R-3

Obverse III²10 – Doubled 18 in date. 1 doubled below upper crossbar. First 8 doubled at top left inside of lower loop and has a short die chip spike at top left inside of upper loop.
Reverse C³a – A long thin die gouge runs from D through O to L in DOLLAR.

19	III²11 • C³a (Doubled 1-1)	(176)	I-2	R-3

Obverse III²11 – Doubled 1-1 in date. First 1 doubled strongly below upper crossbar. Second 1 also doubled faintly below upper crossbar. First 8 has a short die chip spike at top left inside of upper loop.

20	III²12 • C³a (Doubled 18)	(176)	I-2	R-3

Obverse III²12 – Doubled 18 in date. First 1 doubled slightly at top right of vertical shaft. First 8 doubled at top and right inside and bottom outside of lower loop with die chip at top left inside of upper loop.

21	III²1 • C³h (O/O Top Right)	(176)	I-2	R-3
22	III²13 • C³d (Doubled 1-1, O Tilted Left)	(176)	I-2	R-3

Obverse III²13 – Doubled 1-1 in date. First 1 doubled at top right of vertical shaft as a notch. Second 1 doubled at top of upper serif and on lower left side of vertical shaft.

23	III²1 • C³k (O Set Left)	(176)	I-2	R-3

Obverse III²1 – First 8 has a short die chip at top left inside of upper loop.
Reverse C³k – II O mint mark centered, upright and set to left. Eagle's right wing is overpolished on some specimens.

24	III²14 • C³a (Doubled Second 1)	(176)	I-2	R-3

Obverse III²14 – Second 1 doubled at lower left side on vertical shaft as a notch.

25	III²1 • C³l (O/O Right)	(176)	I-2	R-3

Reverse C³l – II O mint mark centered and tilted left with doubling on right inside and die chips on lower right outside. Eagle's right wing and left wreath are overpolished.

26	III²15 • C³a (Doubled 18)	(176)	I-2	R-3

Obverse C³a – Doubled 18 in date. First 1 doubled slightly at top right of vertical shaft. First 8 doubled at top outside, left inside and right outside of upper loop.

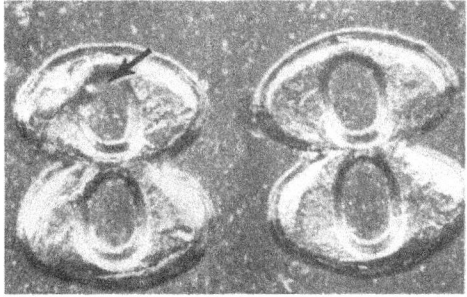

14 O First 8 Doubled

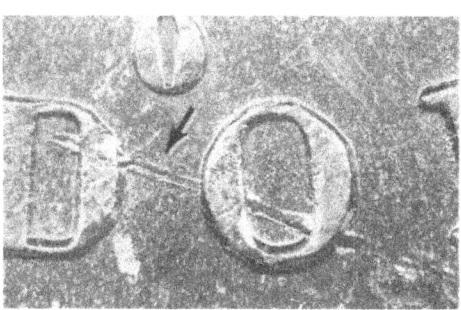

14 R Die Gouges

1881-O

15 O Doubled 1

16 O Doubled 1

(Photo Not Available)

17 O Dash Under 8

(Photo Not Available)

20 O Doubled 18

18 O Doubled 18

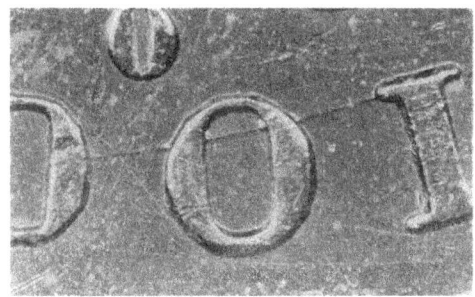

18 R Die Gouge DOL

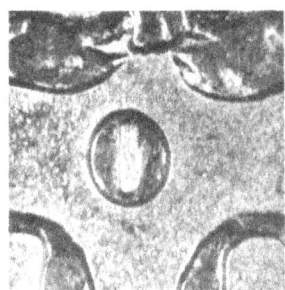

23 R O Set Left

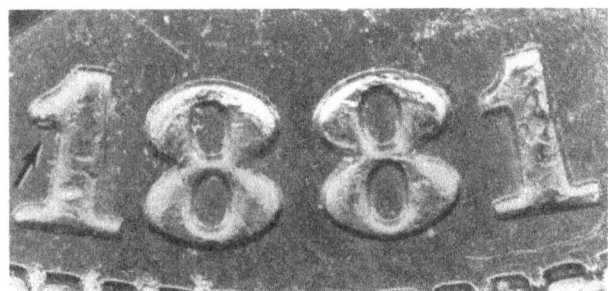

19 O Doubled 1-1

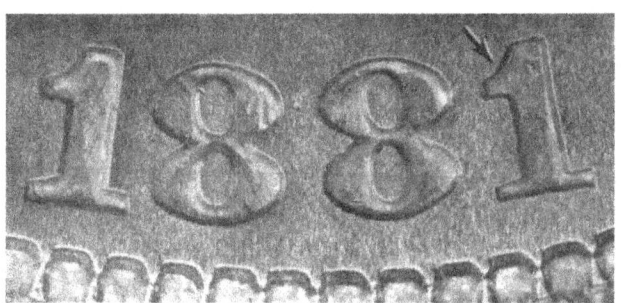

22 O Doubled 1-1

24 O Second 1 Doubled

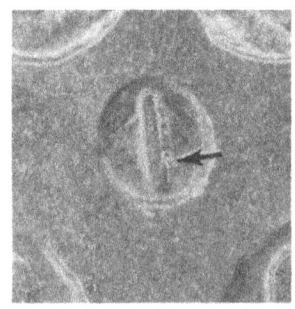

25 R O/O

26 O Doubled 18

225

1881-S

The typical 1881-S is fully struck with outstanding luster. Even though it was a high mintage issue the average number of coins per die pair struck was fairly low so not many coins were struck with worn dies. Apparently this issue escaped significant melting during 1918-1920 and were not mishandled or shipped all over the country. Thus, they are the most plentiful Morgan dollars in nice condition. Numerous die varieties exist but none are particularly significant.

It is readily available in proof-like condition although most are brilliant with little contrast. Many are semi-proof-like or one sided proof-like. The excellent luster of the issue can give proof-like appearance and the coins should be checked to see if clear mirrors exist on both sides when purchasing proof-like specimens. Two-sided cameo proof-likes are scarcer for this date than any other early S mint.

1   III^{2}1 • C^{3}a (Normal Die)   (189)   I-1   R-1
    Obverse III^{2}1 – Normal die of III^2 type. Some specimens show die chips between loops on both sides of first 8.
    Reverse C^{3}a – Normal die of C^3 type with a medium IV S mint mark centered and upright.

1A   III^{2}1 • C^{3}a (Spike in 8's)   (186, 189)   I-2   R-4
    Obverse III^{2}1 – First 8 has a short die chip inside the upper loop at 11 o'clock. Second 8 has die flakes in lower loop. Some specimens also show a short die chip inside the upper loop at 11 o'clock on the second 8 and die flakes at top inside of lower loop of first 8.

2   III^{2}2 • C^{3}a (Doubled 8)   (184)   I-2   R-3
    Obverse III^{2}2 – The first 8 in the date is doubled inside and below the lower loop.

3   III^{2}3 • C^{3}a (Dash Under 8)   I-2   R-3
    Obverse III^{2}3 – The second 8 in the date has a dash under 8.

4   III^{2}4 • C^{3}a (Doubled 18-1)   (185)   I-2   R-3
    Obverse III^{2}4 – Die chip between the loops on the right of the first 8 with a short die chip at top left inside of upper loop, surface doubling on bottom outside of lower loop and tripled on top left inside of lower loop. First 1 doubled slightly below upper crossbar. Second 1 doubled slightly on left side of vertical shaft.

5   III^{2}1 • C^{3}b (S/S Left)   (186)   I-3   R-4
    Obverse III^{2}1 – Spike in first 8 upper loop.
    Reverse C^{3}b – Mint mark is repunched and tilted slightly to left with original showing as a long vertical spike within the middle of the upper loop opening and an arc to the right of the lower loop opening.

6   III^{2}4 • C^{3}b (S/S Left)   (186)   I-3   R-4

7   III^{2}5 • C^{3}c (S/S Left and Up, Doubled Date)   (187)   I-3   R-4
    Obverse III^{2}5 – Top of lower crossbar of both 1's and inside bottom of both loops in both 8's slightly doubled.
    Reverse C^{3}c – Mint mark is repunched with original showing as a short vertical spike to the right of the upper loop opening and an arc within the middle of the lower loop opening.

8   III^{2}1 • C^{3}d (S/S Right)   1-2   R-4
    Reverse C^{3}d – Mint mark is repunched with original showing as a vertical bar to right of top serif. Loops of mint mark filled.

8A   III^{2}1 • C^{3}d (S/S Right)   (183)   I-2   R-4
    Obverse III^{2}1 – First 8 has a short die chip inside the upper loop at 11 o'clock. Second 8 has die chips in lower loop. A spiked die chip is also at top left outside of second 8.

9   III^{2}6 • C^{3}a (Doubled and Spiked 8's)   I-2   R-4
    Obverse III^{2}6 – First 8 has a short die chip inside the upper loop at 11 o'clock and spike die chip between the loops on the right. Second 8 has short spike of metal inside the upper loop at 11 o'clock and strongly doubled at bottom right inside.

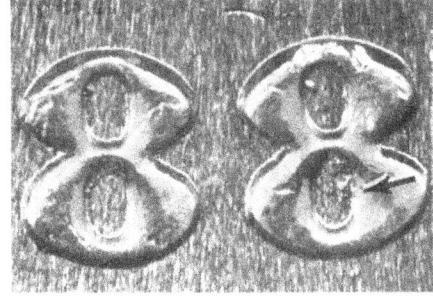

1A O Spike in 8's

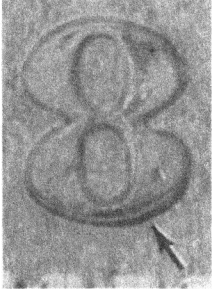

2 O Doubled 8

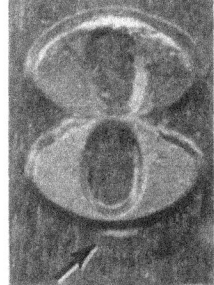

3 O Dash

1881-S

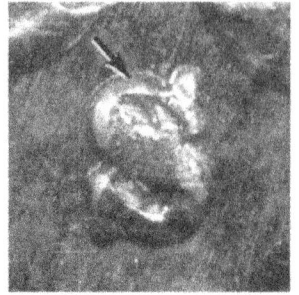
5 R S/S Left

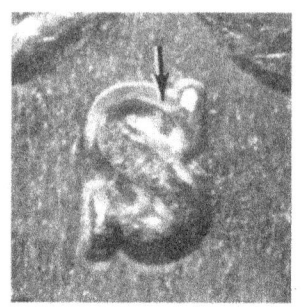
7 R S/S Left and Up

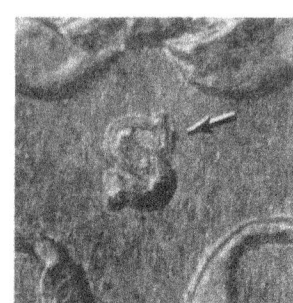
8 R S/S Right

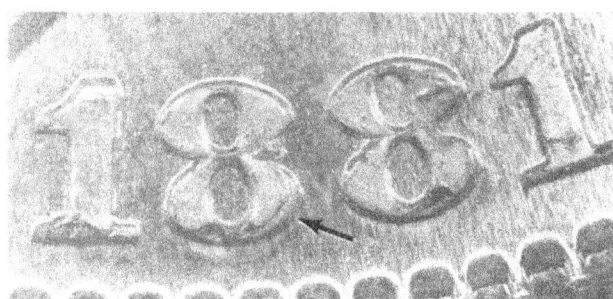
4 O Doubled 18-1

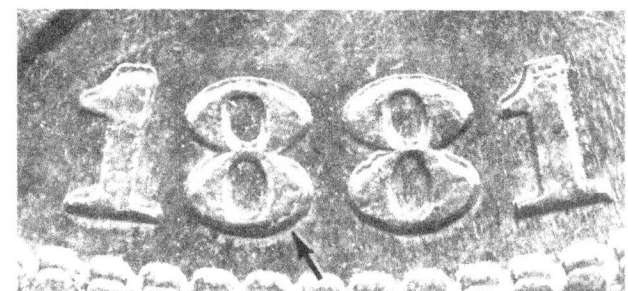
7 O Doubled Date

8A O Spike 8

9 O Doubled 8's

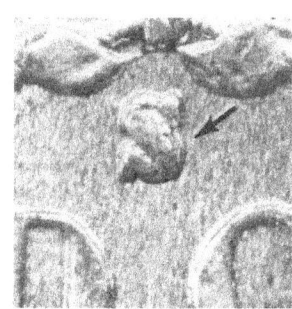
12 R S/S Surface

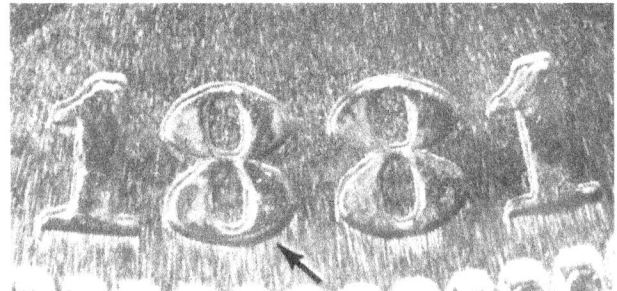
11 O Doubled 18-1

13 R S/S Left

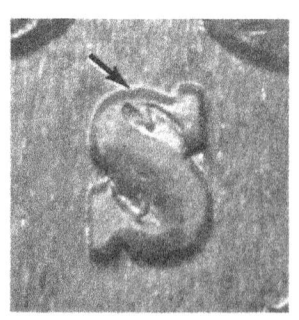
14 R S/S Far Left

1881-S

10	III²6 • C³b (S/S Left)		I-3	R-4

11 III²7 • C³a (Doubled 18-1) (184) I-2 R-3
Obverse III²7 – 18-1 in date doubled slightly at very top. In addition, first 8 is doubled on surface at top left inside and lower right outside of upper loop and right inside and bottom outside of lower loop.

12 III²1 • C³e (S/S Surface) (184) I-2 R-4
Obverse III²1 – Die chips in 8's.
Reverse C³e – Mint mark is repunched with surface doubling on right side of upper serif and lower loop.

13 III²1 • C³f (S/S Left) (186) I-3 R-4
Obverse III²1 – Spike die chip in upper loop on second 8 barely shows.
Reverse C³f – Mint mark is repunched with original showing as a spike at left of upper loop opening and an arc in the middle of lower loop opening. Loops are partially filled.

14 III²1 • C³g (S/S Far Left) I-3 R-4
Reverse C³g – Mint mark is repunched with original showing as a short spike at far left inside of upper loop opening.

15 III²8 • C³g (Doubled 88, S/S Far Left) (185) I-3 R-3
Obverse III²8 – Doubled 88 in date. First 8 doubled on top surface inside and bottom outside of lower loop and left inside and right outside of top loop. Second 8 has a bulge at top left outside of lower loop.

16 III²8 • C³a (Die Chip in Leaves) I-2 R-4
Reverse C³a – Large die chip on wreath leaf opposite NI of UNITED on some specimens.

17 III²9 • C³h (Doubled 18-1, S/S Down) (187) I-3 R-4
Obverse III²9 – Doubled 18-1 in date. First 1 doubled slightly at very bottom. First 8 doubled on surface at bottom outside of lower loop with die chip in left inside of upper loop. Second 1 doubled at lower left of vertical shaft with two vees at bottom of vertical shaft.
Reverse C³h – Mint mark is repunched with original showing as thin horizontal line in middle of upper loop and faint diagonal line at top inside of lower loop.

18 III²4 • C³i (S/S Down) I-3 R-4
Reverse C³i – Mint mark is repunched with original showing as a thin line diagonal line curved at top in middle of upper loop and faint diagonal line at top inside of lower loop.

19 III²10 • C³f (Doubled Date, S/S Left) (186) I-3 R-4
Obverse III²10 – All digits in date slightly doubled. First 1 doubled at very top and on surface at bottom of upper crossbar. First 8 doubled slightly at very top and tripled at bottom outside of lower loop. Second 8 doubled very slightly at lower left outside of upper loop and at bottom outside of lower loop. Second 1 doubled at bottom of left vertical shaft.

20 III²20 • C³j (S/S Up) (185) I-2 R-4
Reverse C³j – Mint mark is repunched with curved line at bottom inside of lower loop. Partially filled loops of mint marks. Small dots of metal all over eagle.

21 III²8 • C³k (Doubled 88, S Tilted Right) (183) I-2 R-3
Reverse C³k – Medium IV S mint mark centered and tilted right with loops partially filled.

22 III²11 • C³l (Slanted Date, S Set Left) (185) I-2 R-3
Obverse III²11 – Date slanted with first 1 close to rim.
Reverse C³l – IV S mint mark set left with slight tilt to right.

23 III²12 • C³k (Doubled 18, S Tilted Right) (183) I-2 R-3
Obverse III²12 – Doubled 18 in date. First 1 doubled on right side. First 8 tripled at bottom surface and edge of lower loop, doubled at top inside of lower loop, and doubled at top inside and lower left outside of upper loop. Second 8 has a bulge at top left outside of lower loop.

24 III²13 • C³c (Doubled 18-1, S/S Left and Up) (185) I-3 R-4
Obverse III²13 – Doubled 18-1 in date. 1 doubled slightly at top left of lower crossbar, bottom left and top right of vertical shaft. First 8 doubled strongly on surface at top and right inside and bottom outside of lower loop. Second 1 doubled slightly at top left of upper crossbar.

25 III²12 – C³a (Doubled 18) (184) I-2 R-3
Obverse III²12 – Die polished down somewhat.

26 III²10 • C³c (Doubled Date, S/S Left and Up) (186) I-3 R-4

1881-S

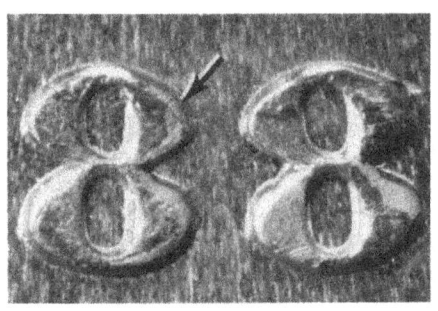
15 O Doubled 88

16 R Die Chip in Leaves

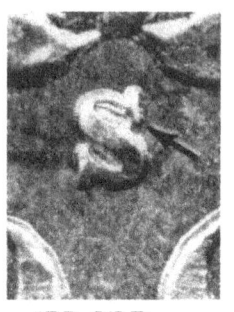
17 R S/S Down

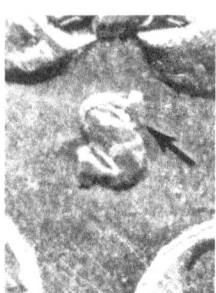
18 R S/S Down

17 O Doubled 18-1

19 O Doubled Date

20 R S/S Up

21 R S Tilted Right

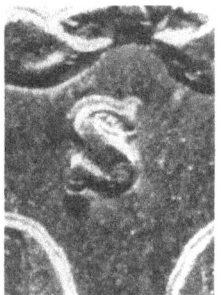
22 R S Set Left

23 O Doubled 18

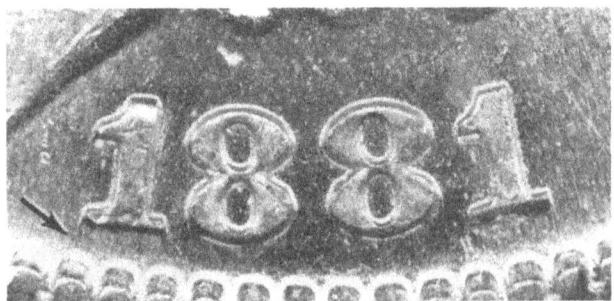
22 O Slanted Date

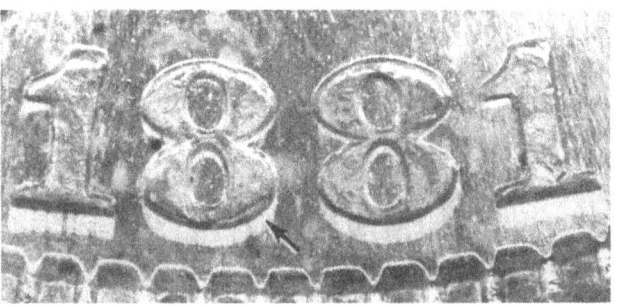
24 O Doubled 18-1

1881-S

27	III² 14 • C³ a (Doubled 18-1)	(185)	I-2	R-3

Obverse III² 14 – Doubled 18-1 in date. First I doubled slightly at top right of vertical shaft and at top left and right of bottom crossbar. First 8 is doubled slightly at top inside and strongly at bottom outside of lower loop. Upper loop of first 8 has spike at left inside. Second 1 doubled slightly at lower left side of vertical shaft.

28	III² 15 • C³ m (Doubled 1-1, S/S Left)	(186)	I-3	R-4

Obverse III² 15 – Doubled 1-1 in date. First 1 doubled below upper crossbar and on right side of vertical shaft. Second 1 doubled at lower left of vertical shaft.

Reverse C³ m – Mint mark is repunched with original showing as a diagonal line at right of upper loop opening and an arc at the right of the lower loop opening. IV S mint mark is set high.

29	III² 16 • C³ a (Doubled First 8)	(186)	I-2	R-3

Obverse III² 16 – First 8 is doubled on surface at right inside of both loops. Both 8's show short die chip inside upper loop at 11 o'clock.

30	III² 1 • C³ c (S/S Left and Up)	(187)	I-3	R-4
31	III² 17 • C³ a (Doubled 18)	(185)	I-2	R-3

Obverse III² 17 – Doubled 18 in date. First 1 doubled on surface of right side of shaft. First 8 doubled faintly on right inside and lower right outside of bottom loop. First 8 has a short die chip in upper loop at 11 o'clock.

32	III² 8 • C³ n (Doubled 88, S Set Left)	(184)	I-2	R-3

Reverse C³ n – IV S mint mark set left with slight tilt to left. TED, TATES, AMERICA, motto and right wreath tip slightly doubled towards rim.

33	III² 18 • C³ o (Doubled 8, High S)	(186)	I-2	R-3

Obverse III² 18 – Doubled first 8 on lower right inside of upper loop and right inside of lower loop. Both 8's have a die chip at top left inside of upper loop.

Reverse C³ o – Medium IV S mint mark centered and set high.

34	III² 19 • C³ 9 (Doubled 188, S/S Far Left)	(185)	I-2	R-3

Obverse III² 19 – Doubled 188 in date. 1 doubled slightly at top right of vertical shaft. First 8 doubled at left inside and on surface at right outside of upper loop and top inside and bottom outside of lower loop. Second 8 tripled at top inside of upper loop.

35	III² 20 • C³ a (Doubled 18)	(185)	I-2	R-3

Obverse III² 20 – Doubled 18 in date. 1 doubled on left top of base. First 8 doubled strongly on surface at right outside of upper loop, top and right inside and bottom outside of lower loop. First 8 has short die chip at top left inside of upper loop.

36	III² 1 • C³ k (S Tilted Right)	(184)	I-2	R-3
37	III² 14 • C³ p (Doubled 18-1, S Tilted Left)	(186)	I-2	R-3

Reverse C³ p – Medium IV S mint mark centered and tilted slightly left.

38	III² 6 • C³ o (Doubled 18-1, Spiked 8's, High S)	(186)	I-2	R-4
39	III² 21 • C³ a (Doubled 18-1, Dash Under 8)	(186)	I-2	R-3

Obverse III² 21 – Doubled 18-1 in date. First 1 doubled at top right. First 8 doubled at top inside of lower loop with short die chip inside upper loop at 11 o'clock. Second 1 doubled at left side of vertical shaft. Second 1 doubled at left side of vertical shaft. Second 8 has dash just below lower loop.

40	III² 22 • C³ m (Doubled 18-1, S/S Left)	(185)	I-2	R-3

Obverse III² 22 – Doubled 18-1 in date. First 1 doubled slightly at upper right of vertical shaft. First 8 doubled at top left inside of both loops and slightly at bottom right outside of lower loop. Second 1 doubled at very top and slightly at lower left side of vertical shaft.

27 O Doubled 18-1

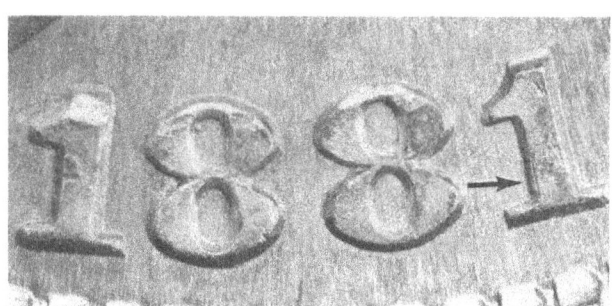

28 O Doubled 1-1

1881-S

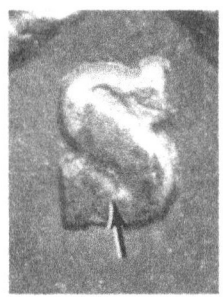

28 R S/S

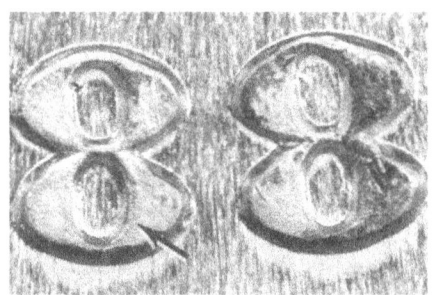

29 O First 8 Doubled

31 O Doubled 18

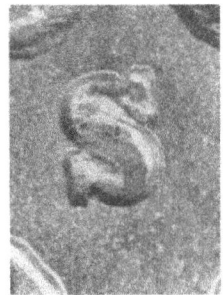

32 R S Set Left

33 O First 8 Doubled

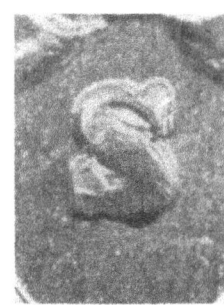

33 R High S

34 O Doubled 188

35 O Doubled 18

37 R S Tilted Left

39 O Doubled 18-1, Dash Under 8

40 O Doubled 18-1

1881-S

41   III²23 • C³q (Doubled 8-1, S/S Line)   (184)   I-2   R-3
Obverse III²23 – Doubled 8-1 in date. First 8 doubled on surface at lower right outside of upper loop and top inside of lower loop. Second 1 doubled slightly and left side of vertical shaft.
Reverse C³q – Mint mark is repunched with original showing as a thin diagonal line at right of upper loop opening and an arc at right of lower loop opening. IV S mint mark set slightly high.

42   III²1 • C³p (S Tilted Left)   (186)   1-2   R-3
Obverse III²1 – Short die chip inside upper loop of first 8 at 11 o'clock.

43   III²1 • C³r (S/S Curve)   (182)   I-2   R-3
Reverse C³r – IV S mint mark repunched slightly as curved line at right inside of lower loop. Some specimens show die chip in wreath leaf opposite U of UNITED.

44   III²24 • C³p (Tripled 8, S Tilted Left)   (189)   I-2   R-3
Obverse III²24 – First 8 tripled on lower right outside of both loops, tripled at top left inside of upper loop and doubled at top inside of lower loop. Upper loop has a spike of metal at top left inside.

45   III²25 • C³s (Doubled 18, S/S)   (185)   I-2   R-3
Obverse III²25 – Doubled 18 in date. 1 doubled at top left and right of lower crossbar. First 8 doubled at top right inside of lower loop and on lower right surface of upper loop.
Reverse C³s – IV S mint mark doubled at lower left of lower serif.

46   III²2 • C³o (Doubled First 8, S Set High)   (184)   I-2   R-3

47   III²26 • C³a (Doubled 18)   (184)   I-2   R-3
Obverse III²26 – Doubled 18 in date. 1 doubled slightly at top right of vertical shaft. First 8 doubled at upper left inside and right outside of upper loop and right inside and bottom right outside of lower loop.

48   III²23 • C³a (Doubled 8-1)   (184)   1-2   R-3

49   III²26 • C³l (Doubled 18, S Set Left)   (184)   1-2   R-3

50   III²27 • C³t (Doubled 18, S/S)   (186)   I-2   R-3
Obverse III²27 – Doubled 18 in date. 1 doubled at top right of vertical shaft. First 8 doubled on surface of right outside of both loops.
Reverse C³t – IV S mint mark repunched with top serif doubled on right outside and lower serif doubled as a notch on lower left outside.

51   III²26 • C³p (Doubled 18, S Tilted Left)   (184)   I-2   R-3

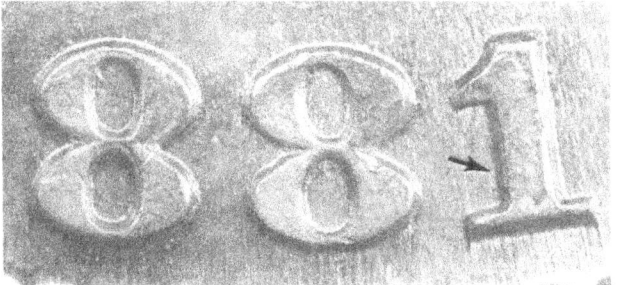
41 O Doubled 8-1

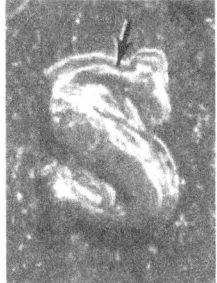
41 R S/S Line

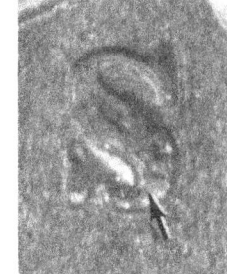
43 R S/S

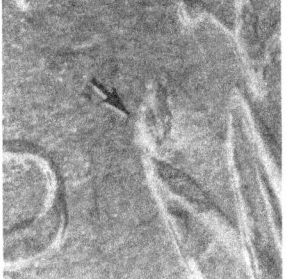
43 R Die Chips in Wreath

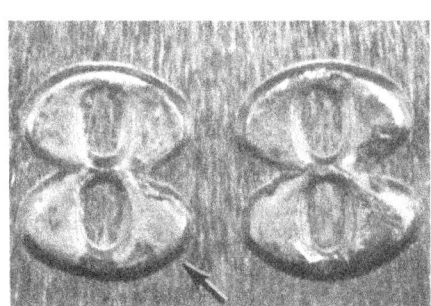
44 O Tripled 8

45 O Doubled 18

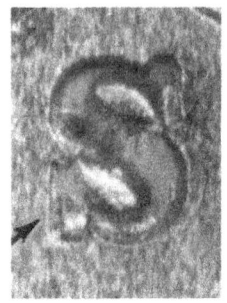

45 R S/S

47 O Doubled 18

50 O Doubled 18

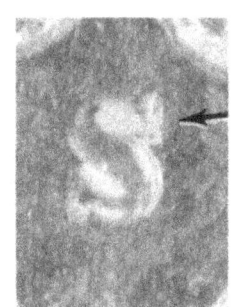

50 R S/S

1882-P

Full strike specimens are available although slightly weakly struck examples exist. Luster is generally better than earlier P mint coins and some show nice frosted devices. A fair number of minor die varieties exist but none are significant.

As with all early P mints proof-like specimens are fairly scarce. Some cameo proof-likes exist however. Most proofs show good cameo contrast and nice ones are available.

1	III² 1 • C³ a (Closed 2)		(180)	I-1	R-1

Obverse III² 1 – Normal die of III² type with thick 1 in date. The top knob and serif of the tail almost touch the curve of the 2. Some specimens show die chip between loops on left of first 8.
Reverse C³ a – Normal die of C³ type.

1A	III² 1 • C³ a (Dot 2)	(179)	I-2	R-4

Obverse III² 1 – Small dot of metal on surface in middle of bottom crossbar.

1B	III² 1 • C³ a (Metal in 2)	(180)	I-2	R-3

Obverse III² 1 – Both loops of 2 have die chips and diagonal polishing marks.

1C	III² 1 • C³ a (Metal in Date)	(180)	I-2	R-3

Obverse III² 1 – Metal in both 8's and the 2 in the date caused by die flaking, chipping and insufficient polishing. Some specimens only have metal in the 2.

1D	III² 1 • C³ a (Metal in 82)	(180)	I-2	R-3

Obverse III² 1 – Second 8 has die chip in bottom right inside of lower loop. Both loops of 2 are filled with shallow metal from die chips and flakes with horizontal polishing marks.
Reverse C³ a – Some specimens show die rust pits around E of ONE.

2	III² 2 • C³ a (Open 2)		I-1	R-2

Obverse III² 2 – Normal die of III² type with thin 2. Knob and serif of tail do not touch body of 2.

3	III² 3 • C³ a (Doubled 8)		I-2	R-3

Obverse III² 3 – Second 8 in date is doubled on top left. Open 2 variety.

4	III² 4 • C³ a (Doubled 2)		I-2	R-3

Obverse III² 4 – 2 is doubled slightly on right side of the ball at top. Upper loop of 2 is filled with shallow metal from die chips with horizontal polishing marks.

1882-P

1A O Dot 2

1B O Metal in 2

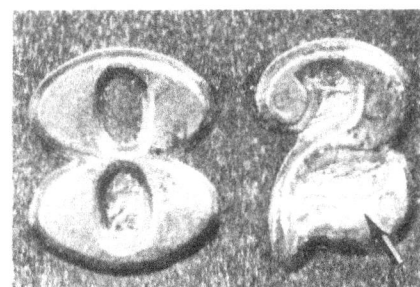
1D O Metal in 82

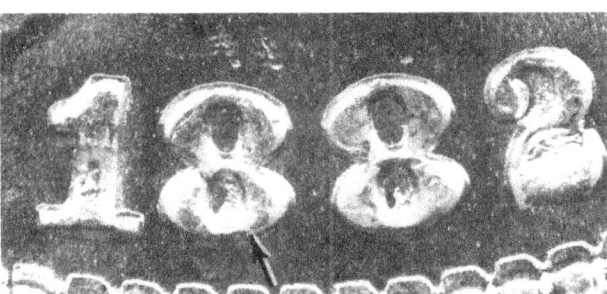
1C O Metal in Date

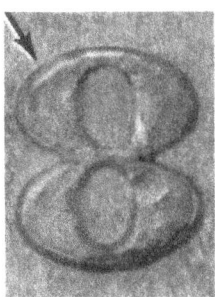
3 O Doubled 8

1D R Pitted Die

5	III²5 • C³a (Doubled 1)	(180)	I-2	R-3

Obverse III²5 – 1 in date doubled at top right of the stem. The 882 is partially filled at top and bottom. Closed 2 variety.

6	III²6 • C³a (Doubled 18)		I-2	R-4

Obverse III²6 – 18 in date doubled. 1 is doubled at top right of the stem. Upper loop of first 8 is doubled on left. Open 2 variety.

7	III²7 • C³a (Doubled 1-82)	(178)	I-2	R-4

Obverse III²7 – 1-82 in date slightly doubled. 1 is doubled at the top right of the stem. Second 8 doubled on left side of upper loop and right side of lower loop. 2 doubled on left side of upper loop.

8	III²8 • C³a (Doubled 2)		I-2	R-4

Obverse III²8 – 2 in date doubled strongly at top inside of upper loop.

9	III²9 • C³a (Doubled 82)	(180)	I-2	R-3

Obverse III²9 – 82 in date doubled. Second 8 is doubled slightly on left outside of upper loop and bottom outside of lower loop. 2 doubled slightly at top and right outside of upper loop. First 8 has die chip on left side between loops.

10	III²10 • C³a (Doubled 82)		I-2	Proof

Obverse III²10 – 82 in date is doubled. Second 8 is doubled strongly on left outside of upper loop. 2 is doubled slightly on left side of shaft.

11	III²11 • C³a (Doubled Date)	(180)	I-2	R-4

Obverse III²11 – Entire date is slightly doubled. 1 is doubled slightly at bottom of upper crossbar. First 8 is doubled slightly at right inside and left outside on upper loop. Second 8 is doubled at top outside of upper loop and doubled slightly on left outside of lower loop. 2 is doubled slightly at top left outside of upper loop.

12	III²12 • C³a (Doubled Date)	(181)	I-2	R-3

Obverse III²12 – Entire date is doubled. 1 is doubled slightly at very bottom. First 8 is doubled slightly at right outside of upper loop. Second 8 is doubled strongly at left outside of upper loop and slightly at bottom outside of lower loop. 2 is doubled slightly at left outside of upper loop.

13	III²13 • C³a (Doubled 188)	(181)	I-2	R-3

Obverse III²13 – 188 in date is doubled. 1 is doubled faintly below top crossbar. First 8 is doubled faintly at bottom left outside and top left inside of upper loop and at bottom right outside of lower loop. Second 8 doubled at left outside of upper loop and faintly at bottom outside of lower loop.

14	III²14 • C³a (Doubled 882)	(180)	I-2	R-3

Obverse III²14 – Faintly doubled 882 in date. First 8 doubled at left inside of upper loop. Second 8 doubled at left outside of both loops. 2 doubled on right side of upper loop.

1882-P

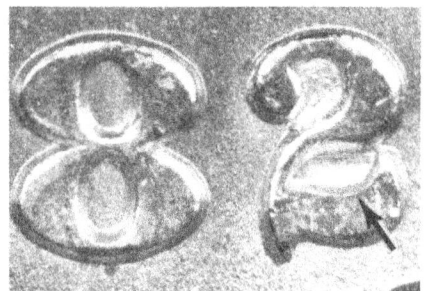

4 O Doubled 2 • 5 O Doubled 1 • (Photo Not Available) 6 O • 8 O Doubled 2

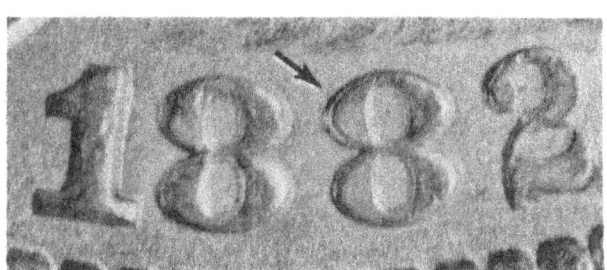
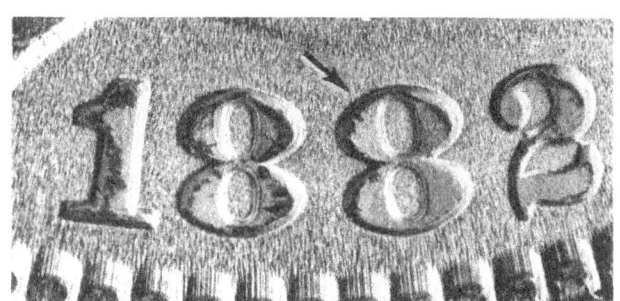

7 O Doubled 1-82 • 11 O Doubled Date

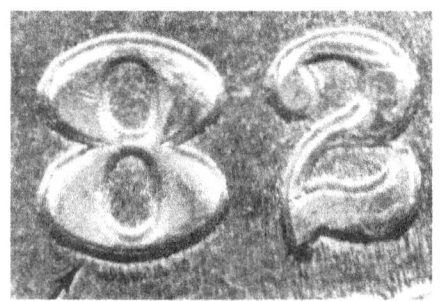
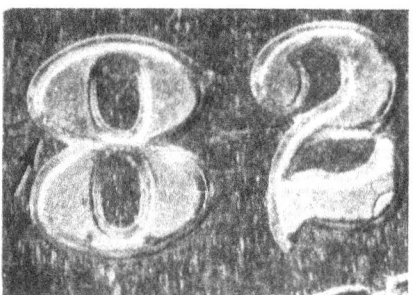

9 O Doubled 82 • 10 O Doubled 82 • 13 O Doubled 188

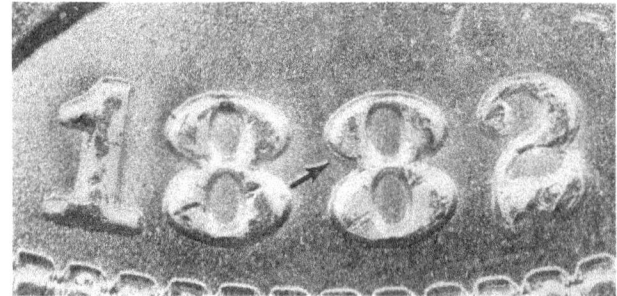
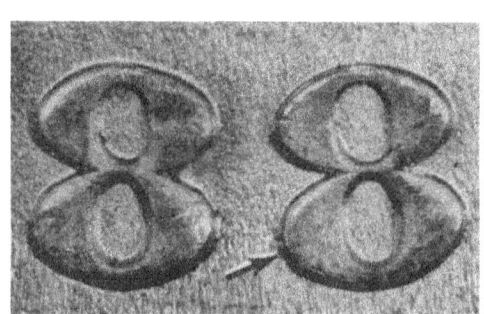

12 O Doubled Date • 14 O Doubled 88

1882-P

15	III² 15 • C³a (Doubled 8-2)	(179)		I-2	R-3

Obverse III² 15 – Doubled 8-2 in date. First 8 doubled at left outside and right inside of upper loop. Upper ball of 2 doubled on right side.

16	III² 16 • C³a (Doubled Date)	(180)		I-2	R-3

Obverse III² 16 – Entire date doubled. 1 doubled slightly at top right of vertical shaft. First 8 doubled slightly at lower left outside of upper loop. Second 8 doubled strongly on left outside of upper loop and at bottom left of lower loop. 2 doubled at left and right outside of upper loop.

17	III² 17 C³a (Doubled Date)	(179)		I-2	R-3

Obverse III² 17 – Entire date is doubled. 1 doubled below upper serif. First 8 doubled slightly at right inside and left outside of upper loop. Second 8 is doubled strongly at top outside of upper loop and slightly at left outside of lower loop. 2 doubled strongly at top outside of upper loop and on right side of ball, upper loop, shaft and serif.

18	III² 18 • C³a (Doubled Date)	(179)		I-2	R-3

Obverse III² 18 – Entire date is doubled. 1 doubled slightly on upper right surface of vertical shaft. First 8 doubled at left outside of upper loop. Second 8 doubled at top outside of upper loop and upper left outside of lower loop. 2 doubled at top outside of upper loop.

19	III² 19 • C³a (Doubled Date)	(181)		I-2	R-3

Obverse III² 19 – Entire date is doubled. 1 doubled slightly below upper crossbar. First 8 tripled at top inside and lower left outside of upper loop and doubled slightly at bottom outside of lower loop. Second 8 doubled strongly at left outside of upper loop and at bottom outside of lower loop. 2 doubled slightly on right side of ball and right outside of upper loop.

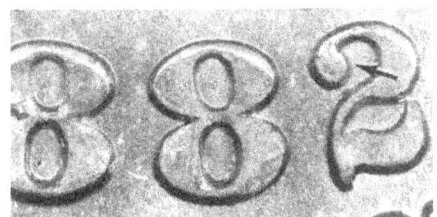

15 O Doubled 8-2

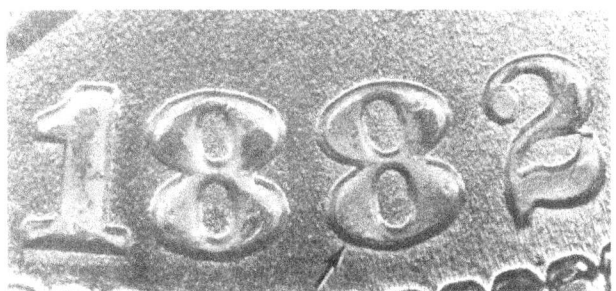

16 O Doubled Date

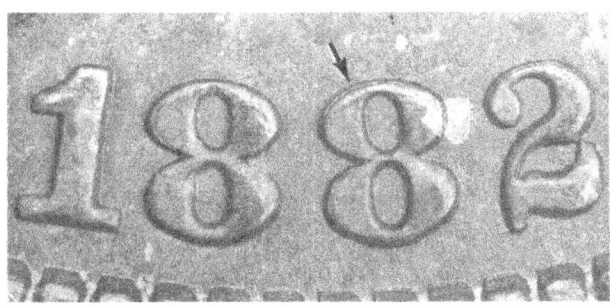

17 O Doubled Date

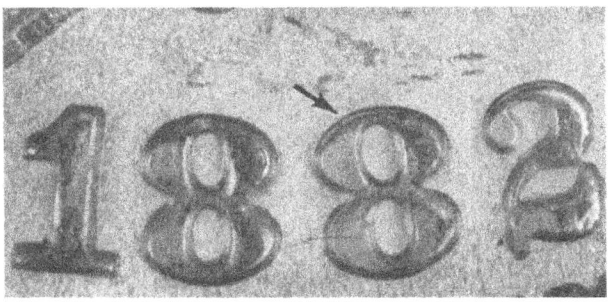

18 O Doubled Date

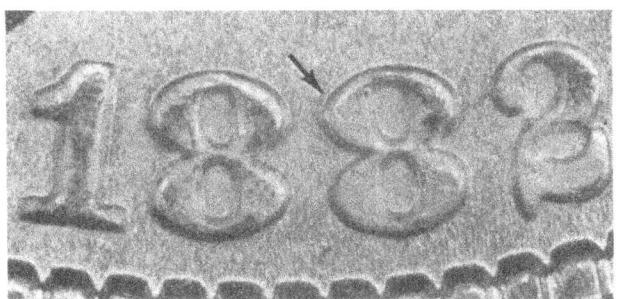

19 O Doubled Date

1882-CC

Half the mintage was in the GSA sales so BU specimens are readily available. Usually the strike is full and luster good. Several die varieties exist but none are significant.

A significant number of proof-like specimens exist and some have very deep mirrors with cameo contrast.

1   **III² 1 • C³ a (Open 2)**   I-1   R-2
     Obverse III² 1 – Normal die of III² type with open 2 at top.
     Reverse C³ a – Normal die of C³ type with large open V CC mint mark.

2   **III² 2 • C³ b (Doubled 882 and Reverse)**   (177, 178)   I-2   R-3
     Obverse III² 2 – Doubled 882 in date. First 8 doubled slightly at right outside of upper loop and left inside of lower loop. Second 8 doubled strongly on left outside of upper loop and slightly on bottom outside of lower loop. 2 doubled slightly at top outside of upper loop. Some specimens show first two stars on right with fine polishing marks below them and a heavy diagonal polishing mark below the first 8 on later die states.
     Reverse C³ b – All legend letters and stars doubled near rim.

3   **III² 3 • C³ c (Doubled 1-82)**   (177)   I-2   R-3
     Obverse III² 3 – 1 doubled below bottom crossbar on some specimens. Second 8 and 2 slightly doubled at top and upper left side. Date set low close to rim. Some specimens show die chip between loops of second 8 on right. Open 2 variety.
     Reverse C³ c – Right C of mint mark set low.

4   **III² 4 • C³ a (Closed 2)**   I-1   R-3
     Obverse III² 4 – Normal die of III² type with closed 2.

5   **III² 5 • C3 a (Doubled 882)**   (178)   I-2   R-3
     Obverse III² 5 – 882 doubled in date. First 8 doubled slightly on right outside with dot at top inside of upper loop. Second 8 doubled slightly at top outside and lower left outside of upper loop and on right outside of lower loop. 2 doubled at top outside and inside of upper loop plus right outside of upper loop. Closed 2 variety.

6   **III² 6 • C³ a (Doubled Date)**   (178)   I-2   R-3
     Obverse III² 6 – Entire date is doubled. 1 is slightly doubled at top left of lower crossbar. First 8 is doubled at top outside and right inside of upper loop and on right outside of lower loop. Second 8 is doubled at top and outside of upper loop and right outside of lower loop. 2 doubled at top and right outside of upper loop.

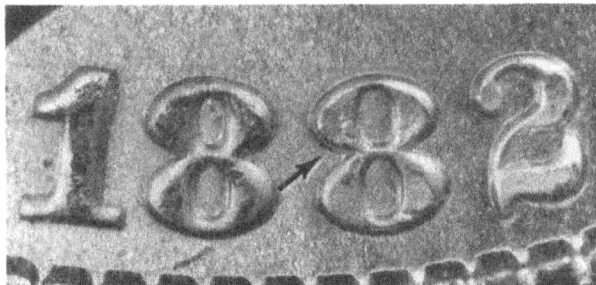

2 O Doubled 882

3 O Doubled 82

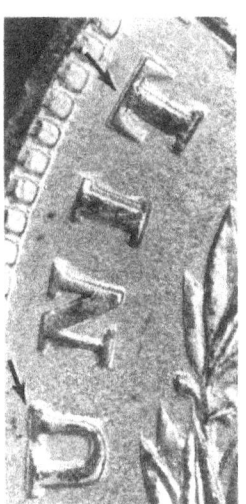

2 R Doubled Legend

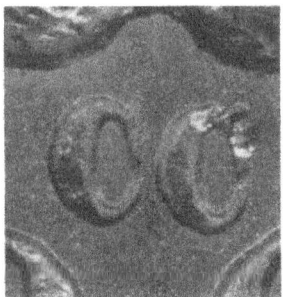

3 R Low Right C

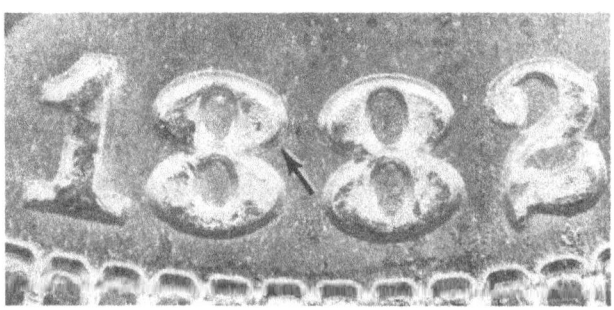

5 O Doubled 882

1882-CC / 1882-O

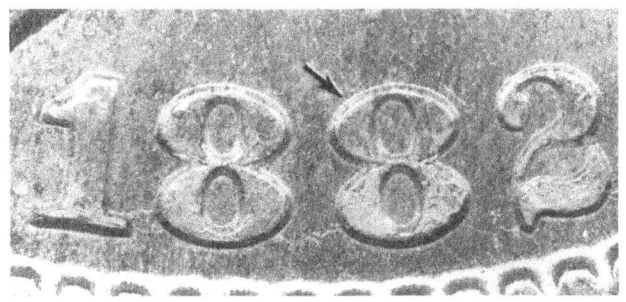

6 O Doubled Date

1882-O

Like the 1881-O, the 1882-O tends to be fully struck but with subdued luster. The reverse tends to be weaker struck more often however. Slider coins are are also fairly common. A large number of die varieties exist and a few are significant. Three very visible O/S mint marks (VAM's 3, 4 and 5) are fairly scarce and command substantial premiums in higher grades. Earlier die states of O/S exist but are not as visible. The O/S reverses show raised dots due to rusted dies and proof-likes are unknown. A very strongly doubled O mint mark of VAM 7 is visible below and within the O and carries a modest premium.

Proof-likes are fairly available and quite a few have cameo contrast.

1   III²1 • C³a (Open 2)   (181)   I-1   R-2
     Obverse III²1 – Normal Die of III² type with open 2 at top. The open 2 is more common than the closed 2.
     Reverse C³a – Normal die of C³ type with tall oval medium II O mint mark centered and upright.

2   III²2 • C³a (Closed 2)   (181)   I-1   R-2
     Obverse III²2 – Normal die of III² type with closed 2.

3   III²3 – C³b (O/S Flush)   (181)   I-5   R-3/4
     Obverse III²3 – Second 8 in date doubled on lower left outside of upper loop and bottom outside of lower loop. 2 doubled on right outside of upper loop. Polishing marks inside ear with area around neck overpolished. Open 2 variety.
     Reverse C³b – O over S variety with the center shaft of the S flush within the O. Small dots of metal all over eagle probably due to rusted die. An earlier die state shows a thin diagonal line (formerly VAM 6)

4   III²4 • C³c (O/S Depressed)   (181)   I-5   R-3
     Obverse III²4 – Polishing marks inside ear. Second 8 doubled at left outside of both loops. 2 doubled on right outside of upper loop. Small dots of metal all over the Liberty Head. Open 2 variety.
     Reverse C³c – O over S variety with the center shaft of the S depressed within the O. Small dots of metal all over eagle and wreath. An earlier die state shows as a diagonal tear drop at lower part of opening.

5   III²5 • C³d (O/S Broken)   (181)   I-4   R-3
     Obverse III²5 – Second 8 in date doubled on left side of loop. 2 doubled faintly at top outside. Die chip between loops on left side of first 8. Polishing marks inside ear. Open 2 variety.
     Reverse C³d – O over S variety with the center shaft of the S broken within the O. Small dots of metal all over eagle and wreath. An earlier die state shows as a triangular dot at left side of loop opening and as a fine line in the middle.

6*   III²2 • C³e (O Tilted Left)   (181)   1-2   R-3
     Reverse C³e – II O mint mark, tilted left and some have a heavy horizontal die scratch at the bottom of the opening.
     VAM 6 was formerly O/S line

7   III²6 • C³f (O/O Low)   (176)   I-4   R-4
     Obverse III²6 – 882 in date is slightly doubled. First 8 doubled at right inside and outside of upper loop. Loops of second 8 doubled on left outside. 2 doubled at top outside. Open 2 variety.
     Reverse C³f – Mint mark repunched with the original showing below and inside.

8   III²1 • C³g (O/O Right)   I-2   R-4
     Reverse C³g – Mint mark repunched with the original showing on the right side and top of the opening.

1882-O

3 O Doubled 82

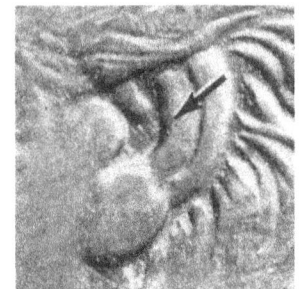
3 O Polishing Marks

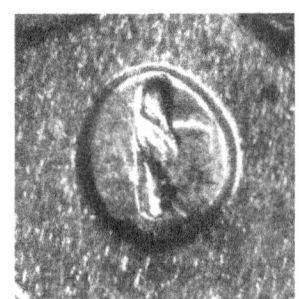
3 R O/S Flush

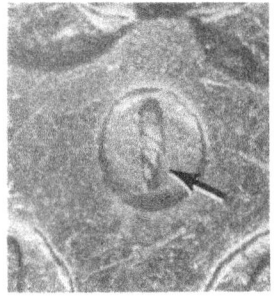
4 R O/S Depressed

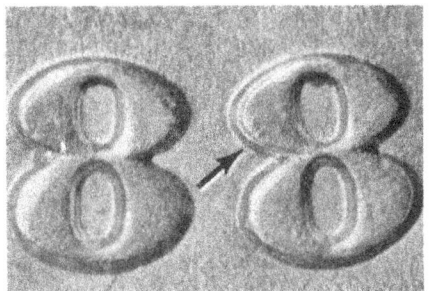
5 O Doubled 82

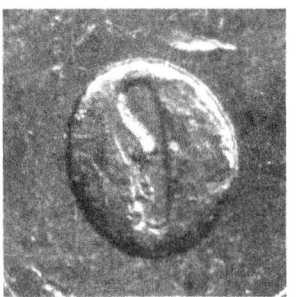
5 R O/S Broken

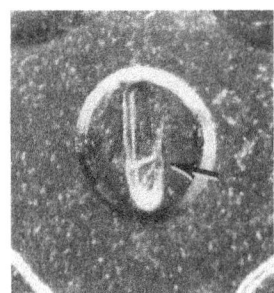
6 R Die Scratch in O

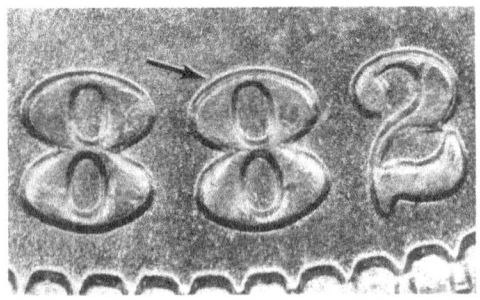
7 O Doubled 882

7 R O/O Low

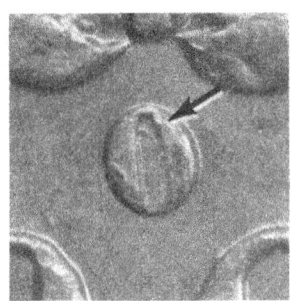
8 R O/O Right

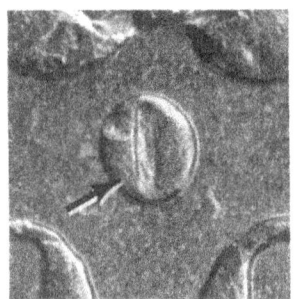
9 R O/O Left

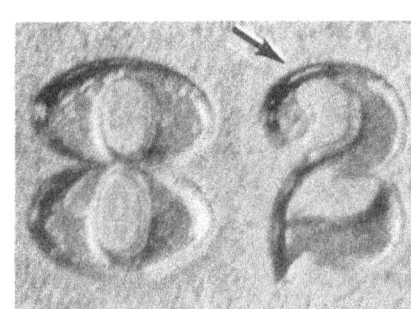
10 O Doubled 82

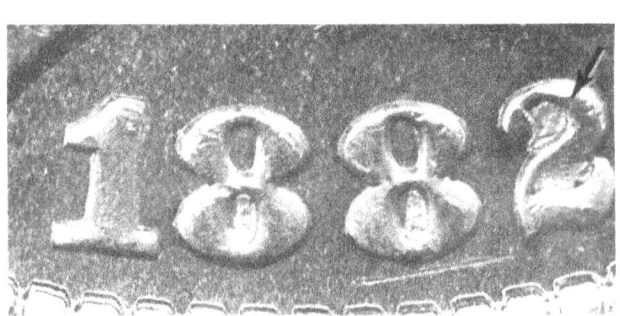
10 O Doubled 18, Filled Date

239

1882-O

9   III² 10 • C³ a (Doubled 18)   I-2   R-4
Obverse III² 10 – Metal in 882. Both 8's have die flakes on right side of lower loop opening. 2 has die flakes in upper loop with curved horizontal step at lower left side of loop opening. Lower loop of 2 is also filled and has heavy horizontal polishing marks. In addition, 1 doubled slightly at top right outside and first 8 is doubled slightly at top inside of loops.

10   III² 7 • C³ a (Doubled 82)   (176)   I-2   R-3
Obverse III² 7 – 82 in date is doubled. Top loop of second 8 is doubled at top and bottom loop at top right. 2 is doubled faintly at top. Short die chips between loops of first 8 on left and some coins show both sides. Open and closed 2 variety.

11   III² 8 • C³ a (Doubled 8)   I-2   R-3
Obverse III² 8 – Second 8 in date doubled on left side of upper loop. Open 2 variety.

12   III² 2 • C³ f (O/O Low)   I-4   R-4

13   III² 9 • C³ h (O/O Lower Left, Doubled 2)   I-2   R-4
Obverse III² 9 – 2 in date is doubled with a horizontal curved line just above bottom crossbar.
Reverse C³ h – Mint mark repunched with the original showing on the lower left side of opening.

14   III² 10 • C³ h (O/O Lower Left, Doubled 18)   (181)   I-2   R-4

15   III² 2 • C³ i (O/O Left)   (181)   I-2   R-4
Reverse C³ i – II O Mint mark repunched with original showing as a vertical bar on left side of loop opening and die chips with polishing marks at bottom inside of loop.

16   III² 8 • C³ e (O Tilted Left)   I-2   R-3
Obverse III² 8 – With closed 2.

17   III² 10 • C³ e (Metal in 882, O tilted Left)   (181)   I-2   R-4
Obverse III² 10 – Die has a long horizontal die crack above date and first three stars on left.

18   III² 11 • C³ a (Doubled 882 Left)   (176)   I-2   R-3
Obverse III² 11 – 882 in date doubled. First 8 doubled slightly at lower left outside of upper loop and right outside of lower loop. Top loop of second 8 doubled at top left and bottom loop doubled on left side and faintly at bottom. 2 doubled all across the very top and right side of lower serif.

19   III² 12 • C³ a (Doubled 82)   (176)   I-2   R-3
Obverse III² 12 – 82 in date is doubled. Second 8 is doubled at top and left outside of upper loop. 2 is doubled at top and left outside of upper loop and slightly on right side of lower left serif.
Reverse C³ a – Some specimens show overpolished die with field showing through eagle's right wing.

20   III² 13 • C³ a (Doubled 1-8)   (181)   I-2   R-3
Obverse III² 13 – Doubled 1-8 in date. 1 is doubled on top right side of shaft. First 8 has die chip with polishing mark at top right inside of upper loop, at bottom inside of lower loop, and a small mark on left outside of upper loop. Second 8 is doubled slightly at top inside of upper loop. Both loops of 2 have die chips at lower inside.

21   III² 14 • C³ a (Doubled 882)   (176)   I-2   R-4
Obverse III² 14 – Doubled 882 in date. First 8 doubled slightly on right outside of upper loop. Second 8 doubled at top left outside of upper loop and slightly at bottom right of lower loop. 2 doubled strongly on left outside of upper loop and on right side of lower left serif.

22   III² 11 • C³ j (Doubled 82 and Reverse)   (176)   I-3   R-3
Reverse C³ j – Outer portion doubled with letters doubled outward in a radial direction for UN-ED, STATES OF AMERICA, R of DOLLAR, both stars, motto, tip of eagle's right wing, top outside of right wreath. Die overpolishing with disconnected leaves in the wreath and field showing through eagle's left wing.

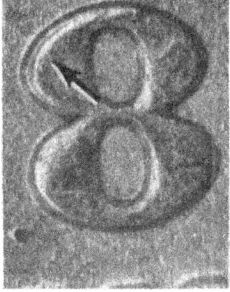 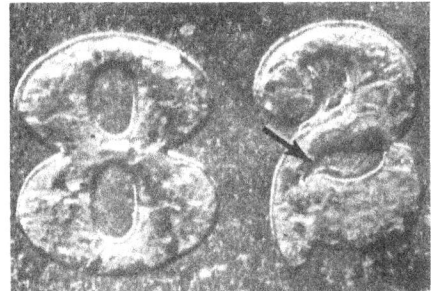 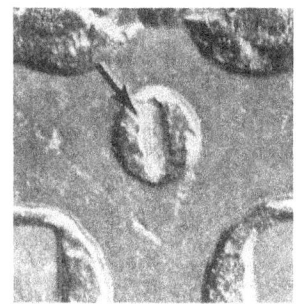

11 O Doubled 8   13 O Doubled 2   15 O O/O Left

1882-O

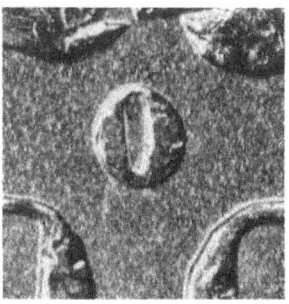
16 O O Tilted Left

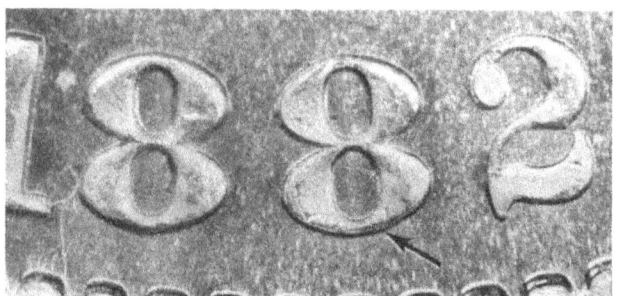
18 O Doubled 82 Left

19 O
Overpolished Wing

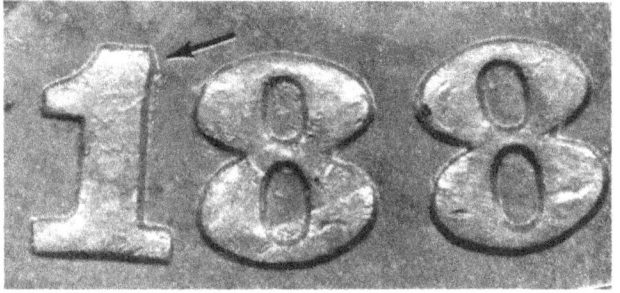
20 O Doubled 1-8

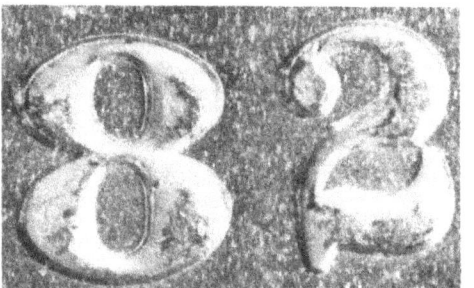
19 O Doubled 82

21 O Doubled 882

22 R Doubled Reverse

23 O Doubled 18

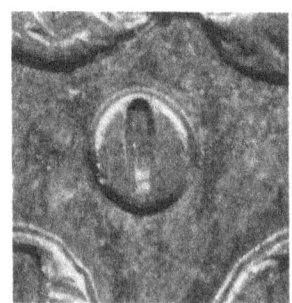
23 R O Tilted Left

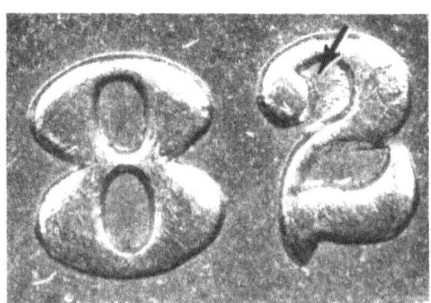
24 O Doubled 2

1882-O

23 III² 15 • C³ k (Doubled 18, O Tilted Left)   (181)   I-2   R-3
Obverse III² 15 – Doubled 18 in date. 1 doubled below upper crossbar at top right of vertical shaft. First 8 doubled at top right inside of lower loop.
Reverse C³ k – II O mint mark set left and tilted left.

24 III² 16 • C³ k (Doubled 2, O Tilted Left)   (181)   I-2   R-3
Obverse III² 16 – 2 in date doubled on right side of knob. Die chips and polishing lines in upper loop and at bottom of lower loop of 2.

25 III² 16 • C³ l (Doubled 2, O/O Left)   (181)   I-2   R-3
Reverse C³ l – II O mint mark repunched with original showing as a vertical bar on left side of loop opening but slightly more pronounced then C³ i with diagonal polishing lines on right side of opening. Heavy horizontal polishing lines in eagle's tail feathers and in wreath bow.

26 III² 17 • C³ a (Doubled 2)   (181)   I-2   R-3
Obverse III² 17 – 2 in date doubled on right side of knob but slightly stronger than VAM 24. Lower loop has horizontal line at top inside.

27 III² 18 • C³ e (Doubled 1-82)   (181)   1-2   R-3
Obverse III² 18 – Doubled 1-82 in date. 1 doubled slightly below upper crossbar. Second 8 doubled at left outside of upper loop. 2 doubled slightly at right outside of upper loop.

28 III² 19 • C³ e (Doubled Date and Stars)   I-3   R-3
Obverse III² 19 – Entire date is doubled. 18 doubled slightly at very bottom. Second 8 doubled at left outside of upper loop. 2 doubled slightly at right outside of upper loop. All left and right stars doubled towards rim. Tops of E PLUR doubled towards rim and right lower serif of M doubled at top.

29 III² 20 • C³ a (Doubled Date)   (181)   I-2   R-3
Obverse III² 20 – Entire date is doubled. 1 is doubled at top right vertical shaft. First 8 is doubled at top inside of lower loop. Second 8 is doubled at left outside of both loops. 2 is doubled at top right outside of upper loop.

30 III² 21 • C³ g (Doubled 1-2, Dash, O/O Right)   (181)   I-2   R-4
Obverse III² 21 – Doubled 1-2 in date. 1 doubled strongly below upper crossbar. 2 doubled slightly on right side of upper ball. Second 8 has a faint dash below lower loop.

31 III² 22 • C³ a (Doubled Date)   (181)   I-2   R-3
Obverse III² 22 – Entire date doubled. 1 doubled at top right of vertical shaft. First 8 doubled at top inside of upper loop. Second 8 doubled at left outside of upper loop. 2 doubled at left outside and right inside of upper loop.

32 III² 23 • C³ a (Doubled 882)   (181)   I-2   R-3
Obverse III² 23 – Doubled 882 in date. First 8 doubled at right inside of upper loop. Second 8 doubled at left outside of both loops. 2 doubled at left outside and right inside of upper loop.

33 III² 24 • C³ a (Doubled 882)   (181)   I-2   R-3
Obverse III² 24 – Doubled 882 in date. First 8 doubled slightly at bottom outside of upper loop. Second 8 doubled at left outside of upper loop. 2 doubled strongly at right outside of upper loop and slightly at right side of upper ball.

34 III² 25 • C³ a (Double Date)   (181)   I-2   R-3
Obverse III² 25 – All digits in date are doubled. 1 doubled slightly below upper crossbar and at top of lower crossbar. First 8 doubled slightly at lower left outside of upper loop. Second 8 doubled at top and left outside of upper loop. 2 doubled at top and left and right outside of upper loop and on right side of lower serif.

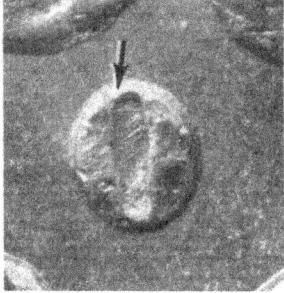
25 R O/O Left

26 O Doubled 2

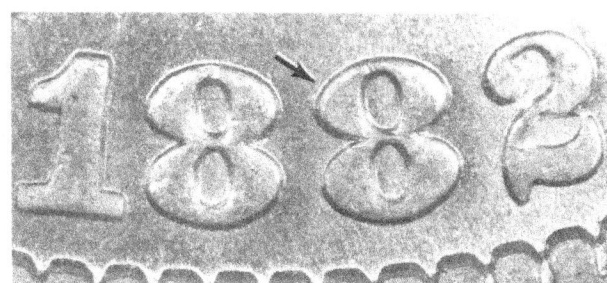
27 O Doubled 1-82

1882-O

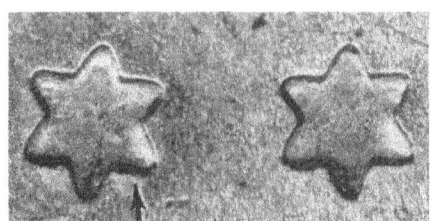

28 O Doubled Stars

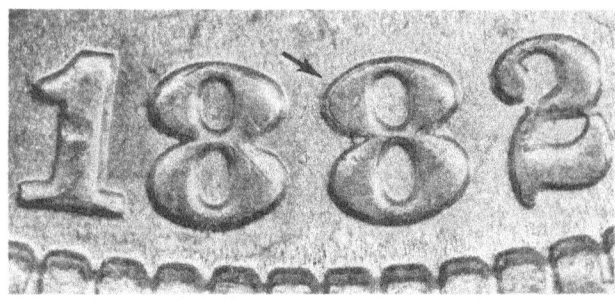

28 O Doubled Date

29 O Doubled Date

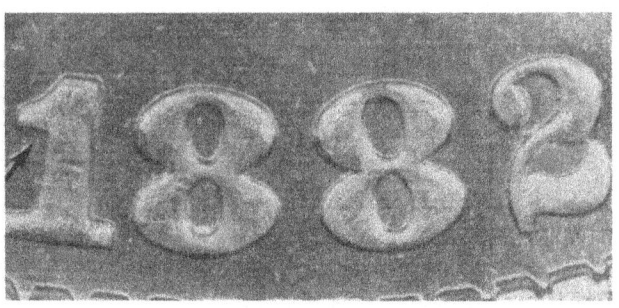

30 O Doubled 1-2, Dash Under 8

31 O Doubled Date

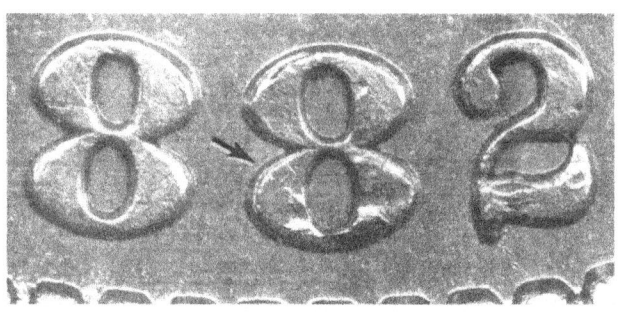

32 O Doubled 882

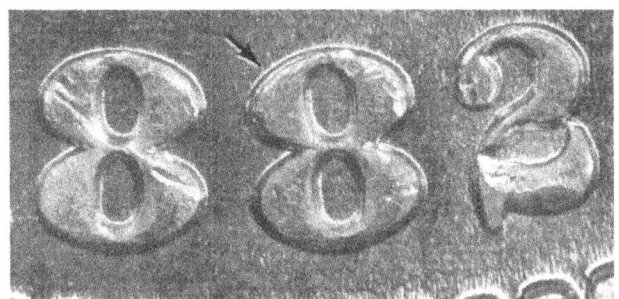

33 O Doubled 882

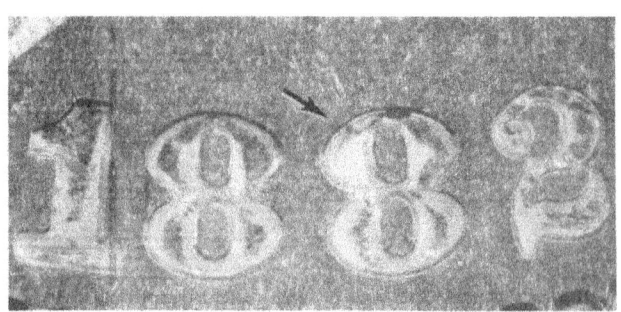

34 O Doubled Date

1882-S

Most specimens are fully struck although a few exist with slight weakness. Luster is usually excellent. This last year of the four common date S mint years, 1879-1882, is fairly available in nice condition although not quite as much as 1880-S and 1881-S. Quite a few minor die varieties exist but none are significant. VAM 20 has one of the farthest tilted S mint mark to the left known.

Proof-likes are fairly available but not quite as much as earlier S mints. Most tend to be brilliant and many are one-sided proof-like. Two-sided cameo proof-likes are fairly scarce like that for 1881-S.

1   III^{2}1 • C^{3}a (Open 2)   (187)   I-1   R-2
     Obverse III^{2}1 – Normal die of III^2 type with open 2 in which tail does not touch body of 2. Some specimens show die chips between loops of both 8's on right side or on first 8 right side and second 8 left side.
     Reverse C^{3}a – Normal die of C^3 type with a medium IV S mint mark centered and upright.

2   III^{2}2 • C^{3}a (Doubled 882)   (183)   I-2   R-3
     Obverse III^{2}2 – Doubled 882 in date. First 8 doubled at left and top outside and right inside of upper loop and right outside of lower loop. Second 8 doubled strongly at left outside and faintly at top outside of upper loop and at bottom and right outside of lower loop. 2 doubled at top and right outside and top inside of upper loop.

3   III^{2}3 • C^{3}b (Doubled 82)   (187)   I-2   R-3
     Obverse III^{2}3 – 82 in date doubled slightly at top. Die chip on right side of first 8 and on left side of second 8 between loops. Open 2 variety.
     Reverse C^{3}b – IV S mint mark is filled and titled left.

4   III^{2}4 • C^{3}a (Doubled 88)   (187)   I-2   R-3
     Obverse III^{2}4 – Doubled 88 in date. The first 8 is doubled on the left inside of the upper loop. The second 8 is doubled on the left outside of the upper loop. Both open and closed 2 varieties.

5   III^{2}5 • C^{3}a (Doubled 882)   (186)   I-2   R-3
     Obverse III^{2}5 – Doubled 882 in date. The first 8 is doubled on the right outside of both loops. Second 8 doubled at top and top right of lower loop. The 2 is doubled at top right.

6   III^{2}1 • C^{3}c (S/S)   I-3   R-4
     Reverse C^{3}c – IV S mint mark repunched with original showing as a thin diagonal line on right side of upper loop and curved line at right inside of lower loop with tilt to far left.

7   III^{2}6 • C^{3}a (Doubled 82)   I-2   R-3
     Obverse III^{2}6 – Doubled 82 in date. Second 8 is doubled slightly on left inside of upper loop. 2 is doubled very slightly on right outside of upper loop. Both 8's have die chips between loops an left and right sides.

8   III^{2}7 • C^{3}a (Doubled 8-2)   (187)   I-2   R-3
     Obverse III^{2}7 – Doubled 8-2 in date. First 8 doubled on inside of upper loop. 2 doubled slightly at top outside. 82 in date very shallow due to over polished die.

9   III^{2}8 • C^{3}a (Doubled 18-2)   I-2   R-3
     Obverse III^{2}8 – Doubled 18-2 in date. 1 is doubled slightly on surface of right side of vertical shaft. First 8 is doubled on right outside of upper loop. 2 is doubled at top and right outside of upper loop and has die chip at left inside of lower loop.

10   III^{2}9 • C^{3}a (Doubled 1-82)   (187)   I-2   R-3
     Obverse III^{2}9 – Doubled 1-82 in date. 1 is doubled on top right side of shaft. First 8 has die chip at top inside of upper loop, at bottom inside of lower loop with polishing marks and a small mark on left outside of upper loop. Second 8 and 2 are doubled slightly on right outside of upper loop.

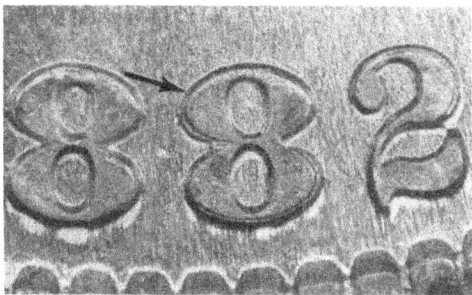
2 O Doubled 882

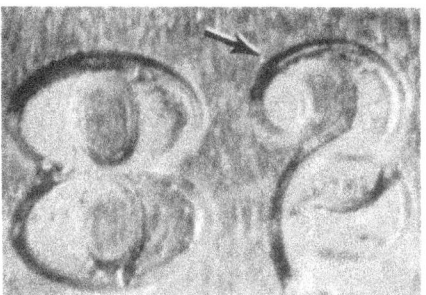
3 O Doubled 82

3 R S Filled, Tilted Left

1882-S

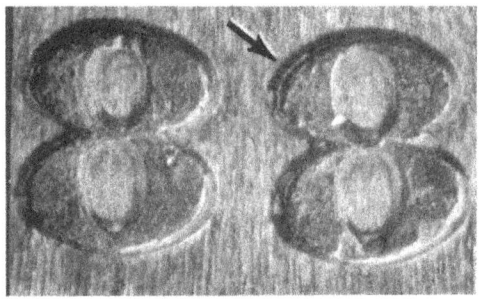
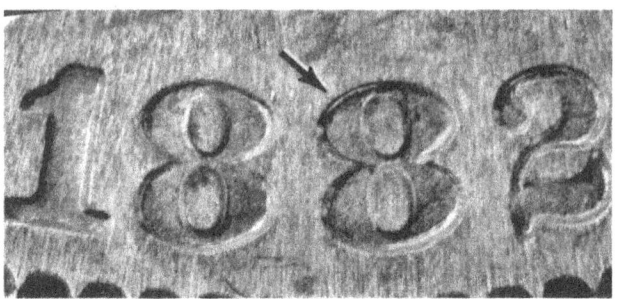
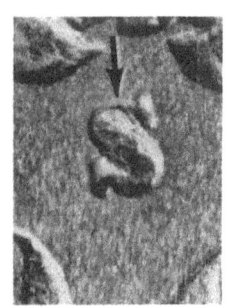

4 O Doubled 88   5 O Doubled 882   6 R S/S

7 O Doubled 82   8 O Doubled 8-2

9 O Doubled 18-2   10 O Doubled 1-82

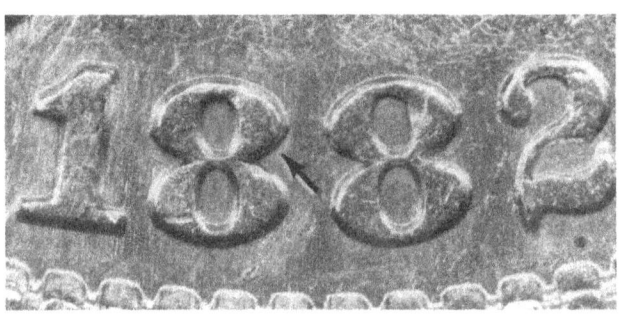

11 O Doubled 882   12 O Doubled 882

245

1882-S

11	III² 10 • C³ b (Doubled 882)	(187)	I-2	R-4

Obverse III² 10 – Doubled 882 in date. First 8 is doubled strongly on left inside and slightly on right outside of upper loop with spikes of metal between loops on both sides. Second 8 is doubled strongly on left outside of upper loop, slightly at bottom outside of lower loop and has a die chip between loops on right side. 2 is doubled on left side of upper loop.

12	III² 11 • C³ a (Doubled 882)		I-2	R-3

Obverse III² 11 – Doubled 882 in date. First 8 is doubled slightly on lower right outside and lower left inside of upper loop. Second 8 doubled slightly on top left outside of upper loop and right outside of lower loop. 2 doubled on right outside. First U in PLURIBUS has shallow die gouge showing as a diagonal line in bottom inside of U.

13	III² 12 • C³ a (Doubled Date)	(186)	I-2	R-3

Obverse III² 12 – 1 in date doubled slightly on right side of vertical shaft and top right of lower crossbar. The first 8 is doubled on the left outside of the top loop. The second 8 is doubled on the bottom inside of the top loop and the bottom and right side of the lower loop. Closed 2 variety with upper loop doubled slightly at top left outside.

13A	III² 12 • C³ a (Doubled Date)	(186)	I-2	R-3

Reverse C³ a – Die break below uppermost berries in left wreath.

14	III² 13 • C³ a (Doubled Date)	(185)	I-2	R-4

Obverse III² 13 – Entire date doubled. 1 doubled on right side of vertical shaft. First 8 strongly doubled on left inside and right outside of both loops. Second 8 doubled strongly at very top and left outside of top loop and is doubled slightly at bottom left outside and top right outside of lower loop. 2 doubled at top and right outside of upper loop and on right side of bottom serif.

15	III² 14 • C³ a (Doubled 882)		I-2	R-4

Obverse III² 14 – Doubled 882 in date. First 8 is doubled slightly on surface at bottom right of lower loop and lower left inside of upper loop. Second 8 is tripled at top outside of upper loop and doubled on right outside of lower loop. 2 is doubled at very top outside.

16	III² 15 • C³ a (Doubled Date)	(186)	I-2	R-4

Obverse III² 15 – Entire date doubled. 1 doubled at top left of lower crossbar. First 8 doubled on right outside of both loops with die chip between loops on right side. Second 8 is doubled at top outside of upper loop and right outside of lower loop. 2 is doubled at top and right outside of upper loop and has a die chip on surface on right of lower crossbar. Open 2 variety.

17	III² 5 • C³ c (Doubled 882, S/S)		I-3	R-4
18	III² 13 • C³ b (Doubled Date, S Tilted Left)	(186)	I-2	R-4
19	III² 16 • C³ d (Doubled Date, S/S)		I-2	R-3

Obverse III² 16 – Entire date doubled. 1 doubled at top of lower crossbar on both sides and as a fine horizontal line well below the upper crossbar. First 8 doubled at top left outside of upper loop and at right outside of lower loop. Second 8 doubled at top left outside of upper loop and at bottom and right outside of lower loop. 2 doubled at top and right outside of upper loop.

Reverse C³ d – IV S mint mark slightly doubled at bottom outside of lower loop.

20	III² 17 • C³ e (Doubled Date, S Tilted Far Left)	(186)	I-2	R-3

Obverse III² 17 – Entire date doubled. 1 doubled slightly on top right side of vertical shaft. First 8 doubled slightly on right outside of lower loop. Second 8 doubled slightly on left inside and strongly on right outside of upper loop. 2 doubled strongly on right outside of upper loop.

Reverse C³ e – IV S mint mark tilted far to left and shifted slightly to left. One of the farthest S tilts known.

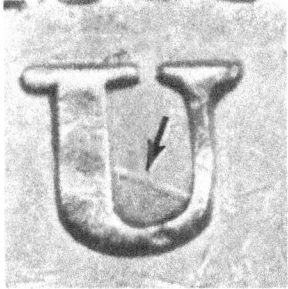

12 O Die Gouge

13 O Doubled Date

1882-S

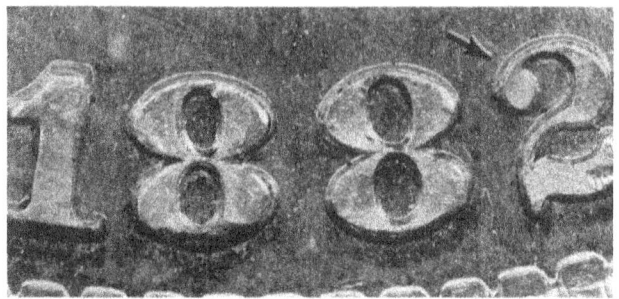

14 O Doubled Date

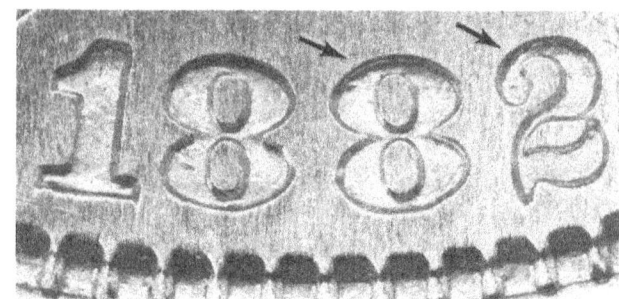

15 O Doubled 882

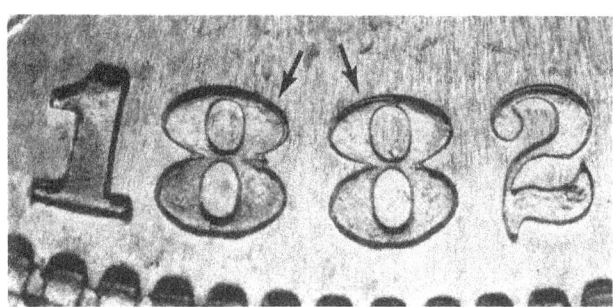

16 O Doubled Date

19 O Doubled 882

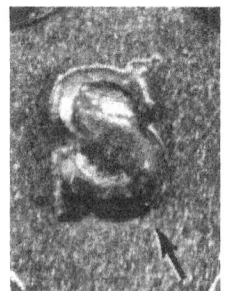

19 R S/S

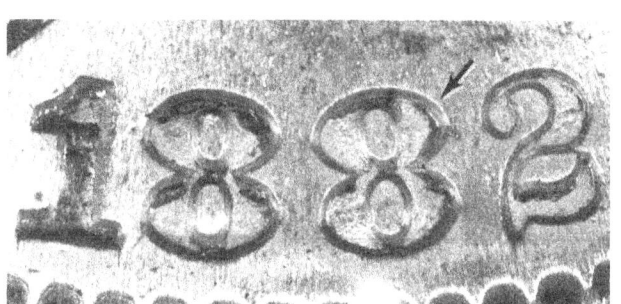

20 O Doubled Date

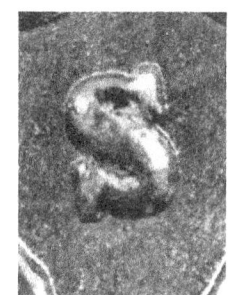

20 R S Tilted Left

21   III² 18 • C³ b (Doubled 882)   (187)   1-2   R-3

        Obverse III² 18 – Doubled 882 in date. First 8 doubled slightly at left outside and right inside of upper loop and right outside of lower loop. Second 8 doubled strongly at left outside of upper loop and right and bottom outside of lower loop. 2 doubled at top outside of upper loop.

22   III²10 • C³a (Doubled 882)   (186)   I-2   R-4

23   III²9 • C³b (Doubled 1-82, S Tilted Left)   (186)   I-2   R-3

24   III² 19 • C³ a (Doubled Date)   (187)   I-2   R-3

        Obverse III² 19 – Entire date is doubled. 1 is doubled slightly on surface at top right of shaft. First 8 doubled on right outside and slightly on lower left inside of upper loop. Second 8 doubled on left outside of upper loop with die chip between loops on right side. 2 doubled on right outside of upper loop and slightly on right side of lower serif.

25   III² 15 • C³ b (Doubled Date, S Tilted Left)   (186)   I-2   R-3

26   III² 18 • C³ a (Doubled 882)   (185)   I-2   R-3

27   III² 17 • C³ a (Doubled Date)   (187)   I-2   R-3

1882-S / 1883-P

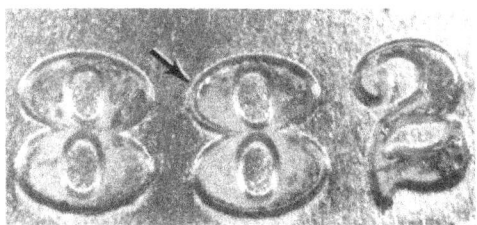

21 O Doubled 882

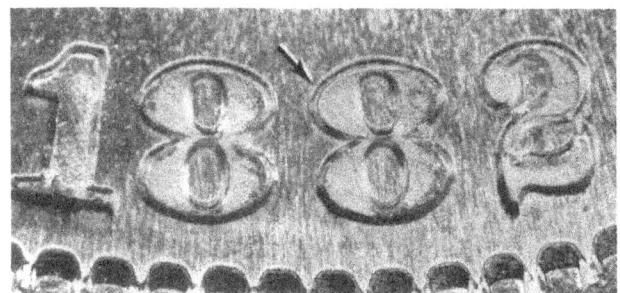

24 O Doubled Date

1883-P

This issue generally is fully struck although slightly weak struck examples exist, particularly on the reverse. Luster is usually fairly good. Some specimens exhibit a surface roughness on the devices which are fine raised dots due to rusted dies. A number of minor die varieties exist but two are unusually interesting. VAM 4 has strong doubling above the 83 and VAM 10 has all left and right stars quadrupled to sextupled towards the rim.

It is the most available 1879-1884-P proof-like but is still fairly scarce. Most have fairly good contrast and a number have very deep mirrors with cameo devices on both sides. The proofs have fairly good contrast but generally not as good as the 1880-1882 years and are more difficult to obtain in nice condition.

1   **III² 1 • C³ a (Normal)**   (180)   I-1   R-1
     Obverse III² 1 – Normal die of III² type. Some specimens show a die chip between the loops of the first 8 on left.
     Reverse C³ a – Normal die of C³ type.
     Note: Some specimens show rusted obverse and reverse dies with fine pits over Liberty head and eagle.

2   **III² 2 • C³ a (Low Dash Under 8)**   (193)   I-2   R-3
     Obverse III² 2 – Normal die with a dash well below the second 8.

3   **III² 3 • C³ a (High Dash Under 8, Doubled 8-3)**   I-2   R-3
     Obverse III² 3 – Normal die with a dash just below the second 8. First 8 doubled at bottom outside of lower loop. 3 doubled at bottom inside of lower loop.

4   **III² 4 • C³ a (Doubled 1-83)**   (180)   I-3   R-3
     Obverse III² 4 – Doubled 1-83 in date. 1 is doubled below top crossbar and at top right. 83 is doubled strongly at top left and right outside. In addition, the lower loop of second 8 is doubled at top right outside. Also, the top of the lower serif of the 3 is doubled and the lower loop has a notch at lower left.

5   **III² 5 • C³ a (Doubled 1-3, High 8)**   (180)   I-2   R-3
     Obverse III² 5 – 1 doubled at left end of lower crossbar. 3 in date doubled at bottom inside of lower loop and shows as a notch in loop. Second 8 set higher than other numerals. A short, shallow dash set low shows between the 1 and first 8.

6   **III² 6 • C³ a (Low 3, Doubled 1-3)**   (180)   I-2   R-3
     Obverse III² 6 – 3 set lower than the rest of the date. 1 doubled as notch on left side of lower crossbar. 3 doubled at bottom inside of lower loop.

7   **III² 7 • C³ a (Doubled 18-3)**   (180)   I-2   R-3
     Obverse III² 7 – Doubled 18-3 in date. 1 doubled slightly at top right outside of vertical shaft. First 8 doubled at top inside of upper loop. 3 doubled slightly at bottom of lower loop.

8   **III² 8 • C³ a (Doubled 18-3)**   (180)   I-2   R-3
     Obverse III² 8 – Doubled 18-3 in date. 1 is doubled on left of upper serif and base. First 8 is doubled at top inside of lower loop. 3 is doubled on right side of upper serif.

9   **III² 9 • C³ a (Doubled 18-3, Stars and Motto)**   (180)   I-3   R-4
     Obverse III² 9 – Doubled 18-3 in date. 1 doubled at bottom of upper crossbar and base plus left side of vertical shaft. First 8 doubled at left inside of both loops and at bottom outside of lower loop. 3 is doubled slightly at bottom inside of lower loop. All stars and motto letters are doubled next to rim in radial direction.

1883-P

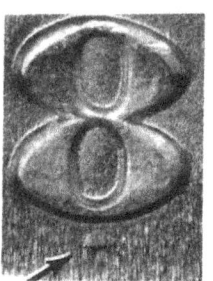

2 O Low Dash

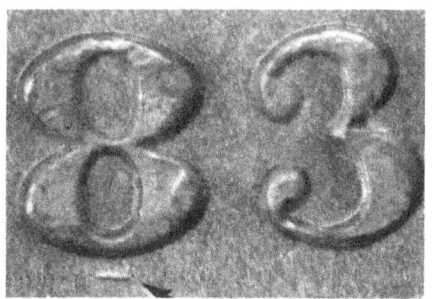

3 O High Dash

5 O Doubled 3, High 8

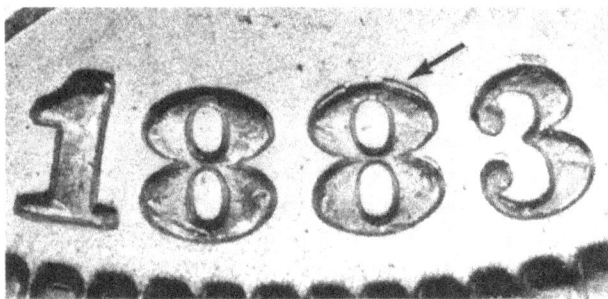

4 O Doubled 83

5 O High 8

6 O Low 3

8 O Doubled 18-3

7 O First Doubled 8

9 O Doubled Stars, Motto

1883-P

10   **III² 10 • C³ a (Doubled Date, Dash 8, Sextupled Stars)**   (180)   I-3   R-4
Obverse III² 10 – Entire date is doubled. 1 doubled strongly below upper and lower crossbars. First 8 doubled strongly below lower loop. Second 8 doubled below lower loop as a thin line in middle. 3 doubled slightly at bottom left inside of lower loop. Second 8 has a long curved dash set well below lower loop. All left and right stars and tops of UNUM letters quadrupled to sextupled towards rim with first five stars on right having large shifts.

11   **III² 11 • C³ a (Doubled 18-3)**   (188)   I-2   R-3
Obverse III² 11 – Doubled 18-3 in date. 1 doubled on surface at bottom of upper crossbar and base. First 8 doubled faintly on lower inside of both loops. 3 doubled faintly at top inside of upper loop and at bottom inside of lower loop.

12   **III² 12 • C³ a (Doubled 18)**   (188)   I-2   R-3
Obverse III² 12 – Doubled 18 in date. 1 doubled on surface on right side of vertical shaft. First 8 doubled on surface on left inside of lower loop.

13   **III² 13 • C³ a (Slanted Date, Doubled 1-3)**   (192)   I-2   R-3
Obverse III² 13 – Date slanted with 83 high above rim. 1 doubled below bottom crossbar. 3 doubled at bottom inside of lower loop.

14   **III² 14 • C³ a (Doubled 18-3)**   (188)   I-2   R-3
Obverse III² 14 – Doubled 18-3 in date. 1 doubled at top right of vertical shaft. First 8 doubled at top left inside of both loops. 3 doubled slightly at bottom right outside of lower loop.

15   **III² 15 • C³ a (Doubled 8-3)**   (181)   I-2   R-3
Obverse III² 15 – Doubled 8-3 in date. First 8 doubled slightly on right outside of lower loop. 3 doubled slightly at bottom inside of lower loop.

9 O Doubled 18-3

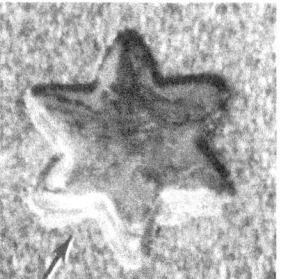

10 O Sextupled Stars

10 O Doubled Date

11 O Doubled 18-3

12 O Doubled 18

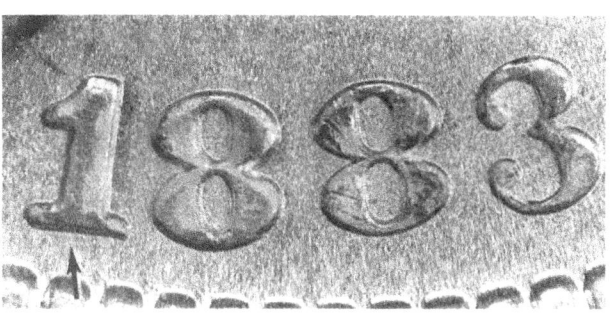

13 O Doubled 1-3, Slanted Date

14 O Doubled 18-3

15 O Doubled 8-3

1883-CC

Over half the mintage was in the GSA sale so BU specimens are readily available. Usually the strike is full and the luster good. A few die varieties exist but the only significant one is VAM 4 with an unusually strong doubled date.

A fair proportion of this issue are deep mirror proof-likes with good contrast. A sizeable number are cameo proof-likes.

1    $III^2 1 \cdot C^3 a$ (Normal Die)   I-1   R-2
     Obverse $III^2 1$ – Normal die of III^2 type. Some specimens show die chip between loops of first 8 on right.
     Reverse $C^3 a$ – Normal die of $C^3 a$ type with large centered V CC mint mark.

2    $III2\ 1 \cdot C^3 b$ (Slanted CC)   (178)   1-2   R-3
     Reverse $C^3 b$ – Large V CC slanted with left C set high. Both C's have polishing marks inside.

3    $III^2 3 \cdot C^3 b$ (Dash Under 8)   (178)   I-2   R-3
     Obverse $III^2 3$ – Dash under second 8 in date. First 8 doubled at top inside of lower loop. Some specimens show only a dot left of the dash.

4    $III^2 4 \cdot C^3 c$ (Doubled Date, Dash Under 8)   (178)   I-3   R-3
     Obverse $III^2 4$ – All digits in date are doubled. The 1 is doubled on the right side of the vertical bar and above the bottom right serif. First 8 is doubled at the top inside of the upper loop and metal is on the left outside. Second 8 is doubled at top and a short dash appears well below the bottom loop. The 3 is doubled at top and metal is also at top and right and just above the end of the lower loop.
     Reverse $C^3 c$ – First C has diagonal line at top inside of loop and metal within it. Second C has metal at bottom inside of loop and short line at very top inside of loop.

5    $III^2 5 \cdot C^3 a$ (Doubled 18-3)   (178)   I-2   R-3
     Obverse $III^2 5$ – Doubled 18-3 in date. 1 doubled on surface on lower part of upper crossbar, on right side of vertical shaft and on top of right side of lower crossbar. First 8 doubled on left inside of lower loop. 3 doubled at bottom inside of lower loop.

6    $III^2 6 \cdot C^3 a$ (Doubled 18, Dash 8)   (178)   1-2   R-3
     Obverse $III^2 6$ – Doubled 18 in date. 1 doubled on surface at right side of vertical shaft. First 8 doubled on surface at left inside of both loops. A very short dot dash appears under second 8 on some specimens.

7    $III^2 7 \cdot C^3 d$ (Doubled Date, CC/CC)   (178)   1-2   R-3
     Obverse $III^2 7$ – Entire date is slightly doubled. 1 is doubled on surface at bottom of upper crossbar, on right side of vertical shaft and at top of bottom crossbar. First 8 doubled on surface at left inside of both loops. Second 8 doubled slightly at top right outside of lower loop. 3 doubled slightly on right side of upper ball and at bottom inside of lower loop.
     Reverse $C^3 d$ – First C in mint mark is doubled at bottom inside. Second C is doubled slightly at lower left of upper serif.

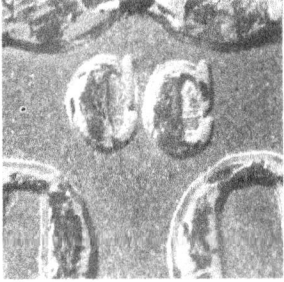

2 R Slanted CC Left

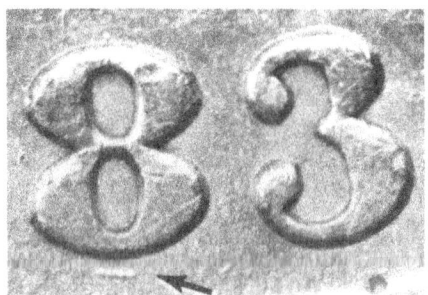

3 O Dash

4 R Doubled CC

1883-CC / 1883-O

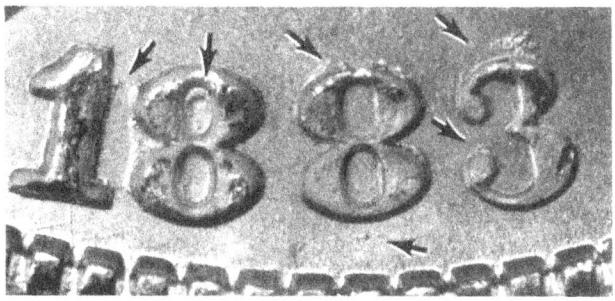

4 O Doubled Date

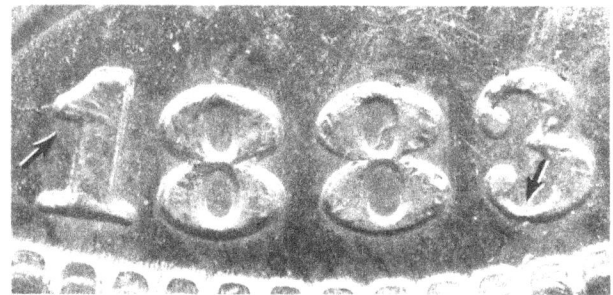

5 O Doubled Date

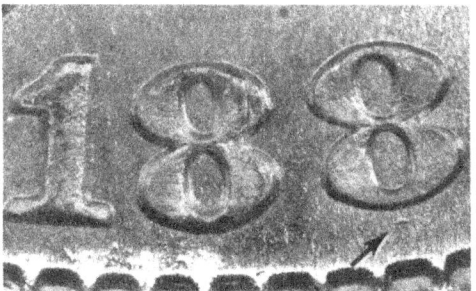

6 O Doubled 18, Dash 8

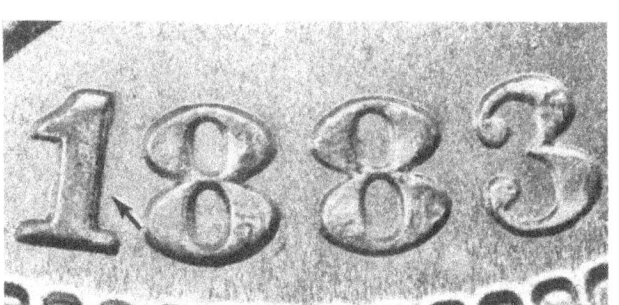

7 O Doubled Date

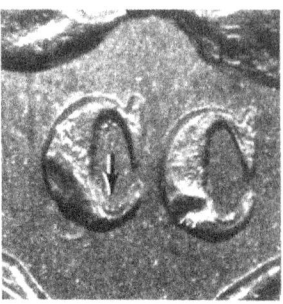

7 R CC/CC

1883-O

The first of the common date O mints, the strike runs the gamut from extremely flat to razor sharp. However, full strikes are fairly easy to locate. Luster is generally good but can be dull on some coins from dies that were used in the coining presses a long time. This issue is not plagued by an abundance of sliders as the earlier O mint issues were. Although numerous die varieties exist, only VAM 4 with a doubled O mint mark below the O is very significant.

Proof-likes are available but not as readily as the early S mints. Generally the contrast is fairly good and very deep mirror cameos can occasionally be found. Twelve branch mint proofs were reported struck and two are known.

1   III²1 • C³a (Normal Die)   (181)   I-1   R-2
     Obverse III²1 – Normal die of III² type. Some specimens show a die chip between loops of first 8 on left.
     Reverse C³a – Normal die of C³ type with tall oval medium II O mint mark centered and upright.

1A   III²1 • C³a (Die Flake in 8)   (181)   I-2   R-4
     Obverse III²1 – Die flake in lower loop of first 8 and under loop on lower right outside.

1B   III²1 • C³a (Gouge In 8)   (181)   I-2   R-4
     Obverse III²1 – Diagonal die gouge on top left inside of lower loop of first 8.

2   III²2 • C³a (Dash Under 8)   (181)   I-2   R-3
     Obverse III²2 – Dash under second 8 in date. Some specimens show 1 doubled well below upper crossbar as a short spike.

3   III²9 • C³b (O/O Right)   (181)   I-2   R-3
     Obverse III²9 – 1 doubled at bottom of crossbar and on left top side of vertical shaft.
     Reverse C³b – Mint mark repunched with the original showing on the right side of the opening.

4   III²3 • C³c (O/O Down, Doubled 1)   (181)   I-2   R-3
     Obverse III²3 – 1 in date doubled slightly at top left and on top right of stem plus at bottom of lower crossbar. Second 8 is set high. Date shallow from overpolished die.
     Reverse C³c – II O mint mark repunched with the original showing at the top of the opening and below at left and right sides.

5   III²1 • C³d (O/O Right and High)   (181)   I-2   R-3
     Reverse C³d – Mint mark repunched with the original showing at the top and right side of the opening.

6   III²1 • C³e (O/O High)   (181)   I-2   R-4
     Reverse C³e – Mint mark repunched with the original showing at the top of the opening.

1883-O

7   III²4 • C³a (Doubled 18-3)   (181)   I-2   R-3
    Obverse III²4 – Doubled 18-3 in date. 1 doubled slightly at top left. First 8 doubled at bottom outside of lower loop. 3 doubled at bottom left inside of lower loop.

8   III²1 • C³f (O Tilted Far Right)   (181)   I-2   R-3
    Reverse C³f – Normal die with II O mint mark tilted far to right.

9   III²5 • C³e (High 8, O/O High)   (181)   I-2   R-4
    Obverse III²5 – Second 8 in date set higher than first 8 and 3. Faint doubling at bottom of 1 and at bottom inside of 3 lower loop.

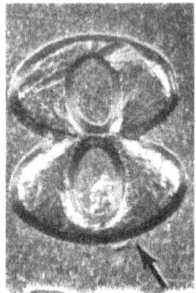
1A O Die Flake In First 8

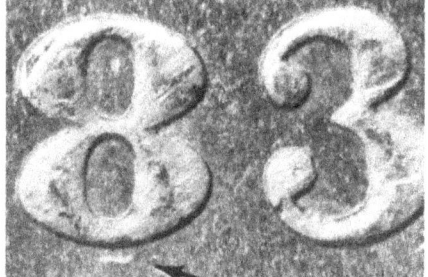
2 O Dash

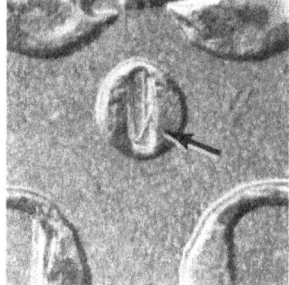
3 R O/O Right

1B O Gouge in 8

3 O Doubled 1

4 O Doubled 1

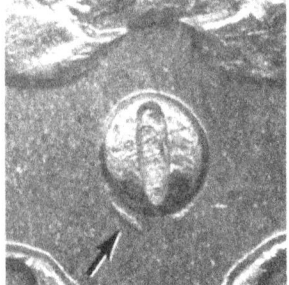
4 R O/O Down

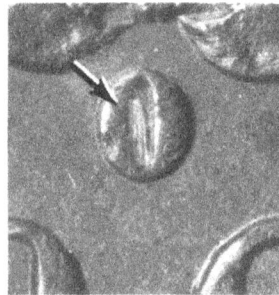
5 R O/O Right

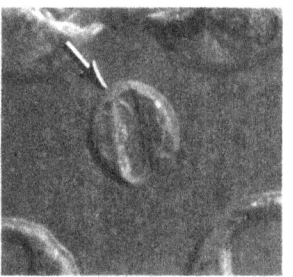
6 R O/O High

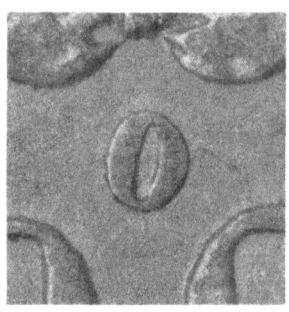
8 R O Tilted Right

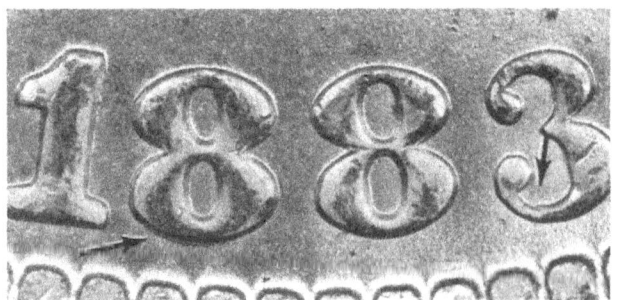
7 O Doubled 18-3

9 O High 8

1883-O

10	III²5 • C³g (High 8, O/O Low)	(181)	I-2	R-3

Reverse C³g – II O mint mark repunched with original showing as a diagonal line at bottom of loop opening.

11	III²5 • C³h (O Tilted Slightly Right, High 8)	(181)	I-2	R-3

Reverse C³h – II O mint mark centered and tilted slightly right.

12	III²1 • C³i (O Set Left)	(181)	I-2	R-3

Reverse C³i – II O mint mark set slightly to left.

13	III²1 • C³j (O/O Right and Down)	(181)	I-2	R-3

Reverse C³j – II O mint mark repunched with the original showing at top inside and lower right outside.

14	III²6 • C³a (Doubled 1-3)	(181)	I-2	R-3

Obverse III²6 – 1 in date doubled at bottom of crossbar and on top left side of shaft. 3 doubled slightly at bottom left inside of lower loop.

15	III²7 • C³a (Slanted Date)	(181)	I-2	R-3

Obverse III²7 – Date slanted with 83 higher than normal.

16	III²5 • C³k (O/O Line)	(181)	I-3	R-4

Reverse C³k – High upright II O mint mark repunched with the original showing as a high raised line in the center of the opening and curving to the left at top.

17	III²8 • C³l (Low 3, O Tilted Left)	(181)	I-2	R-3

Obverse III²8 – 3 in date punched low with bottom close to rim.
Reverse C³l – II O mint mark tilted slightly to the left.

18	III²5 • C³a (High 8)	(181)	I-2	R-4

Reverse C³a – II O mint mark has fine diagonal polishing line at bottom of opening.

19	III²9 • C³1 (Doubled 1)	(181)	I-2	R-3

Obverse III²9 – 1 doubled slightly at top left and at top right of stem.

20	III²10 • C³f (Doubled 3, O Tilted Right)	(181)	I-2	R-3

Obverse III²10 – 3 in date doubled slightly at bottom left inside of lower loop.

21	III²11 • C³a (Doubled 18)	(181)	I-2	R-3

Obverse III²11 – Doubled 18 in date. 1 doubled on surface to top right of vertical shaft. First 8 doubled slightly at lower left inside of upper loop.

22	III²3 • C³a (Doubled 1)	(181)	I-2	R-3

Reverse C³a – Some specimens show an E die clash below eagle's tail feathers.

23	III²12 • C³a (Doubled 1)	(181)	I-2	R-3

Obverse III²12 – 1 doubled on surface at top right of vertical shaft. Slight slant to date with 1 closest to rim.

24	III²1 • C³m (Doubled Reverse)	(181)	I-2	R-3

Reverse C³m – Middle leaves in clusters of left and right wreaths doubled towards rim. Top inside of wreath bow and designer's initial, M, doubled.

25	III²10 • C³i (Doubled 3, O Set Left)	(181)	I-2	R-3
26	III²4 • C³i (Doubled 18-3, O Set Left)	(181)	I-2	R-3
27	III²12 • C³n (Doubled 1, O/O Surface)	(181)	I-2	R-3

Reverse C³n – II O mint mark repunched with doubling on surface at lower left and right sides.

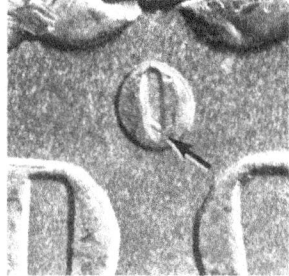   

10 R O/O Low   11 R O Tilted Slightly Right   12 R O Set Left   13 R O/O Right 4 Down

1883-O

14 O Doubled 1

15 O Slanted Date

16 O O/O Line

17 O Low 3

17 R O Tilted Left

19 O Doubled 1

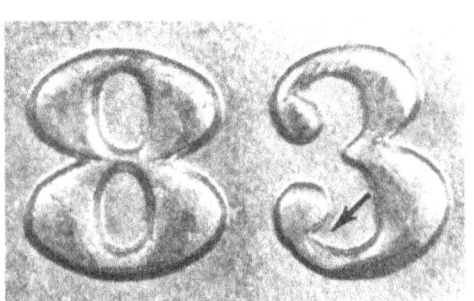
20 O Doubled 3

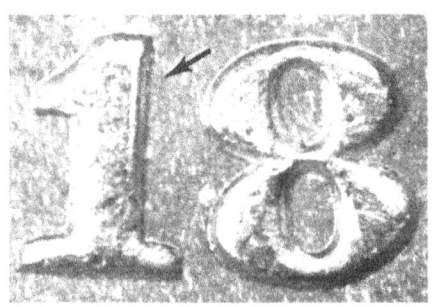
21 O Doubled 18

23 O Doubled 1

24 O Doubled Wreath

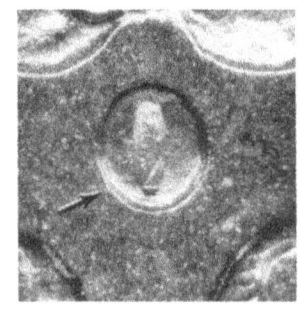
27 R O/O

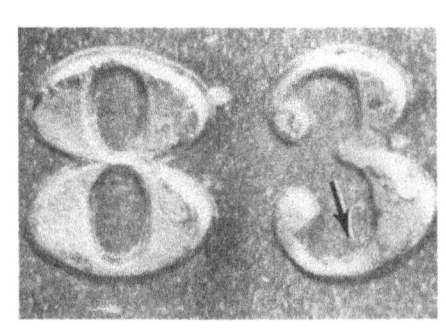
28 O Doubled 3

1883-O

28	III² 14 • C³ a (Doubled 3)		(181)	I-2	R-3

Obverse III² 14 – 3 doubled at bottom left inside of lower loop.

29	III² 14 • C³ o (Doubled 3, O/O)		(181)	I-2	R-3

Reverse C³ o – II O mint mark repunched with doubling at lower right inside.

30	**III² 2 • C³ h (Dash Under 8, O Tilted Slightly Right)**		(181)	I-2	R-3

31	III² 15 • C³ a (Doubled 18-3)		(181)	I-2	R-3

Obverse III² 15 – Doubled 18-3 in date. 1 doubled slightly below bottom crossbar. First 8 doubled slightly at top inside of upper loop. 3 doubled at bottom left inside of lower loop.

32	III² 16 • C³ a (Dash Under 8)		(181)	I-2	R-3

Obverse III² 16 – Long thin dash under second 8 in date. Some specimens show weakly struck periphery of stars and letters.

33	III² 10 • C³ p (Doubled 3, O/O Right)		(181)	I-2	R-3

Obverse III² 10 – Also shows diagonal die gouge at top left inside of lower loop of first 8.
Reverse C³ p – II O mint mark repunched with doubling at right inside and polishing line at top inside.

34	III² 17 • C³ j (Doubled 18-3, O/O Right and Down)		(181)	I-2	R-3

Obverse III² 17 – Doubled 18-3 in date. 1 doubled as line on top left of lower crossbar. First 8 doubled at left inside of both loops. 3 doubled at bottom inside of lower loop.

35	III² 18 • C³ a (Doubled 18 and Stars)		(181)	I-2	R-3

Obverse III² 18 – Doubled 18 in date. 1 doubled below upper crossbar and on surface at top and right of vertical shaft. First 8 doubled slightly at top inside of both loops and bottom left outside of upper loop. All right stars, first left star and UNUM strongly doubled towards rim.

36	III² 19 • C³ a Doubled 18-3)		(181)	I-2	R-3

Obverse III² 19 – Doubled 18-3 in date. 1 doubled at top left of upper crossbar as two notches and at bottom of lower crossbar with a notch at right. First 8 doubled slightly at top inside of upper loop. 3 doubled slightly in middle bottom inside of lower loop.
Reverse C³ a – Some specimens show a partial die clash E below eagle's tail feathers.

37	III² 20 • C³ a (Doubled 8-3)		(181)	I-2	R-3

Obverse III² 20 – Doubled 8-3 in date. First 8 doubled slightly at lower left inside of both loops. 3 doubled at top outside of upper loop and right outside and bottom inside of lower loop.

38	III² 21 • C³ a (Doubled 18-3)		(181)	I-2	R-3

Obverse III² 21 – Doubled 18-1 in date. 1 doubled below upper crossbar and on right side of vertical shaft. First 8 doubled at left inside of both loops. 3 doubled at bottom inside of lower loop.

29 R O/O

31 O Doubled 18-3

32 O Dash Under 8

33 R O/O Right

34 O Doubled 18-3

35 O Doubled 18

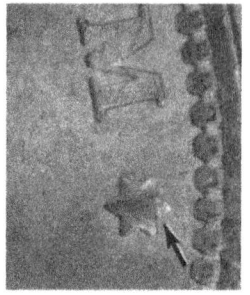
35 O Doubled Stars, M

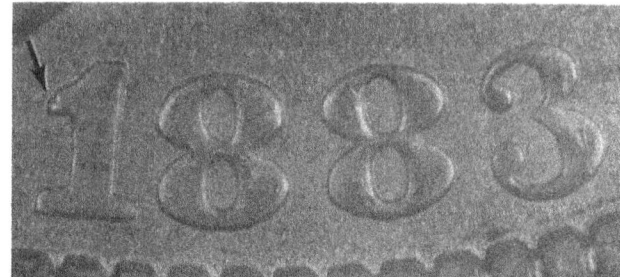
36 O Doubled 18-3

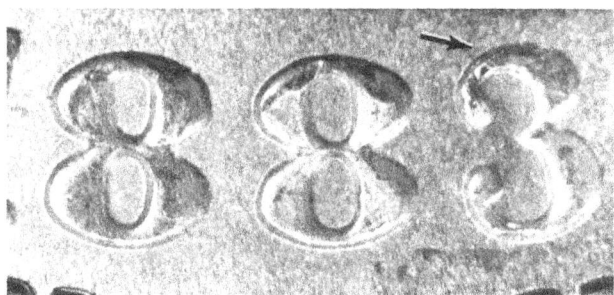
37 O Doubled 8-3

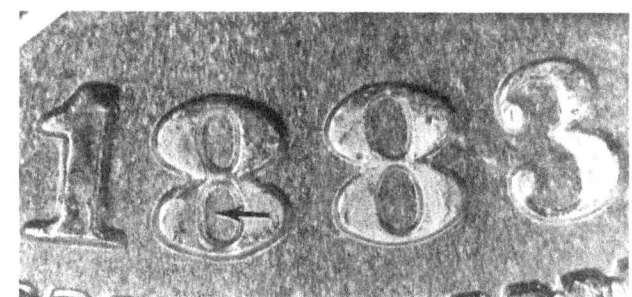
38 O Doubled 18-3

1883-S

This year is the beginning of the scarcer uncirculated S mints. Apparently this and some of the later S mints were extensively melted during 1918-1920 thus making uncirculated specimens scarce while circulated specimens are common. As with the earlier S mints, the 1883-S generally has a full strike and good luster. A few die varieties exist but none are significant. Proof-likes on both sides are difficult to locate and most tend to be brilliant although some cameos are known. Beware of one sided proof-likes or coins with good luster being passed off as fully proof-like.

1   III^{2}1 • C^{3}a (Normal Die)   (187)   I-1   R-2
Obverse III^{2}1 – Normal die of III^2 type. Some specimens show a die chip between loops of second 8 on right.
Reverse C^{3}a – Normal die of C^3 type with medium IV S mint mark centered and upright.

2   III^{2}1 • C^{3}b (S Tilted Right)   I-2   R-3
Reverse C^{3}b – Normal die with IV S mint mark tilted slightly to right.

3   III^{2}2 • C^{3}a. (Doubled 18)   (186)   I-2   R-3
Obverse III^{2}2 – Doubled 18 in date. 1 is doubled at top left of upper crossbar as two notches at bottom of upper crossbar and top left of vertical shaft. First 8 doubled on left inside of upper loop.

4   III^{2}3 • C^{3}a (Doubled 1-3)   (186)   I-2   R-3
Obverse III^{2}3 – Doubled 1-3 in date. 1 doubled slightly below upper crossbar and strongly at upper right of vertical shaft with a triangular projection sticking out on the field. 3 doubled at bottom left inside of lower loop. First 8 has horizontal polishing marks at right inside of upper loop.

5   III^{2}4 • C^{3}a (Doubled 18)   (186)   I-2   R-3
Obverse III^{2}4 – Doubled 18 in date. 1 doubled on surface at bottom of upper crossbar and left and right sides of vertical shaft. First 8 doubled on surface at left inside of upper loop with die chips on left and right side of upper loop.

6   III^{2}5 • C^{3}a (Doubled 18-3)   (187)   I-2   R-3
Obverse III^{2}5 – Doubled 18-3 in date. 1 doubled on surface at top and right side of shaft. First 8 doubled at top inside of upper loop and left inside of lower loop. 3 doubled slightly at bottom inside of lower loop.

7   III^{2}6 • C^{3}a (Tripled First 8, Doubled 1-3)   (187)   I-2   R-3
Obverse III^{2}6 – First 8 tripled on left inside of both loops and doubled at top inside of lower loop. 1 doubled on top right of vertical shaft and at top right of lower crossbar. 3 doubled slightly at bottom inside of lower loop.

1883-S

8   III²7 • C³a (Doubled 8-3)   (187)   I-2   R-3

Obverse III²7 – Doubled 8-3 in date. First 8 doubled on left inside of both loops. 3 doubled at bottom inside of lower loop and ball of lower loop. 1 has die chip on vertical shaft.

Reverse C³a – Some specimens show die chip in wreath opposite N of UNITED.

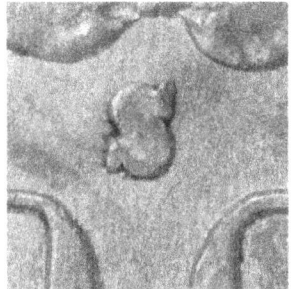

2 R S Tilted Right

3 O Doubled 18

5 O Doubled 18

4 O Doubled 1-3

6 O Doubled 18-3

7 O Doubled 18-3

8 O Doubled 8-3

8 R Die Chip in Wreath

1884-P

This date is usually fairly well struck although slightly weak strikes occasionally surface. Luster can be good to slightly below average in keeping with its high mintage. A few varieties exist. The one significant variety shows a small dot next to the designer's initial, M, on obverse and reverse in two different sizes. These dots were to identify working dies when the date was made smaller in 1884. The dot variety brings a moderate premium.

Proof-likes are quite scarce and are usually brilliant. Some very deep mirror cameos exist however. Proofs have fairly good contrast and are available with few hairlines.

1 III²1 • C³a (Normal Die)   (187, 189)   I-1   R-1
   Obverse III²1 – Normal die of III² type
   Reverse C³a – Normal die of C³ type.

2 III²2 • C³a (Dash Under 8)   (188)   I-2   R-3
   Obverse III²2 – Dash under second 8 in date. Date set further right than normal.
   Reverse C³a – Some specimens show a partial E under the eagle's tail feathers.

3 III²3 • C³b (Large Dot)   (188)   I-4   R-4
   Obverse III²3 – Large dot after the engraver's initial M. Date set further right than normal.
   Reverse C³b – Small dot after engraver's initial M.

4 III²4 • C³b (Small Dot)   (189)   I-4   R-4
   Obverse III²4 – Small dot after engraver's initial M. Date set further right than normal.
   Reverse C³b – Dot is in slightly different position than in VAM 3.

5 III²5 • C³a (Doubled 18)   (188)   I-3   R-3
   Obverse III²5 – Doubled 18 in date. 1 is doubled slightly at top left. First 8 is doubled at top left and right outside. Ear doubled
      on left inside and right outside.

6 III²6 • C³a (Low Dash Under 8)   (189)   I-2   R-4
   Obverse III²6 – Thin dash set very low below second 8. Date set further right than normal.

7 III²7 • C³a (Slanted Dash Under 8)   I-2   R-4
   Obverse III²7 – Slanted dash set left of center below second 8. Date set very much further right than normal.

8 III²8 • C³a (Far Date)   (189)   I-2   R-3
   Obverse III²8 – Date set further right than normal.

9 III²9 • C³a (Very Far Date)   I-2   R-3
   Obverse III²9 – Date set much further right than normal. Second 8 has a big dot on surface of right side of upper loop.

10 III²10 • C³a (Doubled 188 and Stars)   (187)   I-2   R-3
   Obverse III²10 – Doubled 188 in date with digits doubled at very top outside. All left stars, first two on right and E – P doubled
      at 12 o'clock. Lips and chin of Liberty head slightly doubled. Date set much further right than normal.

11 III²12 • C³a (Low Dash Under 8)   (188)   I-2   R-3
   Obverse III²12 – Long dash set well below second 8 and centered. Date set further right than normal.

12 III²1 • C³c (Doubled Motto)   (187)   I-2   R-3
   Reverse C³c – Doubled tops of IN GOD WE TRUST letters. Tops of lower serifs of TATES OF AM also doubled at top right of
      right wreath.

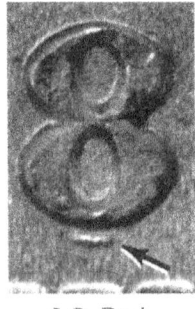   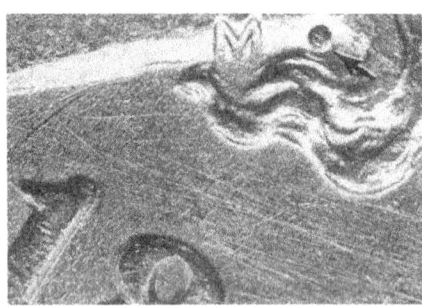   

2 O Dash   3 O Large Dot   3 R Dot

1884-P

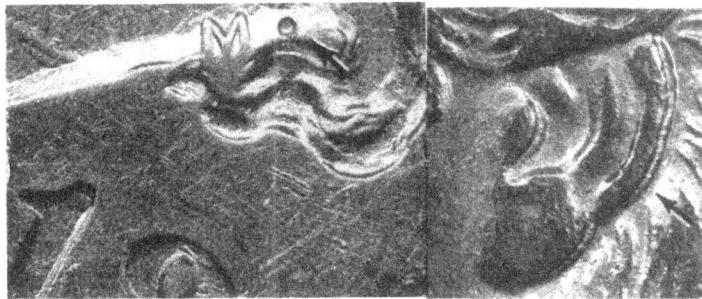 

4 O Small Dot   5 O Doubled Ear   5 O Doubled 18

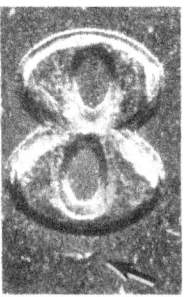  

6 O Low Dash Under 8   7 O Slanted Dash Under 8   10 O Doubled Stars and E

9 O Very Far Date, Dot 8   10 O Doubled 188

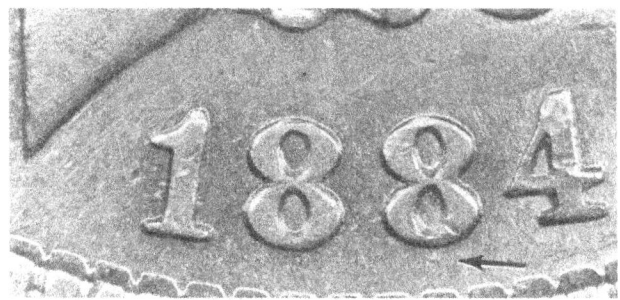 

11 O Far Date, Partial Dash Under 8   12 R Doubled Motto

1884-CC

Eighty-five percent of the mintage was in the GSA sales resulting in general availability of BU specimens. Generally the strike is full and luster good, but some slightly weakly struck specimens exist. A few minor die varieties exist but none command a premium.

Like the 1882-CC and 1883-CC a fair proportion are proof-like with good contrast and some are very deep mirror cameos.

1   III²1 • C³a (Normal Die)   I-1   R-3
       Obverse III²1 – Normal die of III² type.
       Reverse C³a – Normal die of C³ type with large V CC mint mark.

2   III²2 • C³b (Doubled 18 Top)   (177)   I-2   R-3
       Obverse III²2 – Doubled 18 in date. The 1 is a wide curved vertical spike above the top point and is doubled slightly above the bottom crossbar. The left outside of the loops of the first 8 are doubled. Some specimens show a thick die break through the bottom of the date digits.
       Reverse C³b – First C of mint mark is doubled on the left inside.

3   III²3 • C³a (Doubled 18 Left)   (177)   I-2   R-3
       Obverse III²3 – Doubled 18 in date. 1 doubled below top crossbar and to the left of bottom crossbar. The inside right of the top and bottom loops of the first 8 have die chips and right outside of upper loop is slightly doubled. Some specimens show a die break through the bottom of the date digits.

4   III²4 • C³a (Spiked Date)   (177)   I-2   R-4
       Obverse III²4 – There is a vertical spike of metal from the top of the 1 in the date. Some specimens show a horizontal spike to the left of the lower loop of the first 8. A thin die break line shows below the designer's initial M. The third star on the left has a hook at the bottom point due to a die chip.
       Reverse C³a – Some specimens show a horizontal die gouge through E in STATES.

5   III²5 • C³c (CC/CC)   (177)   I-2   R-4
       Obverse III²5 – Doubled 18 in date. 1 is doubled to left showing as horizontal lines from upper and lower crossbars. The first 8 is doubled at the top left side of both loops and the upper right inside of lower loop. Date set further right than normal.
       Reverse C³c – Mint mark doubled with first C doubled at top inside and bottom left outside and second C doubled at right inside.

6   III²6 • C³b (Doubled First 8)   I-2   R-4
       Obverse III²6 – First 8 is doubled on the right side of the lower loop and at top right outside of upper loop.

7   III²7 • C³a (Doubled 18 Bottom)   (177)   I-3   R-4
       Obverse III²7 – Doubled 18 in date. 1 is doubled at bottom and a spike of metal extends to left from left side of the bottom crossbar. The first 8 is doubled strongly all along the bottom and on the bottom left of the upper loop.

8   III²1 • C³d (CC Tilted Left)   I-2   R-3
       Reverse C³d – Large V CC mint mark tilted left.

9   III²8 • C³a (Dash Under 8)   I-2   R-4
       Obverse III²8 – Dash under second 8 in date.

10   III²9 • C³d (Far Date, CC Tilted Left)   (178)   I-2   R-3
       Obverse III²9 – Date set further right than normal.

11   III²10 • C³a (Doubled 18)   (177)   I-2   R-3
       Obverse III²10 – Doubled 18 in date. 1 doubled at top as a as a notch on left side of lower crossbar. First 8 doubled on top left outside of lower loop with die chips on right inside of both loops.

2 O Doubled 18 Top   2 R Doubled C   3 O Doubled 18 Left

1884-CC / 1884-O

12 III²8 • C³d (Dash Under 8, CC Tilted Left)　　　　(178)　　I-2　　R-3

4 O Spiked Date

5 O Doubled Date

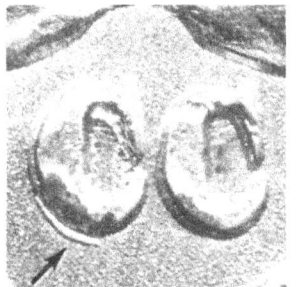
5 R Doubled CC

6 O Doubled First 8

7 O Doubled 18 Bottom

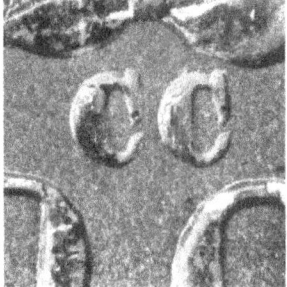
8 R CC Tilted Left

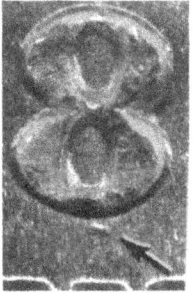
9 O Dash Under 8

11 O Doubled 18

1884-O

This O mint has a wide variation in strike from flat to full. Full strike specimens are fairly easy to locate, however. Luster is average but can range from very good to dull. Numerous die varieties exist but only VAM 6 with doubling on the left outside and inside of the O mint mark is very significant and commands a modest premium.

Proof-likes are somewhat available like the 1883-O and 1885-O and have fairly good contrast. Very deep mirror cameos can occasionally be found.

1　　III²1 • C³a (Oval O)　　　　　　　　　　　　(181)　　I-1　　R-2
　　Obverse III²1 – Normal die of III² type.
　　Reverse C³a – Normal die of C³ type with a tall oval medium II O mint mark centered and upright.

2　　III²1 • C³b (Round O)　　　　　　　　　　　(181)　　I-1　　R-2
　　Reverse C³b – Normal die of C³ type with circular III O mint mark with narrow slit.

1884-O

3	III²2 • C³r (Doubled 1, O/O Line on Left)	(181)		I-2	R-3

Obverse III²2 – The top of the 1 is doubled to left. Date set further right than normal.
Reverse C³r – II O mint mark doubled on left inside as a line and at top inside as a diagonal line.

4   III²3 • C³a (Doubled 18) (181) I-2 R-3

Obverse III²3 – Doubled 18 in date. 1 shows a curved vertical spike at top left and a short horizontal spike to left of bottom crossbar. First 8 is slightly doubled on left outside of lower loop and has a large bulge to right outside lower loop. Entire head is covered with dots of metal from a pitted die.

5   III²4 • C³a (Far Date) (181) I-2 R-3

Obverse III²4 – Date set further right than normal.
Reverse C³a – II O mint mark. Opening filled almost flush on some specimens.

6   III²4 • C³c (O/O Left and Down) (181) I-3 R-4

Reverse C³c – II O mint mark repunched with original showing on left side of opening, a spike below the O and line outside the lower left.

7   III²4 • C³d (O/O Tilted Left) (181) I-2 R-3

Reverse C³d – II O mint mark repunched with original showing diagonally within opening. Right wreath doubled on outside and TATES OF AMERICA doubled at bottom.

8   III²5 • C³e (O/O Center) (181) I-2 R-3

Obverse III²5 – Date set much further right than normal.
Reverse C³e – II O mint mark repunched with original showing upright within all but extreme left of opening.

9   III²1 • C³f (O/O Right) (181) I-2 R-3

Reverse C³f – II O mint mark repunched with original showing upright within half of opening.

10   III²4 • C³g (O/O Left) (181) I-2 R-3

Reverse C³g – II O mint mark repunched with original showing as a wavy vertical line within left side of opening. So-called O/CC variety.

11   III²3 • C³f (Doubled 18, O/O Right) (181) I-2 R-3

Obverse III²3 – 1 doubled as dot to left of the bottom of the crossbar and at very top. First 8 doubled at left outside of top loop and right outside of bottom loop.

12   III²1 • C³h (O/O Line) (181) I-2 R-3

Reverse C³h – II O mint mark repunched with original showing as a thin vertical line on left side of opening.

13   III²1 • C³i (O/O Centered High) (181) I-2 R-3

Reverse C³i – II O mint mark repunched with original showing as curved line centered at top of opening.

14   III²4 • C³j (O/O Right High) (181) I-2 R-3

Reverse C³j – II O mint mark repunched with original showing as a curved line at top of opening shifted slightly to the right.

15   III²5 • C³k (O/O Far Right) (181) I-2 R-3

Reverse C³k – II O mint mark repunched with original showing as a thin vertical line curved slightly at top and on inside and upper right side of opening.

16   III²5 • C³a (Very Far Date) (181) I-2 R-3

17   III²1 • C³l (O/O Far Left) (181) I-2 R-3

Reverse C³l – II O mint mark repunched with original showing as a vertical bar in middle and right side of opening and very thin space on left side.

 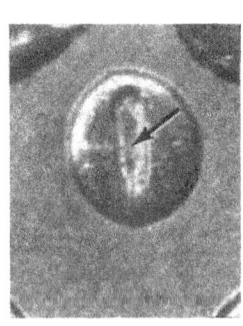  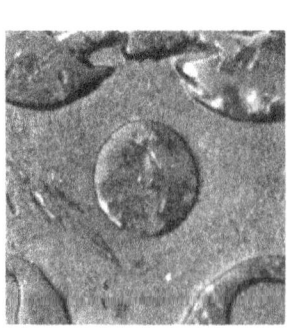

3 O Doubled 1   3 R O/O Line   4 O Doubled 18   5 R Filled O

1884-O

18   III²6 • C³b (Dash Under 8)   (181)   I-2   R-3
  Obverse III²6 – Dash under second 8 in date with date set further right than normal.

19   III²7 • C³a (Doubled 18)   (181)   I-2   R-3
  Obverse III²7 – Doubled 18 in date. Top of 1 doubled faintly as a thin line starting at middle of upper curve to almost the right side. First 8 doubled faintly at top left outside. Date set much further right than normal.

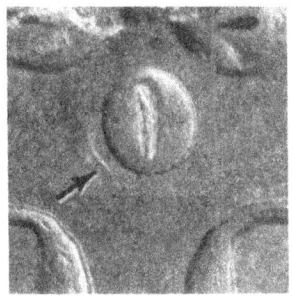 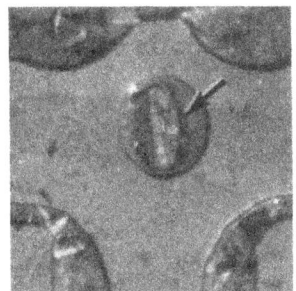 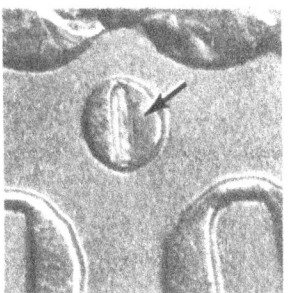 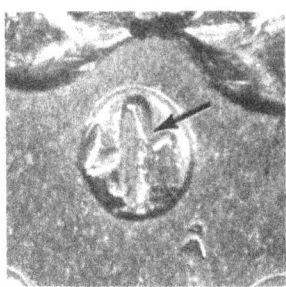

6 R O/O Left and Down   7 R O/O Tilted Left   8 R O/O Center   9 R O/O Right

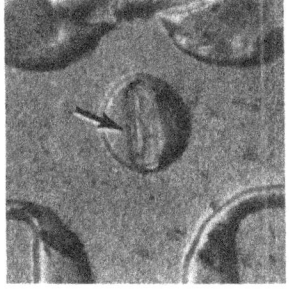  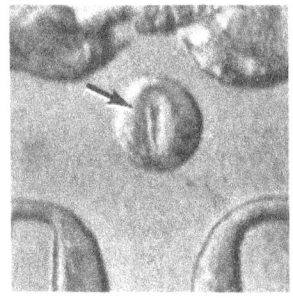 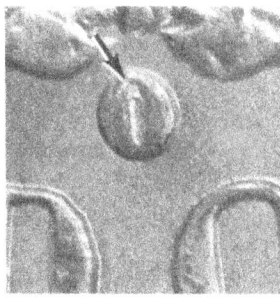

10 R O/O Left   11 O Doubled 18   12 R O/O Line   13 R O/O Centered High

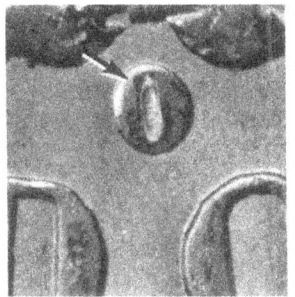 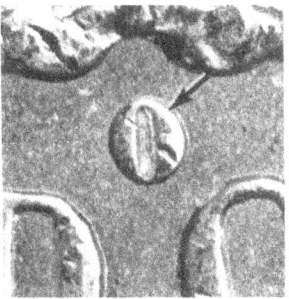 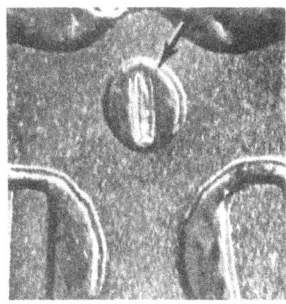 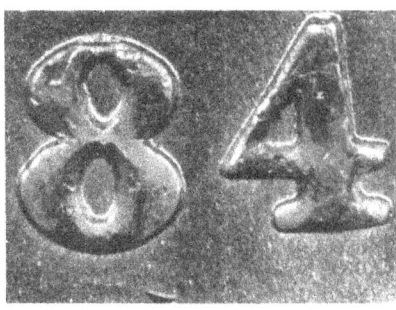

14 R O/O Right High   15 R O/O Far Right   17 R O/O Far Left   18 O Dash Under 8

 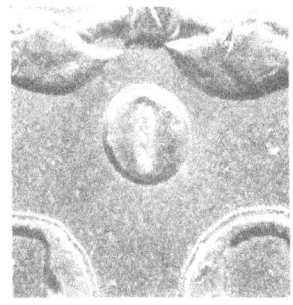 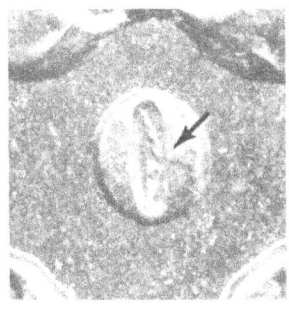

19 O Doubled 1   20 R High O   21 R O/O Curved

1884-O

| 20 | III² 2 • C³ m (Doubled 1, High O) | (181) | I-2 | R-3 |

Reverse C³ m – II O mint mark set high and upright.

| 21 | III² 5 • C³ n (Very Far Date, O/O Curved) | (181) | I-2 | R-3 |

Reverse C³ n – II O mint mark repunched with original showing as a raised curved line in middle of opening.

| 22 | III² 8 • C³ o (Slanted Low Date, O/O Tilted) | (181) | I-2 | R-3 |

Obverse III² 8 – Date set much further right than normal and slanted with 1 very close to rim.
Reverse C³ o – II O mint mark repunched with original showing as a vertical bar in right half of opening. Mint mark centered and tilted to left.

| 23 | III² 9 • C³ a (Doubled 1-4) | (181) | I-2 | R-4 |

Obverse III² 9 – 1 and 4 in date doubled at very top. Date set further right than normal.

| 24 | III² 10 • C³ a (Doubled 18) | (181) | I-2 | R-3 |

Obverse III² 10 – 1 doubled as a slanted line to left of lower crossbar. First 8 doubled at top left and right outside of upper loop.

| 25 | III² 1 • C³ p (O/O Centered Low) | (181) | I-2 | R-3 |

Reverse C³ p – II O mint mark tilted left, repunched with original showing as a curved line centered at bottom of opening.

| 26 | III² 11 • C³ a (Doubled 18) | (181) | I-2 | R-3 |

Obverse III² 11 – Doubled 18 in date. 1 is doubled at top of upper crossbar. First 8 doubled at top outside of upper loop as a broken line and as a vertical bar at top of loop.

27	III² 4 • C³ b (Far Date)	(181)	I-2	R-3
28	III² 6 • C³ a (Dash Under 8)	(181)	I-2	R-4
29	III² 4 • C³ i (O/O Centered High)	(181)	I-2	R-3
30	III² 11 • C³ q (Tripled 1, O/O Bar)	(181)	I-2	R-3

Obverse III² 11 – 1 tripled at very top. Date set further right than normal.
Reverse C³ q – II O mint mark doubled with original showing as a raised band on left inside of opening.

22 O Slanted Date

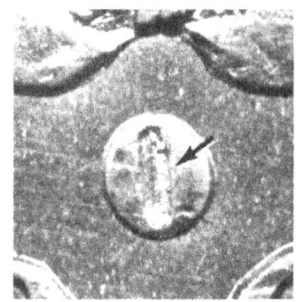

22 R O/O Tilted

23 O Doubled 4

24 O Doubled First 8

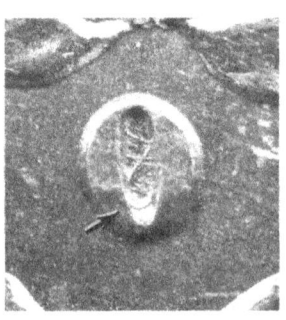

25 R O/O Centered Low

26 O Doubled 18

1884-O / 1884-S

31   III²5 • C³s (Very Far Date, O/O Line On Right)   (181)   I-2   R-3
     Reverse C³s – II O mint mark doubled on right inside as a thin shaft curved slightly left at very top.
32   III²5 • C³t (Very Far Date, O Tilted Left)   (181)   1-2   R-3
33   III²7 • C³t (Doubled 18, O Tilted Left)   (181)   I-2   R-3
34   III²12 • C³a (Doubled 18)   (181)   I-2   R-3
     Obverse III²12 – Doubled 18 in date. 1 doubled at top left and right of upper crossbar. First 8 doubled at top right outside of
     upper loop and left inside of lower loop as a short hook.
35   III²13 • C³u (Doubled Eyelid, Reverse)   (181)   I-2   R-3
     Obverse III²13 – Eyelid doubled at lower edge and eye in front. Date set further right than normal.
     Reverse C³u – TATES AMER and top of right wreath doubled towards rim.
36   III²3 • C³a (Doubled 18)   (181)   I-2   R-3

  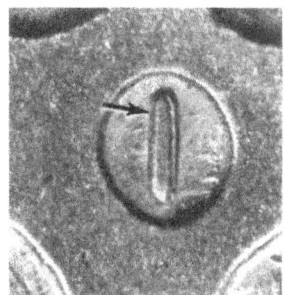

30 O Tripled 1   30 R O/O Bar   31 R O/O Line on Right

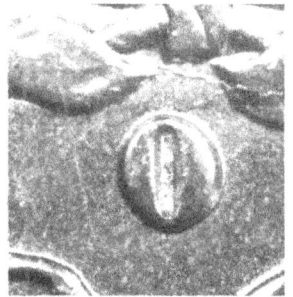 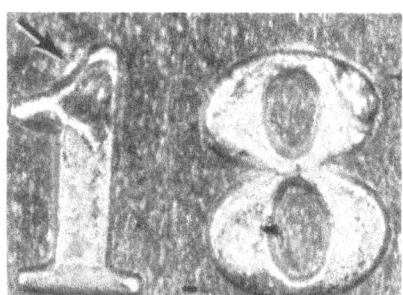

32 R O Tilted Left   34 O Doubled 18

1884-S

The 1884-S is a rarity in uncirculated condition although it is fairly common in the circulated grades. There are quite a few sliders around and some bring substantial premiums because of the large uncirculated price increases. A few higher grade MS65 specimens are known. Generally the strike is fairly good but some have slight weakness on the reverse. Luster is typically good. A few die varieties exist but none are significant.

Proof-like uncirculated 1884-S are extremely rare with only a couple known. Some with semi-proof-like on one side and proof-like on the other are known. Some fully proof-like AU specimens exist.

1   III²1 • C³a (Normal Die)   I-1   R-2
     Obverse III²1 – Normal die of III² type.
     Reverse C³a – Normal die of C³ type with medium IV S mint mark centered and upright.

2   III²1 • C³b (S Tilted Right)   (187)   I-2   R-3
     Reverse C³b – Normal die of C³ die with IV S mint mark shifted left and tilted right.

1884-S / 1885-P

3	III²2 • C³c (S/S Left)		I-3	R-3

Obverse III²2 – Date set further right than normal.
Reverse C³c – IV S mint mark is repunched with original showing as a short spike of metal at top of upper loop opening and a vertical spike of metal at left of the lower loop opening.

4	III²2 • C³a (Far Date)	(187)	I-2	R-3
4A	III²2 • C³a (Far Date)		I-2	R-3

Reverse C³a – Die chip at very top of right wreath.

5	III²3 • C³a (Very Far Date)	(187)	I-2	R-3

Obverse III²3 – Date set much further right than normal.

6	III²2 • C³d (Far Date, S Set Left)	(187)	I-2	R-3

Reverse C³d – IV S mint mark upright and set to left with loops filled.

7	III²3 • C³e (S/S High, Very Far Date)	(187)	I-2	R-3

Reverse C³e – IV S mint mark doubled with diagonal line in upper loop and curved line in lower loop.

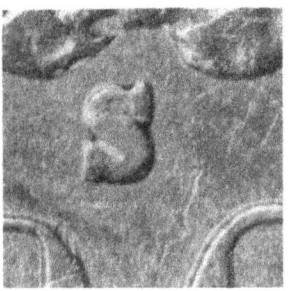

2 R S Tilted Right

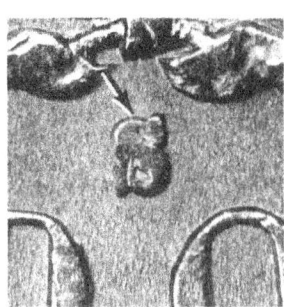

3 R S/S Left

4A R Die Chip in Wreath

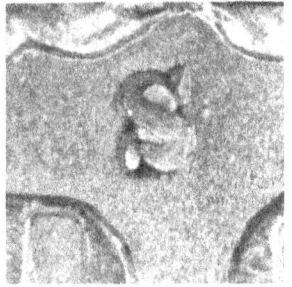

6 R S Set Left

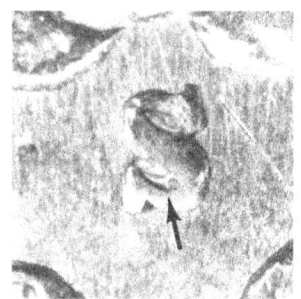

7 R S/S

1885-P

This is the first so-called common P mint from 1885 to 1887. The strike is generally good as is the luster. A number of minor die varieties exist. VAM 6 is significant with strongly doubled date digits at top and brings a modest premium.

Proof-likes are fairly available and a high percentage of them are very deep mirror frosted or cameos. Proofs usually have average contrast and are plagued by hairlines.

1	III²1 • C³a (Normal Die)		I-1	R-1

Obverse III²1 – Normal die of III² type.
Reverse C³a – Normal die of C³ type.

1A	III²1 • C³a (Pitted Reverse)		I-2	R-3

Reverse C³a – Die is pitted below left wreath around ONE D.

1B	III²1 • C³a (Pitted Reverse)	(189)	I-2	R-3

Reverse C³a – Die is pitted around DOL of DOLLAR.

1885-P

2	III² 2 • C³ a (Doubled 5)	(189)		I-2	R-3

Obverse III² 2 – 5 in date doubled all across the top. Some specimens show a faint dash well below the second 8. Date set on right side of normal position tolerance.

3	III² 3 • C³ a (High Dash Under 8)	(188)		I-2	R-3

Obverse III² 3 – 5 in date doubled all across the top. Short dash under and touching second 8.

4	III² 4 • C³ a (Low Dash Under 8)	(188)		I-2	R-3

Obverse III² 4 – Dash well below second 8 shifted right.

5	III² 5 • C³ a (Doubled 85)	(188)		I-2	R-3

Obverse III² 5 – 85 in date doubled at bottom. Date set further right than normal.

6	III² 6 • C³ a (Doubled Date)	(189)		I-4	R-4

Obverse III² 6 – All numerals in date doubled at very top with large shift.

7	III² 7 • C³ a (Low Dash Under 8)	(189)		I-2	R-3

Obverse III2 7 – Dash well below second 8 shifted left.

8	III² 8 • C³ a (Thick Dash Under 8)			I-2	R-4

Obverse III² 8 – Thick dash under and touching second 8.

9	III² 9 • C³ a (Far Date)	(188)		I-2	R-3

Obverse III² 9 – Date set further right than normal.

10	III² 10 • C³ a (Doubled 5)			I-2	R-3

Obverse III² 10 – 5 in date doubled all across the top. Date set in middle of normal position tolerance. There is a small vertical mark on tenth denticle from point of Liberty Head neck.

11	III² 11 • C³ a (Tripled 5)			I-2	R-3

Obverse III² 11 – 5 in date is tripled all across the top. Date set on left side of normal position tolerance.

12	III² 12 • C³ a (Doubled 5)	(188)		I-2	R-3

Obverse III² 12 – 5 in date is doubled at top outside as a thin line set well above top of 5.

13	III² 13 • C³ a (Doubled 5)	(189)		I-2	R-3

Obverse III² 13 – 5 in date is doubled all across the top outside with doubling slightly stronger on right side.

14	III² 14 • C³ a (Doubled 5)	(188)		I-2	R-3

Obverse III² 14 – 5 in date is doubled at top outside as a thin broken line set very far above top of 5.

15	III² 15 • C³ a (Doubled 18-5)	(188)		I-3	R-4

Obverse III² 15 – 18-5 doubled in date. 1 doubled at very top as a thin curved line. First 8 doubled strongly at bottom inside of lower loop as a thick bar. 5 doubled slightly at very top as a thin line.

16	III² 6 • C³ a (Doubled First 8)	(189)		I-2	R-3

Obverse III² 16 – First 8 in date doubled at top inside of upper loop.

17	III² 17 • C³ a (Slanted Date)	(188)		I-2	R-3

Obverse III² 17 – Date slanted with 1 closer to rim.

18	III² 18 • C³ a (High Dash Under 8)	(188)		I-2	R-3

Obverse III² 18 – Short dash just under and against bottom outside of second 8 lower loop.

1A R Pitted Reverse

1B R Pitted Reverse

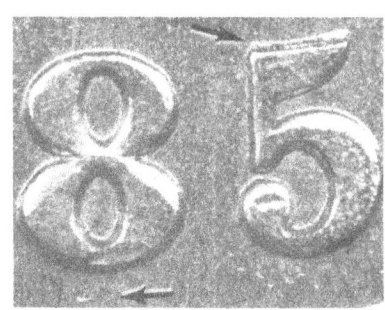

2 O Dash Under 8, Doubled 5

1885-P

3 O Dash Doubled 5

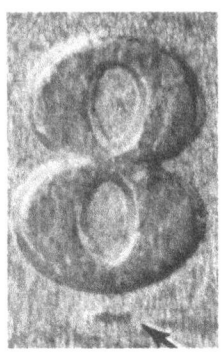
4 O Low Dash

5 O Doubled 85

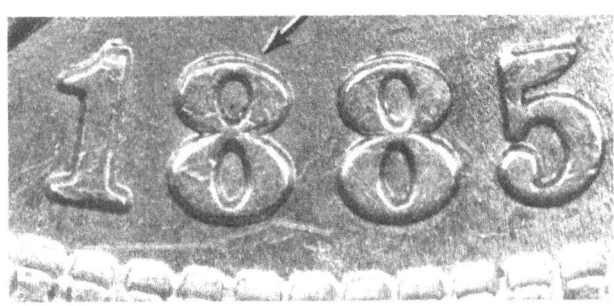
6 O Doubled Date

7 O Low Dash Under 8

8 O Thick Dash Under 8

10 O Doubled 5

11 O Tripled 5

12 O Doubled 5

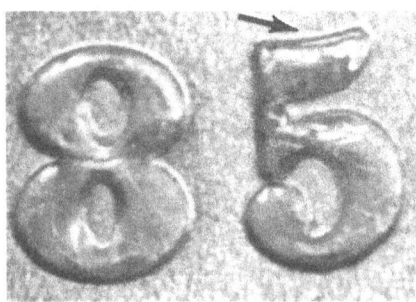
13 O Doubled 5

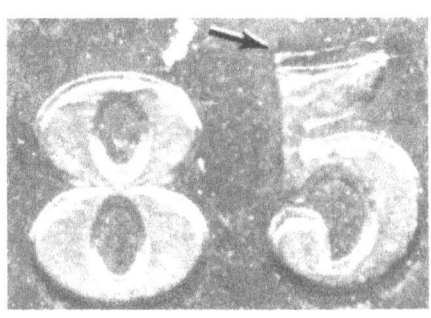
14 O Doubled 5

1885-P / 1885-CC

19	III²19 • C³a (Doubled First 8)	(189)	I-2	R-3

Obverse III²19 – First 8 doubled inside lower loop as an arc at top and line at left.

20	III²20 • C³a (Low Dash Set Right)	(188)	I-2	R-3

Obverse III²20 – Faint short dash set well below second 8 and to the right over 10th denticle.

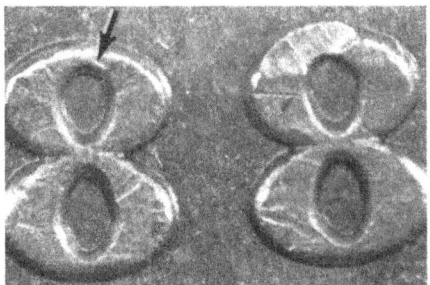

15 O Doubled 18-5

17 O Slanted Date

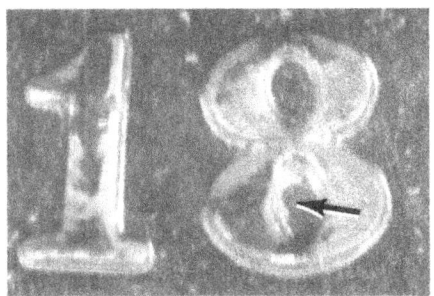

16 O Doubled First 8

18 O High Dash Under 8

19 O Doubled First 8

20 O Low Dash Set Right

1885-CC

Over half the mintage was in the GSA sales. So even though it has the third lowest mintage (excluding non-available 1895-P business strike) it is readily available in BU. It is quite rare in circulated grades however. The strike is generally full although there are some slightly weakly struck with planchet striations in the hair above the ear. Only a couple of minor die varieties are known. One has a very thick dash below the second 8, but it does not command any premium. As with the 1881-CC a considerable percentage are proof-likes and quite a few of these are deep mirror cameos.

1	III²1 • C³a (Normal Die)		I-1	R-3

Obverse III²1 – Normal die of III² type.
Reverse C³a – Normal die of C³ type with large V CC mint mark.

270

1885-CC / 1885-O

2   III²2 • C³a (Dash Under 8)   I-2   R-3
    Obverse III²2 – 5 in date doubled slightly at bottom for about half the curve. Dash under second 8.

3   III²1 • C³b (CC Tilted Left)   I-2   R-4
    Reverse C³b – Large V CC mint mark tilted left with right C almost touching wreath.

4   III²3 • C³a (Thick Dash Under 8)   I-2   R-4
    Obverse III²3 – Thick dash under and touching second 8 with die chips at bottom inside of lower loop. Bottom of dash is faintly doubled. One of the largest dashes known.
    Reverse C³a – Die chips within both mint mark C's.

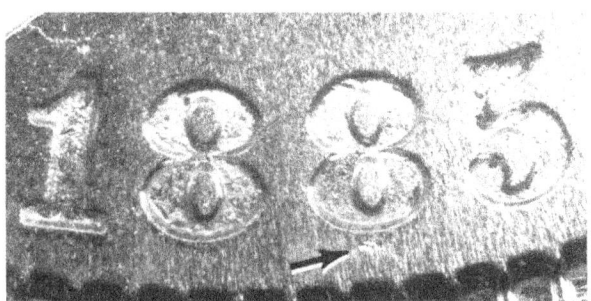 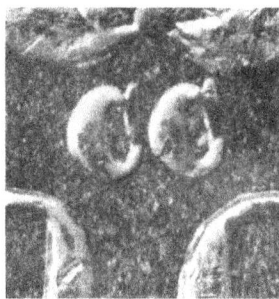 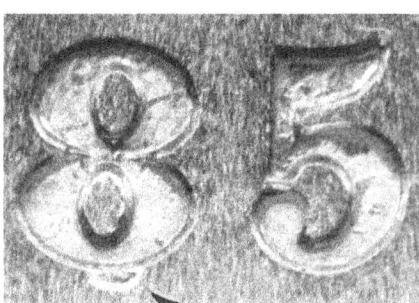

2 O Dash Doubled 5   3 R CC Tilted Left   4 O Thick Dash Under 8

1885-O

This is another common date O mint that has wide variations in strike although fully struck specimens are available. The luster can also vary considerably. A number of minor die varieties exist and the most interesting is VAM 9 which has a moderate shift in a doubled date. Proof-likes are somewhat available but many have a shallow depth. Deep mirror cameos are fairly scarce.

1   III²1 • C³a (Normal Die)   (181)   I-1   R-2
    Obverse III²1 – Normal die of III² type.
    Reverse C³a – Normal die of C³ type with circular medium III O mint mark centered and upright.

1A   III²1 • C³a (Rusted Wing)   (181)   I-2   R-4
    Reverse C³a – Top of eagle's left wing and neck covered with raised spots due to rusted die.

2   III²2 • C³a (Doubled 5)   (181)   I-2   R-3
    Obverse III²2 – 5 in date doubled at top.

3   III²3 • C³a (Doubled 18)   (181)   I-2   R-3
    Obverse III²3 – 1 in date doubled below the top bar. First 8 doubled slightly at top right inside of upper loop.

4   III²4 • C³a (Doubled 18)   (181)   I-2   R-3
    Obverse III²4 – 18 in date doubled. Bottom crossbar of 1 doubled at top and appears as a short spike on the left and a slight bulge to the right of the stem. Inside lower loop of first 8 doubled at bottom and left.

5   III²5 • C³a (Slanted Date)   (181)   I-2   R-3
    Obverse III²5 – Date set high and slanted to make 5 higher than 1. Date set further left than normal.

6   III²6 • C³a (Low Date)   (181)   I-2   R-3
    Obverse III²6 – Date set low with slight slant down to right so that 5 is very close to rim.

7   III²7 • C³a (Dash Under 8)   (181)   I-2   R-4
    Obverse III²7 – Small short dash well below second 8 with vertical mark on denticle underneath 8.

8   III²1 • C³b (O Shifted Right)   (181)   I-2   R-3
    Reverse C³b – Normal die with III O mint mark shifted to the right.

9   III²8 • C³a (Doubled 885)   (181)   I-3   R-3
    Obverse III²8 – Large vertical shift in 885 in date. Both 8's show a curved spike slanting down to left from middle right inside of lower loop. 5 has a faint horizontal curved line at lower inside of loop, and a vertical bar at left outside of loop opening.

1885-O

10   III² 9 • C³ a (Dash Under 8, Bar Ear) (181)   I-2   R-3

Obverse III² 9 – Small short dash just under second 8. Vertical die gouge in front of ear.

1A R Rusted Wing and Neck

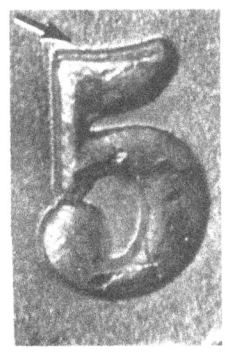
2 O Doubled 5

3 O Doubled 18

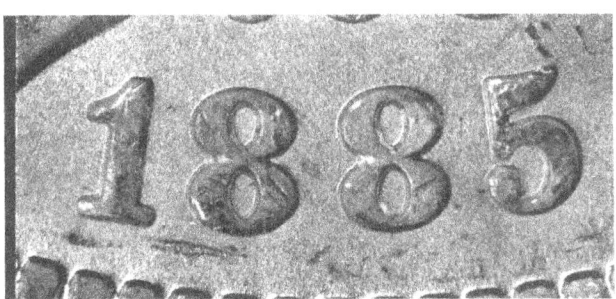
5 O Slanted Date

6 O Low Date

4 O Doubled 18

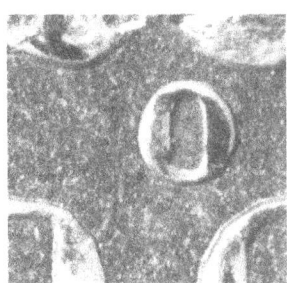
8 R O Shifted Right

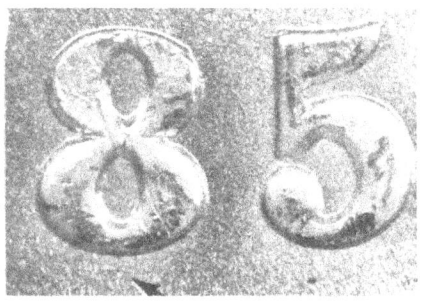
10 O Dash Under 8

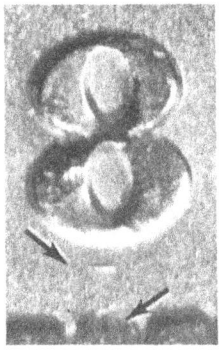
7 O Dash Under 8

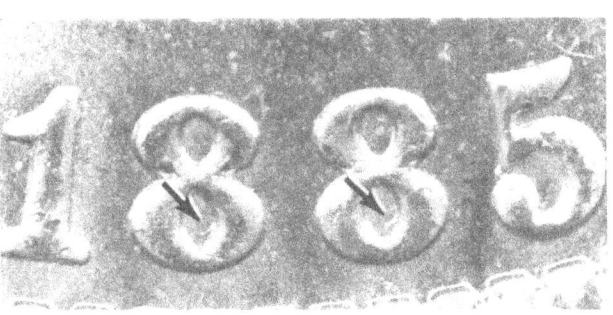
9 O Doubled 885

10 O Bar Ear

11	III²10 • C³c (Far Date, High O)	(181)	I-2	R-3
	Obverse III²10 – Date set farther right than normal.			
	Reverse C³c – Normal die with III O mint mark set high.			
12	III²1 • C³d (O/O Left)	(181)	I-2	R-4
	Reverse C³d – III O mint mark repunched with original showing as a vertical bar on left side of loop opening.			
13	III²10 • C³a (Far Date)	(181)	I-2	R-3
14	III²7 • C³b (Dash Under 8, O Shifted right)	(181)	I-2	R-3

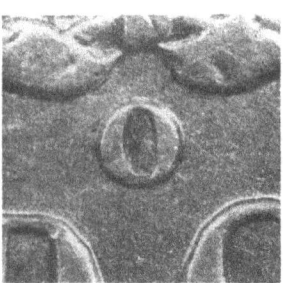 

11 R High O   12 R O/O Left

1885-S

The typical strike has a touch of weakness and some are fairly flat on the reverse. Bold strikes can be found however. The luster tends to be good. Several minor die varieties exist but VAM 6 has significant doubling of the S mint mark on the left side.

Proof-likes are quite scarce and a few deep mirror cameos exist. Quite a number of one sided proof-likes are available and the reflection depth should be checked on both sides when buying proof-likes.

1	III²1 • C³a (Normal Die)	(185, 187)	I-1	R-2
	Obverse III²1 – Normal die of III² type.			
	Reverse C³a – Normal die of C³ type with a medium IV S mint mark centered and upright.			
1A	III²1 • C³a (Die Flake in Wreath)	(187)	I-2	R-3
	Reverse C³a – Large die flake in wreath leaves opposite NI of UNITED. Same as VAM 7.			
2	III²2 • C³a (Doubled 5)		I-2	R-3
	Obverse III²2 – 5 in date doubled at top appearing as two short dashes on the left and right side.			
3	III²3 • C³a (Doubled 8)		I-2	R-3
	Obverse III²3 – Second 8 in date doubled faintly at the top and lower loop doubled on the top left.			
4	III²4 • C³a (Doubled 18)	(185)	I-2	R-4
	Obverse III²4 – Doubled 18 in date. 1 doubled slightly below upper crossbar and on left and right side of lower crossbar. First 8 doubled strongly on left outside of upper loop and lower left outside of lower loop.			
5	III²5 • C³a (Far Date)	(187)	I-2	R-3
	Obverse III²5 – Date set further right than normal.			
6	III²1 • C³b (S/S)		I-3	R-4
	Reverse C³b – IV S mint mark strongly doubled with original showing as vertical spike to left of lower serif, a thin diagonal line to left of upper loop, a curved line on right inside of lower loop, and a thin diagonal line on right inside of upper loop.			
7	III²6 • C³a (Doubled Date)	(187)	I-2	R-3
	Obverse III²6 – Entire date doubled slightly at very top of digits.			
	Reverse C³a – Some specimens show a large die flake in wreath leaves opposite NI of UNITED.			

1885-S / 1886-P

2 O Doubled 5

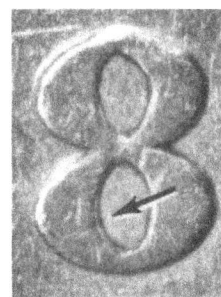

3 O Doubled 8

4 O Doubled 18

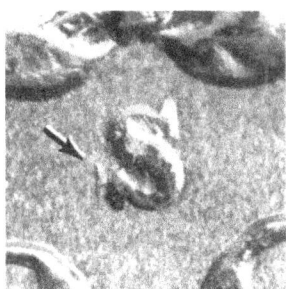

6 R S/S

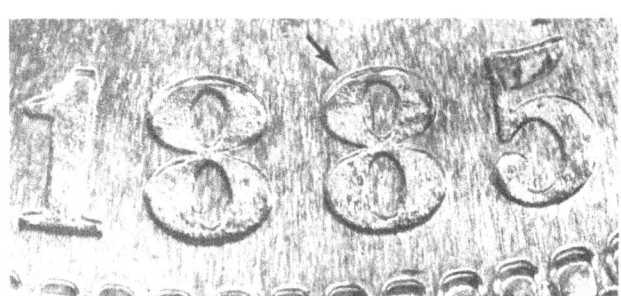

7 O Doubled Date

7 R Die Break in Leaves

1886-P

The usual strike on this issue is full although there are some specimens with a touch of weakness. Luster is generally good but a sizeable proportion are dull due to worn dies. These coins exhibit surface roughness and radial flow lines in the fields due to die erosion by the planchet metal moving against the die surfaces when struck. This dull luster from worn dies is common for the 1886-1891-P mint coins. A fair number of minor die varieties exist with doubled dates but none are very significant.

Proof-likes are somewhat available but most have only moderate mirror depth and light frosted contrast. Some very deep mirror cameos do exist however. Proofs have adequate but not striking contrast and many coins are plagued with hairlines.

1	III²1 • C³a (Closed 6)		(189)	I-1	R-1

Obverse III²1 – Normal die of III² type with closed 6. Upper knob touches lower loop. Some specimens show die chip between loops of first 8 on left side and some show die chips in upper loop of 6.
Reverse C³a – Normal die of C³ type.

1A	III²1 • C³a (Line in 6)		I-2	R-4

Obverse III²1 – Thick horizontal line curving down at right end in lower part of upper loop of 6.

1B	III²1 • C³a (Die Gouge in M)		I-2	R-4

Obverse III²1 – Die gouge in designer's initial M at base of neck showing as a horizontal curved line.

2	III²2 • C³a (Open 6)		(189)	I-1	R-2

Obverse III²2 – Normal die of C³ type with open 6. Upper knob distinctly separate from lower loop.

3	III²3 • C³a (Doubled 1 Weak)			I-2	R-3

Obverse III²3 – 1 in date doubled below the crossbar. Closed 6 variety. Some specimens show a thin dash well below second 8.

4	III²4 • C³a (Doubled 18 Strong)		(190)	I-3	R-3

Obverse III²4 – 18 in date doubled. 1 doubled below top crossbar. First 8 doubled at top inside of upper loop and slightly at right outside of lower loop. Doubling more pronounced than III²3 obverse. Closed 6 variety.

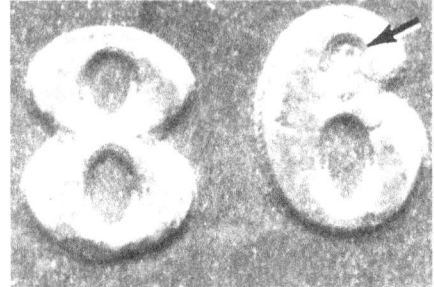  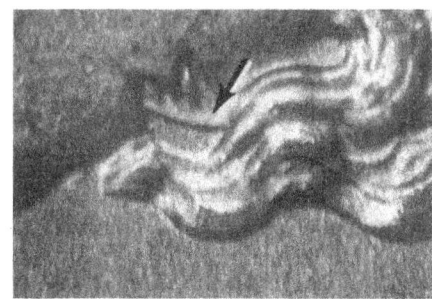

1 O Die Chips in 6   1A O Line in 6   1B O Die Gouge in M

3 O Doubled 1 Weak   4 O Doubled 1 Strong   5 O Doubled 18

| 5 | III²5 • C³a (Doubled 18) | (190) | I-3 | R-3 |

Obverse III²5 – 18 in date doubled. Doubling of the 1 appears as a line under the top crossbar and projecting out from the stem. Loops of the 8 are doubled inside at top. Closed 6 variety.

| 6 | III²6 • C³a (High 6) | (188) | I-2 | R-3 |

Obverse III²6 – 6 in date punched higher than normal.

| 7 | III²7 • C³a (High Date) | (190) | I-2 | R-3 |

Obverse III²7 – Entire date set higher than normal. Open and closed 6 varieties.

| 8 | III²8 • C³a (Far Date, High 6) | | I-2 | R-3 |

Obverse III²8 – Date set further right than normal with closed 6 set slightly high.

| 9 | III²9 • C³a (Doubled 1-6) | (189) | I-3 | R-4 |

Obverse III²9 – 1-6 doubled strongly. 1 is doubled strongly at very bottom. Closed 6 is doubled strongly at top. Date set further right than normal.

| 10 | III²10 • C³a (Doubled 18) | | I-2 | R-3 |

Obverse III²10 – 18 in date doubled. 1 doubled well below as a thin line. First 8 doubled at bottom and on right side of lower loop as a thin line. High 6 in date.

| 11 | III²11 • C³a (Doubled 188) | | I-3 | R-4 |

Obverse III²11 – 188 in date doubled. 1 is doubled strongly below crossbar. First 8 doubled at upper right inside of upper loop and at bottom right outside. Second 8 doubled on lower left inside of bottom loop.

| 12 | III²12 • C³a (Doubled Date) | (189) | I-2 | R-4 |

Obverse III²12 – Entire date doubled. 1 has short horizontal spike just below upper crossbar. First 8 is slightly doubled on left bottom outside of upper loop showing as a thin curved line. Second 8 is doubled slightly at top inside of upper loop. Both loops of the 6 are doubled inside at the top left with the top one being strong and ending bluntly on the right side.

| 13 | III²13 • C³a (Near Date) | (189) | I-2 | R-4 |

Obverse III²13 – Date set further left than normal with closed 6. Second with horizontal die chip at top inside of upper loop of second 8.

| 14 | III²14 • C³a (Dash Under 8) | (189) | I-2 | R-4 |

Obverse III²14 – Faint dash under second 8 in date.

1886-P

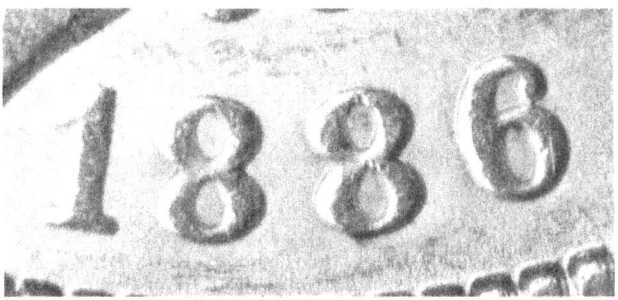
6 O High 6

7 O High Date

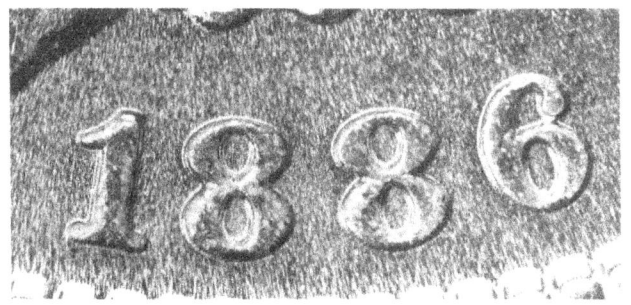
8 O High 6

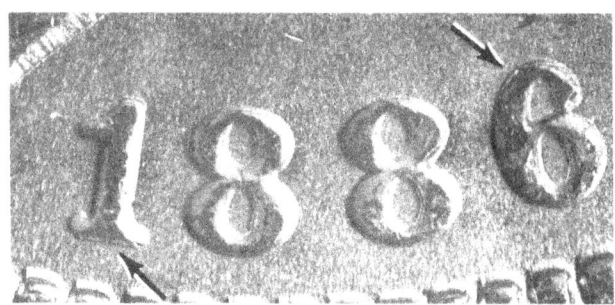
9 O Doubled 1-6

10 O Doubled 18

13 O Near Date, Bar 8

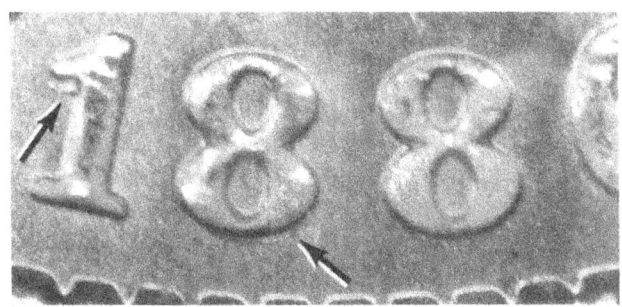
11 O Doubled 188

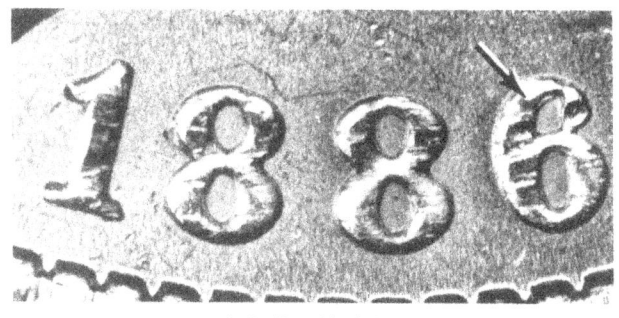
12 O Doubled Date

1886-P / 1886-O

15	III²15 • C³a (Doubled 18-6, Dash 8)	(179)		I-2	Proof

Obverse III²15 – Doubled 18-6 in date. 1 doubled below upper crossbar as a thin line and slightly below bottom crossbar. First 8 doubled at top inside of upper loop and bottom outside of lower loop. 6 doubled slightly at bottom outside of lower loop. Second 8 has a thick dash adjacent to bottom of lower loop.

16	III²15 • C³a (Doubled 1)	(189)		I-2	R-3

Obverse III²15 – 1 doubled at bottom of base.

17	III²1 • C³b (Doubled Arrows)	(190)		I-2	R-3

Reverse C³b – Lower three arrow feathers doubled at bottom, wreath bow doubled at top inside, and olive branch doubled at far left.

18	III²16 • C³a (Doubled 6)	(189)		I-2	R-3

Obverse III²16 – 6 doubled at very top outside as a curved line.

14 O Dash Under 8

16 O Doubled 1

18 O Doubled 6

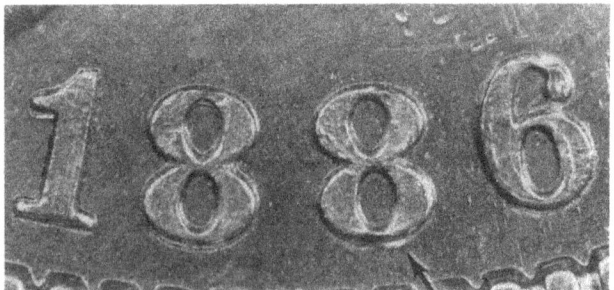
Proof 15 O Doubled 18-6, Dash Under 8

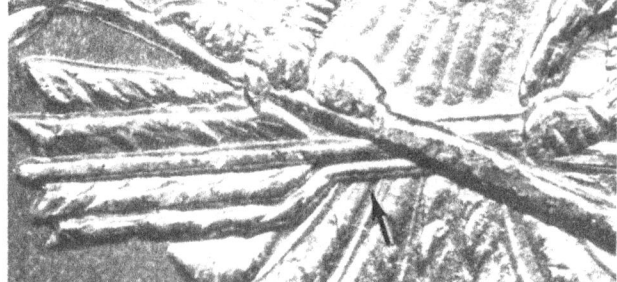
17 R Doubled Arrows

1886-O

This issue is typically fairly well struck but some weak strikes are around and sliders are plentiful. Luster is usually average but can vary considerably. A number of die varieties exist. The only significant one is VAM 1A with an "E" under the eagle's tail feathers due to clashed dies. It is fairly scarce in circulated grades and quite rare in uncirculated condition. Higher grade circulated and uncirculated VAM 1A specimens command some price premiums. Fully prooflike specimens in general are extremely rare and vary considerably in strike and contrast. However, what many consider to be the most spectacular Morgan dollar in terms of depth of mirror, cameo contrast, lack of abrasions and rarity is the 1886-O formerly in the Wayne Miller collection.

1	III²1 • C3 a (Normal Die)	(181)		I-1	R-2

Obverse III²1 – Normal die of III² type with closed 6.
Reverse C³a – Normal die of C³ type with circular medium III O mint mark centered and upright.

1A	III²1 • C³a (E on Reverse)	(181)		I-4	R-4

Reverse C³a – Clashed die with full E under eagle's tail feathers on left side.

2	III²2 • C³a (High 6)	(181)		I-2	R-3

Obverse III²2 – Normal die with high 6 in date.

1886-O

3	III²6 • C³a (Open 6)	(181)		I-2	R-3

Obverse III²6 – Normal die of III² type with open 6.

4	III²1 • C³b (O Tilted Left)	(181)		I-2	R-3

Reverse C³b – Normal die with III O mint mark tilted to the left.

5	III²3 • C³a (Doubled 18)	(181)		I-2	R-3

Obverse III²3 – 18 in date doubled. Short stem of original 1 projects below bottom crossbar of new 1. First 8 is doubled to the lower left just below bottom loop. Closed 6 variety.

6	III²4 • C³c (Doubled 1)	(181)		I-2	R-3

Obverse III²4 – 1 in date doubled at top. Closed 6 variety.
Reverse C³c – Normal die with III O mint mark tilted to the right.

7	III²1 • C³d (O/O Down)	(181)		I-3	R-4

Reverse C³d – Mint mark repunched with original showing as two arcs at bottom.

8	III²2 • C³e (O Set High)	(181)		I-2	R-3

Reverse C³e – III O mint mark set high.

9	III²5 • C³a (Doubled 6)	(181)		I-2	R-4

Obverse III²5 – 6 in date doubled at top outside as a thin curved line.

10	III²6 • C³e (Doubled 18-6)	(181)		I-3	R-4

Obverse III²6 – Doubled 18-6 in date. 1 doubled as a thin line on right side below lower crossbar. First 8 doubled below lower loop. 6 doubled at top outside of upper loop.

11	III²7 • C³e (Near Date, O Set High)	(181)		I-2	R-3

Obverse III²7 – Date set further left than normal and set slightly high.

12	III²8 • C³a (Doubled 6)	(181)		I-2	R-3

Obverse III²8 – 6 doubled at top inside of upper loop. Date set further left than normal.

13	III²9 • C³a (Doubled 1)	(181)		I-2	R-3

Obverse III²9 – 1 doubled slightly below upper crossbar.

14	III²10 • C³a (Far Date)	(181)		I-2	R-3

Obverse III²10 – Date set further right than normal.

15	III²1 • C³f (O Set Right)	(181)		I-2	R-3

Reverse C³f – Medium III O mint mark upright and set slightly to right.

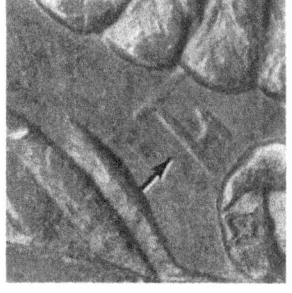

1A R E

2 O High 6

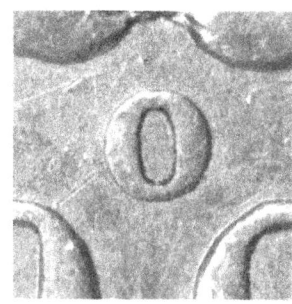

4 R O Tilted Left

5 O Doubled 18

6 O Doubled 1

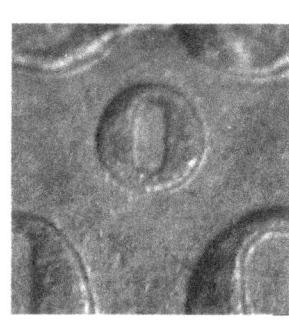

6 R O Tilted Right

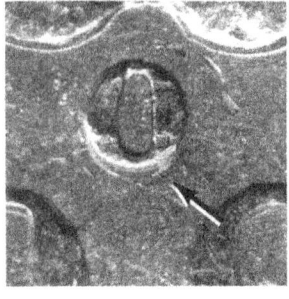 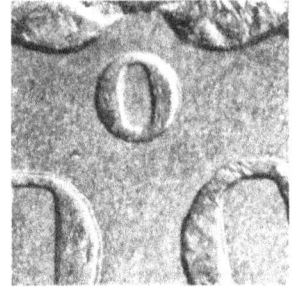 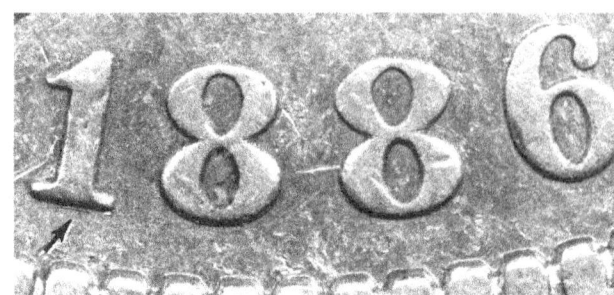

7 R O/O   8 R O Set High   10 O Doubled 18-6

9 O Doubled 6 *Photo Not Available*

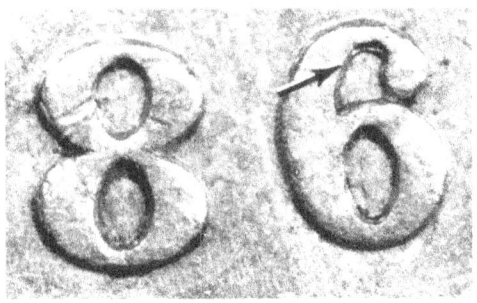 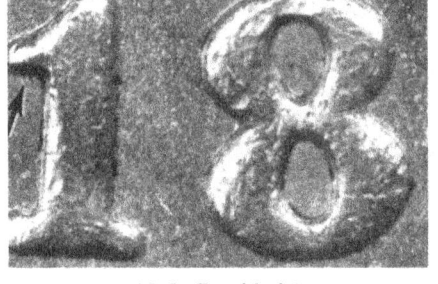 

12 O Doubled 6   13 O Doubled 1   15 R O Set Right

1886-S

The 1886-S usually comes fully struck with good luster. Because of the fairly low mintage, many semi prooflike specimens exist. Full proof-likes are somewhat available with a few of these being deep mirror cameos. Only a couple minor die varieties exist.

1   III²1 • C³a (Normal Die)   I-1   R-3
     Obverse III²1 – Normal die of III² type with closed 6.
     Reverse C³a – Normal die of C³ type with a medium IV S mint mark centered and upright.
     Note: Some specimens show die chips in bottom of top loop of 6 and in I, G and E of IN GOD WE and O of OF on the reverse.

1A   III²1 • C³a (Lines in 6)   (187)   I-2   R-3
     Obverse III²1 – 6 in date has horizontal polishing lines in lower loop.

2   III²1 • C³b (S/S)   (187)   I-2   R-4
     Obverse III²1 – Some specimens have die chips in 6 all across opening of top loop and in the upper part of the lower loop.
     Reverse C³b – Doubled IV S mint mark tilted left with thin vertical line to right of top serif and metal at top left side of bottom serif.

3   III²2 • C³c (Doubled 18-6, S Tilted Left)   (187)   I-2   R-3
     Obverse III²2 – 18-6 in date doubled. 1 and first 8 are doubled at very bottom next to field. 6 is doubled slightly at very top outside of upper loop next to field. 6 also shows die chips in lower part of upper loop.
     Reverse C³c – IV S mint mark centered with slight tilt to left and doubled on outside of upper and lower serifs.

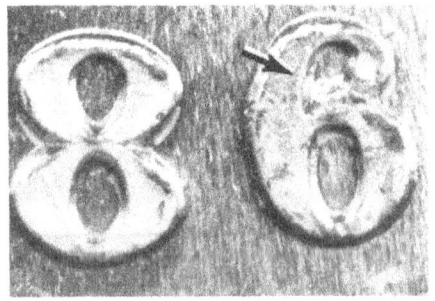 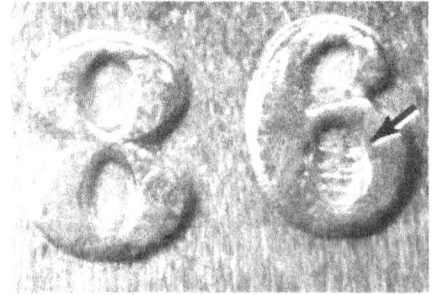 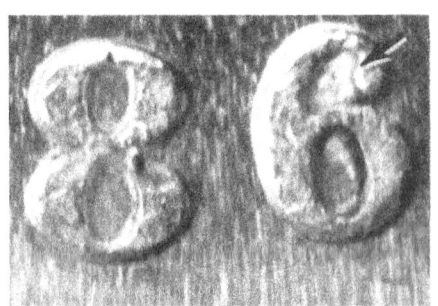

1 O Die Chips in 6   1A O Lines in 6   2 O Die Chips in 6

1886-S / 1887-P

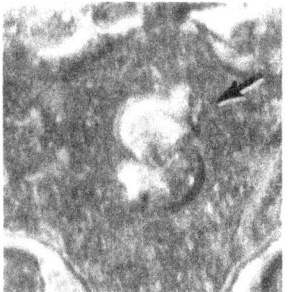  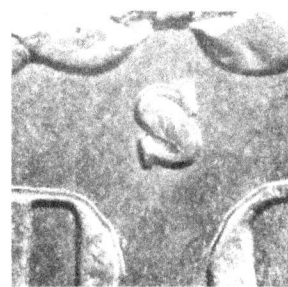

2 R S/S   3 O Doubled 18-6   3 R S Tilted Left

1887-P

On the average this issue is not quite as fully struck nor is the luster as good as the 1886-P. However, because of the high mintage fully struck lustrous specimens can be found. The 1887-P frequently has indentations in the jaw and neck area due to grease and debris having collected in the deepest recesses of the die cavity. If large and distracting, these indentations can lower the value of an otherwise high grade BU coin. A fair number of minor die varieties exist with most of these being doubled date digits. How ever, VAM 2 7/6 overdate has remains of the 6 showing as curved lines on either side of the bottom of the 7 and brings a substantial premium in all grades.

Proof-like are somewhat available as for the 1886-P, but the contrast tends to be less. A few deep mirror cameos are available. Proofs have adequate but not striking contrast.

1   III^{2}1 • C^{3}a (Normal Die)   (190)   I-1   R-1
     Obverse III^{2}1 – Normal die of III^2 type. Some specimens show die chips between loops of 8's in various combinations such as on both sides of first 8, on left side of second 8, on left side of first 8 and on both sides of second 8, on right side of both 8's, on left side of first 8 and on right side of second 8, on right side of first 8 and both sides of second 8.
     Reverse C^{3}a – Normal die of C^3 type.

1A   III^{2}1 • C^{3}a (D With Tail)   I-2   R-6
     Reverse C^{3}a – Die break on D in DOLLAR to form tail.

2   III^{2}2 • C^{3}a (7/6)   (189)   I-5   R-4
     Obverse III^{2}2 – 7 repunched over 6 in date. The bottom loop of the 6 shows as a long curved line starting up slightly from the lower right bottom of the 7 and extending upwards one-third the digit height. On the left side of the stem, a short spike slants upwards at a point one-third the way up on the stem height. A short vertical spike shows at the very top of the 7 crossbar in the middle. A short spike also slants upwards from the middle right side of the crossbar.

3   III^{2}3 • C^{3}a (Doubled 1-7)   (189)   I-3   R-4
     Obverse III^{2}3 – 1-7 in date doubled. 1 is doubled below upper crossbar. 7 is doubled strongly at very top. Entire date is set further left than normal. Some specimens show a die chip between loops of first 8 on left and second 8 on right.

4   III^{2}4 • C^{3}a (Doubled 18-7)   (190)   I-2   R-4
     Obverse III^{2}4 – Doubled 18 and 7 in date. The 1 and 8 are doubled slightly at bottom. First 8 also doubled at top inside of lower loop. 7 is doubled all across the top and there is a vertical spike above the top left serif. Date set further left than normal.

5   III^{2}5 • C^{3}a (Doubled Date)   (190)   I-4   R-4
     Obverse III^{2}5 – Entire date doubled. The 1 is doubled slightly on top left side of lower crossbar. First 8 is doubled at top inside of upper loop and die chip is between the loops on the left side. Second 8 is doubled strongly at top inside of upper loop and die chips between the loops on both sides. The 7 is doubled below the crossbar and on the right side. Date set further left than normal.

6   III^{2}6 • C^{3}a (Spiked Tail Feather, Low Date)   (189)   I-2   R-3
     Obverse III^{2}6 – Entire date set lower and further right than normal with die chip between loops of first 8 on left side.
     Reverse C^{3}a – Third tail feather has a die gouge under it showing as a thin horizontal line.

7   III^{2}7 • C^{3}a (Doubled 18 Weak)   (190)   I-2   R-3
     Obverse III^{2}7 – 18 in date doubled slightly at bottom. Date set further left than normal.

8*   III^{2}8 • C^{3}a (Far Slanted Date)   (190)   I-2   R-3
     Obverse III^{2}8 – Date set further right than normal and slanted with 1 closest to rim.
     * The former VAM 8 is the same as VAM 11.

1887-P

9   III²9 • C³a (Doubled 18 Strong)   (189)   I-3   R-4
Obverse III²9 – 18 in date doubled strongly all across bottom.

10   III²10 • C³a (Doubled 18)   (189)   I-2   R-3
Obverse III²10 – 1 doubled weakly at bottom. First 8 in date doubled at bottom with die chip to left of loops on some specimens.

1A R D with Tail

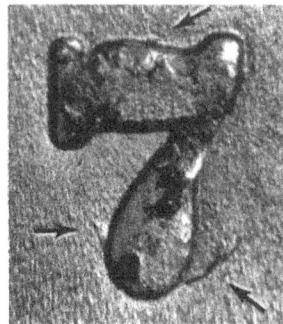
2 O 7/6

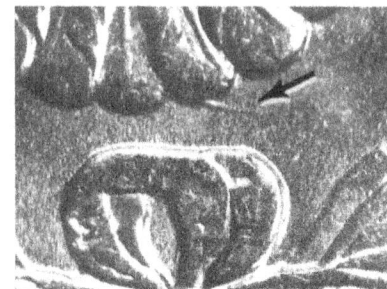
6 R Die Gouge

3 O Doubled 1-7

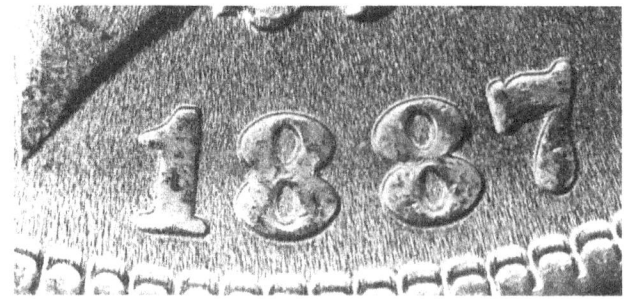
6 O Low and Far Date

4 O Doubled 18-7

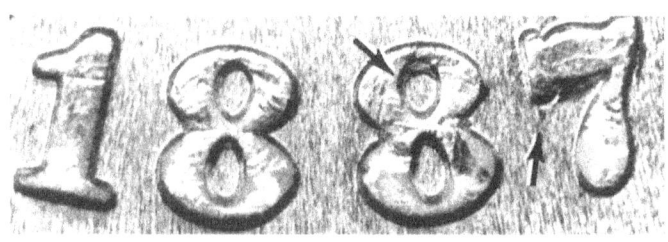
5 O Doubled Date

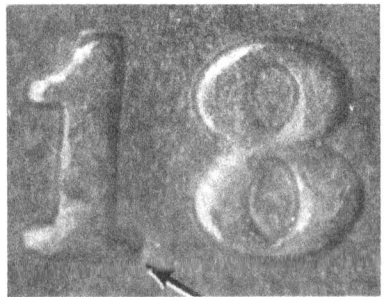
7 O Doubled 18 Weak

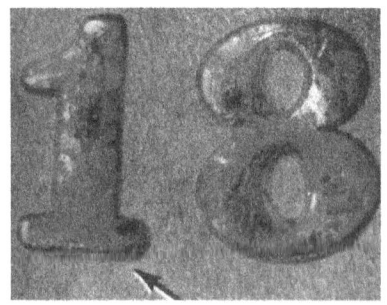
9 O Doubled 18 Strong

10 O Doubled 18

1887-P

11	III²11 • C³a (Doubled 18-7)	(189)	I-3	R-4

Obverse III²11 – Doubled 18 and 7 in date. The 1 and first 8 are doubled all across the bottom. 7 doubled at top. The first 8 has a die chip between the loops on the left in some specimens.

12	III²12 • C³a (Doubled LIBERTY)	(190)	I-2	R-3

Obverse III²12 – Stars on each side of the date are doubled at bottom. Letters PLURIB are doubled at top. LIBERTY is doubled to the right.

13	III²13 • C³a (Doubled Stars)	(190)	I-3	R-4

Obverse III²13 – First four stars on right and first two stars on left doubled at bottom with first two on right showing strong shifts.

14	III²14 • C³a (Near Date)	(189)	I-2	R-3

Obverse III²14 – Date set further left than normal.

15	III²15 • C³a (Doubled Stars and Motto)	(189)	I-3	R-4

Obverse III²15 – First three stars on right, all stars on left and motto letters RIB doubled towards rim. Front of eye doubled and LIBERTY slightly doubled on right side.

16	III²1 • C³b (Doubled Reverse Legend)	(190)	I-2	R-3

Reverse C³b – Doubled ITED STATES OF AMERICA AR, right star towards rim and some outer edges or right wreath leaves.

8 O Far Slanted Date

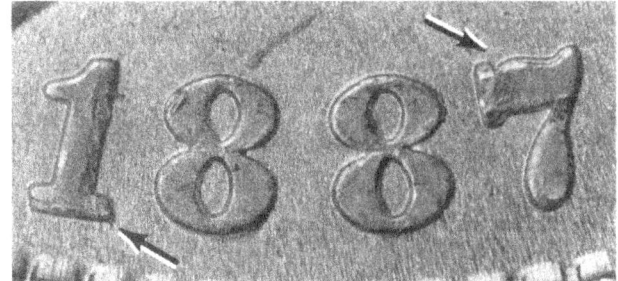

11 O Doubled 18-7

12 O Doubled LIBERTY

13 O Doubled Stars

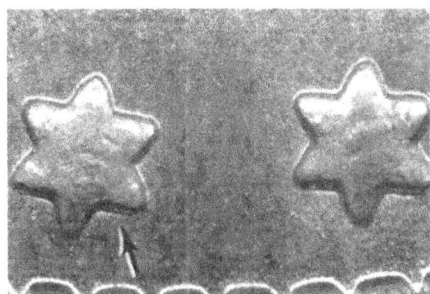

15 O Doubled Stars

16 R Doubled AMERICA

1887-O

Strike on this issue ranges from very weak to full with most coins having some trace of weakness. Luster is quite variable as well. Because of the high mintage lustrous fully struck specimens can be located however. Like the 1887-P there is one die variety, VAM 3, with the 7/6 overdate. The curved lines of the 6 base is not quite as prominent at the bottom of the 7 however. It is a little scarcer in most grades than the 1887-P 7/6 overdate but rare in MS64 and above. Most of the 1887-O 7/6 are slightly weakly struck and some later die states are very weak. Fully proof-like overdates are unknown in contrast to the P mint overdate where some are fully proof-like. A number of other die varieties exist but all are minor except VAM 2. This variety shows remains of the 1-7 first punch way to the left of the date which is the largest shift of date doubling in the Morgan dollar series.

Proof-likes are somewhat available but they tend to have soft strikes. A fair proportion are deep mirror cameos exist. According to Wayne Miller, the Amon Carter, Jr. collection had a branch mint 1887-O which is the only one known.

1   III^2 1 • C^3 a (Normal Die)   (181)   I-1   R-1
     Obverse III^2 1 – Normal die of III^2 type. Some specimens show die chips between loops on both sides of first 8.
     Reverse C^3 a – Normal die of C^3 type with circular medium III O mint mark centered and upright.

2   III^2 2 • C^3 a (Doubled 1, Tripled 7)   (181)   I-5   R-4
     Obverse III^2 2 – The entire date has been doubled with shift to the right. The top point of the original 1 is visible to the left of the new 1 with dot of metal at top. The 7 is tripled with doubling at the top and a dot of metal to the left of the crossbar and metal at the extreme lower left. One of the largest shifts of date doubling known.

3   III^2 3 • C^3 a (7/6)   (181)   I-5   R-4
     Obverse III^2 3 – 7 repunched over 6 in date. The bottom loop of the 6 shows as a long curved line starting from the lower right bottom of the stem of the 7 and extending upwards almost half the digit height. On the left side of the stem, a short spike curves to the left and then up at a point one third the way up on the stem height.
     Reverse C^3 a – Some specimens show depression in eagle's breast due to weak strike.

4   III^2 4 • C^3 a (Doubled 1-7)   (181)   I-2   R-3
     Obverse III^2 4 – Doubled 1-7 in date. The 1 is doubled at the top and the 7 is doubled at the bottom.

5   III^2 5 • C^3 a (Doubled Stars and Motto)   (181)   I-5   R-5
     Obverse III^2 5 – A doubled die in the radial direction causing all stars and lettering to be doubled next to rim. Denticles are filled below and to the left of date. Die chips between loops of first 8 on left and second 8 on right.

6   III^2 6 • C^3 a (Doubled 188)   (181)   I-3   R-3
     Obverse III^2 6 – 1 in date doubled all across very bottom. Both 8's doubled at bottom inside at lower loop.

7   III^2 7 • C^3 a (Doubled 18)   (181)   I-2   R-3
     Obverse III^2 7 – 1 and 8 in date doubled slightly all the way across very bottom.

8   III^2 8 • C^3 a (Doubled 87)   (181)   I-2   R-4
     Obverse III^2 8 – 87 in date doubled at bottom. Second 8 has thin curved line at bottom left side. The 7 has a short diagonal line well below bottom also on the left side. The first 8 has a die chip between the loops on the left side.

9   III^2 9 • C^3 a (Doubled 1-7 Top)   (181)   I-2   R-4
     Obverse III^2 9 – Doubled 1-7 in date. The 1 is doubled strongly at bottom of upper serif and 7 is doubled slightly all across the top.

10   III^2 10 • C^3 a (Doubled 87)   (181)   I-2   R-3
     Obverse III^2 10 – Doubled 87 in date. Second 8 doubled at lower left outside. 7 doubled slightly at very top. Die chips between loops of first 8 on left and right and on second 8 on right.

1A R Pitted Reverse

2 O Doubled 1, Tripled 7

1887-O

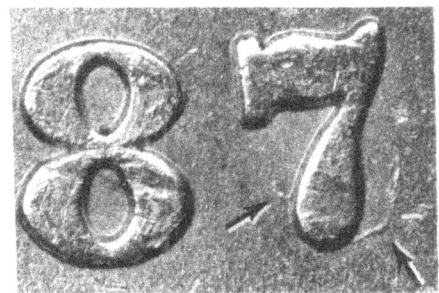
3 O 7/6

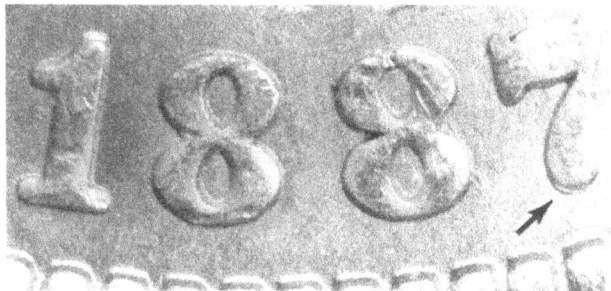
4 O Doubled 1-7

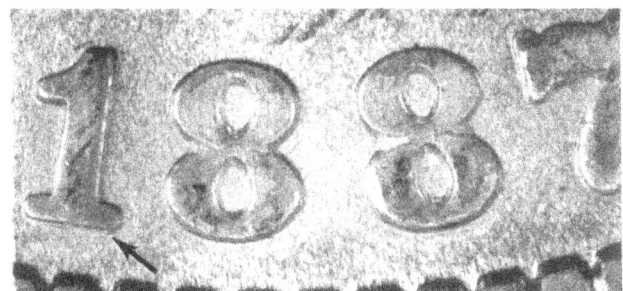
6 O Doubled 188

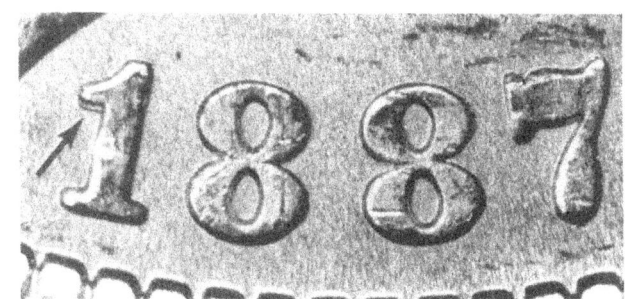
9 O Doubled 1-7 Top

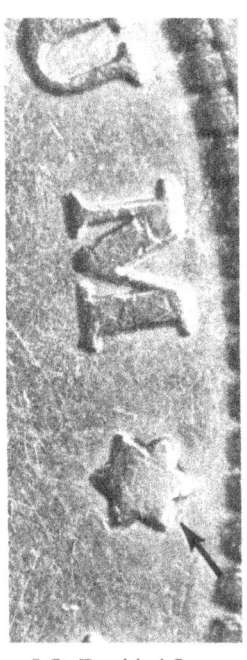
5 O Doubled Stars and Motto

7 O Doubled 18

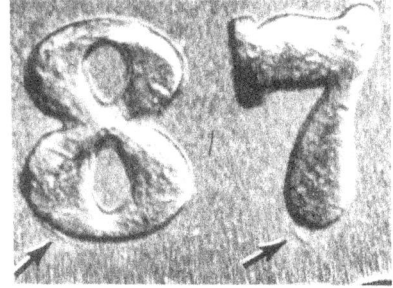
8 O Doubled 87

10 O Doubled 87

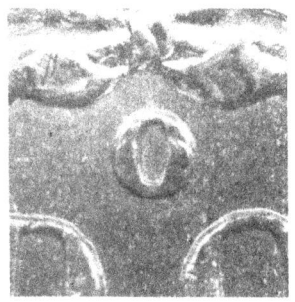
13 R O Set Right

11	III² 11 • C³ a (Near Date)	(181)	I-2	R-3
	Obverse III² 11 – Date set further left than normal.			
12	III² 12 • C³ a (Far Date)	(181)	I-2	R-3
	Obverse III² 12 – Date set further right than normal.			
13	III² 13 • C³ b (Near Date, O Shifted Right)	(181)	I-2	R-3
	Reverse C³ b – Normal die with III O mint mark shifted slightly left.			

1887-O

| 14 | III² 13 • C³ a (Low Date) | (181) | I-2 | R-3 |

Obverse III² 13 – Date set further left than normal with 1 close to rim.

| 15 | III² 14 • C³ a (Doubled 1-87) | (181) | I-2 | R-3 |

Obverse III² 14 – Doubled 1-87 in date. 1 doubled at top left of lower crossbar. 8 doubled faintly at top outside of upper loop. 7 doubled strongly all across very top. Date set much further left than normal.

| 16 | III² 15 • C³ a (Doubled 1) | (181) | I-2 | R-3 |

Obverse III² 15 – 1 doubled slightly below upper crossbar. Date set further right than normal.

| 17 | III² 16 • C³ a (Doubled 8-7) | (181) | I-2 | R-3 |

Obverse III² 16 – Doubled 8-7 in date. First 8 doubled slightly on bottom right outside of lower loop. 7 doubled about upper serif. Date set further right than normal.

18	III² 8 • C³ b (Far Date, O Shifted Right)	(181)	I-2	R-3
19	III² 1 • C³ b (O Shifted Right)	(181)	I-2	R-3
20	III² 17 • C³ a (Doubled 88)	(181)	I-2	R-3

Obverse III² 17 – Doubled 88 in date. First 8 doubled at bottom outside of lower loop. Second 8 doubled very slightly also at bottom outside of lower loop.

| 21 | III² 1 • C³ c (O Tilted Right) | (181) | I-2 | R-3 |

Reverse C³ c – III O mint mark centered and tilted slightly to right.

| 22 | III² 18 • C³ a (Doubled Eyelid & Stars, Pitted Reverse) | (181) | I-3 | R-3 |

Obverse III² 18 – All left stars doubled towards rim and eyelid doubled underneath.
Reverse C³ a – Pitted die below eagle's tail feathers.

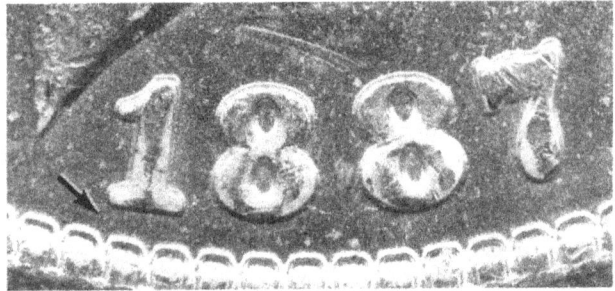
14 O Low Date

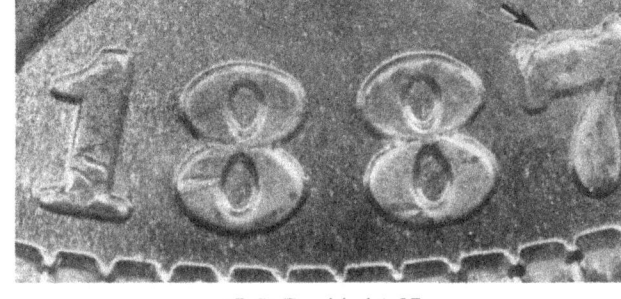
15 O Doubled 1-87

16 O Doubled 1, Far Date

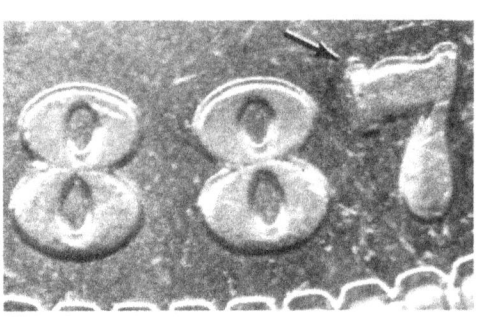
17 O Doubled 8-7

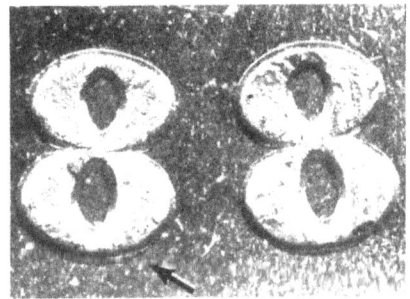
20 O Doubled 88

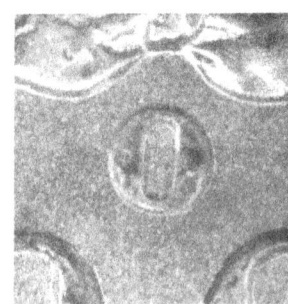
21 R O Tilted Right

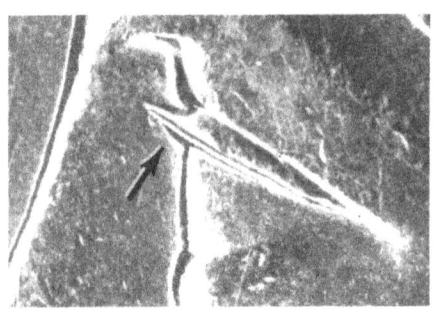
22 O Doubled Eyelid

1887-S

Typically the strike is good as well as the luster for this issue. It is difficult, however, to find specimens without excessive bag marks. A few die varieties exist but all are fairly minor. Proof-likes are fairly scarce and some are cameos. One sided proof-likes are not uncommon.

1   **III²1 • C³a (Normal Die)**   (185)   I-1   R-2
    Obverse III²1 – Normal die of III² type. Some specimens show die chips between the loops of the first 8 on the left side and second 8 on the right side.
    Reverse C³a – Normal die of C³ type with a medium IV S mint mark, centered and upright.

2   **III²1 • C³b (S/S Left)**   (187)   I-3   R-4
    Obverse III²1 – Some specimens show die chip between loops of second 8 on the right side.
    Reverse C³b – Mint mark repunched with original showing arcs within the top and bottom loops.

3   **III²2 • C³a (Slanted Date, Doubled 7)**   (187)   I-2   R-3
    Obverse III²2 – Both 8's have die chips between loops on left side. 7 is doubled at bottom of crossbar. Date set high with right side slanted up.

4   **III²3 • C³a (Doubled 1-7)**   I-3   R-3
    Obverse III²3 – Doubled 1 and 7 in date. The 1 is doubled at top left as two curved lines well away from 1. The 7 has a dot and short vertical line to left of top left serif. Liberty head profile slightly doubled. Date set further left than normal.

5   **III²4 • C³a (Near Date)**   I-2   R-3
    Obverse III²4 – Date set further left than normal with die chip between loops of first 8 on left.

6   **III²5 • C³a (Very Near Date)**   (186)   I-2   R-3
    Obverse III²5 – Date set much further left than normal.

7   **III²1 • C³c (High S)**   (185)   I-2   R-3
    Reverse C³c – IV S mint mark set high.

8   **III²6 • C³a (Far Date)**   (186)   I-2   R-3
    Obverse III²6 – Date set further right than normal.

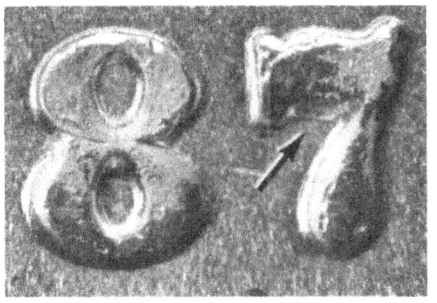

3 O Doubled 7

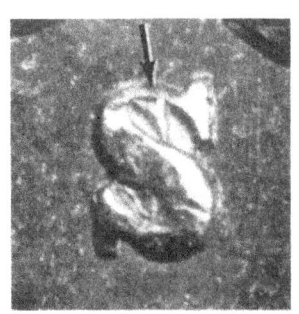

2 R S/S Left

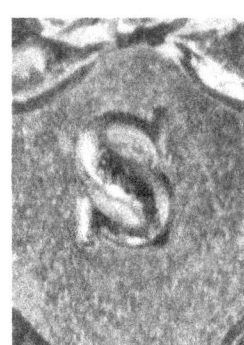

7 R High S

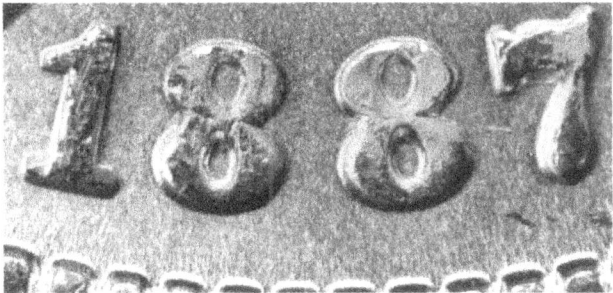

3 O Slanted Date

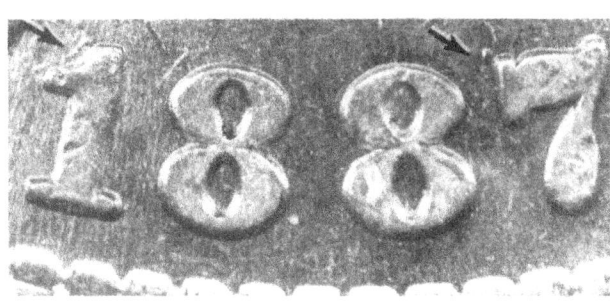

4 O Doubled 1-7

1888-P

An average strike is typical for this issue although a number of weak strikes are around. Luster tends to be fairly good. Nice fully struck specimens with good luster can be located with some searching. A number of minor die varieties exist but none are very significant. Proof-likes are fairly scarce and most have only moderate contrast. Proofs have fairly good contrast but a number have slight weakness in strike in the hair over the ear.

1   III²1 • C³a (Normal Die)   (188, 190)   I-1   R-1
Obverse III²1 – Normal die of III² type. Some specimens show die chip between loops of first 8 on right side.
Reverse C³a – Normal die of C³ type.

2   III²2 • C³a (Near and High Date)   (190)   I-2   R-3
Obverse III²2 – Date set further left and higher than normal.

3   III²3 • C³a (Very Near Date)   (190)   I-2   R-3
Obverse III²3 – Date set much further left than normal.

4   III²1 • C³b (Doubled Reverse)   I-3   R-4
Obverse III²1 – Die crack through bottom of date with die chip on lower left bottom of first 8.
Reverse C³b – Outer portion doubled with lower inside of lettering doubled in UNITED STATES OF AMERICA and top inside of NE-OL-AR. Outside of eagles right wing, motto, upper part of left wreath on outside and lower outside of right wreath slightly doubled.

5   III²4 • C³a (Doubled 1)   (190)   I-2   R-3
Obverse III²4 – 1 doubled at top as thin, short, curved line.

6   III²1 • C³c (Doubled Reverse)   I-3   R-4
Reverse C³c – Outer portion doubled with letters doubled in outward direction in UNITED STATES, F, ONE, D-LAR and left star. IN GOD WE and left wreath slightly doubled.

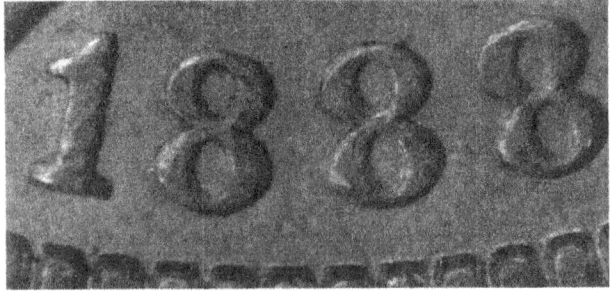

2 O Near and High Date

4 R Doubled Legend

4 R Doubled Legend

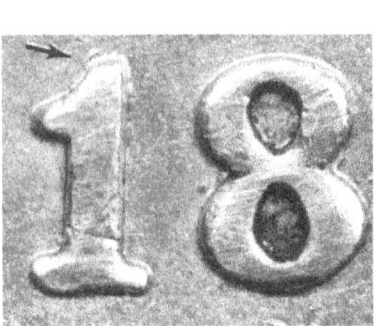

5 O Doubled 1

6 R Doubled Reverse

1888-P

7	**III²5 • C³d (Near Slanted Date, Doubled Reverse)**		I-3	R-4

Obverse III²5 – Date set further left than normal and slanted with 1 close to rim.
Reverse C³d – Top left doubled with NITED doubled towards rim and STATES OF AMERIC and motto doubled towards the left. Outside edge of eagle's right wing, left middle outside of eagle's left wing, top of eagle's beak, and upper left outside of left wreath slightly doubled. Upper left field is rough with polishing lines and fine die chips. Large long horizontal polishing lines across eagle's tail feathers and arrow shafts.

8	**III²6 • C³a (Near Slanted Date)**	(190)	I-2	R-3

Obverse III²6 – Date set further left than normal and slanted with last 8 far from rim. Date set higher than VAM 7.

9	**III²7 • C³a (High Date)**	(190)	I-2	R-2

Obverse III²7 – Date set higher than normal.

10	**III²8 • C³a (Slanted Date)**	(190)	I-2	R-3

Obverse III²8 – Date slanted with last 8 far from rim. Date lateral position is normal.

11	**III²9 • C³a (Doubled Ear)**		I-3	R-4

Obverse III²9 – Ear strongly doubled on right outside of large lobe and on right side of small inner lobe. Hairline just above ear is slightly doubled.

12	**III²7 • C³e (High Date, Doubled Reverse)**	(190)	I-2	R-3

Reverse C³e – Lower inside of letters doubled in U-TED STATES OF AMERICA, right wreath top inside of LLAR and right star towards rim. Left and right wreath doubled towards rim. W-RUST in motto doubled at top.

13	**III²10 • C³a (Far Date)**	(190)	I-2	R-3

Obverse III²10 – Date set further right than normal.

14	**III²11 • C³a (Doubled Stars, Near Date)**	(190)	I-2	R-3

Obverse III²11 – All left and right stars doubled towards rim. Lower parts of UNUM doubled towards rim. Date set further left than normal.

15	**III²12 • C³a (Doubled Last 8)**	(190)	I-3	R-4

Obverse III²12 – Last 8 in date doubled in lower loop as two thick vertical lines.

16	**III²13 • C³f (Doubled 1, Doubled Lower Reverse)**	(190)	I-2	R-3

Obverse III²13 – 1 doubled slightly below upper crossbar.
Reverse C³f – Lower reverse doubled including lower wreath and bow, bottom arrow shaft and NE DOL-AR.

17	**III²1 • C³g (Die Chips in 8's, Doubled Reverse)**	(189)	I-2	R-3

Obverse III²1 – Die chips in lower loops of first and third 8's.
Reverse C³g – Doubled outside of left and right wreaths, IN GOD WE TRUST, MERICA and E-AR.

7 O Near Slanted Date

7 R Doubled Reverse

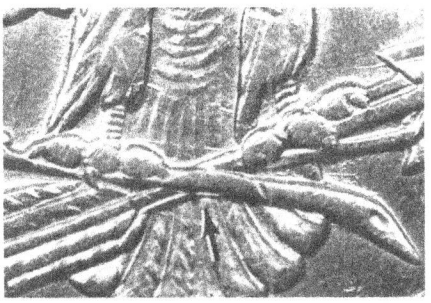

7 R Doubled Reverse

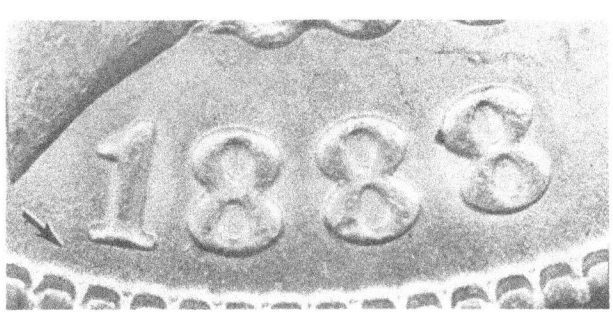

8 O Near Slanted Date

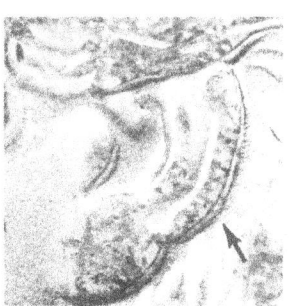

11 O Doubled Ear

1888-P

18   III² 14 • C³ a (Doubled Eyelid)   (188)   I-2   R-3
   Obverse III² 14 – Eyelid strongly doubled. Hair above ear and bottom edge of lower cotton leaf are slightly doubled.

19   III² 15 • C³ a (Doubled Left Stars)   (188)   I-2   R-3
   Obverse III² 15 – All left stars doubled towards rim.

9 O   High Date

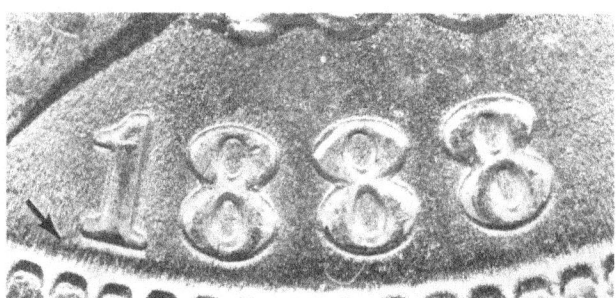
10 O   Slanted Date

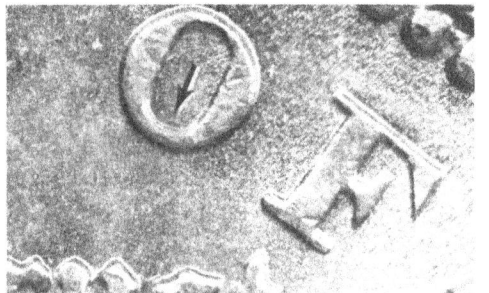
12 R   Doubled Letters

14 O   Doubled Stars

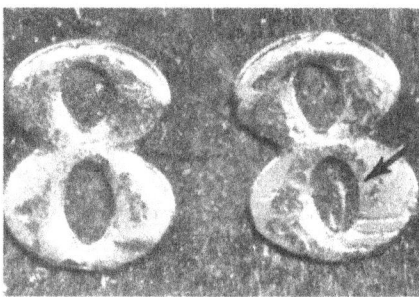
15 O   Doubled Last 8

16 R   Doubled Wreath

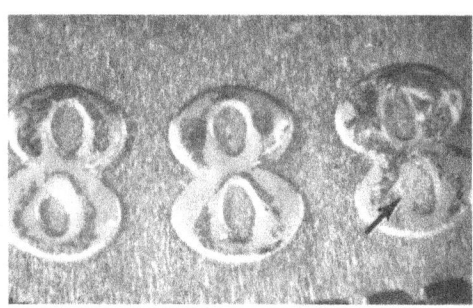
17 O   Die Chips in 8's

17 R   Doubled Wreath

16 O   Doubled 1

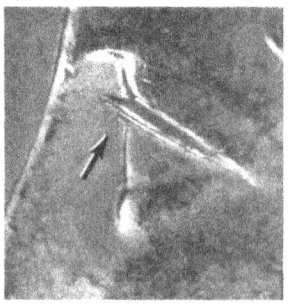
18 O   Doubled Eyelid

1888-O

Typically this issue is slightly weakly struck although because of the large mintage the strike can range from very flat to very sharp. Luster is average to good. A number of die varieties exist but only two are significant. VAM 1B has a long diagonal die break from between "E" and "P" down across the Liberty head, face and neck on late die stages. It is the largest die break in the Morgan dollar series, is fairly scarce and commands a significant premium. VAM 4 has strongly doubled lips, chin, nose and cotton leaves easily visible to the naked eye. It is the strongest doubled obverse of the Morgan dollar series and commands a large premium. It is usually weakly struck and is unknown in uncirculated grades and is scarce in AU. Proof-likes are somewhat difficult to locate and generally only have average contrast. A few deep mirror cameos are known however.

1   III^{2}1 • C^{3}a (Round O)   (181)   I-1   R-1
Obverse III^{2}1 – Normal die of III^2 type.
Reverse C^{3}a – Normal die of C^3 type with centered circular medium III O mint mark with narrow slit, centered and upright.

1A   III^{2}1 • C^{3}a (E on Reverse)   (181)   I-3   R-5
Obverse III^{2}1 – Large die vertical die crack through R in PLURIBUS.
Reverse C^{3}a – Centered, circular, medium II O mint mark. Clashed die with almost full E under eagles tail feathers on left side.

1B   III^{2}1 • C^{3}a (Die Break on Face)   (181)   I-4   R-6
Obverse III^{2}1 – Large diagonal die break extending from rim between E and P across the Liberty Head nose, cheek, neck and lower curls. Early die states show just a line from denticles to dot.

2   III^{2}1 • C^{3}b (Oval O)   (181)   I-1   R-2
Reverse C^{3}b – Normal die of C^3 type with tall oval medium II O mint mark set high.

3   III^{2}2 • C^{3}a (Doubled 18-8)   (181)   I-3   R-4
Obverse III^{2}2 – Doubled 18-8 in date. 1 doubled strongly at top left and on entire left side. First 8 has upper loop doubled strongly at top outside and lower loop doubled at top left outside and lower inside. Lower loop of third 8 doubled strongly at bottom.

4   III^{2}3 • C^{3}a (Doubled Head)   (181)   I-5   R-5
Obverse III^{2}3 – Doubled Liberty head variety with two complete sets of lips, chin and nose clearly visible. Hair is filled and also lower parts of ERT in LIBERTY. The wheat and cotton leaves above LIBERTY are doubled strongly to the right.

5   III^{2}4 • C^{3}b (Doubled 1)   (181)   I-2   R-3
Obverse III^{2}4 – 1 in date doubled below upper crossbar. There is a faint doubling of the upper lip and nose of the Liberty head.

6   III^{2}5 • C^{3}b (Doubled 8)   (181)   I-2   R-3
Obverse III^{2}5 – Last 8 in date doubled faintly at top.

7   III^{2}1 • C^{3}c (O Set High)   I-2   R-3
Reverse C^{3}c – III O mint mark set high.

8   III^{2}1 • C^{3}d (O Set Very High)   (181)   I-3   R-3
Reverse C^{3}d – III O mint mark set very high and to right so it almost touches the wreath.

1A R Die Crack

1B O Die Break Dot

1B O Die Crack

1888-O

9   III²1 • C³e (Doubled Wreath)   (181)   I-3   R-5
Reverse C³e – Doubled lower reverse with middle outside of right wreath strongly doubled. Top inside of ONE DOLLAR and bottom inside of ERICA letters doubled. Right star doubled on left side. Bottom of eagle's tail feathers, arrow shafts and olive leaves slightly doubled. III O mint mark.

10   III²6 • C³a (Slanted Date)   (181)   I-2   R-3
Obverse III²6 – Date slanted with 1 close to rim.

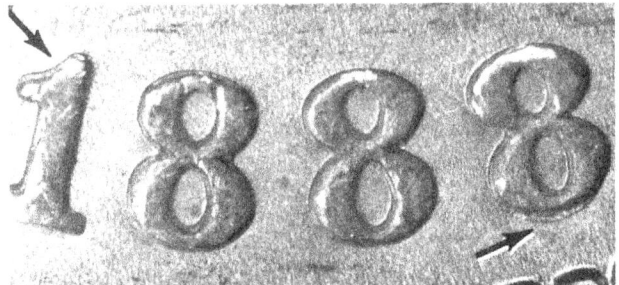

3 O Doubled 18-8

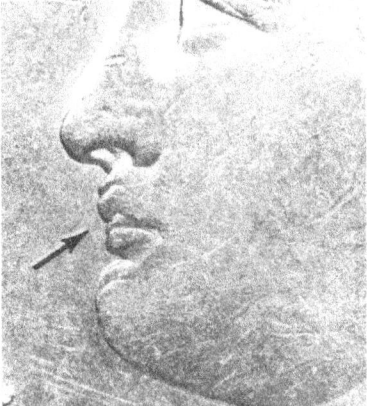

4 O Doubled Head

2 R High O

4 O Doubled Head

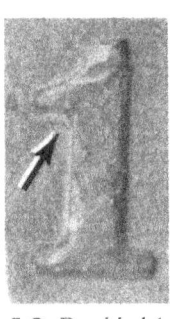

5 O Doubled 1

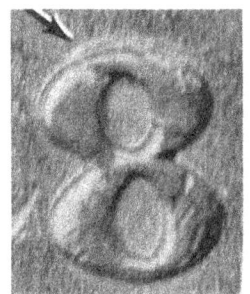

6 O Doubled 8

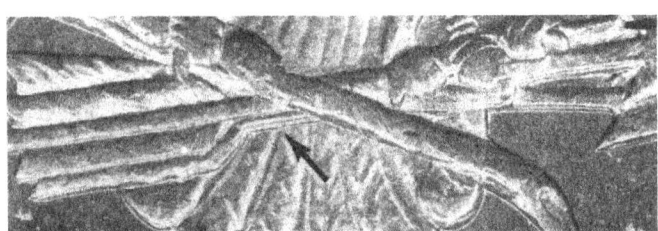

9 R Doubled Arrows

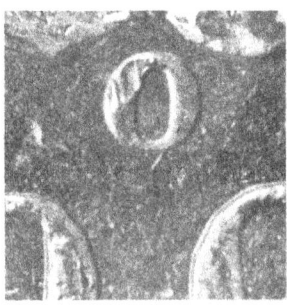

7 R O Set High

8 R O Set Very High

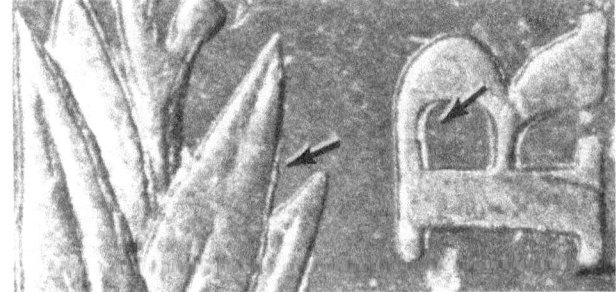

9 R Doubled Wreath

10 O Slanted Date

1888-O

11 III²7 • C³a (Doubled 1) (181) I-2 R-3
Obverse III²7 – 1 doubled slightly below upper crossbar.

12 III²6 • C³f (Slanted Date, Doubled Legend) (181) I-2 R-3
Reverse C³f – Doubled bottom of letters towards rim in TES OF AMERICA, tops and sides in G-D WE TRUST, right side of right star and right side of top leaves in right wreath. Centered III O mint mark.

13 III²8 • C³a (Doubled 88) (181) I-2 R-3
Obverse III²8 – First and second 8's in date doubled slightly at bottom outside of lower loops.

14 III²9 • C³a (High Near Date) (181) I-2 R-3
Obverse III²9 – Date set high and further left than normal.

15 III²1 • C³g (O/O Low, Doubled Legend) (181) I-3 R-4
Reverse C³g – III O mint mark doubled well below the bottom outside. Doubled right wreath and eagle's left wing edge towards rim. F-AMERICA-AR, right star and TRUST strongly doubled towards the rim.

16 III²10 • C³c (Doubled Second 8, Far Date, O Set High) (181) I-2 R-3
Obverse III²10 – Second 8 doubled slightly at bottom outside of lower loop. Date set further right than normal.

17 III²11 • C³b (Near Date, Oval O) (181) I-3 R-3
Obverse III²11 – Date set further left than normal.

11 O Doubled 1

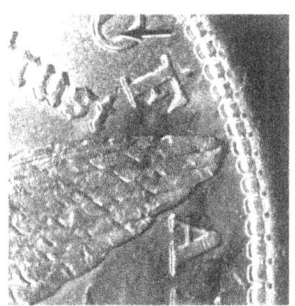

12 O Doubled Letters

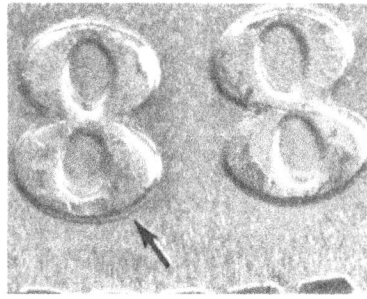

13 O Doubled First and Second 8's

14 O High Near Date

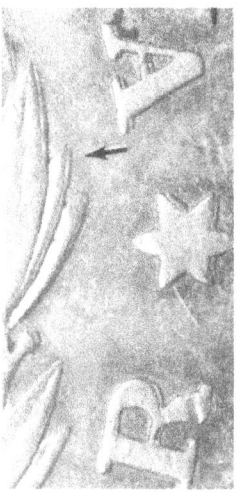

15 R Doubled Wreath and Letters

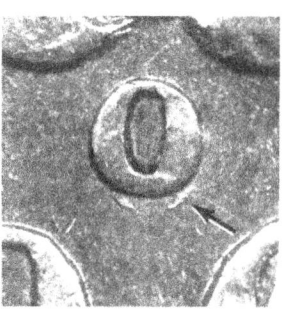

15 R O/O Low

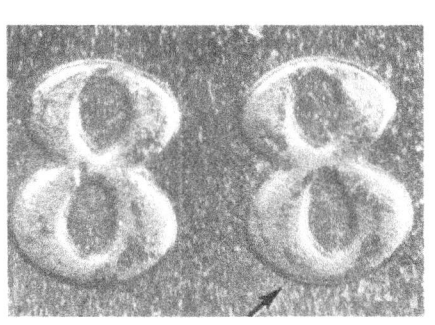

16 O Doubled Second 8

1888-S

The 1888-S generally has an average strike but numerous weakly struck specimens are on the market. Luster is generally good. A few minor die varieties exist but none are significant. As with most S mint issues one sided proof-likes and semi proof-likes are fairly common. Full two-sided proof-likes are fairly scarce and some deep mirror cameos exist.

1	III²1 • C³a (Normal Die)	(186)	I-1	R-3

Obverse III²1 – Normal die of III² type.
Reverse C³a – Normal die of C³ type with a medium IV S mint mark centered and upright.

1A	III²1 • C³a (Extra Claws)	(187)	I-3	R-4

Reverse C³a – Heavy die gouges below eagles right talon, between legs and on the eagle's lower right wing.

2	III²1 • C³b (S/S)	(186)	I-2	R-4

Reverse C³b – IV S mint mark repunched with original showing as a thin curved line on left side of upper loop opening.

3	III²2 • C³a (Doubled 8)		I-2	R-4

Obverse III²2 – Last 8 doubled all across top outside. Date set further left than normal.

4	III²1 • C³c (Overpolished Wing)	(187)	I-2	R-3

Reverse C³c – Eagle's right wing is overpolished with field showing in middle and fine diagonal polishing lines throughout wing.

5	III²3 • C³a (Slanted Date)	(186)	I-2	R-3

Obverse III²3 – Date is slanted with last 8 high above rim.

6	III²4 • C³d (Doubled Date, S/S)	(187)	I-2	R-3

Obverse III²4 – Entire date is doubled. 1 is doubled above top crossbar. All 8's doubled slightly at top outside of upper loop and at top left outside of lower loop.
Reverse C³d – IV S mint mark repunched with original showing as a slanted bar in lower portion of upper loop opening and a short curved line on right side of lower loop opening.

7	III²5 • C³a (Doubled 18-8)	(187)	I-2	R-3

Obverse III²5 – Doubled 18-8 in date. 1 and first 8 slightly doubled at very bottom outside. Last 8 doubled at top outside of upper loop.

1A R Die Gouges

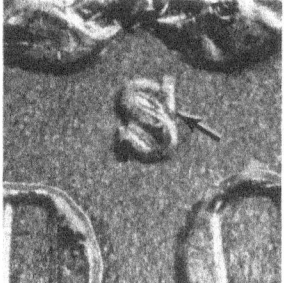
2 R S/S

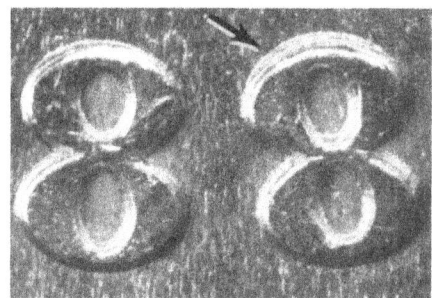
3 O Doubled 8

4 R Overpolished Wing

5 O Slanted Date

1888-S / 1889-P

8   III²6 • C³e (Doubled Stars, S/S)   (187)   I-2   R-3
    Obverse III²6 – All left and right stars plus E PL-R doubled towards rim. Liberty head profile is also doubled. Date set further left than normal.
    Reverse C³e – IV S mint mark repunched with original showing as a horizontal curved line within middle of upper loop opening and lower loop is doubled at top inside. Top serif is doubled on the right side.

9   III²5 • C³b (Doubled 18, S/S)   (186)   I-2   R-3

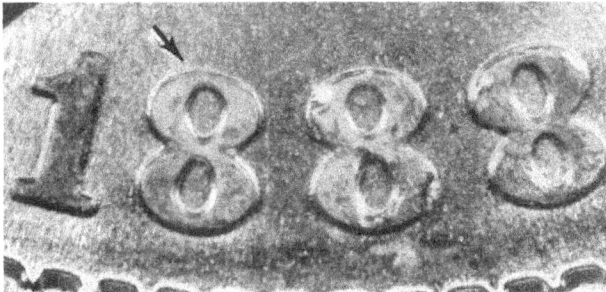
6 O Doubled Date

7 O Doubled 18-8

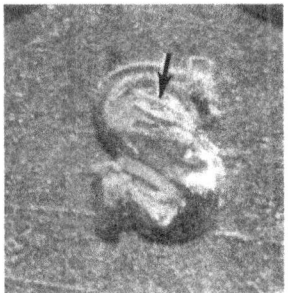
6 R S/S

8 O Doubled Stars

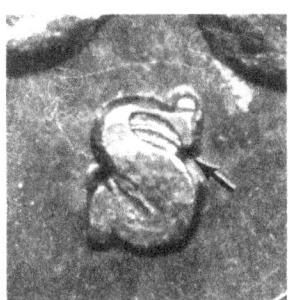
8 R S/S

1889-P

    This large mintage issue generally has a slightly weak strike although extremes of strike can readily be found. The main problem with this issue is the generally dull luster caused by extended use of dies to produce the high mintages. The majority of these coins have rough fields due to worn dies causing the dull luster. A number of minor die varieties exist but none are very significant.

    Proof-likes are quite scarce and exhibit only slight contrast. It is among the scarcest of all 1880's P mint proof-likes. Proofs have fairly good contrast but a few exhibit slight weakness in the strike.

1   III²1 • C³a (Closed 9)   (189)   I-1   R-1
    Obverse III²1 – Normal die of III² type with tail of 9 touching body. Some specimens show die chips between loops of second 8 on right, both 8's on right, or first 8 on right and second 8 on both sides.
    Reverse C³a – Normal die of C³ type.

2   III²2 • C³a (Open 9)   (190)   I-1   R-1
    Obverse III²2 – Normal die with tail of 9 not touching body.

3   III²3 • C³a (Doubled 189)   I-2   R-3
    Obverse III²3 – 1 in date doubled below upper and lower crossbar. Bottom of first 8 and 9 doubled faintly. All right stars doubled slightly towards rim. Closed 9 variety. Date set further right than normal.

4   III²4 • C³a (Very Far Date)   I-2   R-3
    Obverse III²4 – Die chip between loops of first 8 on right. Open 9 variety. Date set much further right than normal.

5   III²5 • C³a (Far Date)   (190)   I-2   R-3
    Obverse III²5 – Date set further right than normal. Closed and open 9 varieties.

1889-P

5A	III²5 • C³a (Bar Wing)	(190)	I-2	R-4

Reverse C³a – Die break on to of eagle's right wing showing as a short parallel bar.

6	III²6 • C³a (Doubled 1-9)	(190)	I-3	R-4

Obverse III²6 – 1-9 in date doubled. 1 doubled at bottom and below upper crossbar. 9 doubled strongly at top outside. Closed 9 variety. Some specimens have a die chip between loops of first 8 on right. Date set further right than normal.

7	III²7 • C³a (High 9)	(190)	I-2	R-3

Obverse III²7 – 9 in date is set higher than rest of numerals by about 20 percent. Some specimens show die chip between loops of second 8 on right.

8	III²8 • C³a (Very Far Date, High 9)		I-2	R-3

Obverse III²8 – Date set much further right than normal. Open 9. High 9. Both 8's have die chips at top inside of lower loop. 9 has die chips at bottom inside of upper loop and top right inside of upper loop.

9	III²9 • C³a (Slanted Date)	(190)	I-2	R-3

Obverse III²9 – Date slanted with 9 higher than 1 and set further right than normal. Open 9.

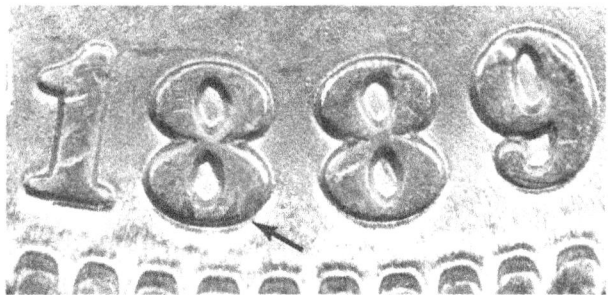

3 O Doubled 18-9

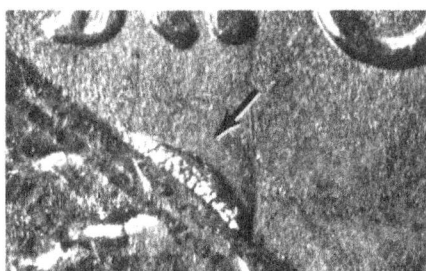

5A R Bar Wing

6 O Doubled 1-9

7 O High 9

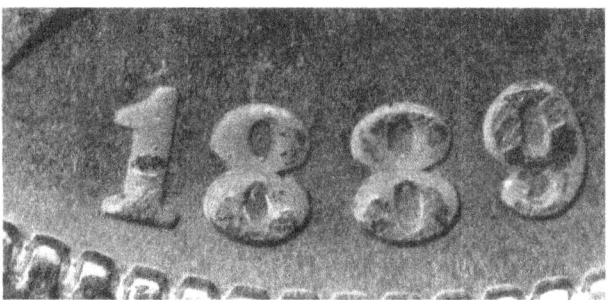

8 O Very Far Date, High 9

9 O Slanted Date

1889-P

10	III² 10 • C³ a (Doubled First 8)		I-2	R-3

Obverse III² 10 – Date set further right than normal and first 8 is doubled at very top outside as a thin arc.

11	III² 11 • C³ a (Doubled 18)		I-3	R-4

Obverse III² 11 – 1 in date doubled very strongly at top. First 8 doubled slightly at top outside center. Date slanted with 9 higher than 1. Open 9 variety.

12	III² 12 • C³ a (Doubled 1)	(190)	I-2	R-3

Obverse III² 12 – 1 doubled slightly below upper crossbar. Date set further right than normal with 9 set high.

13	III² 13 • C³ a (Very Far Slanted Date)	(190)	I-2	R-3

Obverse III² 13 – Date slanted with 1 close to rim and 9 far from rim and set much further right than normal. Closed 9 variety.

14	III² 14 • C³ a (Doubled 1-9)	(190)	I-2	R-3

Obverse III² 14 – Doubled 1-9 in date. 1 doubled at lower right bottom crossbar. 9 doubled slightly at top outside of upper loop. Some specimens show a die chip between the loops of first 8 on right.

15	III² 15 • C³ a (Doubled 889)	(190)	I-2	R-3

Obverse III² 15 – Doubled 889 in date. First 8 doubled at top inside of lower loop. Second 8 doubled slightly at top inside of upper loop. 9 doubled at top inside of upper loop and at right top inside of lower loop.

16	III² 16 • C³ a (Doubled Ear)	(189)	I-3	R-3

Obverse III² 16 – Ear is doubled on lower left outside and left inside. Hair above ear is doubled on lower edge. Right stars doubled towards rim. Date set further right than normal.

17	III² 17 • C³ a (Doubled 18)	(189)	I-2	R-3

Obverse III² 17 – 18 doubled in date. 1 doubled as a short horizontal spike below upper crossbar. First 8 doubled at top inside of upper loop. Date set further right than normal.

18	III² 18 • C³ a (Doubled Ear)	(190)	I-2	R-3

Obverse III² 18 – Ear is doubled on right outside and right side of inner ear fill or concha. Hair above ear is doubled on lower edge. Lower edge of cotton leaves are doubled. Date is set much further right than normal with slight slant so 1 is further from rim than rest of date.

19	III² 1 • C³ b (Doubled Reverse)	(190)	I-2	R-3

Reverse C³ b – Doubled left wreath leaves, TED, and IN GOD WE TRUST toward rim.

20	III² 19 • C³ a (Doubled Ear)	(190)	I-2	R-3

Obverse III² 19 – Ear is doubled on right outside and right side of inner ear fill or concha. Hair above ear is doubled on lower edge. Doubled forehead. Date is in normal position.

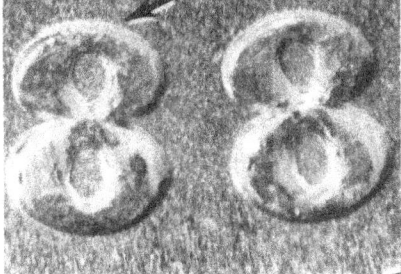

10 O Doubled First 8

11 O Doubled 18

12 O Doubled 1

12 O Far Date and High 9

13 O Very Far Slanted Date

1889-P / 1889-CC

21   **III² 20 • C³ a (Doubled Ear)**   (190)   I-2   R-3

Obverse III² 20 – Ear is doubled on right outside. Hair above ear is doubled on lower right edge. Date is set further right than normal.

14 O Doubled 1-9

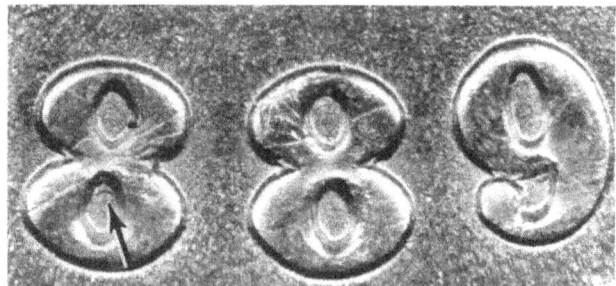

15 O Doubled 889

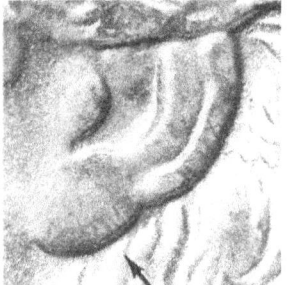

16 O Doubled Ear

17 O Doubled 18

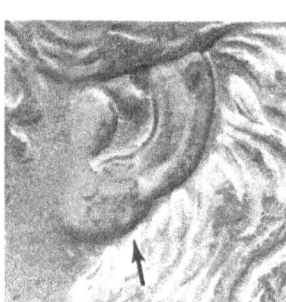

18 O Doubled Ear

19 R Doubled Wreath

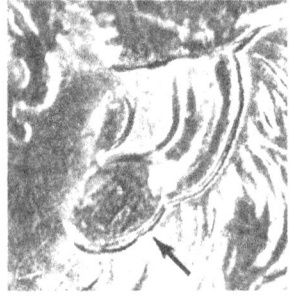

20 O Doubled Ear

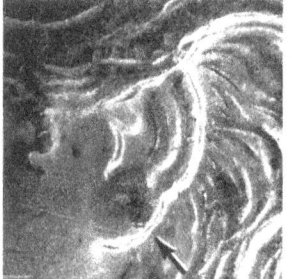

21 O Doubled Ear

1889-CC

This rarest of the Carson City dollars is generally well struck with good luster because of the low mintage. The few dies used did not have to strike an excessive number of coins to achieve the mintage. A significant percentage of the issue are proof-likes and most have good contrast. Only a couple minor die varieties are known.

1   **III² 1 • C³ a (Normal Die)**   I-1   R-3

Obverse III² 1 – Normal die of III² type.
Reverse C³ a – Normal die of C³ type with large centered V CC mint mark.

2   **III² 2 • C³ b (High 9, Doubled 1)**   (177)   I-2   R-4

Obverse III² 2 – 9 in date higher than rest of numerals by about 15 percent. 1 doubled below upper crossbar.
Reverse C³ b – V CC mint mark set slightly to right.

3   **III² 3 • C³ c (Far Date)**   I-2   R-4

Obverse III² 3 – Date set further right than normal.
Reverse C³ c – V CC mint mark tilted slightly to left.

1889-CC / 1889-O

2 O High 9

2 O Doubled 1

2 R CC Set Right

3 R CC Tilted Left
(Photo courtesy F.C.I.)

1889-O

The typical 1889-O has a weak strike with fairly good luster although full struck specimens do exist as well as ones with dull luster. A number of minor die varieties exist but two are significant. VAM 1A shows the "E" of LIBERTY below the eagle's tail feathers as in the 1886-O and 1891-O, but it is much scarcer than for those two dates and only one BU specimen is known. VAM 6 has a strongly doubled date below the 1 and above the 9 and is worth a modest premium.

Proof-likes are fairly scarce but have fairly good contrast.

1   **III^2 1 • C^3 a (Round O)**   (181)   I-1   R-1
      Obverse III^2 1 – Normal die of III^2 type. Open 9. Some specimens show die chips between loops of second 8 on left, both 8's on right side and both 8's on both sides.
      Reverse C^3 a – Normal die of C^3 type with circular medium III O mint mark centered and upright.

1A   **III^2 1 • C^3 a (E on Reverse)**   (181)   I-4   R-7
      Reverse C^3 a – Centered, circular medium III O mint mark. Clashed die with full E under eagle's tail feathers on left side.

2   **III^2 8 • C^3 b (Oval O)**   (181)   I-2   R-3
      Obverse III^2 8 – Some specimens show die chip between loops of first 8 on right. Date set further right than normal.
      Reverse C^3 b – Normal die of C^3 type with high set, tall, oval, medium II O mint mark, centered and upright.

3   **III^2 8 • C^3 c (O/O Top Left)**   (181)   I-2   R-4
      Reverse C^3 c – Centered, circular medium III O mint mark, doubled at top left.

4   **III^2 1 • C^3 d (O/O Top Right)**   (181)   I-2   R-4
      Obverse III^2 1 – Die chip between loops of second 8 on right.
      Reverse C^3 d – III O mint mark set high and doubled slightly on left top surface and at top right outside.

5   **III^2 2 • C^3 a Doubled 18)**   (181)   I-2   R-3
      Obverse III^2 2 – 18 in date doubled at bottom.

1889-O

6 III²3 • C³a (Doubled 18-9) (181) I-4 R-5
Obverse III²3 – 18 in date doubled strongly at bottom. 9 in date doubled slightly at top and strongly at bottom inside of lower loop. Sometimes a spike shows below the top crossbar of the 1.

7 III²4 • C³a (Doubled 1-89) (181) I-2 R-3
Obverse III²4 – Date doubled with clockwise shift about the first 8. Upper crossbar of 1 doubled at bottom. The upper loop of the second 8 and 9 are doubled at top.

8 III²5 • C³e (O Set High, Tilted Right) (181) I-2 R-3
Obverse III²5 – Normal die of III² type. Closed 9.
Reverse C³e – III O mint mark set high and tilted slightly to right.

9 III²1 • C³f (O Set High) (181) I-2 R-3
Obverse III²1 – Some specimens show die chip between loops of both 8's on right side.
Reverse C³f – III O mint mark set upright and high.

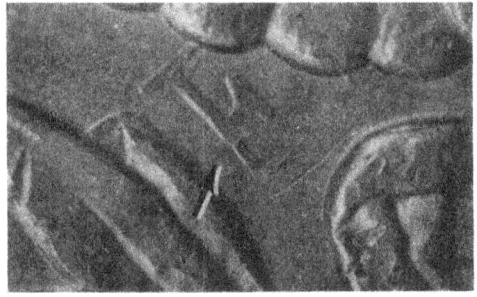
1A R E

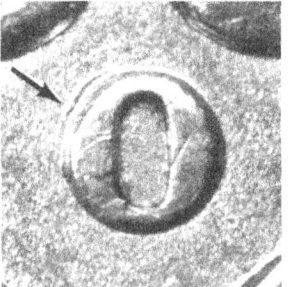
3 R O/O

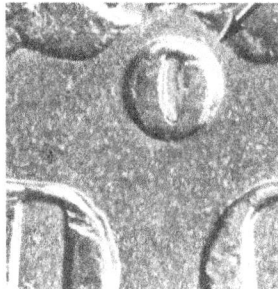
4 R O/O Top Right

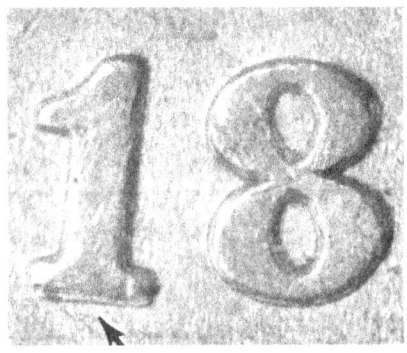
5 O Doubled 18

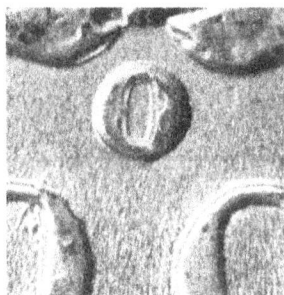
8 R O Set High, Tilted Right

9 R O Set High

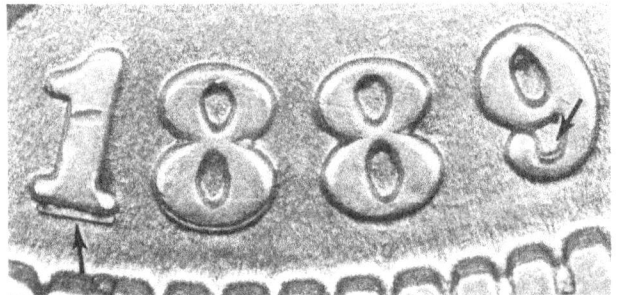
6 O Doubled 18-9

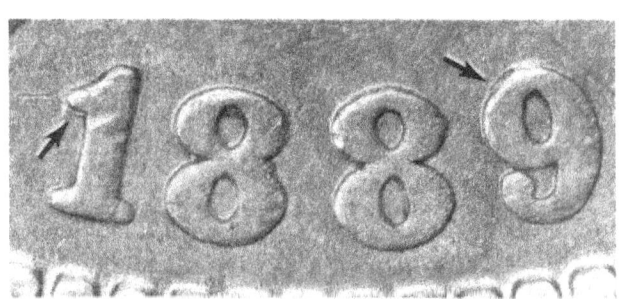
7 O Doubled 1-89

1889-O / 1889-S

10	III²6 • C³f (Wide Date)	(181)	I-2	R-4

Obverse III²6 – 6-9 in date further to the right of the rest of date than normal.

11	III²6 • C³a (Wide Date)	(181)	I-2	R-4
12	III²7 • C³a (Doubled 1, Far Date)	(181)	I-2	R-4

Obverse III²7 – 1 in date is doubled below upper crossbar. First 8 has die chips between loops on both sides. N in UNUM is doubled at top of diagonal bar. Date set further right than normal. Closed 9.

13	III²8 • C³a (Far Date)	(181)	I-2	R-3

Obverse III²8 – Date set further right than normal. Some specimens show die chips between loops of first 8 on left and right.

14	III²9 • C³a (Doubled 9)	(181)	I-2	R-3

Obverse III²9 – 9 doubled slightly at top left outside of upper loop.

15	III²10 • C³a (Doubled 88, Tripled 9)	(181)	I-2	R-3

Obverse III²10 – Both 8's doubled slightly at top outside of upper loop. 9 tripled at top outside of upper loop.

16	III²8 • C³f (Far Date, High O)	(181)	I-2	R-3
17	III²8 • C³g (Far Date, High O)	(181)	I-2	R-4

Reverse C³g – Oval medium II O mint mark and set very high.

10 O Wide Date

12 O Doubled 1

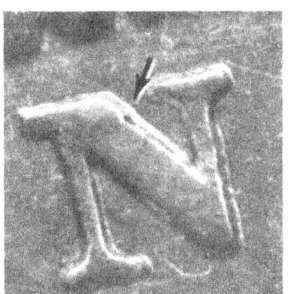
12 O Doubled N

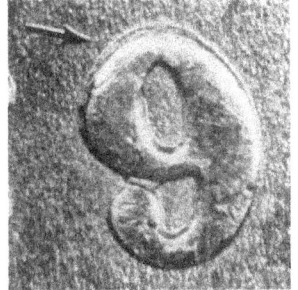
14 O Doubled 9

15 O Doubled 88, Tripled 9

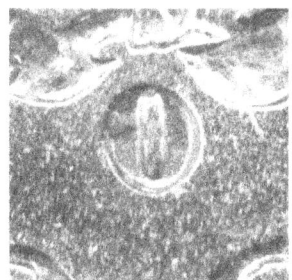
17 R High O

1889-S

This date is generally well struck with good luster. A few die varieties exist but none are particularly significant. Semi proof-like specimens are fairly common but fully proof-like ones are scarce and some of these are cameos.

1	III²1 • C³a (Normal Die)		I-1	R-3

Obverse III²1 – Normal die of III² type with closed 9. Some specimens show a die chip between loops of first 8 on left.
Reverse C³a – Normal die of C³ type with a medium IV S mint mark centered and upright.

2	III²2 • C³b (S Tilted Left)	(188)	I-2	R-3

Obverse III²2 – Date set further right than normal. Closed and open 9.
Reverse C³b – IV S mint mark centered and tilted to the left.

3	III²2 • C³a (Far Date)	(187)	I-2	R-3

1889-S

4   III²2 • C³c (S/S Down)   I-2   R-4
Obverse III²2 – Die chip between first 8 loops on right.
Reverse C³c – IV S mint mark doubled on right side and bottom of lower loop and at bottom of lower serif. Filled loops.

5   III²3 • C³a (High 9)   (184)   I-2   R-4
Obverse III²3 – 9 in date set higher than rest of date numerals and doubled on right side and bottom of lower loop. Later specimens show die chip between loops of first 8 on right. Date set further right than normal.

6   III²4 • C³a (Doubled 9)   I-2   R-4
Obverse III²4 – 9 in date is doubled just above the top loop a thin curved line at top left. Liberty head profile slightly doubled.

7   III²1 • C³d (S/S Middle)   (187)   I-2   R-4
Reverse C³d – IV S mint mark repunched with original showing as a curved horizontal line within middle of upper loop opening.

8   III²5 • C³a (Doubled 1, Far Slanted Date)   (187)   I-2   R-3
Obverse III²5 – 1 is doubled slightly below base. Date set further right than normal with 9 far from rim.

9   III²6 • C³a (Far Slanted Date)   (184)   I-2   R-3
Obverse III²6 – Date set further right than normal and slanted with 9 farther from rim than 1.

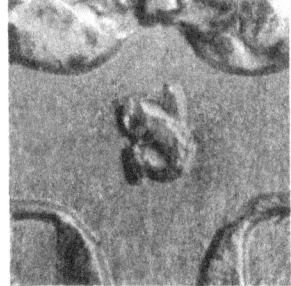
2 R S Tilted Left

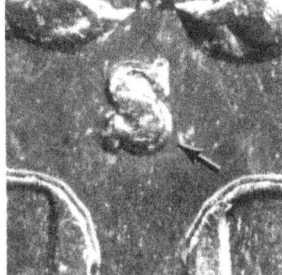
4 R S/S Down

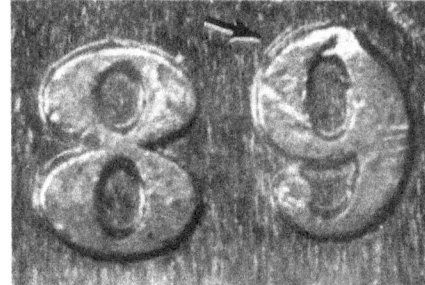
6 O Doubled 9

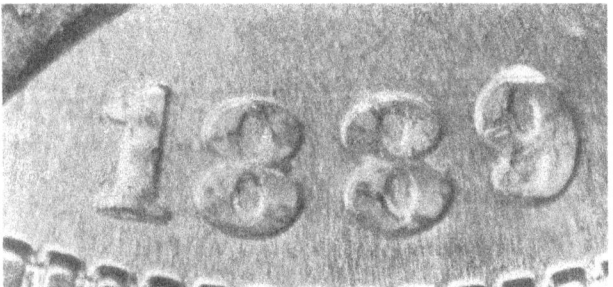
5 O High 9

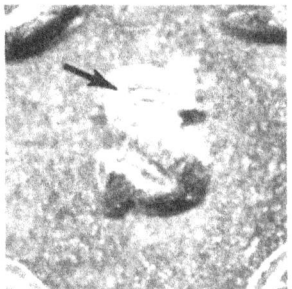
7 R S/S Middle

8 O Doubled 1

9 O Far Slanted Date

8 O Far Slanted Date

10	III²7 • C³e (Doubled Profile, S Set Right)	(187)	I-2	R-3

Obverse III²7 – Nose, lips and chin profile slightly doubled.
Reverse C³e – IV S mint mark centered, upright and set slightly to right.

11	III²8 • C³a (Very Far Date)	(184)	I-2	R-3

Obverse III²8 – Date set much further right than normal.

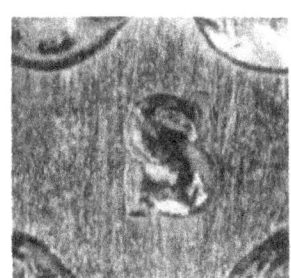

10 R S Set Right

10 O Doubled Profile

1890-P

Coins of this date tend to have a touch of weakness in the strike. Like the 1889-P, the 1890-P generally has dull luster from dies used longer than usual. Some minor die varieties exist. VAM 4 is strongly doubled at the top of 90 and is fairly significant.

Proof-likes are fairly scarce and tend to be dull with little contrast although a few cameos are known. Proofs are fairly scarce because of the low mintage but they have good contrast and are generally fully struck.

1	III²1 • C³a (Closed 9)		I-1	R-1

Obverse III²1 – Normal die of III² type with closed 9.
Reverse C³a – Normal die of C³ type.

2	III²2 • C³a (Open 9)		I-1	R-2

Obverse III²2 – Normal die of III² type with open 9.

3	III²3 • C³a (Doubled 1)	(191)	I-2	R-3

Obverse III²3 – 1 in date doubled with short spike below top crossbar.

4	III²4 • C³a (Doubled 1-90)	(189)	I-3	R-4

Obverse III²4 – 1-90 in date doubled. 1 is doubled below upper crossbar as short horizontal spike. 9 doubled strongly at very top outside. 0 doubled as a long arc at top left outside.

5	III²5 • C³a (Doubled 1-90)		I-3	R-5

Obverse III²5 – 1-90 in date doubled at top. In addition, the bottom crossbar of the 1 is doubled at top.

6	III²6 • C³a (Doubled 0)		I-2	R-3

Obverse III²6 – 0 in date doubled at top.

7	III²7 • C³a (Slanted Date)	(190)	I-2	R-3

Obverse III²7 – Date slanted with 0 higher than 1. Closed 9. Date set further right than normal.

8	III²8 • C³a (Doubled 1-90)		I-2	R-4

Obverse III²8 – 1-90 in date doubled. 1 is doubled below upper crossbar as a short horizontal spike. Closed 9 is slightly doubled at bottom inside of both loops, on left and right to outside of upper loop and at top left outside of lower loop. 0 is slightly doubled at bottom inside and at very top left outside with an additional arc well above on top outside.

1890-P

9   III²9 • C³a (Doubled 89)   I-2   R-3
     Obverse III²9 – 8 and 9 are both doubled at bottom inside of lower loop. Closed 9.
     Reverse C³a – G in GOD has die chip at top inside.

10   III²10 • C³a (Doubled 90, Far Date)   (190)   I-2   R-3
     Obverse III²10 – 90 in date doubled. 9 doubled at top outside of upper loop. 0 doubled slightly as faint broken arc at top left outside. Date set further right than normal. Closed 9.

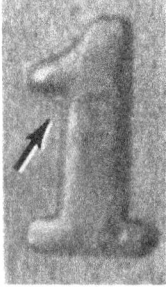
3 O Doubled 1

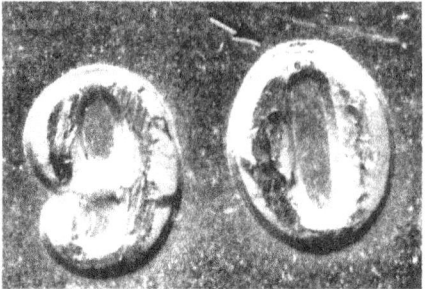
4 O Doubled 1-90   6 O Doubled 0

7 O Slanted Date

8 O Doubled 1-90

(Photo Not Available)

5 O

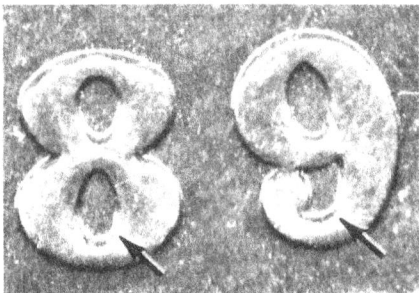
9 O Doubled 89

9 R Die Chip in G

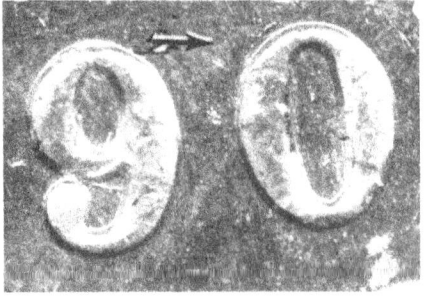
10 O Doubled 90

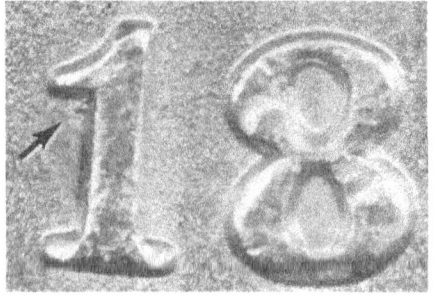
12 O Doubled 18

11   III²11 • C³a (Near Date)   (189)   I-2   R-3
      Obverse III²11 – Date set further left than normal.

12   III²12 • C³a (Doubled 18)   I-2   R-3
      Obverse III²12 – 18 in date doubled. 1 has short spike below top crossbar. 8 doubled at top inside of upper loop.

13   III²13 • C³a (Far Date)   (190)   I-2   R-3
      Obverse III²13 – Date set further right than normal.

14   III²14 • C³a (Doubled Profile, Slanted Date)   (190)   I-2   R-3
      Obverse III²14 – Liberty head profile slightly doubled on nose, lips and chin. Date slanted with 1 closest to rim.

14 O   Slanted Date

1890-CC

     This high mintage CC issue is usually fairly well struck although some coins can be quite flat. Luster is usually good. A few minor die varieties exist and VAM 3 has a significantly doubled 90 at the bottom. The most significant die variety is VAM 4, Tail bar, that has a wide die gouge extending vertically between the eagle's tail feathers and left wreath. This die variety brings a moderate premium in all grades. Proof-likes are fairly available and quite a few are very deep mirror cameos.

1   III²1 • C³a (Normal Die)   I-1   R-2
      Obverse III²1 – Normal die of III² type.
      Reverse C³a – Normal die of C³ type with large centered, V CC mint mark.

2   III²1 • C³b (CC Tilted Left)   I-2   R-3
      Reverse C³b – Normal die with large V CC mint mark leaning to the left with top of second C touching wreath.

3   III²2 • C³c (Doubled 90)   (178)   I-4   R-4
      Obverse III²2 – 90 in date doubled. 9 doubled strongly at bottom and to lower left of top loop. 0 doubled strongly to lower left. Date is set much further right than normal Some specimens are polished with only doubling on lower left outside of 9 showing.
      Reverse C³c – Normal die with centered V CC mint mark tilted to the left.

4   III²3 • C³d (Tail Bar)   (178)   I-5   R-5
      Obverse III²3 – Date set further right than normal. Diagonal die gouge in back of eye.
      Reverse C³d – Die gouge from junction of eagle's tail feathers down to wreath. Centered V CC mint mark tilted to right with vertical spikes of metal at the top of both C's just to the left of the serif.

5   III²1 • C³e (Doubled CC Top)   I-3   R-4
      Obverse III²1 – Some specimens show die wear at top of lower loops of 8 and 9.
      Reverse C³e – Doubled mint mark. First C doubled at left inside with short spike at top. Second C doubled strongly at lower inside. Some specimens only show right C doubled.

6   III²4 • C³f (Doubled 18)   I-3   R-4
      Obverse III²4 – Doubled 18 in date. 1 is doubled strongly all across the top. First 8 is doubled slightly at top.
      Reverse C³f – First C in mint mark doubled with vertical spike just to left of top serif and a short curved line at lower left inside of opening.

1890-CC

7   III²1 • C³g (Doubled CC Inside)   I-3   R-3
Reverse C³g – Doubled mint mark. First C doubled strongly on lower left inside of loop. Second C tilted slightly to right and doubled slightly on lower left inside of loop.

8   III²3 • C³a (Far Date)   I-2   R-3
Reverse C³a – Both C's of mint mark show polishing marks within opening on some coins.

9   III²5 • C³a (Near Date)   (177)   I-2   R-3
Obverse III²5 – Date set further left than normal. Die chips on lower inside of upper loop and on upper inside of lower loop of 8 plus right inside of lower loop of 9.

10   III²6 • C³a (Doubled 18)   (178)   I-2   R-3
Obverse III²6 – Doubled 18 in date. 1 doubled at very bottom and on surface at right of vertical shaft. 8 doubled at top outside of both loops.

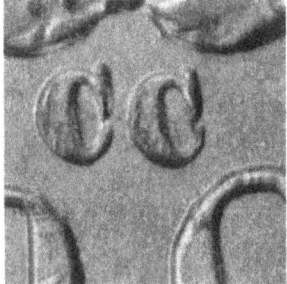
2 R CC Tilted Left

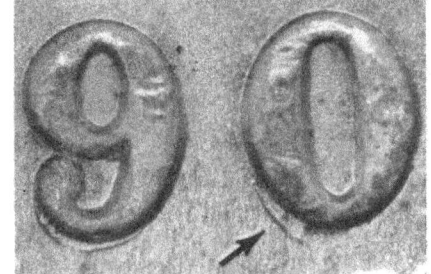
3 O Doubled 90

3 R CC Tilted Left

4 R Tail Bar

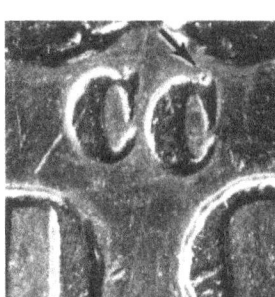
4 R Doubled CC

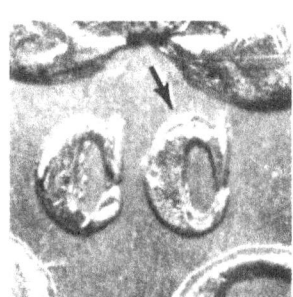
5 R Doubled CC Top

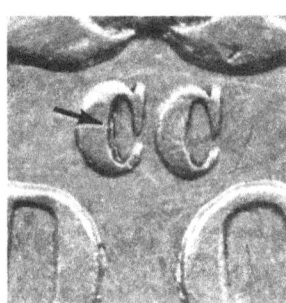
7 R Doubled CC Inside

6 O Doubled 18

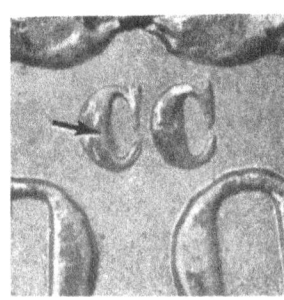
6 R Doubled CC

10 O Doubled 18

1890-CC / 1890-O

11	III²3 • C³b (Far Date, CC Tilted Left)	(178)	I-2	R-3
12	III²3 • C³h (Far Date, Doubled C)	(178)	I-2	R-3

Obverse III²3 – Diagonal die gouge in back of eye.
Reverse C³h – Left C mint mark doubled at top inside.

13	III²7 • C³a (Doubled 1)	(178)	I-2	R-3

Obverse III²7 – 1 doubled at top left and right of lower crossbar. Date set further right than normal.

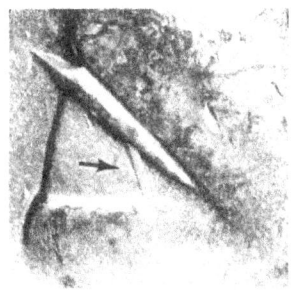 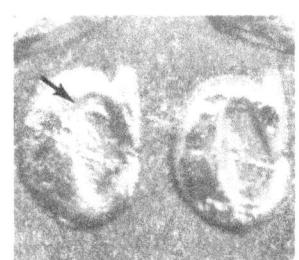 

12 O Line in Eye   12 R Doubled Left C   13 O Doubled 1

1890-O

The usual strike for this date is fairly weak but with good luster. Fully struck specimens can be located because of the high mintage. Some minor die varieties exist and the most significant is VAM 10 with two diagonal die gouges just to the right of the date. Proof-likes are fairly available and usually have good contrast. However, the strike is often weak.

1	III²1 • C³a (Normal Die)	(181)	I-1	R-1

Obverse III²1 – Normal die of III² type.
Reverse C³a – Normal die of C³ type with medium III O mint mark centered and upright.

1A	III²1 • C³b (High O, Die Gouge in E)	(181)	I-2	R-3

Reverse C³b – Diagonal die gouge above and through lower part of E in ONE.

2	III²1 • C³b (High O)	(181)	I-2	R-3

Reverse C³b – Normal die with III O mint mark set high and upright.

3	III²1 • C³c (O Tilted Left)	(181)	I-2	R-3

Reverse C³c – Normal die with III O mint mark set high and tilted slightly to the left.

4	III²2 • C³a (Doubled 0)	(181)	I-2	R-4

Obverse III²2 – 0 in date doubled at top.

5	III²3 • C³a (Doubled 9)	(181)	I-3	R-4

Obverse III²3 – Doubled 9 in date showing as a thick arc above left and thin line at above right. A thin line shows at bottom of upper loop opening.

6	III²1 • C³d (O Set High and Left)	(181)	I-2	R-3

Reverse C³d – III O mint mark set high and left.

7	III²4 • C³b (Slanted Date)	(181)	I-2	R-3

Obverse III²4 – Date slanted with 0 set higher than 1.

8	III²1 • C³e (O Tilted Right)	(181)	I-2	R-3

Reverse C³e – Normal die with III O mint mark at normal height and tilted right.

9	III²5 • C³d (Far Date)	(181)	I-2	R-3

Obverse III²5 – Date set further right than normal.

10	III²6 • C³a (Near Date with Bar)	(181)	I-3	R-4

Obverse III²6 – Date set further left than normal. A wide die gouge down with striations extends diagonally from the 0 in the date down to the right to the rim. A second die gouge also extends diagonally from rim under first star on right.

1890-O

| 11 | III²6 • C³d (Near Date, O Set High and Left) | (181) | I-2 | R-3 |

Obverse III²6 – Date not quite as far left as VAM 10 and does not have die gouge near date.

| 12 | III²1 • C³f (O/O Down) | (181) | I-2 | R-3 |

Reverse C³f – III O mint mark doubled with original showing at top inside and bottom outside.

13	III²6 • C³b (Near Date, High O)	(181)	I-2	R-3
14	III²5 • C³b (Far Date, High O)	(181)	I-2	R-3
15	III²7 • C³g (High Date, O Set Right)	(181)	I-2	R-3

Obverse III²7 – Date set high and further right than normal.
Reverse C³g – III O mint mark at normal height with slight shift to right.

1A R Die Gouge in E

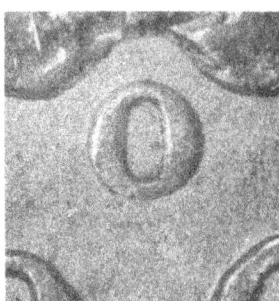

2 R High O

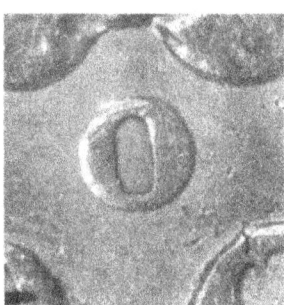

3 R O Tilted Left

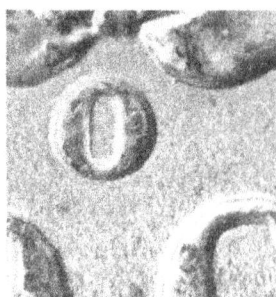

6 R O Set High and Left

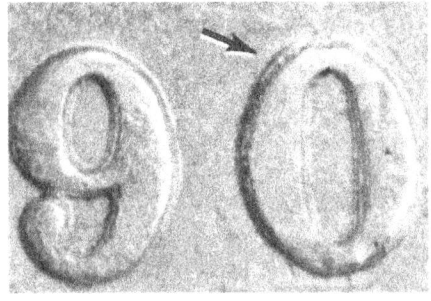

4 O Doubled 0

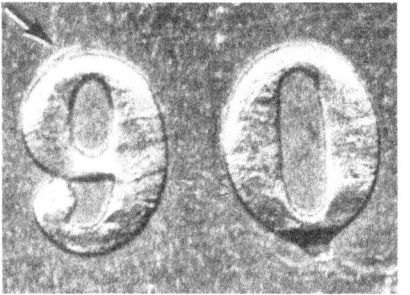

5 O Doubled 9

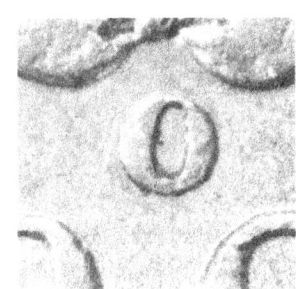

8 R O Tilted Right

7 O Slanted Date

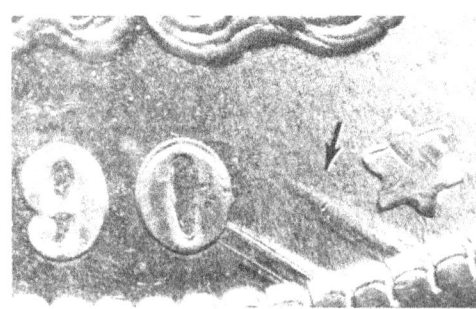

10 O Near Date With Bar

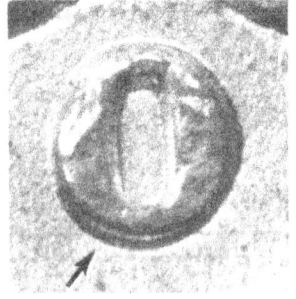

12 R O/O Down

15 O High Far Date

15 R O Set Right

1890-O / 1890-S

16	III²1 • C³g (O Set Right)	(181)	I-2	R-3
17	III²8 • C³b (Very Far Date, High O)	(181)	I-2	R-3

Obverse III²8 – Date set much further right than normal.

18	III²1 • C³h (Doubled Wreath)	(181)	I-2	R-3

Reverse C³h – III O mint mark set high. Left and right wreaths doubled slightly towards rim. N-G-W-U slightly doubled.

19	III²2 • C³i (Doubled 0, O/O Inside)	(181)	I-3	R-3

Reverse C³i – III O mint mark doubled as thick broken line at top inside. Raised dots around NE of ONE and R of DOLLAR and lower wreath from rusted die.

18 R Doubled Wreath

19 R Pitted Reverse

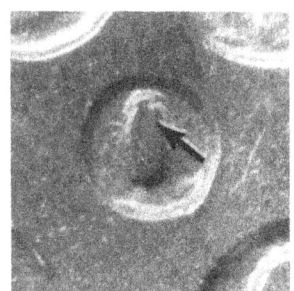

19 R O/O Inside

1890-S

The strike for this issue is usually strong and luster excellent. Sometimes cloudy spots are on the surface, probably due to storage contamination. A fair number of minor die varieties exist but only VAM 12 is significant with strongly doubled 90 at top. VAM 17 has one of the farthest S mint marks tilted to the left. Semi proof-likes and one sided proof-likes are frequently encountered. Two sided mirror proof-likes are fairly scarce and exhibit moderate to good contrast.

1	III²1 • C³a (Normal Die)	(188)	I-1	R-2

Obverse III²1 – Normal die of III² type.
Reverse C³a – Normal die of C³ type with medium IV S mint mark centered and upright.

2	III²1 • C³b (S/S Left)	(188)	I-3	R-4

Reverse C³b – Mint mark repunched with original showing as a broken arc within the upper loop and a complete arc within the lower loop.

3	III²1 • C³c (S/S Down)		I-3	R-4

Reverse C³c – IV S mint mark repunched with original showing as a horizontal curved thin line at lower right of upper loop opening.

4	III²2 • C³c (S/S Right, Doubled 1-9)	(188)	I-3	R-4

Obverse III²2 – Doubled 1 in date shows as a short horizontal spike just below upper crossbar. Some specimens show faint doubling at top outside of 9.

5	III²1 • C³d (S/S Right)		I-2	R-4

Reverse C³d – IV S mint mark repunched with original showing to right of upper serif.

6	III²1 • C³e (S Set High)	(190)	I-2	R-3

Reverse C³e – IV S mint mark set upright and high.

7	III²1 • C³f (S Tilted and Shifted Left)	(187)	I-2	R-3

Reverse C³f – IV S mint mark tilted left and shifted slightly to left.

8	III²1 • C³g (S Tilted Left and Shifted Right)	(190)	I-2	R-3

Reverse C³g – IV S mint mark tilted left and shifted slightly to right.

1890-S

9	III²3 • C³h (Far Date)		I-3	R-3

Obverse III²3 – Date set further right than normal.
Reverse C³h – IV S mint mark very close to wreath and tilted slightly to left.

10	III²3 • C³a (Far Date)	(190)	I-2	R-3

Reverse C³a – Some specimens show die break in left wreath opposite I in UNITED.

11	III²4 • C³a (Near Date)	(190)	I-2	R-3

Obverse III²4 – Date set further left than normal.

12	III²5 • C³a (Doubled 1-90)	(190)	I-4	R-4

Obverse III²5 – 1-90 doubled strongly in date. 1 is doubled below upper serif. 9 doubled at top outside. 0 doubled strongly at top left outside showing as a thick arc.

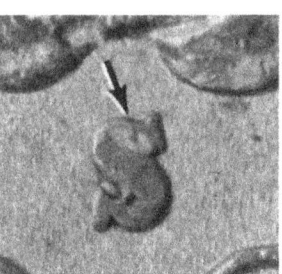
2 R S/S Left

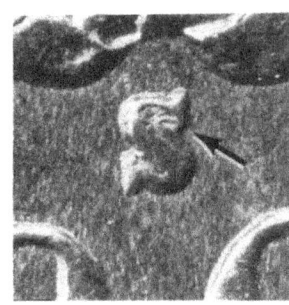
3 R S/S Down

4 O Doubled 1-9

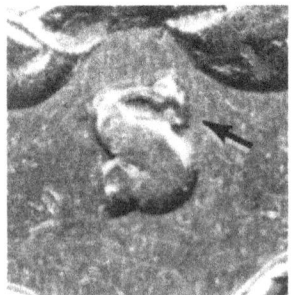
5 R S/S Right

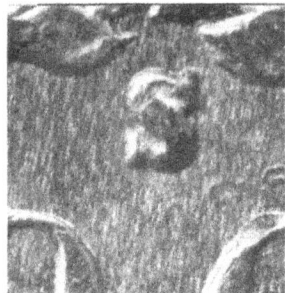
6 R S Set High

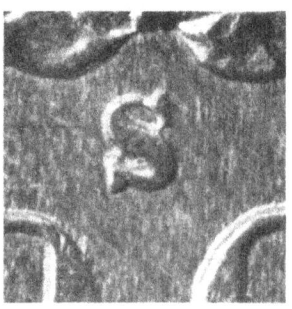
7 R S Tilted and Shifted Left

8 R S Tilted Left and Shifted Right

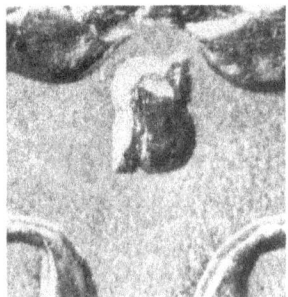
9 R Set High and Titled Left

12 O Doubled 1-90

1890-S

13	III²6 • C³e (Doubled 18)		I-3	R-4

Obverse III²6 – Strongly doubled 18 in date. 1 doubled below upper crossbar showing as short spike ending in fine line. 8 doubled strongly at top of upper and lower loop openings plus at lower left outside of upper loop.
Reverse C³e – Loops of S mint mark are filled in addition to being set high.

14	III²7 • C³i (Doubled O, S Set High and Tilted Left)	(188)	I-2	R-3

Obverse III²7 – 0 doubled slightly at top left outside.
Reverse C³i – IV S mint mark set high and tilted to left with filled loops.

15	III²3 • C³f (Far Date, S Tilted and Shifted Left)	(188)	I-2	R-3
16	III²3 • C³c (S/S Down, Far Date)	(191)	I-3	R-4
17	III²3 • C³j (Far Date, S Tilted Left)	(190)	I-2	R-3

Reverse C³j – IV S mint mark tilted to left. One of the farthest tilts to the left.

18	III²1 • C³k (Doubled Reverse)	(191)	I-2	R-3

Reverse C³k – Letters of legend and motto doubled slightly towards rim. Outside wreath leaves also doubled towards rim.

19	III²3 • C³k (Far Date, Doubled Reverse)	(191)	I-2	R-3
20	III²1 • C³l (S/S and Doubled Arrows)	(190)	I-2	R-3

Reverse C³l – IV S mint mark repunched with original showing to right of upper serif and diagonal line below middle bar. Arrow shafts and feathers doubled at bottom.

21	III²1 • C³j (S Tilted Left)	(187)	I-2	R-3
22	III²3 • C³m (Far Date, S Set Right)	(190)	I-2	R-3

Reverse C³m – IV S mint mark set right and is upright.

23	III²3 • C³i (Far Date, S Set High and Tilted Left)	(190)	I-2	R-3
24	III²8 • C³a (Doubled Profile)	(189)	I-2	R-3

Obverse III²8 – Slightly doubled nose, lips, chin and neck of Liberty head profile.

25	III²1 • C³n (S/S High)	(190)	I-2	R-3

Reverse C³n – IV S mint mark doubled as a shadow outline at very top outside, doubled top serif at top left, and a diagonal line in middle of lower loop.

13 O Doubled 18

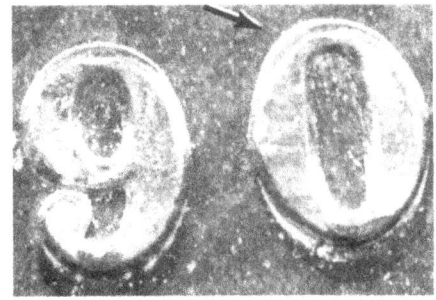
14 O Doubled 0

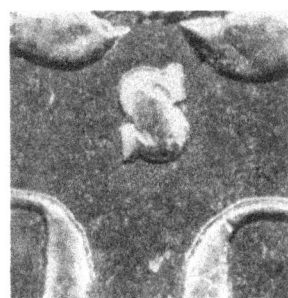
14 R S Set High

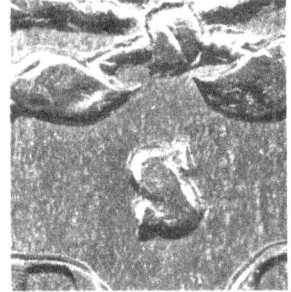
17 R S Tilted Left

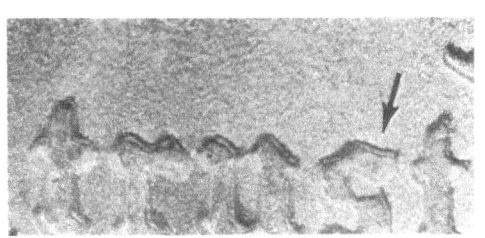
18 R Doubled Reverse

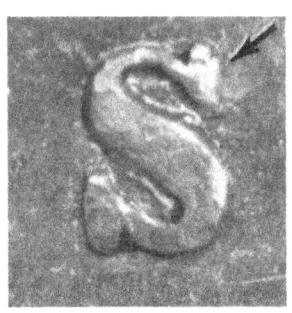
20 R Doubled S

20 R Doubled Arrow Shafts and Feathers

24 O Doubled Profile

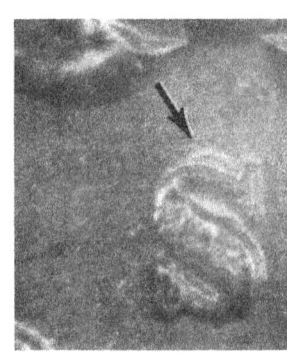
25 R S/S High

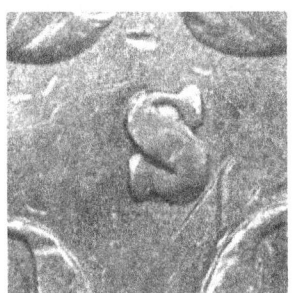
22 R S Set Right

1891-P

The typical 1891-P has a slightly weak strike and dull luster as for the previous two P mint years. A few die varieties exist but none are significant. Full proof-likes are quite scarce and even semi-proof-likes with good luster are very difficult to locate. Proofs have good contrast but often have a touch of weakness in the strike.

| 1 | III²1 • C³a (Normal Die) | (190) | I-1 | R-2 |

Obverse III²1 – Normal die of III² type.
Reverse C³a – Normal die of C³ type.

| 1A | III²1 • C³a (Die Chip on Forehead) | (190) | I-2 | R-4 |

Obverse III²1 – Die chip on forehead above eye.

| 2 | III²2 • C³a (Doubled Ear) | (189) | I-3 | R-4 |

Obverse III²2 – Ear strongly doubled at bottom and halfway up side. Hair strongly doubled just above the ear. Small die chip on forehead just in front of the hairline.

| 2A | III²2 • C³a (Doubled Ear, Mustache) | | I-3 | R-5 |

Obverse III²2 – Die break in front of upper lip.

| 3 | III²3 • C³a (Far Date) | | I-2 | R-3 |

Obverse III²3 – Date set further right than normal with slight slant so that second 1 is higher than first 1.

| 4 | III²4 • C³a (Doubled 1) | (190) | I-2 | R-3 |

Obverse III²4 – Second 1 doubled at top outside.

| 5 | III²5 • C³a (Doubled 1-1) | (190) | I-2 | R-3 |

Obverse III²5 – Doubled 1-1 in date. First 1 is doubled as a line below upper crossbar. Second 1 is doubled slightly at top outside.

| 6 | III²6 • C³a (Slanted Date) | (189) | I-2 | R-3 |

Obverse III²6 – Date slanted in normal lateral position with 1 closest to rim.

| 7 | III²7 • C³a (Doubled 91) | (190) | I-2 | R-3 |

Obverse III²7 – Doubled 91 in date. 9 doubled as thin curved line at bottom inside of both loops. 1 doubled as thin horizontal line above left side of lower crossbar.

1891-P / 1891-CC

1A O Die Chip on Forehead

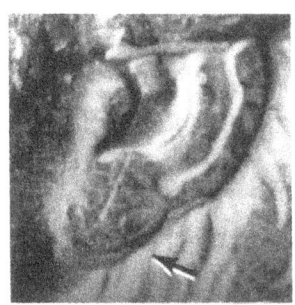

2 O Doubled Ear

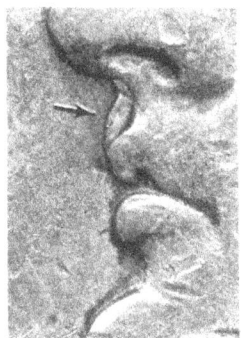

2A O Die Break on Lip

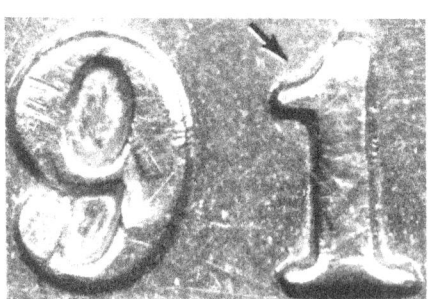

4 O Doubled Last 1

3 O Slanted Date

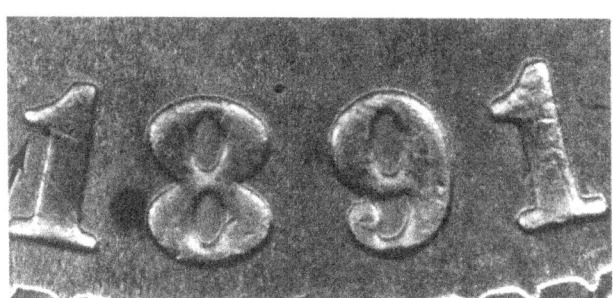

5 O Doubled 1-1

6 O Slanted Date

7 O Doubled 91

1891-CC

This issue is usually fairly well struck although quite a few have a touch of weakness and some are quite flat. Luster is usually good. A couple minor die varieties exist and one is rather unusual. It is VAM 3, spitting eagle, with a small die gouge in front of the eagle's beak. Proof-likes are fairly hard to locate and deep mirrors are scarcer than for 1890-CC. However, their depth of mirror and contrast tend to be only moderate.

1   III² 1 • C³ a (Normal Die)   I-1   R-2
     Obverse III² 1 – Normal die of III² type.
     Reverse C³ a – Normal die of C³ type with V CC mint mark letters set apart with a slight tilt to the left.

2   III² 1 – C³ b (High CC)   (177)   I-2   R-3
     Reverse C³ b – Normal die with V CC mint mark letters close together and set high to the right so that second C almost touches wreath.

3	III²1 • C³c (CC/CC Top and Spitting Eagle)		I-2	R-4

Reverse C³c – Mint mark set wide apart with a slight tilt to the left. The first C is doubled strongly at the top and lower left inside. Second C doubled slightly at top. Later die states show only the left C doubled and a die gouge shows below the eagle's beak as a spitting eagle.

4	III²2 • C³d (C/C Right)		I-2	R-4

Obverse III²2 – Date set further left than normal.
Reverse C³d – Both C's in mint mark tilted slightly left. Left C has horizontal polishing marks within the loop and is doubled slightly on right side of top serif.

5	III²2 • C³a (Near Date)	(177)	I-2	R-3

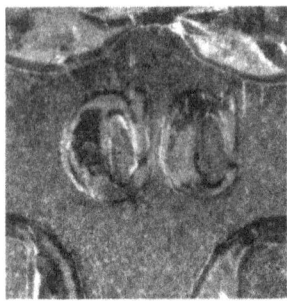 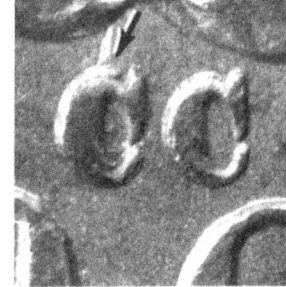 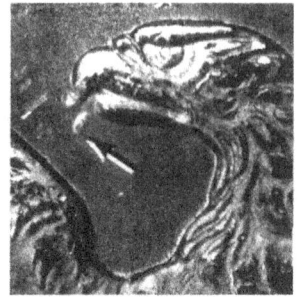 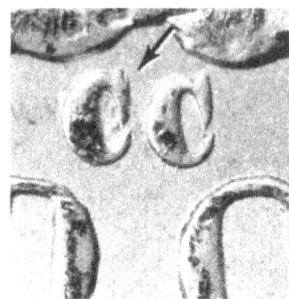

2 R High CC   3 R CC/CC   3 R Spitting Eagle   4 R C/C Right

1891-O

The strike for the 1891-O is usually fairly weak for the hair over the ear and the eagle's breast feathers. But it can vary from bold to very washed out. Luster is usually fairly dull. A few minor die varieties exist but one significant one, VAM 1A, shows an "E" from LIBERTY below the eagle's tail feathers due to clashed dies. It is readily available in lower circulated grades, but scarcer in AU and quite rare in uncirculated. VAM 3 sometimes shows a partial E die clash but in a different position than VAM 1A. Only the 1886-O, 1889-O and 1891-O show a full "E" die clash.

Proof-likes are very scarce for this issue and generally do not have much contrast although some cameos exist.

1	III²1 • C³a (Closed 9)	(181)	I-1	R-2

Obverse III²1 – Normal die of III² type with closed 9 in date.
Reverse C³a – Normal die of C³ type with medium III O mint mark centered and upright.

1A	III²1 • C³a (E on Reverse)	(181)	I-4	R-3

Reverse C³a – Clashed die with full E under eagle's tail feathers on left side.

2	III²2 • C³a (Open 9)	(181)	I-1	R-2

Obverse III²2 – Normal die of III² type with open 9 in date.

3	III²1 • C³b (O Tilted Right)	(181)	I-2	R-3

Reverse C³b – III O mint mark tilted right. Partial E under eagle's tail feathers on left side.

4	III²2 • C³b (O Tilted Right)	(181)	I-2	R-3
5	III²1 • C³c (O/O Top)	(181)	I-2	R-3

Reverse C³c – III O mint mark repunched with original showing as curved line just above top.

6	III²1 • C³d (O/O Down)	(181)	I-3	R-4

Reverse C³d – III O mint mark repunched with original showing fine line well below and to left.

7	III²3 • C³b (Doubled 9)	(181)	I-2	R-3

Obverse III²3 – Open 9 in date doubled at top.

8	III²1 • C³e (O Set High)	(181)	I-2	R-3

Reverse C³e – III O mint mark set high and upright.

9	III²4 • C³e (Far Date, High O)	(181)	I-2	R-3

Obverse III²4 – Date set further right than normal.

1891-O

10 III²5 • C³e (Slanted Date, O Set High) (181) I-2 R-3
   Obverse III²5 – Date slanted with left 1 set closer to rim.

11 III²6 • C³g (Near Date, O Set Right) (181) I-2 R-3
   Obverse III²6 – Date set further left than normal.
   Reverse C³g – III O mint mark is centered, upright and set slightly to right.

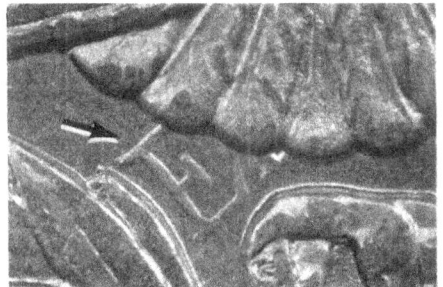
1A R E

3 R O Tilted Right

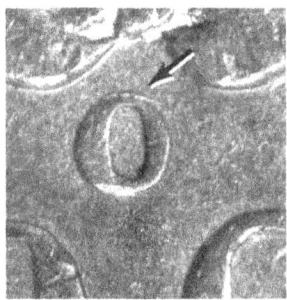
5 R O/O Top

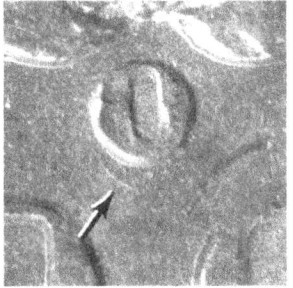
6 R O/O Down

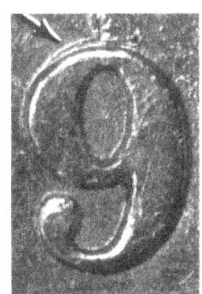
7 O Doubled 9

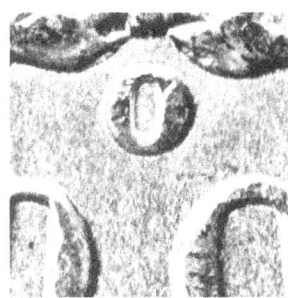
8 R O Set High

10 O Slanted Date

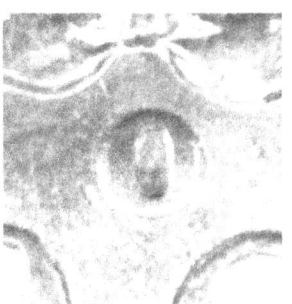
11 R O Set High

1891-S

The 1891-S, like the 1890-S, is usually fully struck and lustrous. It is also plagued by cloudy spots due to storage contamination. A few minor die varieties exist but none are significant. One sided proof-likes and semi proof-likes are fairly common. But two sided proof-likes are fairly scarce, about the same as 1890-S. Some deep mirror cameos exist but these are usually plagued by many bag marks.

1	III²1 • C³a (Normal Die)		I-1	R-2
	Obverse III²1 – Normal die of III² type.			
	Reverse C³a – Normal die of C³ type with IV S mint mark centered and upright.			
1A	III²1 • C³a (Die Gouge in Olive Branch)		I-2	R-5
	Reverse C³a – Die gouge in ends of leaves of olive branch and first adjacent leaf in the wreath.			
1B	III²1 • C³a (Die Gouge Arrow Feathers)		I-2	R-4
	Reverse C³a – Long thin die gouge from olive branch diagonally down to top arrow feather. Fine pit marks all over eagle.			
2	III²1 • C³b (S/S Down)		I-3	R-4
	Reverse C³b – Mint mark repunched with original showing as a short arc within the upper loop and the lower loop is doubled at the bottom.			
3	III²2 • C³a (Doubled Stars)		I-3	R-4
	Obverse III²2 – All stars on left are doubled on side next to rim and eyelid is doubled. Date set further left than normal.			
4	III²3 • C³a (Near Date)	(190)	I-2	R-3
	Obverse III²3 – Date set further left than normal.			
5	III²4 • C³a (Far Date)	(190)	I-2	R-3
	Obverse III²4 – Date set further right than normal.			
5A	III²4 • C³a (Far Date)	(190)	I-2	R-3
	Reverse C³a – Short die break on right side of upper berry cluster of left wreath.			

1A R Die Gouge in Olive Branch

1B R Die Gouge Arrow Feathers

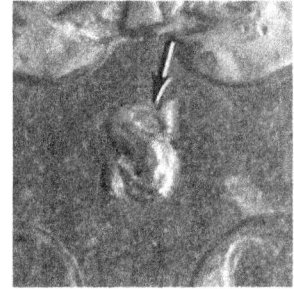

2 R S/S Down

3 O Doubled Stars

5A R Die Break in Wreath

1891-S / 1892-P

6   III²5 • C³a (Doubled 1-1)   (190)   I-2   R-3
Obverse III²5 – Doubled 1-1 in date. First 1 is doubled below upper crossbar as a short horizontal line. Second 1 doubled at top left outside of upper crossbar.

7   III²6 • C³a (Far Slanted Date)   (190)   I-2   R-3
Obverse III²6 – Date set further right than normal with second 1 further from rim than first 1.

8   III²7 • C³a (Doubled Stars)   (185)   I-2   R-3
Obverse III²7 – All stars on left are slightly doubled on side next to rim. Date in normal position.

9   III²8 • C³a (Doubled Stars, Far Date)   (191)   I-2   R-3
Obverse III²8 – All stars on left are slightly doubled on side next to rim. Date set further right than normal.

10   III²4 • C³c (Far Date, High S Mint Mark)   (190)   I-2   R-3
Reverse C³c – IV S mint mark set high.

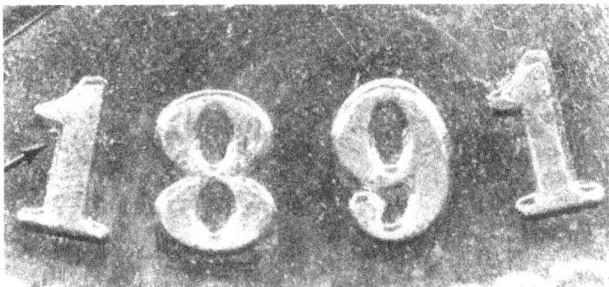
6 O Doubled 1-1

7 O Far Slanted Date

8 O Doubled Stars

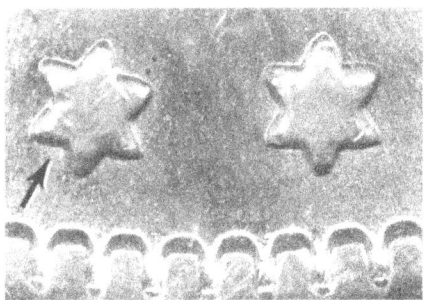
9 O Doubled Stars

1892-P

Usually the 1892-P has a fairly weak strike although full strikes are available. Luster can range from good to fairly dull. A few die varieties exist but none are significant. Fully proof-like specimens are quite rare although a few deep mirror cameos are known. Proofs generally have good contrast but quite a few show some weakness in the strike.

1   III²1 • C³a (Normal Die)   I-1   R-2
Obverse III²1 – Normal die of III² type.
Reverse C³a – Normal die of C³ type.

2   III²2 • C³a (Doubled 1-2)   I-2   R-4
Obverse III²2 – 1-2 in date doubled. 1 is doubled under upper crossbar as a horizontal line. 2 is doubled as a thin line across very top. Open 9. Date set further right than normal.

3   III²3 • C³b (Doubled Reverse)   (190)   I-3   R-4
Obverse III²3 – Lower part of upper crossbar of 1 slightly doubled. Stars on right doubled and stars on left tripled towards rim.
Reverse C³b – Outer portion doubled with lower inside of letters doubled in UNITED STATES OF AMERICA and top inside of ONE DOLLAR. Motto doubled at top. Upper part of left wreath doubled on outside and lower part of right wreath doubled slightly on outside.

1892-P / 1892-CC

4	III²4 • C³a (Near Date)	(190)	I-2	R-3

Obverse III²4 – Date set further left than normal.

5	III²5 • C³a (Doubled Profile, Tripled Motto)	(190)	I-2	R-3

Obverse III²5 – Doubled Liberty head profile including forehead, nose, lips and chin. Tripled bottom inside of letters E PLURIBUS.

6	III²2 • C³b (Doubled 1-2 and Reverse)	(190)	I-3	R-4
7	III²6 • C³a (Doubled Stars, Tripled UNUM)	(190)	I-2	R-3

Obverse III²6 – All left and right stars doubled towards rim. Tops of UNUM letters tripled towards rim.

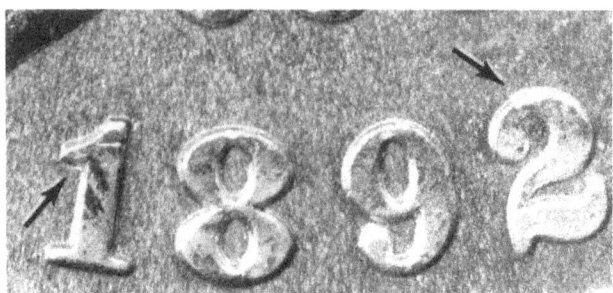
2 O Doubled 1-2

3 R Doubled Motto

3 O Doubled 1

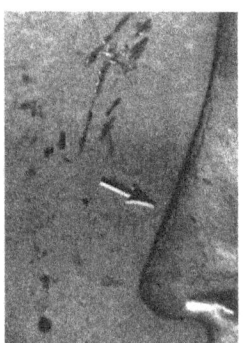
5 O Doubled Profile

7 O Doubled Stars and Letters

1892-CC

The strike is usually fairly good for this date although some specimens can be quite weak. The luster is usually good. Only a few die varieties exist and none are very significant. Proof-likes are scarce but they can be found with deep mirror cameos.

1	III²1 • C³a (Normal Die)	(177)	I-1	R-2

Obverse III²1 – Normal die of III² type with open 2. Some specimens have base of 2 filled in.
Reverse C³a – Normal die of C³ type with V CC mint mark.

2	III²1 • C³b (CC Tilted Left)		I-2	R-3

Reverse C³b – V CC mint mark tilted to left with second C touching wreath.

3	III²2 • C³a (Doubled 2)		I-2	R-3

Obverse III²2 – 2 in date doubled at top.

4	III²1 • C³c (CC/CC Down)	(177)	I-3	R-4

Reverse C³c – First C of V CC mint mark doubled slightly at inside top. Second C doubled strongly at outside left and bottom and in the top inside.

5	III²3 • C³d (Wide CC)		I-2	R-4

Obverse III²3 – Normal die of III² type with closed 2.
Reverse C³d – V CC mint mark set at medium height but with wider spacing than normal.

1892-CC / 1892-O

6	III²1 • C³e (Dropped C)		I-2	R-3
	Reverse C³e – Right C of V CC mint mark set lower than left C.			
7	III²4 • C³a (Slanted Date)		I-2	R-3
	Obverse III²4 – Date slanted with open 2 appreciably higher than 1.			
8	III²5 • C³a (Far Date)	(177)	I-2	R-3
	Obverse III²5 – Date set further right than normal. 8 and 9 show die chips in lower loops.			
9	III²5 • C³b (Far Date, CC Tilted Left)	(177)	I-2	R-3

2 R CC Tilted Left

3 O Doubled 2

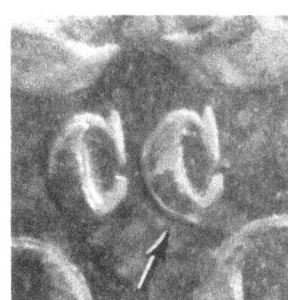

4 R CC/CC

5 R Wide CC

6 R Dropped C

7 O Slanted Date

1892-O

This is probably the most consistently flat struck date of the entire Morgan series. A small number of full strikes exist however. A few die varieties exist but none are significant. Full proof-likes are extremely rare and usually have little contrast. It is among the rarest of Morgan dollars in proof-like.

1	III²1 • C³a (Normal Die)	(181)	I-1	R-2
	Obverse III²1 – Normal die of III² type with open 9.			
	Reverse C³a – Normal die of C³ type with medium III O mint mark centered and upright.			
2	III²2 • C³b (Doubled 2)	(181)	I-2	R-3
	Obverse III²2 – 2 in date doubled at top. Closed 9 variety. Date set further right than normal with slight slant with 1 closer to rim.			
	Reverse C³b – Medium III O mint mark set high.			
3	III²3 • C³a (Closed 9)	(181)	I-1	R-2
	Obverse III²3 – Normal die of III² type with closed 9.			
4	III²3 • C³b (High O)	(181)	I-2	R-3

1892-O / 1892-S

5   III²4 • C³c (Doubled Date)   (181)   I-3   R-4

Obverse III²4 – Entire date doubled. 1 doubled at top left of upper crossbar and top right of lower crossbar. 8 doubled at bottom inside of both loops, at top outside of upper loop and right outside of lower loop. 9 doubled at bottom inside of both loops and at top right outside of upper loop. 2 doubled above lower crossbar, on left inside of upper loop, and at top outside of upper loop. Date set much further left than normal. First two stars on right doubled on right side.

Reverse C³c – Medium III O mint mark set high and tilted slightly to left.

6   III²5 • C³b (Near Date)   (181)   I-2   R-3

Obverse III²5 – Date set further left than normal. Open 9 variety.

7   III²6 • C³d (Doubled Ear, O/O)   (181)   I-3   R-3

Obverse III²6 – Ear strongly doubled on right outside of large lobe and on right side of small inner lobe. Date set much further left than normal.

Reverse C³d – Medium III O mint mark set high and doubled at top left outside.

8   III²7 • C³a (Doubled 1-2)   (181)   I-2   R-3

Obverse III²7 – Doubled 1-2 in date. 1 doubled slightly below upper crossbar as a thin line next to vertical shaft. 2 doubled slightly at top outside.

9   III²8 • C³e (Far Slanted Date, O/O Left)   (181)   I-2   R-3

Obverse III²8 – Date set further right than normal with slant to make 1 closer to rim.

Reverse C³e – Medium III O mint mark set high and doubled on top left outside and top right inside.

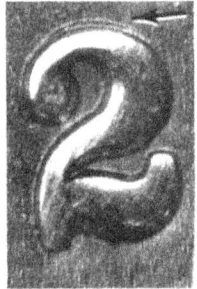 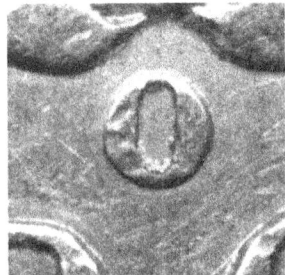 

2 O Doubled 2   4 R High O   5 O Doubled Date

 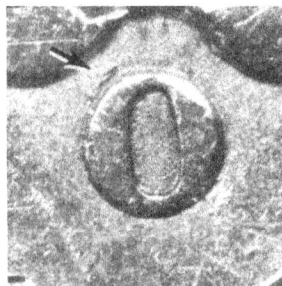 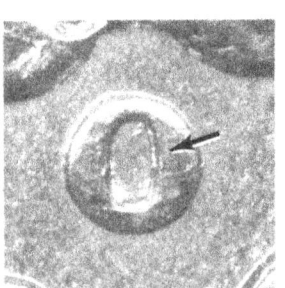 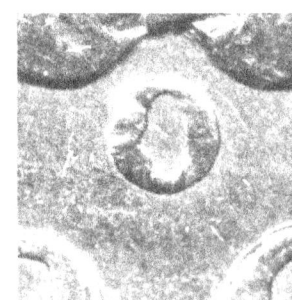

7 O Doubled Ear   7 R O/O   9 R O/O Left   5 R High O, Tilted Left

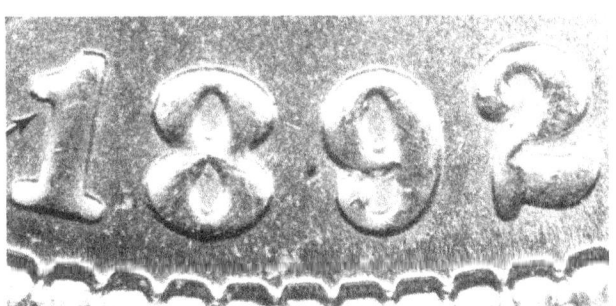 

8 O Doubled 1-2   9 O Far Slanted Date

1892-O / 1892-S

10   III² 9 • C³ f (Doubled 92, O Tilted Right)   (181)   I-2   R-3
     Obverse III² 9 – Doubled 92 in date. 9 doubled at bottom inside of upper loop. 2 doubled at top outside.
     Reverse C³ f – Medium III O mint mark set right and tilted right.

11   III² 10 • C³ g (Doubled Profile)   (181)   I-2   R-3
     Obverse III² 10 – Liberty head profile doubled slightly on nose, lips and chin.
     Reverse C³ g – UNITED and left wreath doubled slightly towards rim.

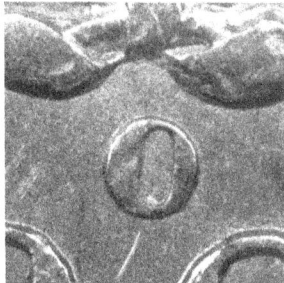

10 O Doubled 92   10 R O Set Right,   11 R Doubled UNITED
                                 Tilted Right

1892-S

Although quite rare in mint state, the 1892-S is usually fully struck and lustrous. Lower grade circulated specimens are quite common. A few die varieties exist and only VAM 2 is significant because of the unusually strongly doubled date and rarity. Proof-like specimens make up a fair proportion of the scarce mint state population, but they are still extremely scarce and generally show little contrast.

1   III² 1 • C³ a (Normal Die)   (190)   I-1   R-2
    Obverse III² 1 – Normal die of III² type. Some specimens have base of 2 filled in.
    Reverse C³ a – Normal die of C³ type with a medium IV S mint mark centered and upright.

2   III² 2 • C³ a (Doubled Date)   (190)   I-4   R-5
    Obverse III² 2 – All digits of date are doubled. 1 doubled at top left. Loops of 8 doubled strongly at top inside and upper loop doubled at lower right. Upper loop of 9 doubled at bottom as thin line in lower loop. 2 doubled below upper knob as triangular patch.

3   III² 3 • C³ a (Far Date)   I-2   R-3
    Obverse III² 3 – Date set further right than normal.
    Reverse C³ a – Medium IV S mint mark centered and upright with shallow filled upper loop and horizontal polishing mark through upper loop.

4   III² 1 • C³ b (S Tilted Right)   I-2   R-3
    Reverse C³ b – IV S mint mark centered and tilted slightly to right.

5   III² 1 • C³ c (S/S Right)   (190)   I-2   R-3
    Reverse C³ c – IV S Mint mark doubled as a curved line in the upper loop, line to the lower right outside of upper serif and line to the right of the bottom of the lower serif.

6   III² 1 • C³ d (High S)   (190)   I-2   R-3
    Reverse C³ d – IV S mint mark set high with slight tilt to right.

7   III² 2 • C³ b (Doubled 892, S Tilted Right)   (190)   I-3   R-4
    Obverse III² 2 – Die has been polished down with only a thin diagonal curved line within upper loops of 8 and 9 and notch on right inside of 2 loop.

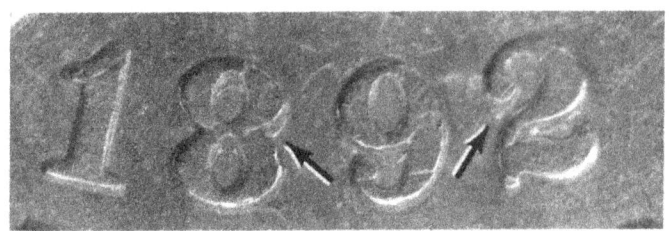

2 O Doubled Date

7 O Doubled 892

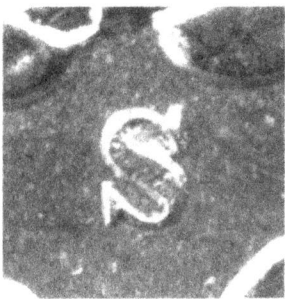

3 R Filled S

4 R S Tilted Left

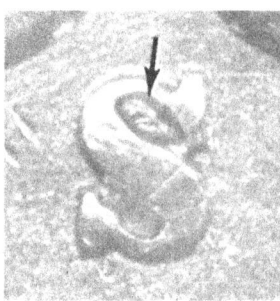

5 R S/S Right

6 R High S, Tilted Right

1893-P

Fully struck specimens with good luster is typical of this issue no doubt due to less extended use of dies to achieve the low mintage. A couple minor die varieties exist. Two of them have the 3 doubled at the top which is not present on 1893-S and is an indication of a counterfeit if seen on the 1893-S. Proof-likes are extremely rare and the few known have little contrast. Proofs generally are fairly weakly struck and are the most poorly struck Morgan proofs. Their contrast ranges from moderate to good.

1   **III²1 • C³a (Normal Die)**   I-1   R-3
    Obverse III²1 – Normal die of III² type with open 3. Upper loop not touching center bar.
    Reverse C³a – Normal die of C³ type.

2   **III²2 • C³a (Doubled 3 Low)**   I-3   R-4
    Obverse III²2 – 3 in date doubled at top and shows as an arc above the 3. Open 3 variety.

3   **III²3 • C³a (Doubled 3 High)**   (189)   I-3   R-4
    Obverse III²3 – 3 in date doubled at top. Closed 3 variety. The original 3 was punched above the new 3 very high. Die chip to right between loops of 3.

4   **III²4 • C³a (Doubled Stars)**   I-3   R-4
    Obverse III²4 – All stars on right and left doubled at bottom. Lower portions of E PL-R-B and first U in UNUM doubled. Closed 9 in date.

5   **III²5 • C³a (Near Date)**   I-2   R-3
    Obverse III²5 – Date set further left than normal. Closed 9 in date.

2 O Doubled 3 Low

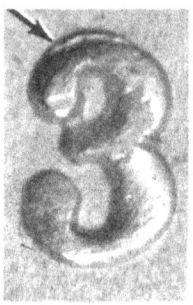

3 O Doubled 3 High

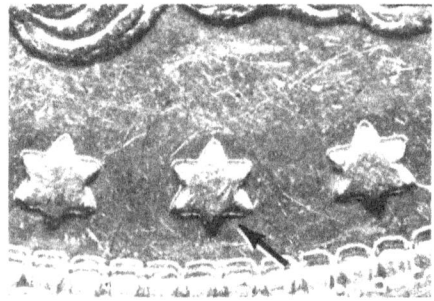

4 O Doubled Stars

1893-CC

A fair proportion of this issue is quite weakly struck with flat hair above the ear and no feather definition on the eagle's breast. Fully struck specimens with good luster are available however. A few die varieties exist but none are significant. Proof-likes are quite rare and are generally weakly struck. Twelve branch mint proofs were struck of this date to commemorate the closing of the Carson City Mint in 1893. Four proof specimens are known and they generally have very-deep mirrors, good contrast and sharp strike.

1   III^{2}1 • C^{3}a (Normal Die)   I-1   R-3
     Obverse III^{2}1 – Normal die of III^2 type with closed 3.
     Reverse C^{3}a – Normal die of C^3 type with centered V CC mint mark.

2   III^{2}1 • C^{3}b (CC Tilted Right)   I-2   R-3
     Obverse III^{2}1 – Some specimens show die chip in 3 on right side between loops.
     Reverse C^{3}b – V CC mint mark tilted to right.

3   III^{2}2 • C^{3}a (Doubled 3)   I-2   R-3
     Obverse III^{2}2 – 3 in date doubled all across very top and has die chip between loops on right.

4   III^{2}3 • C^{3}c (Doubled 3, Far Date, CC Tilted Left)   (178)   I-2   R-3
     Obverse III^{2}3 – 3 in date doubled at top left outside of upper loop. Date set further right than normal.
     Reverse C^{3}c – V CC tilted slightly to left with left C having largest tilt.

5   III^{2}4 • C^{3}a (Doubled Profile)   (178)   I-2   R-3
     Obverse III^{2}4 – Doubled Liberty head profile in forehead, nose, lips, chin and front of eye.

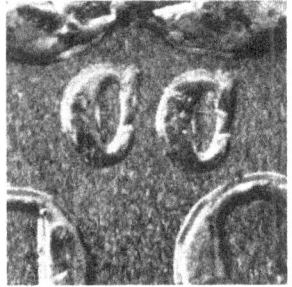

2 R CC Tilted Right

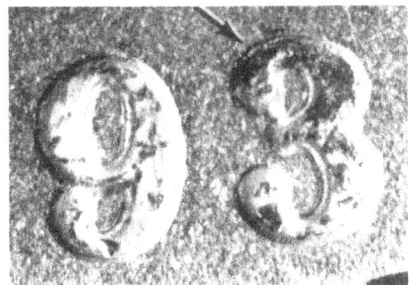

3 O Doubled 3

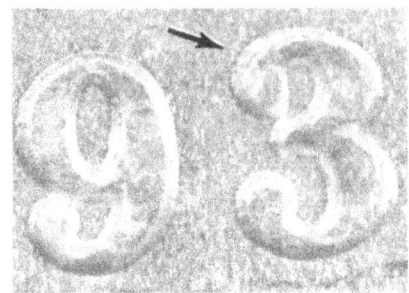

4 O Doubled 3

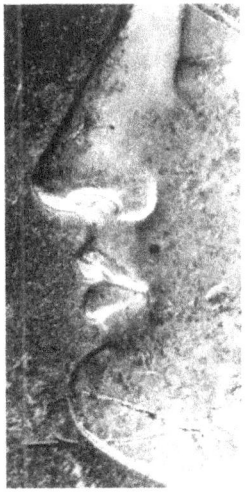

5 O Doubled Profile

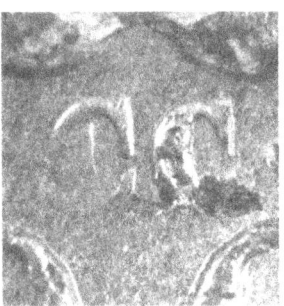

4 R CC Tilted Left

1893-O

Generally this issue is fairly weakly struck although fully struck as well as very flat specimens exist. Luster is generally good because of the low mintage. Only five minor die varieties exist. Full proof-likes on both sides are rare.

1	III²1 • C³a (Normal Die)	(181)	I-1	R-3

Obverse III²1 – Normal die of III² type.
Reverse C³a – Normal die of C³ type with centered medium III O mint mark centered and upright.

2	III²1 • C³b (O Tilted Right)	(181)	I-2	R-3

Reverse C³b – III O mint mark tilted to the right.

3	III²2 • C³a (Slanted Date)	(181)	I-2	R-3

Obverse III²2 – Date slanted with 3 set higher than 1.

4	III²3 • C³b (Doubled 1)	(181)	I-2	R-3

Obverse III²3 – 1 doubled slightly below upper crossbar.

5	III²2 • C³b (Slanted Date, O Tilted Right)	(181)	I-2	R-3

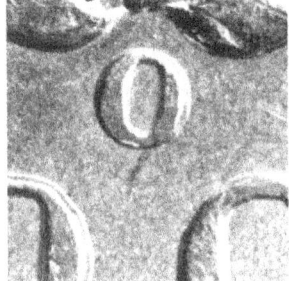  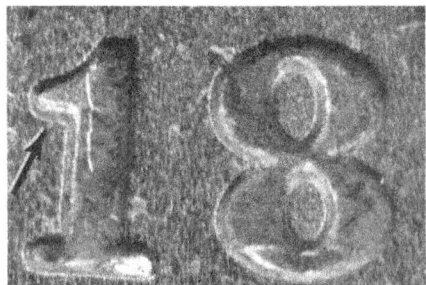

2 R O Tilted Right   3 O Slanted Date   4 O Doubled 1

1893-S

This issue is the lowest mintage and rarest in all grades. It is typically fully struck with good luster. Only one die variety is known and it has a small raised, diagonal die polishing line in the top of T in LIBERTY. This polishing line is diagnostic for a genuine 1893-S. Numerous counterfeits exist with some having added S mint marks to 1893-P or altered 8 to a 3 in an 1898-S. Fully proof-like specimens are extremely rare.

1	III²1 • C³a (Normal Die)	(187)	I-1	R-3

Obverse III²1 – Normal die of III² type with slightly raised 3. Small diagonal polishing mark in top of T in LIBERTY.
Reverse C³a – Normal die of C³ type with a medium IV S mint mark centered and upright.

1894-P

This second lowest mintage issue is generally well struck with good luster. Although the mintage is only 10,000 more than the scarce 1893-S it is more available in all grades. Only two dies varieties are known for this issue. Circulated 1894-P have been counterfeited by removing the O mint mark from 1894-O. Always carefully check the mint mark area for tooling marks and polishing.

Fully proof-like specimens are extremely rare and only a few are known in the uncirculated grade. Proofs are generally nice with full strikes and good contrast. They command a premium over other proofs because of the scarcity of high grade uncirculated business strikes.

1	III²1 • C³a (Normal Die)	(189)	I-1	R-3

Obverse III²1 – Normal die of III² type.
Reverse C³a – Normal die of C³ type.

2	III²2 • C³a (Far Date)	(179)	I-2	Proof

Obverse III²2 – Date set further right than normal.

1894-O

1894-O

Generally this issue is weakly struck but with good luster. Fully struck specimens exist but are almost invariably heavily bag marked. A few minor die varieties exist but none are significant. Fully proof-likes are extremely rare and unknown in high grade uncirculated condition.

1   III²1 • C³a (Normal Die)   (181)   I-1   R-2
      Obverse III²1 – Normal die of III² type.
      Reverse C³a – Normal die of C³ type with medium III O mint mark centered and upright.

2   III²1 • C³b (O Tilted Right)   (181)   I-2   R-3
      Reverse C³b – III O mint mark tilted to the right.

3   III²1 • C³c (O Tilted Left)   (181)   I-2   R-3
      Reverse C³c – III O mint mark tilted slightly to the left.

4   III²2 • C³a (Doubled 1-4)   (181)   I-3   R-4
      Obverse III²2 – 1 and 4 in date doubled. The upper crossbar of the 1 is doubled at bottom. The 4 is doubled at the top left.

5   III²3 • C³a (Doubled 1)   (181)   I-2   R-3
      Obverse III²3 – 1 in date doubled slightly below top crossbar.

6   III²4 • C³a (Very Near Date)   (181)   I-2   R-3
      Obverse III²4 – Date set much further left than normal.

7   III²3 • C³b (Doubled 1)   (181)   I-2   R-4

8   III²5 • C³b (Far Date, O Tilted Right)   (181)   I-2   R-3
      Obverse III²5 – Date set further right than normal.

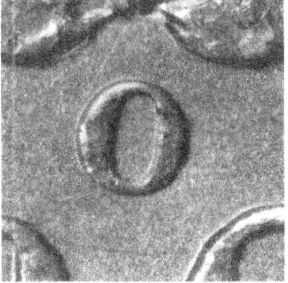   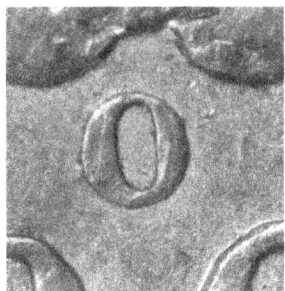

2 R O Tilted Right   3 R O Tilted Left

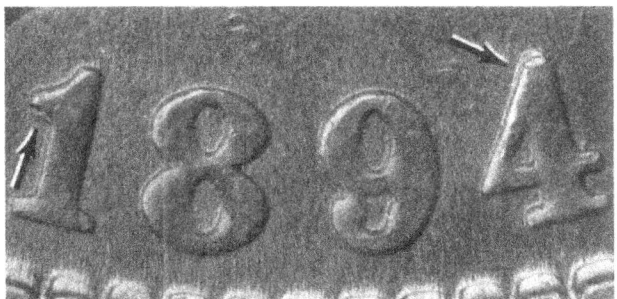   

4 O Doubled 1-4   5 O Doubled 1

1894-S

This date is well struck with good luster. Some specimens show extensive die polishing lines in the fields. Proof-likes are scarce and exhibit moderate to good contrast. They are the most available proof-like by far for the years 1893 to 1895.

1	III²1 • C³a (Normal Die)		I-1	R-2
	Obverse III²1 – Normal die of III² type.			
	Reverse C³a – Normal die of C³ type with a medium IV S mint mark, centered and upright.			
1A	III²1 • C³a (Worm Eye)	(186)	I-2	R-3
	Obverse III²1 – Die polishing line in front of eye as well as lines in back of cap and in hair.			
2	III²1 • C³b (S Tilted and Set Right)		I-2	R-3
	Reverse C³b – IV S mint mark, set right and tilted slightly to the right and doubled at left inside of upper loop.			
3	III²1 • C³c (S Tilted Right)	(185)	I-2	R-3
	Reverse C³c – IV S mint mark centered and tilted slightly to right.			
4	III²2 • C³a (Far Date)	(186)	I-2	R-3
	Obverse III²2 – Date set further right than normal.			
5	III²3 • C³d (Doubled 1, High S)	(190)	I-2	R-3
	Obverse III²3 – 1 in date doubled below upper crossbar.			
	Reverse C³d – Medium III O mint mark set high and upright.			
6	III²1 • C³d (High S)	(185)	I-2	R-3

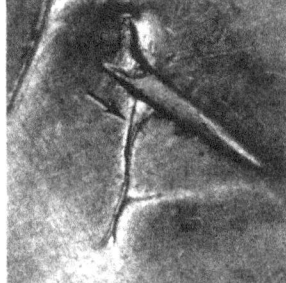

1A O Die Scratch in Eye

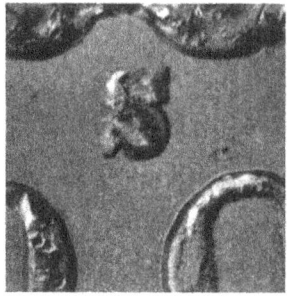

2 R S Tilted Right

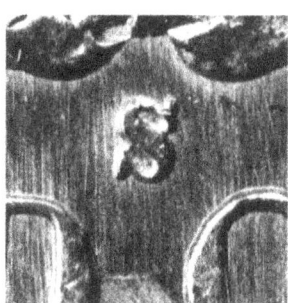

3 R S Tilted Right

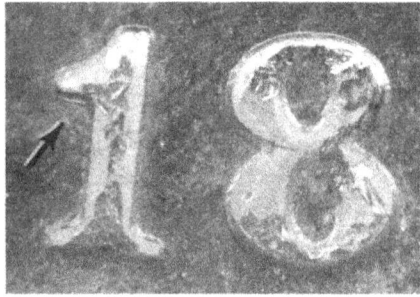

5 O Doubled 1

5 R S Set High

1895-P

No fully documented and authenticated business strikes are known. All of the 12,000 business strikes were apparently melted in the 1918-20 melts. Proofs are fairly available and a fair proportion of these are in top condition with minimal hairlines and good contrast. Three die varieties of the proof are known according to date position.

1   III²1 • C³a (Proof Die)   I-1   Proof
   Obverse III²1 – Proof die of III² type. Only 1895-P proof specimens are known to exist.
   Reverse C³a – Proof die of C³ type.

2   III²2 • C³a (Far Date)   I-2   Proof
   Obverse III²2 – Date set further right than normal.

3   III²3 • C³a (Very Far Date)   I-2   Proof
   Obverse III²3 – Date set much further right than normal.

1895-O

The strike for this issue is generally a little weak although fully struck specimens exist. Luster is usually fairly good because of the low mintage. A high grade uncirculated specimen is an extreme rarity for this issue. A couple die varieties exist but none are significant. Proof-likes are known but are extremely rare.

1   III²1 • C³a (Normal Die)   (181)   I-1   R-3
   Obverse III²1 – Normal die of III² type.
   Reverse C³a – Normal die of C³ type with medium III O mint mark centered and upright.

2   III²1 • C³b (O Tilted Right)   (181)   I-2   R-3
   Reverse C³b – Normal die with III O mint mark tilted slightly to the right.

3   III²2 • C³a (Doubled 5)   (181)   I-2   R-4
   Obverse III²2 – 5 in date doubled at top. Date set further right than normal.

4   III²3 • C³a (Far Date)   (181)   I-2   R-3
   Obverse III²3 – Date set further right than normal.

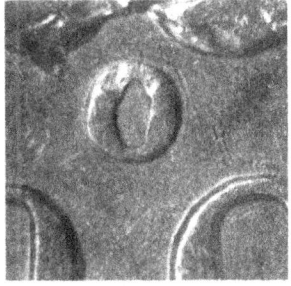

2 R O Tilted Right

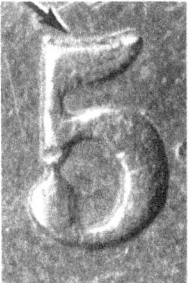

3 O Doubled 5

1895-S

A full strike and good luster is typical for this date. Some specimens show extensive die polishing lines in the fields, particularly on semi and full proof-likes. Only four die varieties are known and two are quite significant. VAM 3 has a repunched S mint mark showing well to the left of the upper loop. It is the largest shift of doubled "S" mint mark known for the Morgan dollar. VAM 4 has a "S" mint mark repunched over a horizontal "S" mint mark. However, because the 1895-S is relatively expensive in all grades, these two interesting die varieties command only modest premiums. Proof-likes are fairly scarce although they make up a significant proportion of this low mintage issue. Most proof-likes have little contrast although some deep mirror cameos are known. Semi proof-likes are abundant in the issue.

1   III²1 • C³a (Normal Die)   (185)   I-1   R-3
   Obverse III²1 – Normal die of III² type.
   Reverse C³a – Normal die of C³ type with a medium IV S mint mark centered and upright.

1895-S / 1896-P

2   III²1 • C³b (S Tilted Right) I-2   R-2
    Reverse C³b – Normal die with IV S mint mark tilted to the right.

3   III²1 • C³c (S/S) I-5   R-5
    Reverse C³c – IV S mint mark tilted to right and repunched. Original mint mark shows as a curved vertical dash at left outside of upper loop, a short spike at top outside of upper loop and a curved line in center of lower loop. Largest shift of S mint mark known for Morgan dollars.

4   III²2 • C³d (S Over Horizontal S) (188) I-5   R-4
    Obverse III²2 – 9 doubled at top left inside of upper loop.
    Reverse C³d – IV S mint mark repunched over a horizontal S. Original S shows as a triangular raised metal to left outside of upright S and as a diagonal line through top and bottom loops of S.

2 R S Tilted Right

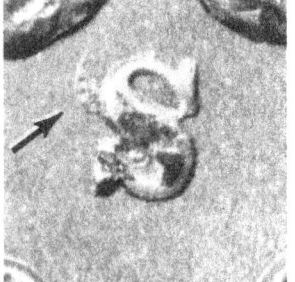
3 R S/S

4 O Doubled 9

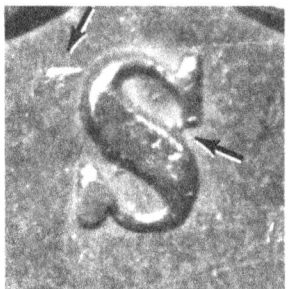
4 R S Over Horizontal S

4 R S Over Horizontal S

1896-P

The strike is usually full and luster good for this issue. A number of minor die varieties exist but only VAM 5 with strongly doubled 1 and 6 is really very significant. Proof-likes are not very scarce but most have only light to moderate contrast. Proofs generally have excellent contrast and are fully struck making them among the best Morgan proofs available.

1   III²1 • C³a (Normal Die) (189) I-1   R-2
    Obverse III²1 – Normal die of III² type.
    Reverse C³a – Normal die of C³ type.

1A III²1 • C³a (Bar 6) (190) I-2   R-5
    Obverse III²1 – 6 in date has vertical die gouge as bar on right inside of lower loop and a short tip at right inside of the upper loop.

1B III²1 • C³a (Pitted Reverse) I-2   R-3
    Reverse C³a – Rust die pits around D and L of DOLLAR.

2   III²2 • C³a (Doubled 6) (186) I-2   R-3
    Obverse III²2 – 6 in date doubled at top. Date set much further left than normal.

1896-P

3 III²3 • C³a (**Doubled 89**)   (190)   I-3   R-4
  Obverse III²3 – 89 in date is doubled with large shift to right within lower loops. The 8 has vertical shaft at top left inside of lower loop. The 9 has a dot to right of lower loop end.

4 III²4 • C³a (**Doubled Stars and 6**)   (191)   I-4   R-5
  Obverse III²4 – All stars right and left doubled with first two on both sides having large shifts. 6 in date doubled on lower left inside of lower loop and at top center of upper loop. Date set low and much further left than normal.

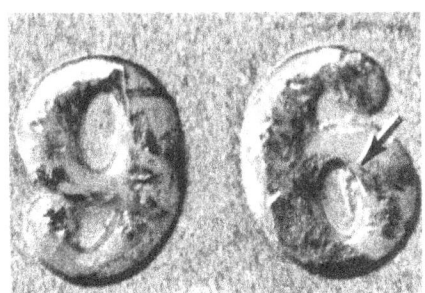
1A O Bar 6

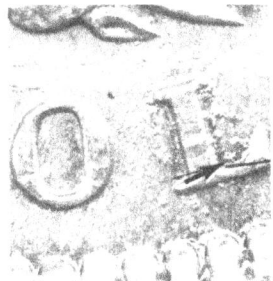
1B R Pitted Reverse

2 O Doubled 6

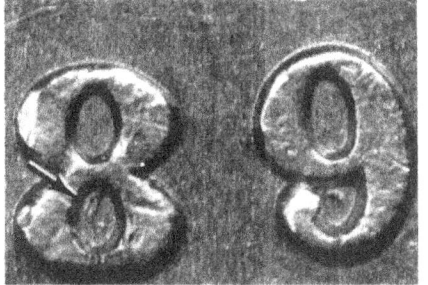
3 O Doubled 89

4 O Doubled 6

4 O Doubled Stars

4 O Doubled Stars

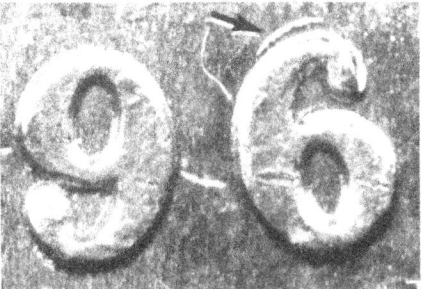
6 O Doubled 6

7 O Doubled 1

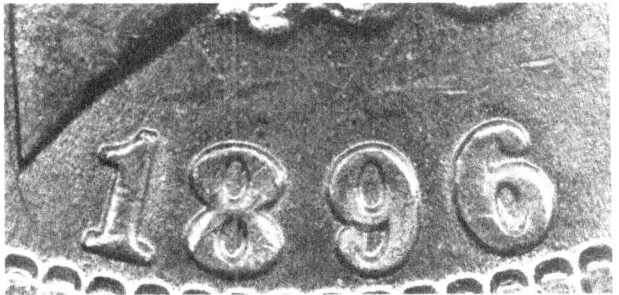
4 O Very Low Near Date

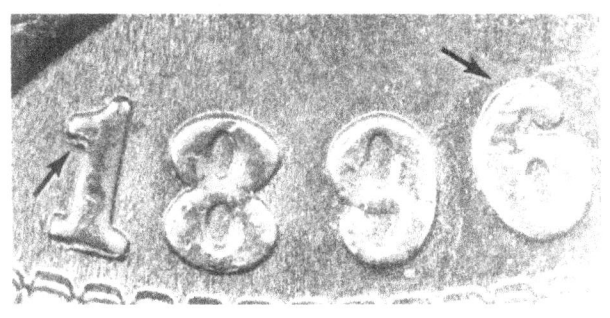
5 O Doubled 18-6

1896-P

5   III² 5 • C³ a (Doubled 18-6)   I-4   R-4
Obverse III² 5 – 18-6 in date doubled strongly. 1 is doubled strongly below upper serif and at lower right of bottom crossbar. 8 is doubled slightly at top inside and lower left outside of upper loop plus at bottom outside of lower loop. 6 is doubled at top outside of upper loop and at top right outside of lower loop.

6   III² 6 • C³ a (Doubled 6)   (190)   I-3   R-4
Obverse III² 6 – 6 in date doubled at top outside of upper loop as thick curved line and at top outside of lower loop as a short thin line. Doubling is set higher and is thicker than VAM 2. Date set further left than normal.

7   III² 7 • C³ 3 (Doubled 1)   I-2   R-3
Obverse III² 7 – 1 in date doubled at top left as short spike and slightly just below upper crossbar. Date set further left than normal.

8   III² 8 • C³ a (Doubled 1-6)   (189)   I-2   R-3
Obverse III² 8 – Doubled 1-6 in date. 1 doubled slightly below top crossbar. 6 doubled at top outside showing as a flat curved line next to top loop.

9   III² 9 • C³ a (Doubled 96)   (186)   I-2   R-3
Obverse III² 9 – Doubled 96 in date. 9 doubled as a faint curved line just above the top loop. 6 doubled as a long curved line and short segment well above top loop.

10   III² 10 • C³ a (Doubled 6, Low Date)   I-2   R-3
Obverse III² 10 – 6 in date doubled just above top outside of upper loop as thin curved segment and dot on right. Date set close to rim.

11   III² 11 • C³ a (Near Date)   (190)   I-2   R-3
Obverse III² 11 – Date set further left than normal.

11A   III² 11 • C³ a (Gouged 8)   I-2   R-4
Obverse III² 11 – Vertical die gouge in left top inside of lower loop of 8.

12   III² 12 • C³ a (Near Slanted Date)   (190)   I-2   R-3
Obverse III² 12 – Date set further left than normal and slanted with 1 close to rim.

13   III² 13 • C³ a (Doubled 1)   (190)   I-2   R-3
Obverse III² 13 – 1 in date doubled below upper crossbar. Date set further left than normal.

8 O Doubled 1-6

10 O Doubled 6, Low Date

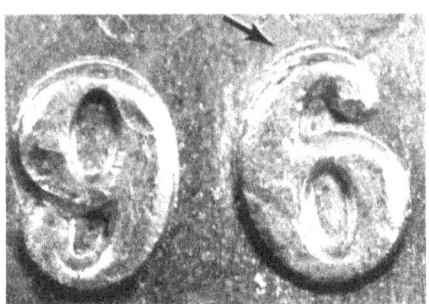

9 O Doubled 96

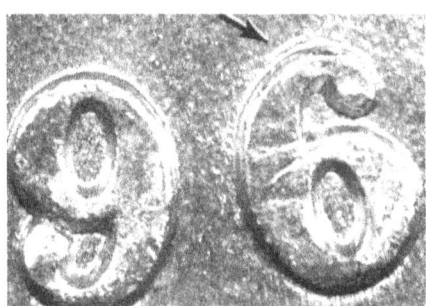

10 O Doubled 6, Low Date

11A O Gouged 8

1896-P / 1896-O

| 14 | III² 14 • C³ a (Doubled 6) | (190) | I-2 | R-3 |

Obverse III² 14 – 6 in date doubled just above top outside of upper loop as a dot on left and thin curved line joining top of loop and doubled slightly at bottom outside of lower loop.

| 15 | III² 15 • C³ a (Doubled 1-9, Tripled 6) | (191) | I-2 | R-3 |

Obverse III² 15 – 1 doubled below upper crossbar. 9 doubled faintly at top outside of upper loop. 6 tripled at top outside of upper loop.

| 16 | III² 16 • C³ a (Doubled 6, Very Low Date) | (191) | I-2 | R-3 |

Obverse III² 16 – 6 doubled at lower left inside of lower loop. Date set much further left than normal and very close to rim. One of the lowest dates in Morgan series.

| 17 | III² 17 • C³ a (Doubled 6, Near Date) | (190) | I-2 | R-3 |

Obverse III² 17 – 6 doubled slightly at top outside. Date set further left than normal.

| 18 | III² 18 • C³ a (Very Near Date) | (189) | I-2 | Proof |

Obverse III² 18 – Date set much further left than normal.

11 O Near Date

12 O Near Slanted Date

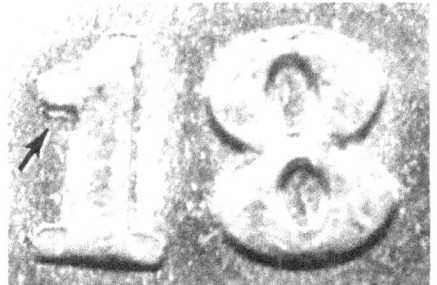

13 O Doubled 1

14 O Doubled 6

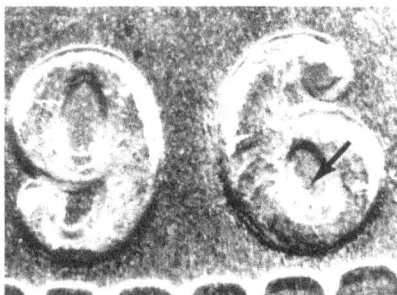

16 O Low Date, Doubled 6

15 O Doubled 1-9, Tripled 6

16 O Low Date, Doubled 6

17 O Doubled 6

1896-O

Typical strike is fairly weak and the luster fairly dull. High grade specimens are quite rare despite the relatively high mintage. Apparently most of the issue was released into circulation after four years of low New Orleans mintages. A number of minor die varieties exist. VAM 7 shows strong doubling below 96 and is worth a modest premium. VAM 4 has a small O mint mark readily detected but is extremely scarce and only known in low circulated grades. Proof-like specimens are extremely rare and generally have little contrast.

1   III² 1 • C³ a (Normal Die)   (181)   I-1   R-2
Obverse III² 1 – Normal die of III² type.
Reverse C³ a – Normal die of C³ type with medium III O mint mark, centered and upright.

1A   III² 1 • C³ a (Gouged Date)   (181)   I-2   R-5
Obverse III² 1 – Heavy die gouges in date. The 8 has die chips at bottom of upper loop opening and a thick horizontal bar die gouge at top of lower loop opening. The 6 has a thick vertical bar die gouge extending from middle of lower loop opening to its top. The upper loop opening of the 6 has a die chip at the very bottom. The 1 has a short horizontal line to the left of bottom of upper serif. There. are polishing lines throughout the lower part of the Liberty's head and within LIBERTY.

2   III² 1 • C³ b (O Tilted Left)   (181)   I-2   R-3
Reverse C³ b – Normal die with medium III O mint mark, tilted slightly left.

3   III² 1 • C³ c (O Tilted Right)   (181)   I-2   R-3
Reverse C³ c – Normal die with medium centered III O mint mark tilted slightly right.

4   III² 1 • C³ d (Small O)   I-4   R-6
Reverse C³ d – Normal die with small I O mint mark, centered and tilted to right

5   III² 2 • C³ a (Doubled 1-6)   (181)   I-2   R-3
Obverse III² 2 – 1-6 in date doubled. 1 doubled slightly on surface below upper crossbar. 6 doubled at top outside.

6   III² 3 • C³ c (Doubled 1-6)   (181)   I-3   R-4
Obverse III² 3 – 1-6 in date doubled. 1 is doubled to the top left. 6 is doubled strongly below and to the left. Date set further right than normal.

7   III² 4 • C³ c (Doubled 96)   (181)   I-4   R-4
Obverse III² 4 – 96 in date doubled strongly at bottom. Date set further left than normal.

   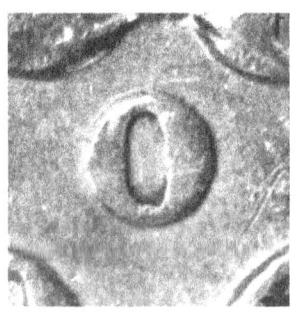   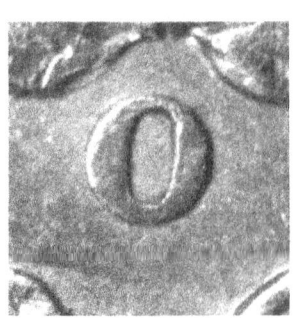

1A O Gouged Date   2 R O Tilted Left   3 R O Tilted Right

1896-O

5 O Doubled 1-6

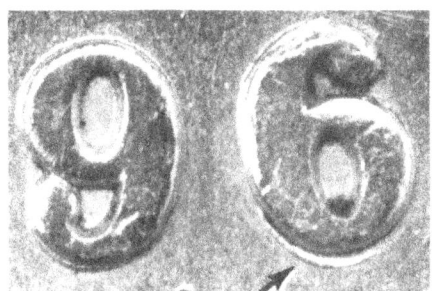

7 O Doubled 96

8 R Oval O

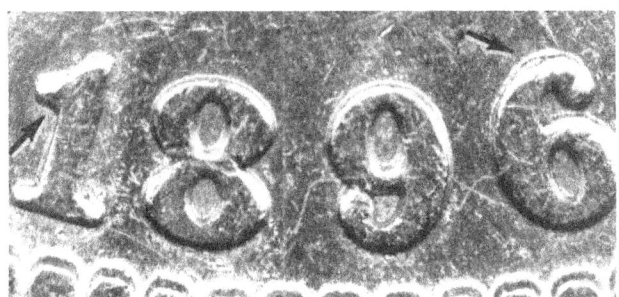

5 O Doubled 1-6

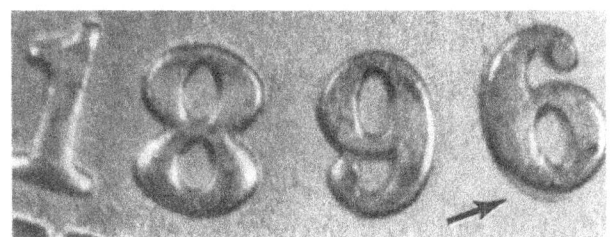

6 O Doubled 1-6

| 8 | III²1 • C³e (Oval O) | (181) | I-3 | R-5 |

Reverse C³e – Normal die of C³ type with an oval II O mint mark.

| 9 | III²5 • C³a (Doubled 1) | (181) | I-2 | R-3 |

Obverse III²5 – 1 doubled at top left as a short curved bar and at left end of top crossbar as a shallow dot.

| 10 | III²6 • C³a (Doubled I) | (181) | I-2 | R-3 |

Obverse III²6 – 1 in date doubled slightly below upper crossbar.

| 11 | III²7 • C³a (Doubled 18) | (181) | I-2 | R-4 |

Obverse III²7 – 18 in date doubled. 1 is doubled strongly at bottom outside of lower loop. 8 is doubled slightly at bottom left outside.

| 12 | III²8 • C³a (Doubled 18-6) | (181) | I-3 | R-4 |

Obverse III²8 – 18-6 doubled in date. 1 doubled strongly below bottom crossbar and slightly below upper crossbar. 8 doubled at bottom left outside of lower loop. 6 doubled strongly on right outside of upper loop and shows as a curved teardrop well away from loop. Date set further left than normal.

| 13 | III²10 • C³f (Near Date, High O) | (181) | I-2 | R-3 |

Obverse III²10 – Date set further left than normal.
Reverse C³f – III O mint mark set slightly high.

| 14 | III²11 • C³c (Doubled 6, O Tilted Right) | (181) | I-2 | R-3 |

Obverse III²11 – 6 doubled slightly at top outside. Date set further left than normal.

| 15 | III²12 • C³c (Doubled 96, O Tilted Right) | (181) | I-2 | R-3 |

Obverse III²12 – 96 doubled very slightly at top outside. Date set further left than normal.

| 16 | III²12 • C³a (Doubled 1, Near Date) | (181) | I-2 | R-3 |

Obverse III²12 – 1 doubled below upper crossbar. Date set further left than normal.

| 17 | III²10 • C³c (Near Date, O Tilted Right) | (181) | I-2 | R-3 |
| 18 | III²10 • C³f (High O) | (181) | I-2 | R-3 |

1896-O / 1896-S

9 O Doubled 1

10 O Doubled 1

11 O Doubled 18

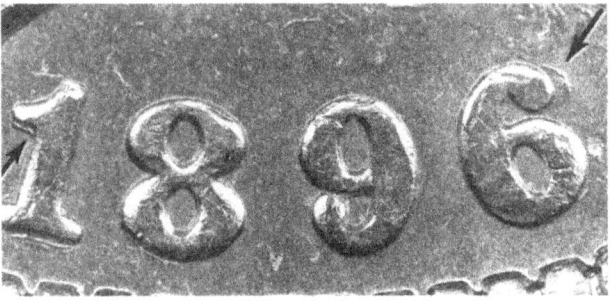
12 O Doubled 18-6

13 R High O

14 O Doubled 6 Top

15 O Doubled 96 Top Slight

16 O Doubled 1

1896-S

Usually this issue has a touch of weakness in the strike although it can vary from full to moderately weak. Luster is generally good. High grade uncirculated specimens with full strike are quite scarce for this relatively high mintage issue and apparently most were released into circulation like the 1896-O after four years of low mintages. A few minor die varieties exist but none are significant except VAM 5 showing S/S with a large shift to the northeast. Proof-likes are very rare with little contrast.

1   III^{2}1 • C^{3}a (Normal Die)   (186)   I-1   R-2
  Obverse III^{2}1 – Normal die of III^2 type.
  Reverse C^{3}a – Normal die of C^3 type with a medium IV S mint mark, centered and upright.

2   III^{2}2 • C^{3}d (Doubled 1-6)   1-2   R-4
  Obverse III^{2}2 – Doubled 1-6 in date. 1 doubled below upper crossbar. 6 doubled at top as a curved thin line just above very top.
  Reverse C^{3}d – IV S mint mark doubled to left of upper serif.

3   III^{2}3 • C^{3}b (S/S)   I-3   R-4
  Obverse III^{2}3 – 8 has vertical spike die gouge within center of lower loop and 9 has dot in center of lower loop.
  Reverse C^{3}b – IV S mint mark repunched with original showing as a thin diagonal line on right side of upper loop opening and as an arc on right side of lower loop opening.

1896-S

4	**III²4 • C³a (Near Date)**		I-2	R-3
	Obverse III²4 – Date set further left than normal.			
5	**III²1 • C³c (S/S Right and Up)**	(188)	I-3	R-4
	Reverse C³c – IV S mint mark repunched with original showing as a short spike above top loop, vertical serif to top right of top serif, curved arc to right of lower loop and vertical serif within lower loop opening.			
6	**III²5 • C³d (Doubled 1, S/S Center)**	(188)	I-3	R-3
	Obverse III²5 – 1 doubled slightly below upper crossbar.			
	Reverse C³d – IV S mint mark repunched with original showing as a curved arc at top of upper loop opening.			
7	**III²6 • C³a (Doubled 6)**	(186)	I-2	R-3
	Obverse III²6 – 6 in date doubled at top outside of upper loop.			
8	**III²6 • C³e (Doubled 6, S/S Down)**	(186)	I-2	R-3
	Reverse C³e – IV S mint mark repunched with original showing as two thin arcs at left side of upper loop opening and middle shaft doubled at bottom.			

2 O Doubled 1-6

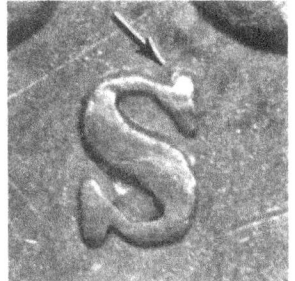

2 R S/S

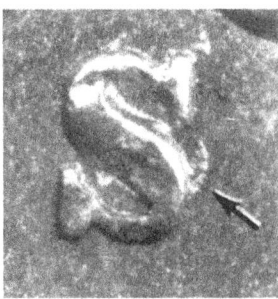

5 R S/S Right and Up

3 O Die Gouge

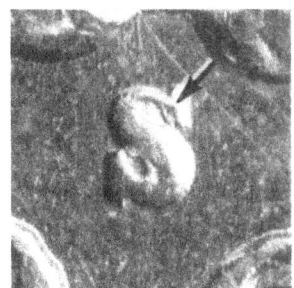

3 R S/S

6 O Doubled 1

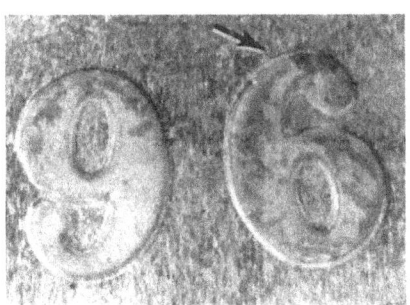

7 O Doubled 6

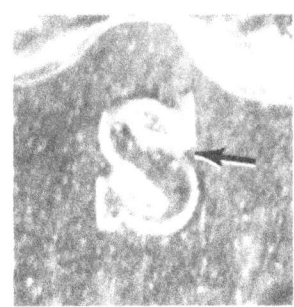

8 R S/S

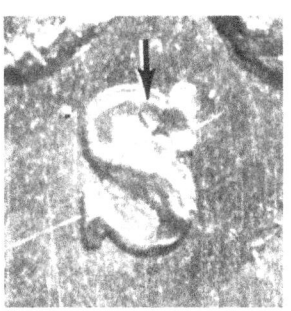

6 R S/S

1897-P

A full strike and good luster is typical for this date. A few minor die varieties exist but none are significant. Proof-likes are fairly scarce and generally have little contrast. Proofs have excellent contrast and are fully struck.

1   III^2 1 • C^3 a (Normal Die)   (189)   I-1   R-2
Obverse III^2 1 – Normal die of III^2 type.
Reverse C^3 a – Normal die of C^3 type.

1A   III^2 1 • C^3 a (Pitted Reverse)   (190)   I-2   R-5
Reverse C^3 a – Die is pitted to left below the eagle's tail feathers and in the lower left wreath.

2   III^2 2 • C^3 a (Doubled 18)   (190)   I-2   R-3
Obverse III^2 2 – Doubled 18 in date. 1 doubled as thin line well below base. 8 in date doubled strongly at bottom outside and top inside of lower loop. Date set further left than normal.

3   III^2 3 • C^3 a (Doubled 1)   (190)   I-2   R-3
Obverse III^2 3 – 1 in date doubled below top crossbar.

4   III^2 4 • C^3 a (Doubled 7)   I-2   R-3
Obverse III^2 4 – 7 is doubled at top left serif and as a fine line just above top of 7.

5   III^2 5 • C^3 a (Doubled 18)   (188)   I-2   R-3
Obverse III^2 5 – 18 in date doubled. 1 is doubled as a short horizontal spike just below the upper crossbar. 8 doubled slightly at top inside of both loops.

6   III^2 6 • C^3 a (Near Date)   I-2   R-3
Obverse III^2 6 – Date set further left than normal.

6A   III^2 6 • C^3 a (Near Date, Pitted Reverse)   (190)   I-2   R-3
Reverse C^3 a – Pitted die below eagle's tail feathers as in VAM 1A.

7   III^2 7 • C^3 a (Slanted Date)   I-2   R-3
Obverse III^2 7 – Date slanted with 1 very close to rim.

8   III^2 8 • C^3 a (Doubled Left Stars)   I-3   R-4
Obverse III^2 8 – Normal date. All left stars doubled strongly towards rim.

1A R Pitted Reverse

2 O Doubled 18

3 O Doubled 1

4 O Doubled 7

5 O Doubled 18

8 O Doubled Stars

1897-P / 1897-O

7 O Slanted Date

1897-O

A touch of weakness in the strike is typical for this issue although specimens can be found with flat strikes and full strikes. Luster is generally dull. A few die varieties exist but none are significant. Proof-likes are extremely rare comparable to the rarity of the 1896-O. Generally the contrast is light although a few cameos are known.

1   III²1 • C³a (Normal Die)   (181)   I-1   R-2
    Obverse III²1 – Normal die of III² type.
    Reverse C³a – Normal die of C³ type with medium III O mint mark centered and upright.

2   III²1 • C³b (O Tilted Right)   (181)   I-2   R-3
    Reverse C³b – Normal die of C³ type with III O mint mark set high and tilted right.

3   III²1 • C³c (O Set High)   (181)   I-2   R-3
    Reverse C³c – Normal die with III O mint mark set upright and high.

4   III²2 • C³b (Doubled 7)   (181)   I-2   R-4
    Obverse III²2 – 7 in date doubled at very bottom. Date set further left than normal.

5   III²1 • C³d (O Set High and Left)   (181)   I-2   R-3
    Reverse C³d – Normal die with III O mint mark set high and to left.

6   III²3 • C³e (Near Date)   (181)   I-2   R-3
    Obverse III²3 – Date set further left than normal.
    Reverse C³e – Normal die with III O mint mark set high and slightly left with tilt to right.

7   III²3 • C³c (Near Date, High O)   (181)   I-2   R-3

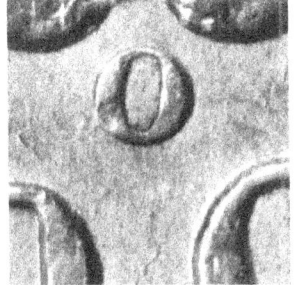

2 R O Tilted Right

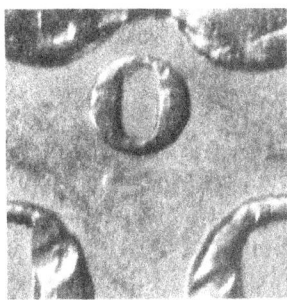

3 R O Set High

4 O Doubled 7

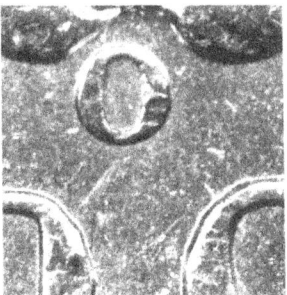

5 R O Set High and Left

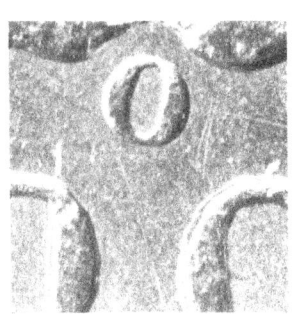

6 R O Set High, Tilted Right

1897-S

The strike is usually full and the luster good. A few minor die varieties exist and only VAM 4 with the doubled 1-7 is of some significance because of the large separation in the doubling. Proof-likes are fairly available and usually have good cameo contrast.

1   III²1 • C³a (Normal Die)   (190)   I-1   R-2
   Obverse III²1 – Normal die of III² type.
   Reverse C³a – Normal die of C³ type with a medium IV S mint mark centered and upright.

2   III²2 • C³a (Doubled 18)   I-2   R-4
   Obverse III²2 – 18 in date doubled. The 1 has a short spike just below the top crossbar. The 8 is doubled inside the top loop.

3   III²1 • C³b (S Tilted Right)   I-2   R-3
   Reverse C³b – IV S mint mark centered and tilted slightly to right.

4   III²3 • C³a (Doubled 1-7)   (186)   I-3   R-4
   Obverse III²3 – 1-7 in date doubled. The 1 has a long horizontal line well below the top crossbar. 7 is doubled at top and shows as a thin broken line.

5   III²4 • C³a (Doubled 1)   (187)   I-2   R-3
   Obverse III²4 – 1 doubled slightly at bottom of upper crossbar.

6   III²4 • C³b (Doubled 1)   I-2   R-3

7   III²5 • C³a (Doubled 1, Tilted 7)   I-3   R-4
   Obverse III²5 – 1 doubled at very top on surface. 7 tilted to left. Date set much further left than normal.

8   III²1 • C³c (S Set High)   (190)   I-2   R-3
   Reverse C³c – IV S mint mark set slightly high.

9   III²6 • C³a (Near Date)   (190)   I-2   R-3
   Obverse III²6 – Date set further left than normal.

10 III²6 • C³b (Near Date, S Tilted Right)   (190)   I-2   R-3

11 III²7 • C³a (Doubled 1-9)   (190)   I-2   R-3
   Obverse III²7 – Doubled 1-9 in date. 1 doubled slightly just below upper crossbar. 9 doubled at top inside of upper loop.

2 O Doubled 18

3 R S Tilted Right

5 O Doubled 1

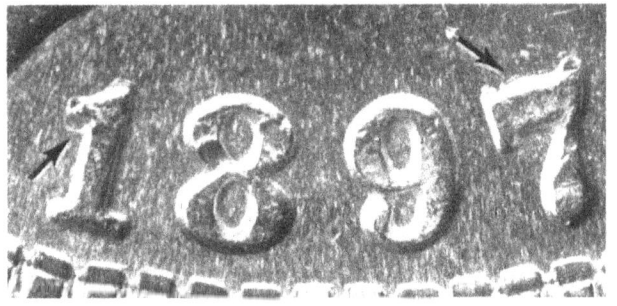

4 O Doubled 1-7

7 O Near Date, Tilted 7

1897-S / 1898-P

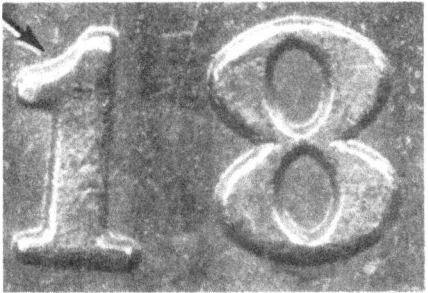
7 O Doubled 1

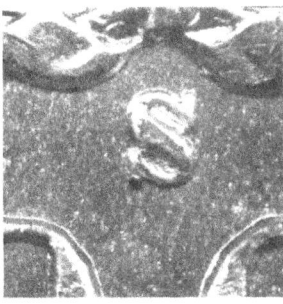
8 R S Set High

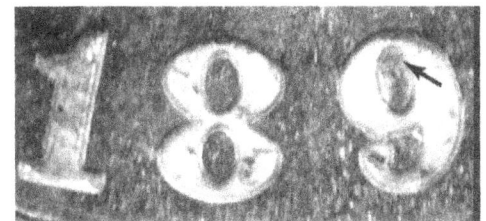
11 O Doubled 1-9

1898-P

This issue has a good strike and good luster. A few die varieties exist but none are significant. Proof-likes are fairly available but generally have little contrast. Proofs are generally of high quality with full strike and very deep cameos.

1 III²1 • C³a (Open 9) (189) I-1 R-2
   Obverse III²1 – Normal die of III² type with open 9.
   Reverse C³a – Normal die of C³ type.

2 III²2 • C³a (Closed 9) I-1 R-2
   Obverse III²2 – Normal die of III² type with closed 9.

3 III²3 • C³a (Near Date) (190) 1-2 R-3
   Obverse III²3 – Date set further left than normal. Open and closed 9's.

4 III²4 • C³a (Doubled 8) I-2 R-4
   Obverse III²4 – Second 8 in date doubled strongly at bottom left outside. Date set further left than normal. Closed 9.

5 III²5 • C³a (Doubled 8) (189) I-2 R-3
   Obverse III²5 – Second 8 in date doubled at top inside of both loops and on lower right outside of upper loop.

6 III²6 • C³a (Doubled First 8) (189) I-2 R-3
   Obverse III²6 – First 8 in date doubled slightly at bottom left outside of lower loop as a thin curved line on field.

7 III²7 • C³a (Doubled Date) (189) I-2 R-3
   Obverse III²7 – Entire date is doubled. 1 doubled at top left and right of bottom crossbar. 898 all doubled at bottom inside of both loops and top outside of upper loops.

8 III²8 • C³a (Doubled 1) (190) I-2 R-3
   Obverse III²8 – 1 doubled below upper crossbar.

9 III²9 – C³a (Slanted Date) (189) I-2 R-3
   Obverse III²9 – Date slanted with 1 closest to rim.

10 III²10 • C³a (Near Date, Doubled Second 8) (189) I-2 R-3
   Obverse III²10 – Second 8 in date doubled at top inside and lower right inside of both loops. Date set further left than normal.

4 O Doubled 8

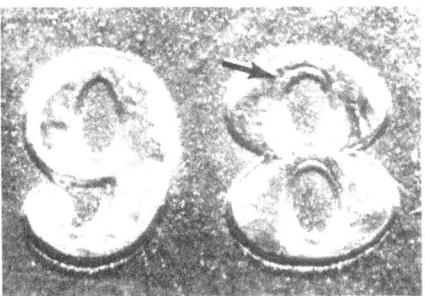
5 O Doubled 8

6 O Doubled First 8

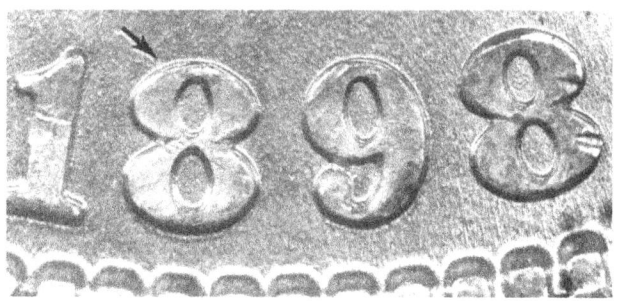
7 O Doubled Date

8 O Doubled 1

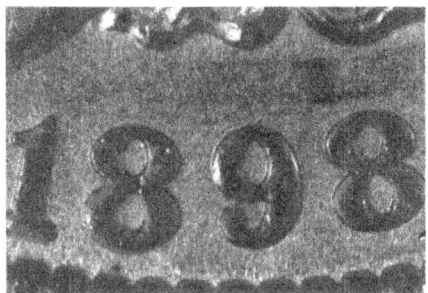
9 O Slanted Date

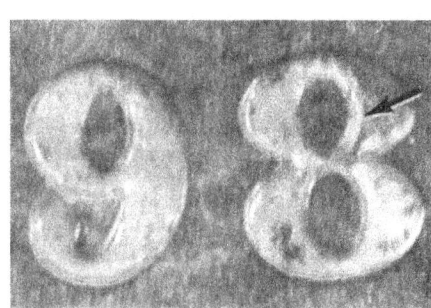
10 O Doubled Second 8

1898-O

Generally the strike is fairly full although it is not uncommon to find slightly weak and weak struck specimens. Luster is generally good. Many thousands of uncirculated bags of 1898-O to 1904-O mint were released by the Treasury in 1962-1964 of these formerly scarce to rare dates. The 1898-O is slightly less available now than the 1904-O which were the two dates released in largest quantities. A number of minor die varieties exist but none are significant. Proof-likes are fairly available and most have little to moderate contrast although a few fairly contrasty proof-likes are known.

1	III²1 • C³a (Normal Die)	(181)	I-1	R-2

Obverse III²1 – Normal die of III² type with open 9.
Reverse C³a – Normal die of C³ type with medium III O mint mark centered and upright.

2	III²2 • C³a (Doubled 8 Bottom)	(181)	I-2	R-3

Obverse III²2 – Second 8 in date doubled slightly at top and right inside of upper loop and top inside and bottom right outside of lower loop. Date set much further left than normal.

3	III²3 • C³a Doubled 18 Top)	(181)	I-2	R-3

Obverse III²3 – 18 in date doubled. 1 doubled at very top as notch. Second 8 in date doubled slightly at top left and bottom right inside of upper loop.

4	III²1 • C³b (O Set High)	(181)	I-2	R-3

Reverse C³b – III O mint mark set high and upright.

5	III²1 • C³c (O Tilted Right)	(181)	1-2	R-3

Reverse C³c – III O mint mark centered and tilted to the right.

6	III²4 • C³a (Near Date)	(181)	I-2	R-3

Obverse III²4 – Date set further left than normal.

7	III²4 • C³b (Near Date)	(181)	I-2	R-3
8	III²4 • C³c (Near Date)	(181)	I-2	R-3

1898-O

9   III²5 • C³a (Doubled 8)   (181)   I-2   R-3
Obverse III²5 – Near date not as close as III²4 obverse with second 8 doubled slightly at top left outside of upper loop and top inside of lower loop.

10   III²5 • C³d (Doubled 8)   (181)   I-2   R-3
Reverse C³d – III O mint mark set high and tilted very far to right.

11   III²6 • C³d (Doubled 898)   (181)   I-2   R-3
Obverse III²6 – Near date not as close as III²4 obverse. Doubled 898 in date. 89 doubled slightly at bottom outside of lower loops. Second 8 doubled slightly on right inside of upper loop and top inside and bottom right outside of lower loop.

12   III²7 • C³b (Doubled 8)   (181)   I-2   R-3
Obverse III²7 – Second 8 in date doubled slightly at top outside of upper loop and strongly on bottom inside of upper loop as thick crescent.

13   III²8 • C³b (Very Near Date)   (181)   I-2   R-3
Obverse III²8 – Date set much further left than normal. Second 8 tripled slightly at top right inside of lower loop.

2 O Doubled 8 Bottom

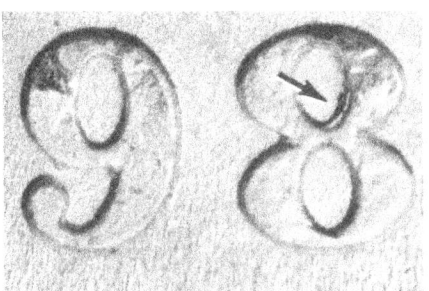
3 O Doubled 8 Top

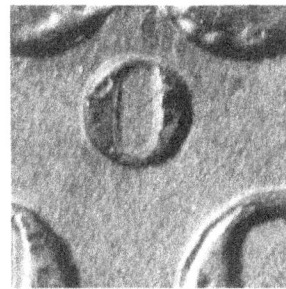
4 R O Set High

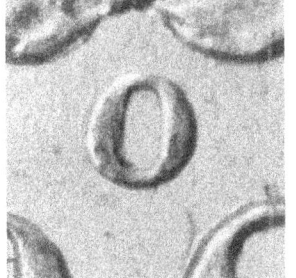
5 R O Tilted Right

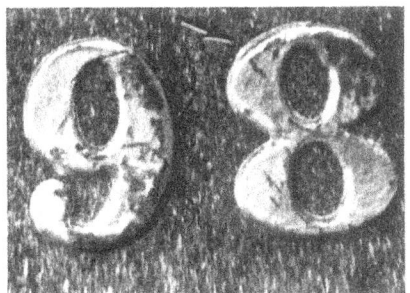
9 O Doubled 8

11 O Doubled 898

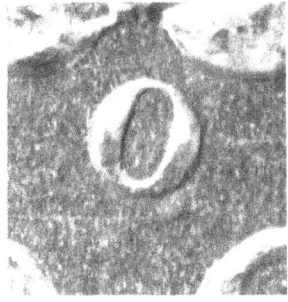
10 R O Set High
Tilted Right

12 O Doubled 8

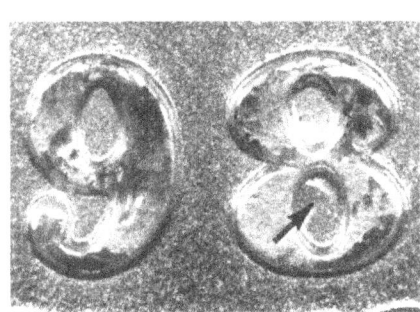
13 O Tripled Second 8

1898-O / 1898-S

| 14 | III²9 • C³a (Doubled First 8) | (181) | I-2 | R-3 |

Obverse III²9 – Date set very near with first 8 doubled slightly on bottom right outside of lower loop.

| 15 | III²10 • C³b (Doubled 1-8, O Set High) | (181) | I-2 | R-3 |

Obverse III²10 – Doubled 1-8 in date. 1 doubled on surface at very top. Second 8 doubled at top and right inside of upper loop and top inside of lower loop. Top of 18 shallow.

| 16 | III²11 • C³b (Doubled Second 8, O Set High) | (181) | I-2 | R-3 |

Obverse III²11 – Second 8 in date doubled at bottom inside of upper loop.

| 17 | III²12 • C³b (Doubled Second 8, O Set High) | (181) | I-2 | R-3 |

Obverse III²12 – Second 8 in date doubled at top right inside of upper loop and top inside and bottom right outside of lower loop. Date at left side of normal position.

| 18 | III²13 • C³a (Doubled First 8) | (181) | I-2 | R-3 |

Obverse III²13 – First 8 doubled slightly at top inside of both loops.

| 19 | III²9 • C³c (Doubled First 8, O Tilted Right) | (181) | I-2 | R-3 |

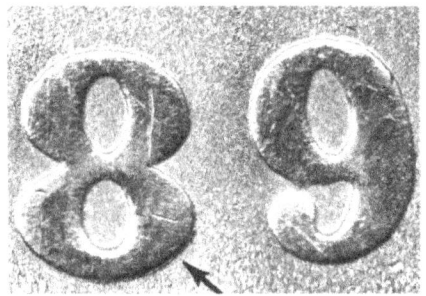

14 O Doubled First 8

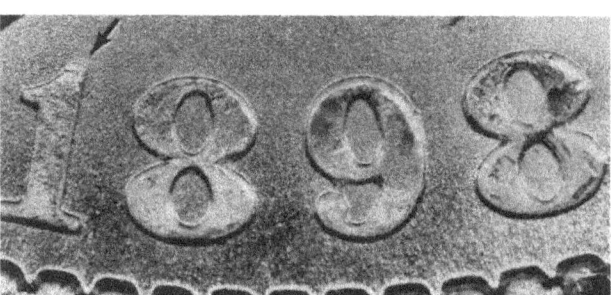

15 O Doubled 1-8

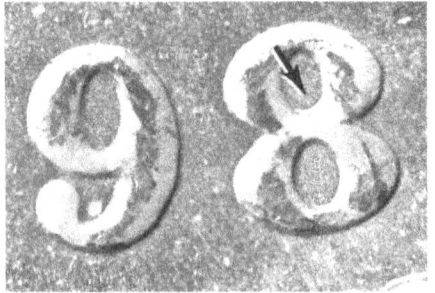

16 O Doubled Second 8

17 O Doubled Second 8

18 O Doubled First 8

1898-S

The strike for this issue is generally fairly full but weakly struck specimens may also be encountered. Luster is generally excellent. A few minor die varieties exist but only VAM 6 with a fairly strongly doubled "S" mint mark with quite a bit of separation downward is of some significance. Proof-likes are fairly scarce and generally have little contrast although a few cameos are known to exist.

| 1 | III²1 • C³a (Closed 9) | | I-1 | R-2 |

Obverse III²1 – Normal die of III² type with closed 9. The bottom loop of the 9 touches the upper loop.
Reverse C³a – Normal die of C³ type with a medium IV S mint mark, centered and upright.

| 2 | III²2 • C³a (Open 9) | | I-1 | R-3 |

Obverse III²2 – Normal die with open 9. The lower loop of the 9 does not touch the upper loop.

| 3 | III²5 • C³b (S/S Center, Doubled 1) | | I-2 | R-3 |

Obverse III²5 – 1 in date doubled below upper crossbar.
Reverse C³b – IV S mint mark doubled below center shaft.

1898-S

4	III²1 • C³c (S/S Right)	(187)	I-3	R-4

Reverse C³c – IV S mint mark doubled to right of top serif and below bottom serif.

5	III²3 • C³d (Doubled 1)	(188)	I-2	R-3

Obverse III²3 – 1 in date doubled slightly just below crossbar. Closed 9.
Reverse C³d – IV S mint mark tilted slightly to the right.

6	III²4 • C³e (Doubled Date, S/S Down)	(187)	I-3	R-4

Obverse III²4 – Entire date is doubled. 1 is slightly doubled below upper crossbar. 898 are doubled at top inside of upper loops. Date set further left than normal. Closed 9.
Reverse C³e – IV S mint mark doubled down with original showing as a curved horizontal line in center of upper loop, slanting line below center shaft and curved horizontal line below lower loop, ending in an extended part of the lower loop on the right and doubled lower serif.

7	III²1 • C³f (S/S Upright)	(188)	I-3	R-4

Reverse C³f – IV S mint mark doubled to right of top serif and below bottom serif but more centered and upright than VAM 4.

8	III²5 • C³d (Near Date, S Tilted Right)	(188)	I-2	R-3

Obverse III²5 – Date set further left than normal.

8A	III²5 • C³d, (Near Date, S Tilted Right)	(187)	I-2	R-4

Reverse C³d – Two thick die gouges through wreath bow loop.

9	III²6 • C³d (Doubled 8, S Tilted Right)	(187)	I-2	R-4

Obverse III²6 – Second 8 doubled at top outside of upper loop. Date set further left than normal.
Reverse C³d – Two thick die gouges through wreath bow loop.

10	III²7 • C³g (Near Slanted Date, S Tilted Far Right)	(187)	I-3	R-4

Obverse III²7 – Near date with slight slant with 1 closest to rim.
Reverse C³g – Medium IV S mint mark centered and tilted very far to the right.

11	III²7 • C³a (Near Slanted Date)	(187)	I-2	R-3
12	III²8 • C³h (Doubled Second 8, S/S High)	(186)	I-2	R-3

Obverse III²8 – Second 8 doubled at top inside of lower loop. Date set further left than normal.
Reverse C³h – IV S mint mark set high and doubled to right of top serif and left side of bottom serif.

13	III²1 • C³d (S Tilted Right)	(187)	I-2	R-3

3 R S/S Center

4 R S/S Right

5 O Doubled 1

5 R S Tilted Right

6 O Doubled Date

6 R S/S Down

7 R S/S Upright

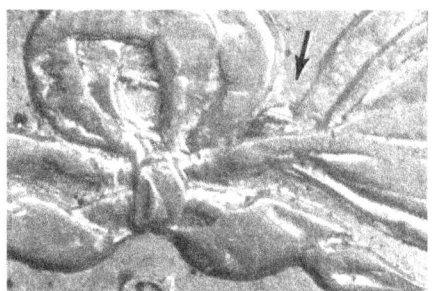

8A R Die Gouge in Bow

9 O Doubled Second 8

10 O Near Slanted Date

10 R S Slanted Far Right

1899-P

The strike is usually fairly good although slightly weakly struck specimens are around. Luster is generally good. Although a low mintage issue, it is not exceptionally scarce. Apparently it escaped being significantly melted. It is highly unlikely that the date continued to be struck into 1900 as it has always been the policy, as required by law, for business strike dies to be dated the year used. Only a few die varieties are known which tend to confirm only a few dies were used for a low total mintage. None of the die varieties are significant however. Proof-likes are fairly scarce and most have moderate contrast although a few very deep mirror cameos are known. Proofs have fairly good contrast but not as much as the few preceding dates.

1	III²1 • C³a (Normal Die)		I-1	R-3
	Obverse III²1 – Normal die of III² type with open 9's.			
	Reverse C³a – Normal die of C³ type.			
2	III²2 • C³a (Doubled 9)		I-2	R-4
	Obverse III²2 – Second 9 in date doubled at top.			
3	III²3 • C³a (Closed 9's)		I-1	R-3
	Obverse III²3 – Normal die with closed 9's.			
4	III²4 • C³a (Doubled 189)	(189)	I-2	R-3
	Obverse III²4 – Doubled 189 in date. 1 is doubled slightly below base. 8 is doubled on right outside of both loops as a thin arc to the right of the upper loop and a thin line to the lower right of the lower loop. First 9 doubled faintly on inside of lower loop.			
5	III²5 • C³a (Doubled 18-9)	(188)	I-2	R-3
	Obverse III²5 – Doubled 18-9 in date. 1 doubled as a short horizontal line below upper crossbar. 8 doubled at top inside of upper loop and at bottom outside of lower loop. Second 9 doubled at top outside of upper loop.			
6	III²6 • C³a (Open and Closed 9's)	(190)	I-2	R-3
	Obverse III²6 – First 9 closed and second 9 open lower loop.			

2 O Doubled 9

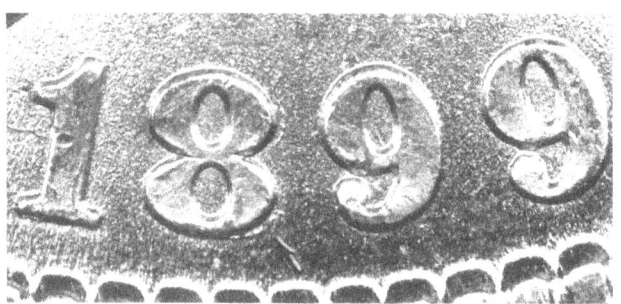
4 O Doubled 189

5 O Doubled 18-9

6 O Open and Closed 9's

1899-O

Generally the 1899-O is well struck. Some weak strikes are around because of the large mintage and some dies were not basined as well as others or the striking pressure was not adequately high in the coining presses. Luster tends to be very good. Quite a few minor die varieties exist. VAM's 4, 5 and 6 have a small "O" mint mark and are quite scarce in any grade and command a significant premium. Only a few uncirculated small "O" specimens are known. Proof-likes are fairly scarce and usually have little contrast although a few very deep mirror cameos exist.

1	III²1 • C³a (Open 9's)		I-1	R-2
	Obverse III²1 – Normal die of III² type with open 9's in date.			
	Reverse C³a – Normal die of C³ type with medium III O mint mark centered and upright.			
2	III²2 • C³b (Closed 9's)		I-1	R-2
	Obverse III²2 – Normal die with closed 9's.			
	Reverse C³b – Normal die with III O mint mark tilted slightly to the right and set slightly high.			
2A	III²2 • C³b (Closed 9's)	(181)	I-1	R-2
	Reverse C³b – Two large die breaks in second leaf cluster from top of left wreath.			
3	III²1 • C³b (O Tilted Right)		I-2	R-3
4	III²2 • C³c (Small O Tilted Right)		I-3	R-4
	Obverse III²2 – Some specimens show die chips in lower loop of second 9.			
	Reverse C³c – Normal die with small I O mint mark tilted to the right and set slightly high and to right.			
5	III²2 • C³d (Small O Set Upright)		I-3	R-4
	Reverse C³d – Normal die with small I O mint mark set high with slight tilt to right.			
6	III²3 • C³c (Near Date, Small O)	(181)	I-3	R-4
	Obverse III²3 – Date set further left than normal.			
7	III²1 • C³e (High O)		I-2	R-3
	Obverse III²1 – Some specimens show die chips in lower loop of second 9.			
	Reverse C³e – III O mint mark set upright and very high.			

1899-O

8	III²4 • C³a (Slanted Date)		I-2	R-3

Obverse III²4 – Date slanted with second 9 higher than 1. Closed 9's.

9	III²4 • C³b (Slanted Date)		I-2	R-3
10	III²4 • C³f (Slanted Date)	(188)	I-2	R-3

Reverse C³f – III O mint mark set high and tilted very far to right.

11	III²5 • C³b (Doubled 1)		I-2	R-3

Obverse III²5 – 1 in date is doubled slightly at bottom of upper crossbar. Open 9's.

12	III²6 • C³b (Doubled 18-9)		I-2	R-4

Obverse III²6 – 18-9 in date doubled. The 1 is doubled at the bottom on the middle and right side. The 8 is doubled all across the bottom and slightly at the top of both loop openings. Second 9 is doubled as a thin curved line at bottom left inside of top loop opening.

13	III²7 • C³g (Doubled 899, O/O)		I-2	R-4

Obverse III²7 – Slightly doubled 899 in date. First 8 has hook of curved metal on right inside of lower loop. Lower ball of first 9 doubled slightly on left side of some specimens. Second 9 shows fine curved line on lower right outside of lower loop.
Reverse C³g – Centered III O mint mark doubled slightly on right inside.

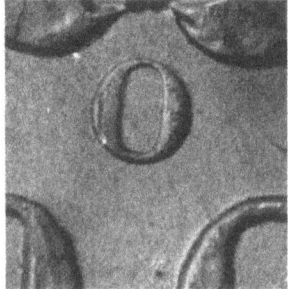 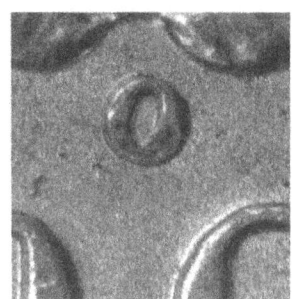 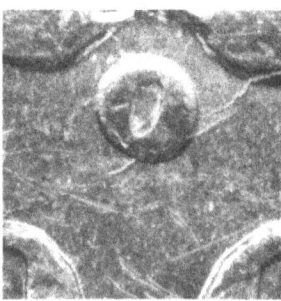 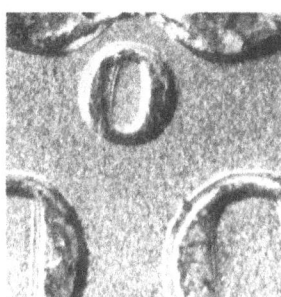

2 R O Tilted Right   4 R O Tilted Right   5 R High O   7 R High O

2A R Die Breaks
in Wreath   8 O Slanted Date   10 R High O Tilted Right

  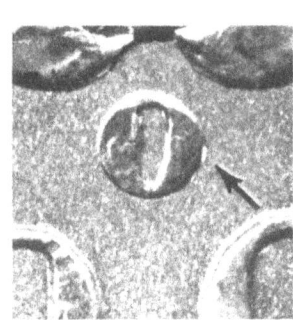

11 O Doubled 1   12 O Doubled 18 9   13 R O/O

1899-O

14	III²8 • C³h (Doubled 89, High O)		I-2	R-3

Obverse III²8 – Slightly doubled 89 in date. 8 and first 9 doubled slightly at top inside of upper loop.
Reverse C³h – Upright III O mint mark set high and shifted slightly to left.

15	III²9 • C³i (Doubled 1-9, High O)		I-3	R-4

Obverse III²9 – Doubled 1-9 in date. 1 doubled slightly below upper crossbar. Second 9 doubled strongly at top outside as thin curved arc and at bottom left inside of upper loop. Date set further left than normal.
Reverse C³i – Upright III O mint mark, set high and shifted slightly to right.

16	III²10 • C³a (Doubled First 9)		I-2	R-3

Obverse III²10 – First 9 doubled at right side and slightly at left outside of lower loop.

17	III²3 • C³e (Near Date, High O)	(181)	I-2	R-3
18	III²1 • C³f (High O Tilted Right)	(181)	I-2	R-3
19	III²11 • C³b (Slanted Date)	(181)	I-2	R-3

Obverse III²11 – Date slanted with second 9 higher than 1 but set further left than III²4. Open 9's.

20	III²5 • C³j (Doubled 1 and Reverse)	(189)	I-3	R-3

Obverse III²5 – First 9 is closed.
Reverse C³j – III O mint mark set high and tilted to right. Doubled UNITED STATES OF AMERI and motto letters towards rim.

21	III²4 • C³e (Slanted Date, High O)	(181)	I-2	R-3
22	III²12 • C³e (Doubled 899, High O)	(181)	I-2	R-3

Obverse III²12 – Doubled 899 in date. 8 and first 9 doubled slightly at bottom outside of lower loop. Second 9 doubled slightly at top outside of upper loop. Date set further left than normal.

23	III²2 • C³a (Closed 9's)	(189)	I-2	R-2
24	III²13 • C³e (Doubled 9, High O)	(181)	I-2	R-3

Obverse III²13 – Second 9 doubled as a thin line above top loop.

25	III²14 • C³a (Doubled 189)	(188)	I-2	R-3

Obverse III²14 – Doubled 189 in date. 1 doubled slightly below base. 8 doubled at right inside of upper and lower loops. First 9 doubled at right inside of lower loop.

26	III²1 • C³k (Doubled Reverse)	(181)	I-2	R-3

Reverse C³k – Legend and motto letters doubled towards rim along with wreath outside edge. III O mint mark set slightly high and upright.

27	III²15 • C³f (Doubled 9)	(181)	I-2	R-3

Obverse III²15 – Second 9 doubled at lower left outside of upper loop as a thin line.

28	III²16 • C³e (Doubled 1-9, High O)	(181)	I-2	R-3

Obverse III²16 – Doubled 1-9 in date. 1 doubled below upper crossbar. Second 9 doubled slightly at very top outside of upper loops. Date set on left side of normal position.

29	III²17 • C³a (Doubled Second 9)	(181)	I-2	R-3

Obverse III²17 – Second 9 doubled on top inside of upper loop.

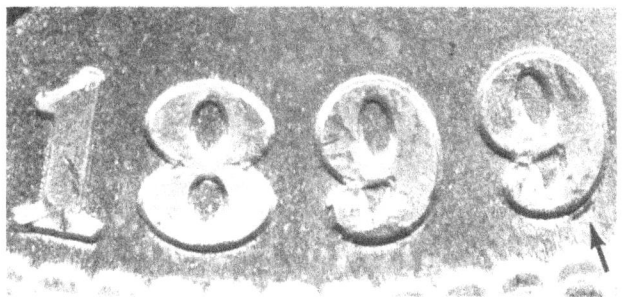
13 O Doubled 889

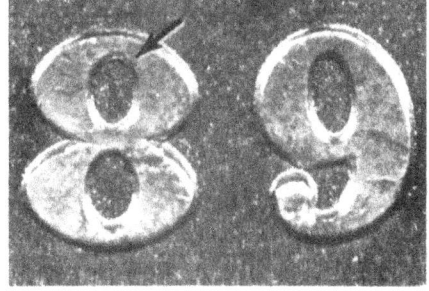
14 O Doubled 89

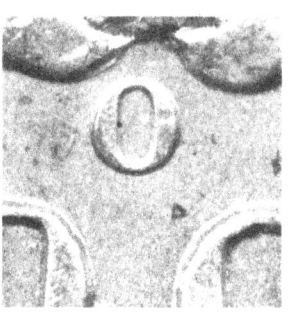
14 R High O Shifted Left

1899-O

15 O Doubled 1-9

15 R High O Shifted Right

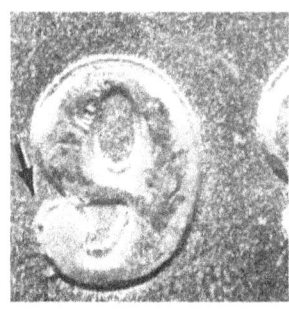
16 O Doubled First 9

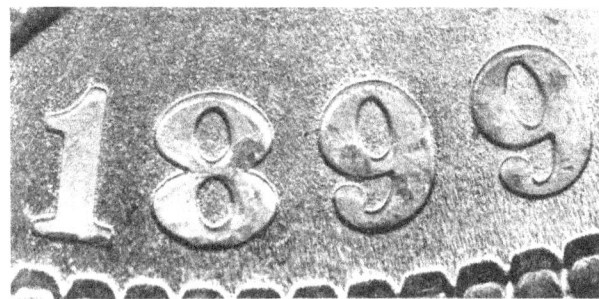
19 O Slanted Date

22 O Doubled 889

20 R Doubled Legend

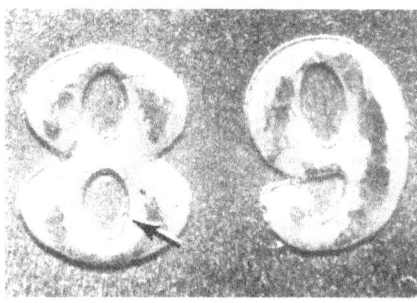
25 O Doubled 89

26 R Doubled Legend Letters

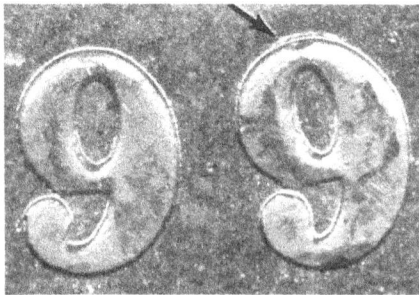
24 O Doubled 9

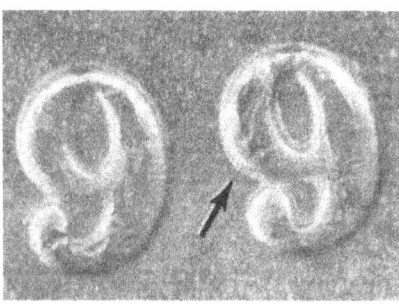
27 O Doubled Second 9

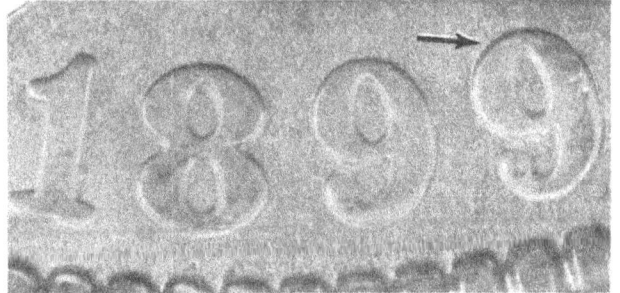
28 O Doubled 1-9

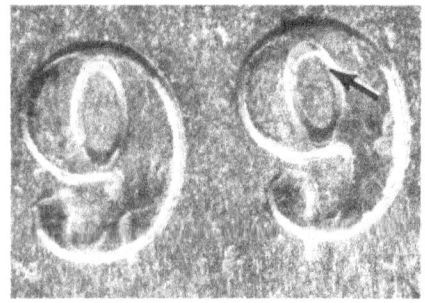
29 O Doubled Second 9

1899-S

A full strike and good luster is typical for the 1899-S. A few minor die varieties exist but the only significant one is VAM 7 with a strongly doubled 1-99. Proof-likes make up a fair proportion of the issue but they have little contrast.

1   III²1 • C³a (Narrow S)   I-1   R-2
     Obverse III²1 – Normal die of III² type with open 9's.
     Reverse C³a – Normal Die of C³ type with narrow, medium IV S mint mark, centered and upright.

2   III²1 • C³b (Wide S)   I-1   R-2
     Reverse C³b – Normal die with wide, large V S mint mark centered.

3   III²1 • C³c (S/S Center)   I-2   R-4
     Reverse C³c – Normal die with IV S mint mark tilted to the right and slightly doubled below upper loop.

4   III²1 • C³d (Spiked S)   I-2   R-4
     Reverse C³d – Normal die with IV S mint mark tilted to the right with a wide spike at top.

5   III²1 • C³e (S Tilted Right)   (186)   I-2   R-3
     Reverse C³e – Normal die with IV S mint mark centered and tilted right.

6   III²2 • C³d (Doubled 99)   (188)   I-2   R-3
     Obverse III²2 – 99 in date doubled. First 9 doubled at bottom right. Second 9 doubled inside the lower loop. Open 9's.

7   III²3 • C³a (Doubled 1-99)   I-3   R-5
     Obverse III²3 – Doubled 1-99 in date. 1 is doubled below upper serif. First and second 9 are both strongly doubled, shifted right and show as spot to right of lower loop end, vertical curved line on left side of upper loop opening and horizontal curved line at top right outside.

8   III²4 • C³b (Doubled 9)   I-2   R-3
     Obverse III²4 – First 9 doubled showing as a thin broken and curved line on right inside of lower loop.

9   III²5 • C³f (Wide S Tilted Right)   I-2   R-3
     Obverse III²5 – Normal die of III² type with closed 9's.
     Reverse C³f – V S mint mark centered and tilted right.

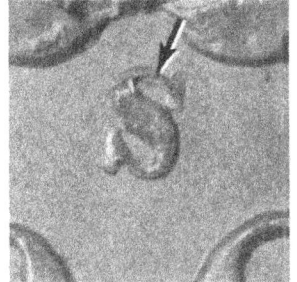 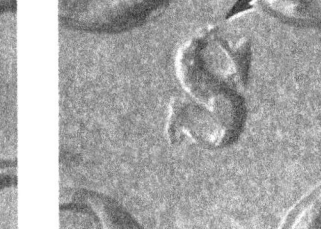 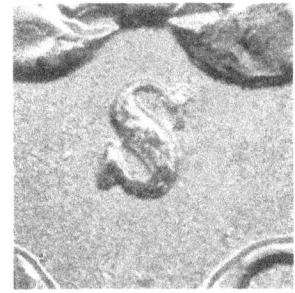 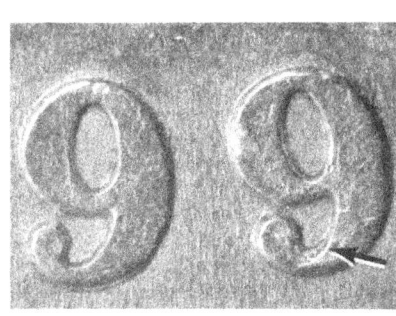

3 R S/S Center   4 R Spiked S   5 R S Tilted Right   6 O Doubled 99

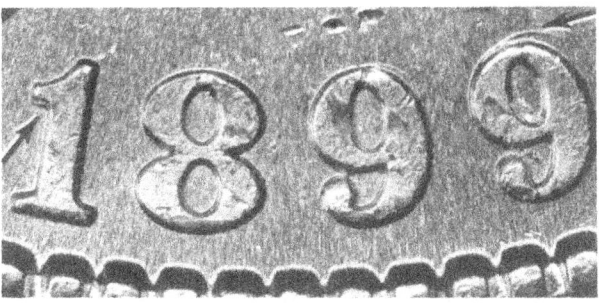  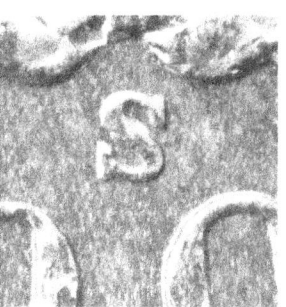

7 O Doubled 1-99   8 O Doubled 9   9 R Tilted S

1899-S / 1900-P

10   III²1 • C³g (S/S Top Serif)   I-2   R-4
   Reverse C³g – Normal die with IV S mint mark set slightly high and tilted right with top serif doubled as a vertical line at top left side and spike inside of lower loop.

11   III²6 • C³e (Near Date, S Tilted Right)   I-2   R-3
   Obverse III²6 – Date set further left than normal.

12   III²1 • C³h (High S, Tilted Right)   (184)   I-2   R-3
   Reverse C³h – IV S mint mark set high and tilted to right. Some specimens show die chip in wreath opposite NI of UNITED.

13   III²7 • C³a (Far Date)   (187)   I-2   R-3
   Obverse III²7 – Date set further right than normal.

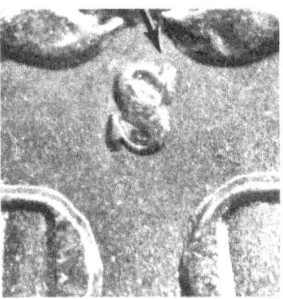   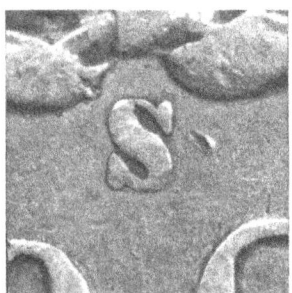

10 R S/S Top Serif   12 R High S Tilted Right

1900-P

The usual strike on this issue is slightly weak and fully struck specimens are fairly difficult to locate. Luster is usually fairly good but can be dull. Quite a few minor die varieties exist but only VAM 11 with slightly doubled bottom of eagle's wings and tail feathers plus arrow shafts is very significant. In this year a slightly modified reverse design type, C⁴, was introduced with less articulated eagle's breast feathers and other minor differences. It was used on some 1900-P, S, 1901-P, O, S, 1902-O and all 1902-P, S, 1903 and 1904. Proof-likes are fairly scarce and are invariably brilliant with little contrast. Some of these show noticeable die polishing lines in the fields. Proofs generally have good contrast but not all of them.

1   III²1 • C³a (Normal Die)   (189)   I-1   R-2
   Obverse III²1 – Normal die of III² type.
   Reverse C³a – Normal die of C³ type.

2   III²1 • C⁴a (Normal Die)   I-1   R-2
   Reverse C⁴a – Normal die of C⁴ type.

3   III²2 • C³a (Doubled Date)   I-2   R-3
   Obverse III²2 – Entire date doubled to ten o'clock.

4   III²3 • C³a (Low Date)   I-2   R-3
   Obverse III²3 – 1 in date closer to rim than normal.

3 O Doubled Date   4 O Low Date

349

1900-P

5	III²4 • C³a (Near Date)	(187, 188, 189)	I-2	R-3	

Obverse III²4 – Date set further left than normal. Open 9.

| 6 | III²5 • C³a (Near Date Set Low) | (189) | I-2 | R-3 |

Obverse III²5 – Date set further left than normal with 1 closer to rim than normal.

| 7 | III²6 • C³a (Very Near Date Set Low) | (189) | I-2 | R-3 |

Obverse III²6 – Date set very much further left than normal with numerals set low next to rim.

| 8 | III²7 • C³a (Doubled 1) | (189) | I-2 | R-3 |

Obverse III²7 – 1 in date doubled below upper crossbar, slightly below lower crossbar and on lower left side of vertical shaft. Closed 9.

| 9 | III²8 • C³a (Doubled 1-0) | (187) | I-2 | R-3 |

Obverse III²8 – Doubled 1-0 in date. 1 doubled at bottom of upper crossbar. First 0 doubled at top outside. Open 9 variety. Date set further left than normal.

| 10 | III²9 • C³a (Doubled 1-00) | | I-2 | R-4 |

Obverse III²9 – 1-00 in date doubled. 1 is doubled strongly at bottom of upper crossbar and bottom crossbar is slightly doubled at bottom right and top left and right. First 0 is doubled slightly at top right outside. Second 0 is tripled slightly at top left and right outside and is doubled all across top outside. Open 9 variety. Date set further left than normal.

| 11 | III²1 • C⁴/C³a (Doubled Eagle, 2 Olive Reverse) | (189) | I-4 | R-5 |

Reverse C⁴/C³a – Extra olive to right of olive connected to olive branch. Doubling on right side of olive leaves in top cluster and first two leaves in the lower cluster, bottom of arrow feathers, shaft and arrow heads, first four tail feather ends, feathers on lower part of eagle's right wing, all of eagle's left wing, eagle's nostril and eye, bottom of top leaves on right wreath and right side of GOD WE-TRU.

| 12 | III²10 • C³a (Doubled Date) | | I-3 | R-4 |

Obverse III²10 – All date digits strongly doubled to twelve o'clock. 1 doubled at top of upper and lower crossbar. 9 doubled at top outside of upper loop and bottom inside of both upper and lower loops. Both 0's doubled at top outside and bottom inside. Date set much further left than normal.

| 13 | III²11 • C³a (Doubled 1-0) | (188) | I-2 | R-3 |

Obverse III²11 – Doubled 1-0 in date. 1 is doubled slightly at bottom of base. First 0 doubled slightly at bottom outside. Date set further left than normal and slanted with 1 close to rim.

| 14 | III²12 • C³a (Near Slanted Date) | (189) | I-2 | R-3 |

Obverse III²12 – Date set further left than normal and slanted with 1 close to rim.

| 15 | III²13 • C³a (Slanted Date) | (189) | I-2 | R-3 |

Obverse III²13 – Date in normal lateral position but slanted with 1 next to rim.

| 16 | III²1 • C⁴/C³b (2 Olive Reverse) | (189) | I-3 | R-3 |

Reverse C⁴/C³b – Extra olive to right of olive connected to olive branch. Doubling at base of left olive leaf cluster, back of lower arrow head, right side of eagle's nostril and eye, and upper feathers of eagle's left wing. Pitting about eagle's neck.

| 17 | III²14 • C³a (Near Date, Doubled Last 0) | (189) | I-2 | R-3 |

Obverse III²14 – Second 0 doubled slightly at top outside. Date set further left than normal.

| 18 | III²1 • C⁴/C³c (2 Olive Reverse) | (189) | I-3 | R-3 |

Reverse C⁴/C³c – Extra olive to right of olive connected to olive branch. Doubling at base of all three olive leaf clusters, top of second arrow feather from top, back of lower arrow head, on right of two innermost right wing feathers next to leg, right side of eagle's nostril and eye, and upper feathers of eagle's left wing.

6 O Near Date Set Low

7 O Very Near Date Set Low

1900-P

8 O Doubled 1

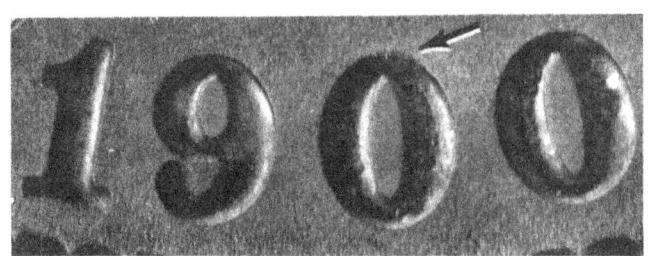
9 O Doubled 1-0

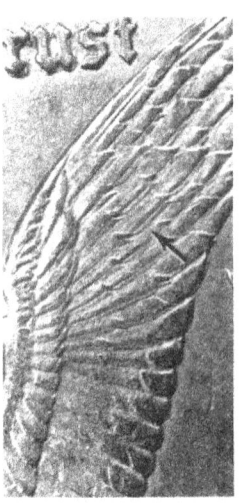
11 R C⁴/C³

10 O Doubled 1-00

11 R Doubled Eagle

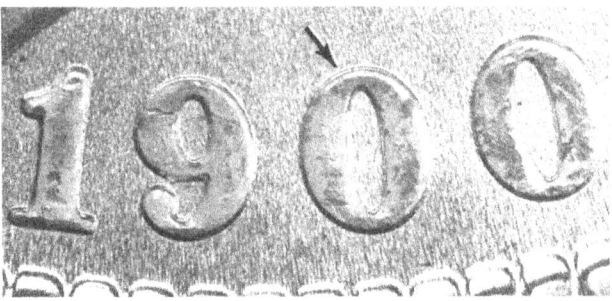
12 O Doubled Date

11 R C⁴/C³

13 O Doubled 1-0

16 R C⁴/C³

17 O Doubled O

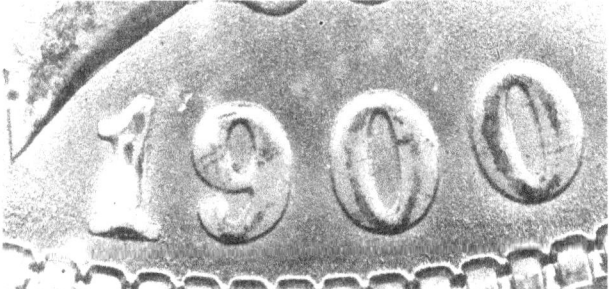
14 O Near Slanted Date

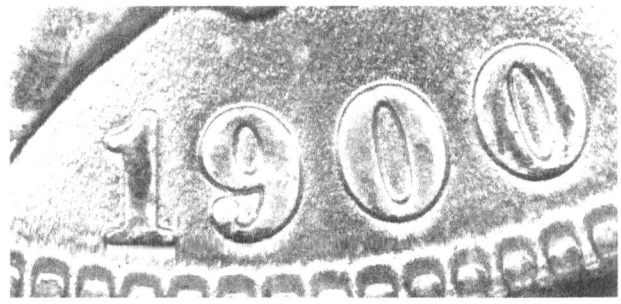
15 O Slanted Date

1900-P

19   III²1 • C⁴/C³ d (2 Olive Reverse)   (189)   I-2   R-3
Reverse C⁴/C³ d – Extra olive to right of olive connected to olive branch. Doubling at base of left and lower olive leaf clusters, back of lower arrow head, and on right of two innermost right wing feathers next to leg.

20   III²15 • C³ a (Near Date, Doubled First 0)   (190)   I-2   R-3
Obverse III² 15 – First 0 in date doubled at lower inside as a curved thick bar. Date set further left than normal.

21   III²16 • C³ a (Doubled 900)   (190)   I-2   R-3
Obverse III² 16 – Doubled 900 in date. 9 doubled faintly at very bottom right outside. Both 0's doubled at lower right inside.

22   III²17 • C³ a (Doubled 19)   (187)   I-2   R-3
Obverse III² 17 – Doubled 19 in date. 1 doubled faintly at bottom right of lower crossbar. 9 doubled at lower left outside of upper loop and at bottom outside of lower loop. Date set further left than normal.

23   III²18 • C³ a (Doubled Stars)   (188)   I-2   R-3
Obverse III² 18 – First two stars on left and right doubled towards rim. Date set low and further left than normal.

18 R 2 Olive Reverse

19 R 2 Olive Reverse

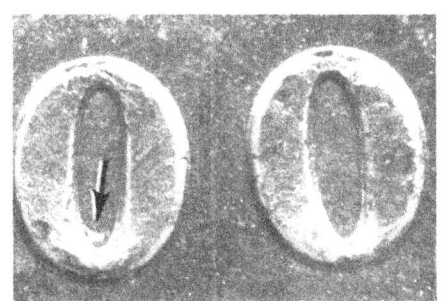
20 O Doubled First 0

21 O Doubled 900

22 O Doubled 19

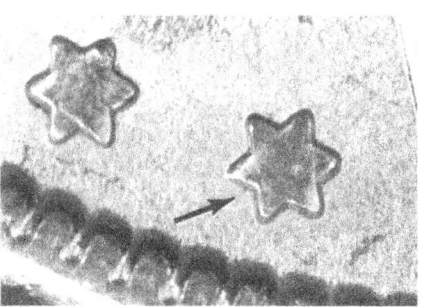
23 O Doubled Stars

1900-O

Generally the strike on this issue is fairly strong but weakly struck specimens are also around because of the high mintage. The luster is usually good. Quite a few minor die varieties exist. The most significant are the O/CC mint marks, VAM's 7-12. Five CC reverse dies left over from the Carson City mint when it closed in 1893 were modified in 1900 by punching the O mint mark over the CC mint mark. Various amounts of the CC remnants show from two low curved lines to the entire "C" s. All O/CC coins command a significant premium and VAM 9 is particularly scarce while VAM's 8, 11 and 12 are the most frequently encountered. VAM 29A has a very large high die break from 19 to the rim and is very scarce and significant. VAM 5 has a small "O" mint mark and is a significant die variety. However, it is very scarce and known only in low circulated grades. Proof-likes are fairly scarce and have little contrast. The O/CC are unknown in full proof-like. Many proof-likes show fine die polishing lines in the fields.

1	III²1 • C³a (Closed 9)		I-1	R-2

Obverse III²1 – Normal die of III² type with closed 9.
Reverse C³a – Normal die of C³ type with medium III O mint mark centered and upright.

2	III²2 • C³a (Open 9)		I-1	R-2

Obverse III²2 – Normal die of with open 9.

2A	III²2 • C³a (Polished Wheat)	(187)	I-3	R-3

Obverse III²2 – Heavy die polishing lines around wheat stalks.

3	III²5 • C³c (O Tilted Right)	(181)	I-2	R-3

Obverse III²5 – Date set further left than normal.
Reverse C³c – Normal die with III O mint mark tilted slightly to the right.

4	III²5 • C³c (O Tilted Left)		I-2	R-3

Reverse C³c – Normal die with III O mint mark tilted slightly to the left.

5	III²3 • C³d (Small O)	(181)	I-3	R-5

Obverse III²3 – Date set much further left than normal. Open 9.
Reverse C³d – Normal die of C³ type with small I O mint mark, tilted to right.

6	III²6 • C³b (O Tilted Right)	(189)	I-2	R-3
7	III²4 • C³e (O/CC Low)	(181)	I-4	R-7

Obverse III²4 – First 0 in date doubled slightly at bottom left.
Reverse C³c – Normal die with III O mint mark, centered and upright punched over CC. The CC mint mark shows as curved lines on the left and right at the bottom of the O.

8	III²5 • C³f (O/O/CC Centered Shifted Left)	(181)	I-5	R-4/5

Reverse C³f – Normal die with III O mint mark, centered and upright, with doubled O punched over CC. O is doubled at top left outside with notch missing at 11 o'clock in doubling and doubled at bottom inside of opening as a thin curved line. The CC mint mark is centered and shifted left under the O and shows as a thin broken curve on the left and two thick projections on the right connected to the O.

8A	III²5 – C³f (O/O/CC Centered, Shifted Left with Rust Spots)		I-5	R-4

Obverse III²5 – Die clash marks are evident.
Reverse C³f – Die rust spots are evident around the mint mark area. Some specimens show clash marks and die polishing in central area.

 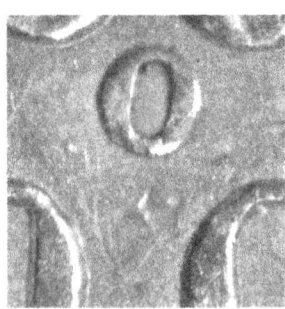 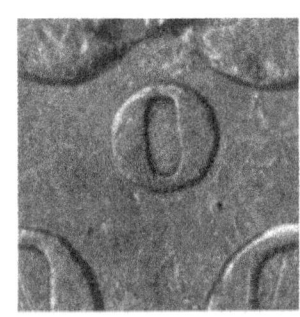

2A O Polished Wheat   3 R O Tilted Right   4 R O Tilted Left

1900-O

9   III²6 • C³g (O/CC Centered Shifted Right)   (181)   I-4   R-7
Obverse III²6 – Doubled 900 in date. 9 doubled at top inside of upper loop. Both 0's doubled at top inside. Date set further left than normal and slanted with 0's higher than 1.
Reverse C³g – Normal die with III O mint mark, centered and upright, punched over CC. The CC mint mark is centered and shifted right under the O and shows as a thin broken curve on the left and two faint projections on the right.

10   III²5 • C³e (O/CC Low)   (181)   I-4   R-4/5
Obverse III²5 – With open 9.

11   III²3 • C³i (O/CC High Shifted Left)   (181)   I-4   R-4
Reverse C³i – III O mint mark, centered and upright, punched over CC. The CC mint mark is high and shifted left under the O and shows as a broad curve on the left and one thick projection on the right connected to the O.

12   III²5 • C³j (O/CC High, Shifted Right)   (181)   I-5   R-4/5
Reverse C³j – III O mint mark centered and upright, punched over CC. The CC mint mark is high and shifted right under the O and shows as a complete thin C high on the left and complete C ends as two thick projections on the right. Heavy horizontal polishing marks are around the wreath bow area.

13   III²7 • C³k (Doubled 19-0)   (181)   I-3   R-4
Obverse III²7 – 19-0 in date doubled. 1 shows short horizontal spike below crossbar. 9 is doubled at top inside of upper loop and slightly at bottom outside. Second 0 doubled strongly at bottom outside. Date set further left than normal. Closed 9.
Reverse C³k – III O mint mark tilted to the right and set right.

14   III²8 • C³l (Doubled 00 Top)   (181)   I-2   R-4
Obverse III²8 First 0 doubled slightly at bottom outside. Last 0 in date is doubled at top. Open 9 variety. Date is set further left than normal.
Reverse C³l – Normal die with III O mint mark set high.

15   III²9 • C³m (Doubled 00 and Stars)   (189)   I-3   R-4
Obverse III²9 – Doubled 00 in date. The first 0 is doubled on the lower left inside and lower right outside. Second 0 doubled slightly on lower left inside. First two stars on right doubled at bottom. Closed 9 variety. Date set further left than normal.
Reverse C³m – III O mint mark set high, upright and shifted slightly left.

16   III²10 • C³b (Doubled 1)   (189)   I-2   R-4
Obverse III²10 – 1 is doubled below upper serif.

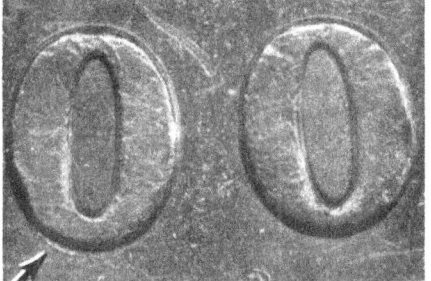
7 O Doubled O

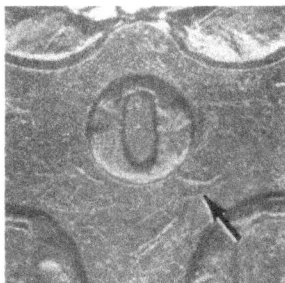
7 R O/CC Low

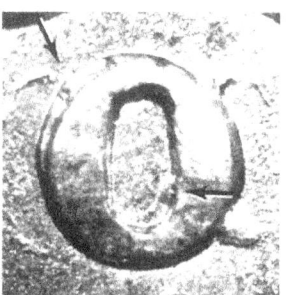
8 R O/O/CC Centered Shifted Left

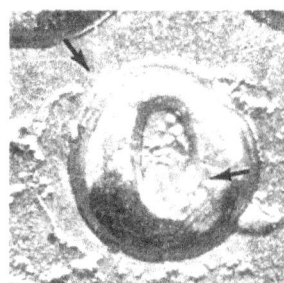
8A R O/CC Centered Die Chips

9 O Doubled 900

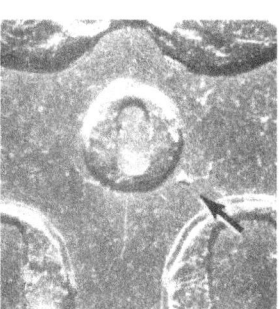
9 R O/CC Centered Shifted Right

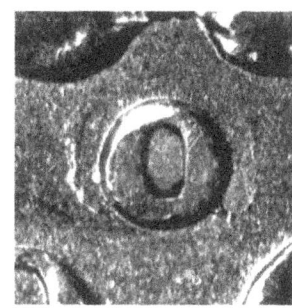
11 R O/CC High Shifted Left

1900-O

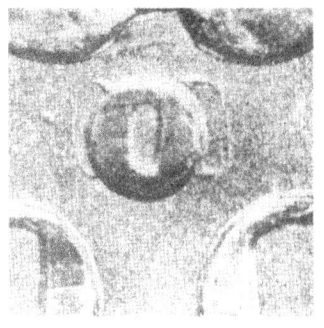
12 R O/CC High Shifted Left

13 O Doubled 19-0

13 R O Tilted Right

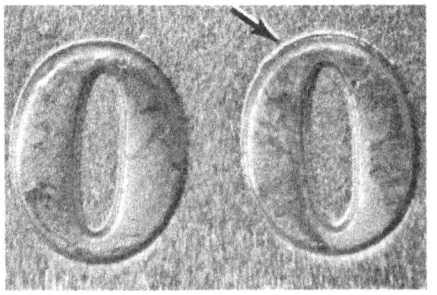
14 O Doubled 0

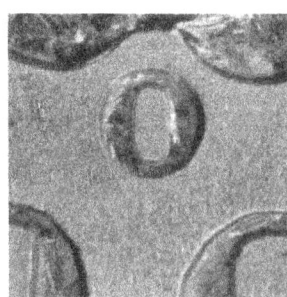
14 R O Set High

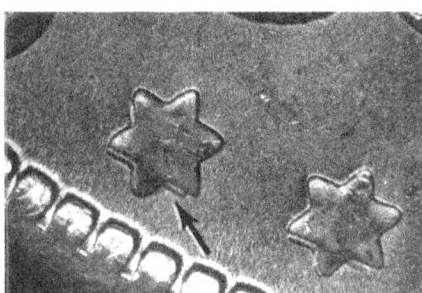
15 O Doubled Stars

16 O Doubled 1

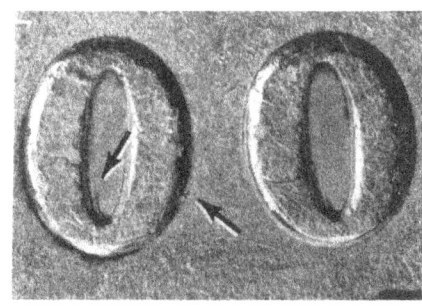
15 O Doubled 00

15 R O Set High Shifted Left

17 O Doubled 9

18 O Doubled 19

19 O Doubled 190

1900-O

17	III² 11 • C³ 1 (Doubled 9)		I-2	R-4

Obverse III² 11 – 9 in date doubled as thin curved line below bottom loop and to lower left and bottom outside of upper loop. Date set further left than normal and slanted with 0's higher than 1. Open 9.

18	III² 12 • C³ a (Doubled 19)		I-3	R-3

Obverse III² 12 – Doubled 19 in date. 1 is doubled as thin horizontal line below bottom crossbar. 9 is doubled as thin curved line below bottom loop and to left bottom outside of upper loop. Date set further left than normal.

19	III² 13 • C³ a (Doubled 190)		I-2	R-4

Obverse III² 13 – Doubled 190 in date. 1 is doubled slightly to left of bottom crossbar. 9 is doubled to left outside of lower loop as thin curved arc and on right inside of lower loop as a thin vertical line. 0 is doubled slightly at lower left outside as short spike. Date is set much further left than normal and slanted with 0's higher than 1. Closed 9.

20	III² 14 • C³ 1 (Doubled 900)		I-2	R-4

Obverse III² 14 – Slightly doubled 900 in date. 9 doubled very slightly on lower right outside of lower loop. First 0 doubled slightly at bottom outside. Second 0 doubled slightly at top outside. Open 9.

21	III² 5 • C³ 1 (Near Date, High O)	(190)	I-2	R-3

Reverse C³ 1 – Some specimens show high die crack through tops of ED STATES OF.

22	III² 3 • C³ a (Very Near Date)	(190)	I-2	R-3
23	III² 15 • C³ 1 (Slanted Date)		I-2	R-4

Obverse III² 15 – Date set further left than normal and slanted with 1 very close to rim.

24	III² 5 • C³ n (O/O Left)		I-2	R-3

Reverse C³ n – III O mint mark set high and doubled on left inside. Mint mark punched very deep into die with narrow center opening.

25	III² 5 • C³ o (O/O Down)		I-2	R-4

Reverse C³ o – III O mint mark doubled at top inside and bottom outside. Mint mark punched very deep into die with narrow center opening.

26	III² 5 • C³ p (O/O Left and Down)		I-2	R-3

Reverse C³ p – III O mint mark set high and doubled on left inside and lower right outside.

27	III² 16 • C³ 1 (Doubled 190 Left)		I-3	R-3

Obverse III² 16 – Doubled 190 in date. 1 doubled at top left of lower crossbar. 9 doubled at lower left outside of bottom loop as thin curved line. 0 doubled at lower left outside as long thin curved line.

28	III² 17 • C³ 1 (Doubled 190 Down)		I-2	R-3

Obverse III² 17 – Doubled 190 in date. 1 doubled strongly below upper crossbar and slightly below bottom crossbar. 9 doubled at top inside of upper loop on surface and at bottom outside of upper and lower loops. First 0 doubled slightly at top inside of loop on surface. Open 9 variety.

29	III² 8 • C³ b (Doubled 00)		I-2	R-3
29A	III² 8 • C³ b (Die Break in Date)		I-4	R-7

Obverse III² 8 – Spectacular large die break through bottom of 190 to rim below vee of neck. Break is as high as date digits above field.

30	III² 18 • C³ b (Doubled 1-0)		I-2	R-4

Obverse III² 18 – Doubled 1-0 in date. 1 is strongly doubled below upper and lower crossbars. Second 0 is doubled at bottom inside and slightly at top right outside. Closed 9 variety.

19 O Slanted Date

20 O Doubled 900

1900-O

23 O Slanted Date

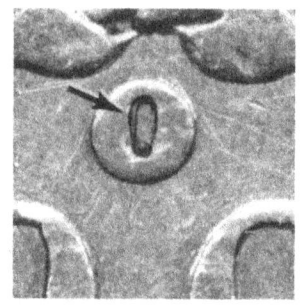
24 R O/O Left

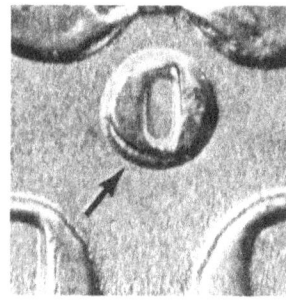
25 R O/O Down

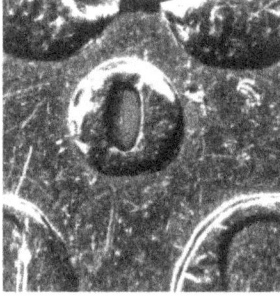
26 R O/O Left and Down

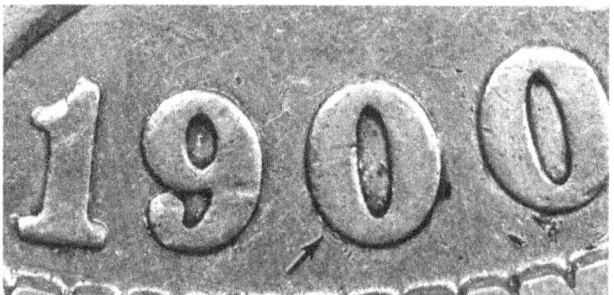
27 O Doubled 190 Left

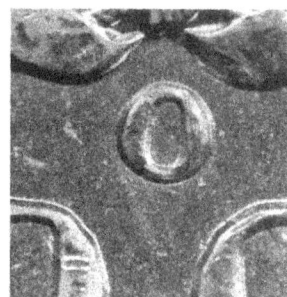
34 R O Set High, Tilted Right

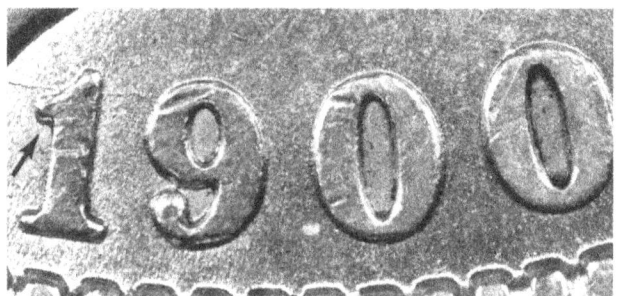
28 O Doubled 190 Down

30 O Doubled 1-0

29A O Die Break

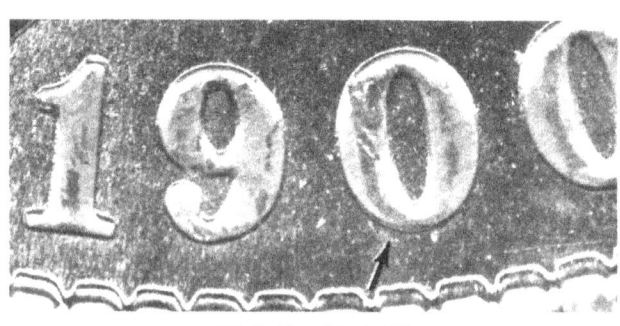
33 O Doubled 190

31 O Slanted Date

34 O Low Date

1900-O / 1900-S

31	III²19 • C³l (Slanted Date)	(181)		I-2	R-3

Obverse III²19 – Date in normal position and slanted with 1 very close to rim.

32	III²2 • C³l (O Set High)	(189)		I-2	R-3
33	III²20 • C³k (Doubled 190, O Tilted and Shifted Right)	(189)		I-2	R-3

Obverse III²20 – Doubled 190 in date. 1 doubled below upper crossbar. 9 doubled at top inside of upper loop. 0 doubled at lower left outside.

34	III²21 • C³q (Low Date, O Set High and Tilted Right)	(181)		I-2	R-3

Obverse III²21 – Date set low to rim and further left than normal.
Reverse C³q – Medium III O mint mark set high and tilted to right.

35	III²22 • C³l (Doubled 900, High 0)	(181)		I-2	R-3

Obverse III²22 – Doubled 900 in date. 9 doubled slightly at top inside of upper loop. Both 0's doubled at top inside. Date set further left than normal.

36	III²23 • C³a (Doubled 00)	(181)		I-2	R-3

Obverse III²23 – Doubled 00 in date. First 0 slightly doubled at lower left outside. Second 0 doubled at top inside as a short arc.

37	III²5 • C³r (Near Date, O/O Left)	(189)		I-2	R-3

Reverse C³r – III O mint mark doubled with large shift to left and showing as a bar in middle of opening and crescent on left outside.

38	III²24 • C³a (Slanted Date)	(187)		I-2	R-3

Obverse III³24 – Date set towards left side of normal position and slanted with 1 closer to rim.

35 O Doubled 900

36 O Doubled 00

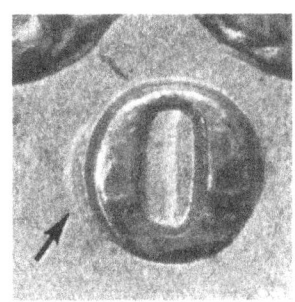
37 R O/O

38 O Slanted Date

1900-S

The usual strike is full but it can vary to very flat. Luster is usually good. A number of die varieties exist but only VAM 3A with wide over narrow "S" mint mark is significant. A slightly wider "S" mint mark was used on some 1899-S and 1900-S and on all 1901-S, 1902-S, 1903-S and 1904-S. Apparently only one die was modified with larger "S" punched on top of narrower "S" (similar to 1879-CC with large CC over small CC). Proof-likes are fairly scarce and have little contrast.

1	III²1 • C³a (Narrow S)	(189)		I-1	R-2

Obverse III²1 – Normal die of III² type with open 9.
Reverse C³a – Normal die of C³ type with narrow IV S mint mark.

1900-S

2	III²1 • C³b (Wide S)	(189)	I-1	R-2

Reverse C³b – Normal die with wide V S mint mark.

2A	III²1 • C³b (Extra Arrow Feather)	(189)	I-2	R-3

Reverse C³b – Heavy die gouge just above top arrow feather.

3	III²2 • C³c (S/S Right)		I-3	R-4

Obverse III²2 – Date set further left than normal.
Reverse C³c – IV S mint mark repunched with original showing as a short vertical spike to right of upper serif.

3A	III²2 • C³c (Wide Over Narrow S)		I-5	R-5

Reverse C³c – Same die as VAM 3 (identical die cracks) except narrow IV S mint mark was repunched with a wide V S mint mark and shows as a thin vertical line on left outside of upper loop and a thick spike on right outside of lower loop.

4	III²3 • C³d (Doubled 00)		I-2	R-4

Obverse III²3 – Both O's in date an doubled all across top outside.
Reverse C³d – V S mint mark set high.

5	III²2 • C³a (Near Date)	(189)	I-2	R-3

Reverse C³a – Normal die of C³ type with wide V S mint mark.

6	III²2 • C³d (Near Date)	(189)	I-2	R-3
7	III²2 • C³e (Doubled O, S/S Right)	(189)	I-2	R-3

Obverse III²4 – Second 0 doubled at top outside. Seventh star on left has two short spikes.
Reverse C³e – IV S mint mark doubled slightly on upper right of top serif and set slightly high and to right.

8	III²5 • C³b (Doubled 190)	(189)	I-2	R-3

Obverse III²5 – Doubled 190 in date. 1 has a spike at top in middle of curve. 9 has a short spike at top left outside and top right inside of upper loop. First 0 has a long curve of metal at top left outside. Date set further left than normal.

9	III²2 • C³f (Near Date, S/S Serifs)	(187)	I-2	R-3

Obverse III²2 – Seventh star on the left has two short spikes.
Reverse C³f – IV S mint mark doubled on lower right of top serif and bottom left of lower serif. S set high and centered.

10	III²2 • C³g (Near Date, High S)	(187)	I-2	R-3

Reverse C³g – IV S mint mark set high.

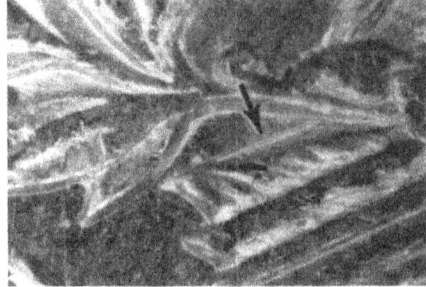
1A R Die Gouge Above Arrow Feathers

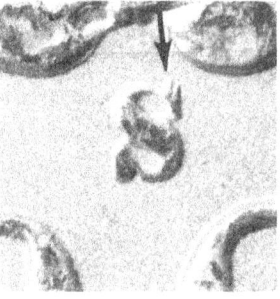
3 R S/S Right

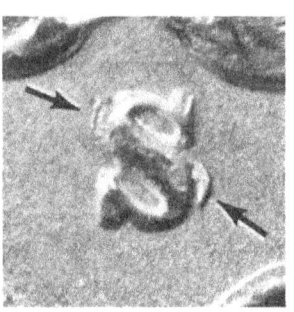
3A R Wide/Narrow S

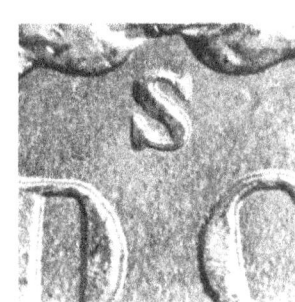
4 R High S

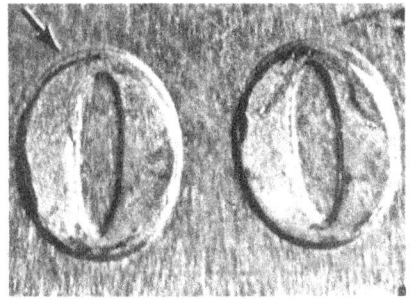
4 O Doubled 00

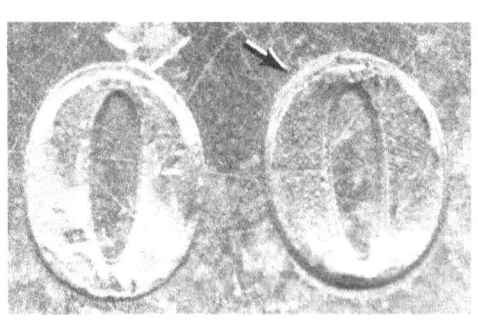
7 O Doubled Second 0

7 R S/S Right

1900-S

11	III²6 • C³b (Doubled 190)	(189)		I-2	R-3

Obverse III²6 – Doubled 90 in date. 1 doubled below upper serif. 9 doubled at top inside of upper loop. First 0 doubled at top outside. Date set further left than normal.

12	III²7 • C³b (Slanted Date)	(189)		I-2	R-3

Obverse III²7 – Slight slant to date with 1 closest to rim.

13	III²8 • C³b (Doubled 9, Tripled 0)	(189)		I-2	R-3

Obverse III²8 – 9 doubled slightly at bottom right inside of lower loop. Second 0 tripled at top inside.

14	III²9 • C³d (Doubled 900, High S)	(189)		I-2	R-3

Obverse III²9 – Doubled 900 in date. 9 doubled at lower inside of lower loop. First 0 doubled slightly at lower inside. Second 0 tripled at top inside and doubled at lower inside.

15	III²1 • C³h (S Set Right)			I-2	R-3

Reverse C³h – V S mint mark set upright and shifted slightly to right.

16	III²2 • C⁴/C³a (Near Date, 2 Olive Reverse)	(189)		I-3	R-4

Reverse C⁴/C³a – Wide V S mint mark centered and upright. Shallow extra olive to right of olive connected to olive branch. Slight doubling at base of left olive leaf cluster and back of lower arrow head.

17	III²2 • C³e (Near Date, S/S Right)	(189)		I-2	R-3

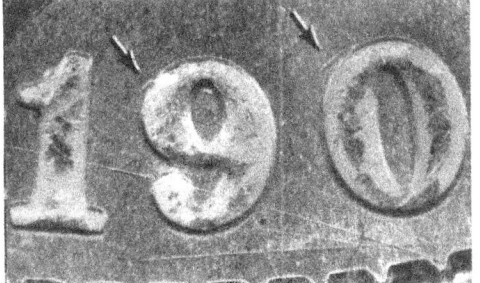

8 O Doubled 190

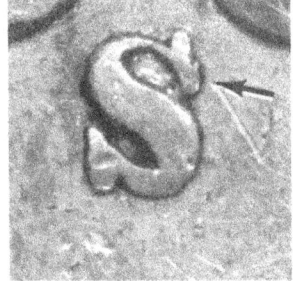

9 R S/S

11 O Doubled 190

12 O Slanted Date

13 O Doubled 9, Tripled Second 0

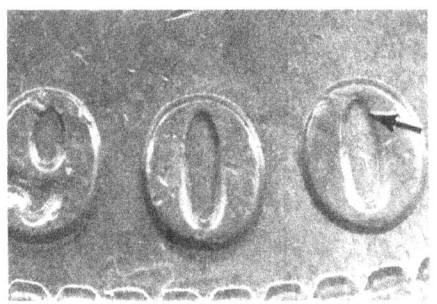

14 O Doubled 900

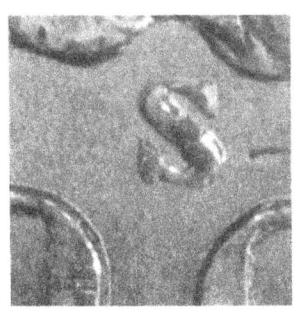

15 R S Set Right

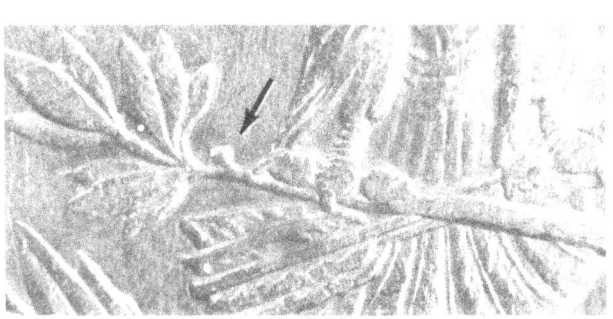

16 R 2 Olive Reverse

1901-P

This issue seems to be split between specimens with a fairly good strike with C^3 reverse and those with a fairly weak strike with C^4 reverse. Luster is usually dull. Lustrous fully struck specimens with minimal bag marks are truly very rare. A few die varieties exist. One of significance is VAM 3 with shifted eagle. It is the strongest doubled reverse die of the Morgan series and shows pronounced doubling of the bottom of the eagle's wings and tail feathers, olive branch and arrow shafts. It commands a large premium in all grades and only two are known in uncirculated. Prooflikes are virtually unknown except for a couple of pieces. The proofs have only moderate contrast. This is probably due to new master dies prepared in 1900 with C^4 reverse having less contrast because of modification of working hubs with less contrast than the original master die. The Philadelphia mint also changed from wood to gas annealing furnaces for planchets in 1901 which may have affected their luster.

1      $III^2 1$ • $C^3 a$ (Normal Die)   (189)   I-1   R-2
Obverse $III^2 1$ – Normal die of III^2 type with closed 9.
Reverse $C^3 a$ – Normal die of C^3 type.

2      $III^2 1$ • $C^4 a$ (Normal Die)   I-1   R-3
Reverse $C^4 a$ – Normal die of C^4 type.

2A $III^2 1$ • $C^4 a$ (Reverse Die Gouges)   (189)   I-2   R-3
Reverse $C^4 a$ – Diagonal die scratches and gouges around NE of ONE and DO of DOLLAR.

3      $III^2 1$ • $C^4 b$ (Shifted Eagle)   (189)   I-5   R-5
Reverse $C^4 b$ – Shifted Eagle variety. Eagle has been shifted to twelve o'clock so that the lower part of the eagle's wings, tail feathers, olive branch and leaves, arrow shafts and arrowheads and eagle's lower beak are strongly doubled. Letters OD and W are doubled below and within the motto IN GOD WE TRUST. The doubling was caused by a misalignment between the hub and die in one of the early blows.

4      $III^2 1$ • $C^4 c$ (Doubled Reverse)   (186)   I-4   Proof
Reverse $C^4 c$ – Doubled lower reverse. UNITED, ONE DOLLAR, MERICA, both stars and wreath are doubled towards rim.

5      $III^2 2$ • $C^4/C^3 a$ (Doubled Ear, 2 Olive Reverse)   (189)   I-3   R-3
Obverse $III^2 2$ – Inner ear lobe, bottom outside of ear lobe, hair above ear, eyelid and lower edge of cotton leaves are slightly doubled.
Reverse $C^4/C^3 a$ – Faint shallow extra olive to right of olive connected to olive branch. Back of lower arrow head, upper feathers of eagle's left wing and right sides of eagle's nostril are slightly doubled.

2A R Die Gouges

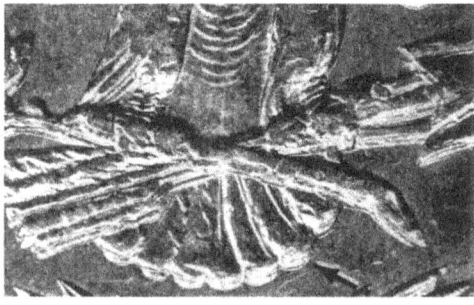

3 R Shifted Eagle

4 R Doubled Reverse

5 O Doubled Ear

5 R C^4/C^3

1901-P

6   III²1 • C⁴/C³ b (2 Olive Reverse)   (189)   I-3   R-3
Reverse C⁴/C³ b – Extra olive to right of olive connected to olive branch. Doubling at base of top and left olive leaf clusters and back of lower arrow head.

7   III²1 • C⁴/C³ c (Doubled Wing and Arrows)   (189)   I-3   R-4
Reverse C⁴/C³ c – Faint shallow extra olive to right of olive connected to olive branch. Eagle's left wing strongly doubled at middle and bottom, arrow heads and eagle's left claws doubled on left side, top of olive branch doubled at bottom, and two innermost eagle's right wing feathers are doubled next to leg.

8   III²3 • C³ a (Doubled Second 1)   (189)   I-2   R-3
Obverse III²3 – Second 1 in date doubled slightly below base.

9   III²1 • C⁴/C³ d (2 Olive Reverse)   (189)   I-3   R-3
Reverse C⁴/C³ d – Extra olive to right of olive connected to olive branch. Doubling on top of olive branch at right of olives, at base of top and left olive leaf cluster, at bottom of leaves of middle and lower olive leaf clusters, eagle's middle talon of right claw, middle of eagle's left wing, right side of eagle's nostril and eye, and on right of two innermost right wing feathers next to leg.

10   III²4 • C⁴ a (Slanted Date)   (189)   I-2   R-3
Obverse III²4 – Date slanted with first 1 closest to rim.

6 R C⁴/C³

7 R Doubled Wing and Arrows

8 O Doubled Second 1

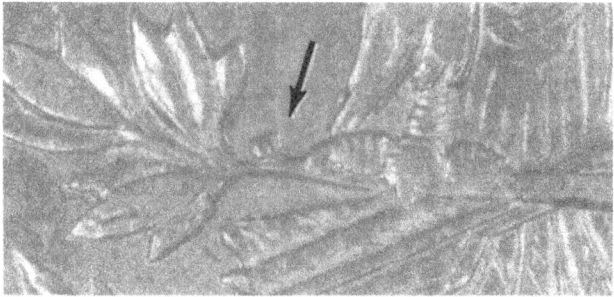

9 R C⁴/C³

10 O Slanted Date

1901-O

A fairly weak strike is typical for this issue although because of the large mintage fully struck specimens can be located. Luster is generally good. Quite a few minor die varieties are known but none are significant. Proof-likes are somewhat scarce but have little contrast.

1 III²1 • C³a (Normal Die) (181) I-1 R-2
   Obverse III²1 – Normal die of III² type with closed 9.
   Reverse C³a – Normal die of C³ type with medium III O mint mark centered and upright.

2 III²2 • C⁴a (Normal Die) (181) I-1 R-1
   Reverse C⁴a – Normal die of C⁴ type with III O mint mark.

3 III²2 • C⁴/C³j (Doubled 1-01, 2 Olive Reverse) (181) I-3 R-3
   Obverse III²2 – 1-01 in date doubled. First 1 doubled below top and bottom crossbars. Lower inside of 0 is doubled. Last 1 doubled at top, above bottom crossbar, and on lower right side of stem.
   Reverse C⁴/C³j – Extra olive to right of olive connected to olive branch. Doubling on top of olive branch at right of olives, at base of olive leaf clusters, top of upper arrow feathers, back of lower arrow head, on right of two innermost right wing feathers next to leg, and right side of eagle's nostril and eye.

4 III²1 • C⁴b (O Tilted Left) I-2 R-3
   Reverse C⁴b – III O mint mark tilted left.

5 III²1 • C⁴c (O Tilted Right) I-2 R-3
   Reverse C⁴c – III O mint mark set high and tilted right.

6 III²1 • C⁴d (High O) I-2 R-3
   Reverse C⁴d – III O set high and to right.

7 III²3 • C⁴a (Double 90) I-2 R-3
   Obverse III²3 – Bottom of 9 slightly doubled. 0 doubled at bottom left outside. Closed 9.

8 III²4 • C⁴a (Doubled 1-01) I-3 R-3
   Obverse III²4 – 1-01 doubled in date. First 1 is doubled slightly at very top left. 0 doubled at lower left and bottom outside. Second 1 doubled strongly below upper crossbar. Closed 9.

9 III²1 • C³b (O Tilted Right) (181) I-2 R-3
   Reverse C³b – III O mint mark set high with slight tilt to right.

3 R C⁴/C³

3 O Doubled 1-01

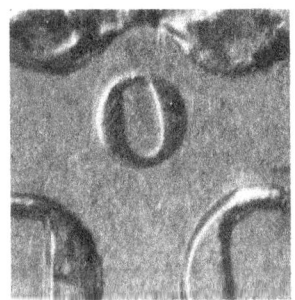

4 R O Tilted Left

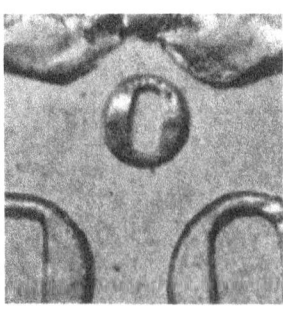

5 R O Tilted Right

6 R High O

1901-O

10 III²5 • C⁴e (Far Date, High O) I-2 R-3
  Obverse III²5 – Date set further right than normal.
  Reverse C⁴e – III O set high and centered.

11 III²6 • C⁴b (Slanted Date) (189) I-2 R-3

12 III²1 • C⁴/C³a (2 Olive Reverse) (181) I-3 R-3
  Reverse C⁴/C³a – Shallow extra olive to right of olive connected to olive branch. Doubling on top of olive branch at right of olives, at base of top and left olive leaf cluster, faintly on end of second arrow feather next to olive branch, back of lower arrow head, right side of eagle's nostril and eye and on right of two innermost right wing feathers next to leg. III O mint mark set slightly to right.

13 III²6 • C⁴/C³b (Slanted Date, 2 Olive Reverse) (181) I-3 R-3
  Reverse C⁴/C³b – Faint shallow extra olive to right of olive connected to olive branch. Doubling on right of eagle's nostril, eye, point of beak, two feathers adjacent to eagle's right leg and back of lower arrow head. III O mint mark set high with tilt to left.

14 III²7 • C⁴/C³c (Near Date, 2 Olive Reverse) (181) I-3 R-3
  Obverse III²7 – Date set further left than normal.
  Reverse C⁴/C³c – Extra olive to right of olive connected to olive branch. Doubling at base of top and left olive leaf cluster, on right of eagle's nostril, and back of lower arrow head. III O mint mark upright and slightly high.

15 III²1 • C⁴/C³d (2 Olive Reverse) (181) I-3 R-3
  Reverse C⁴/C³d – Extra olive to right of olive connected to olive branch. Doubling at base of top olive leaf cluster and back of lower arrow head. III O mint mark tilted left.

16 III²1 • C⁴/C³e (2 Olive Reverse) (181) I-3 R-3
  Obverse III²1 – Strong diagonal polishing line through R of LIBERTY.
  Reverse C⁴/C³e – Faint shallow extra olive to right of olive connected to olive branch. Doubling at base of left olive leaf cluster, faintly on end of second arrow feather next to olive branch, right of eagle's nostril, eye and beak end, two feathers adjacent to eagle's right leg and back of lower arrow head. III O mint mark set high, upright, and set slightly to right.

17 III²1 • C⁴/C³f (2 Olive Reverse) (181) I-3 R-3
  Reverse C⁴/C³f – Extra olive to right of olive connected to olive branch. Doubling on top of olive branch at right of olives, at base of top and left olive leaf cluster, back of lower arrow head, and right side of eagle's nostril and eye. III O mint mark set slightly high and to left with slight tilt to left.

18 III²1 • C⁴/C³g (2 Olive Reverse) (181) I-3 R-3
  Reverse C⁴/C³g – Extra olive to right of olive connected to olive branch. Doubling at base of left olive leaf cluster, back of lower arrow head, feathers at top of eagle's left wing and right side of eagle's nostril. III O mint mark set high, upright and centered.

19 III²1 • C⁴/C³h (2 Olive Reverse) (181) I-3 R-3
  Reverse C⁴/C³h – Extra olive to right of olive connected to olive branch. Doubling at lower edge of lower olive leaves, some leaves at wreath center, and bottom arrow feather plus back of lower arrow head. III O mint mark set high, upright and centered. Gap between the neck and wing appears to be a C³ narrow type but with outline of C⁴ type at edge of wing.

20 III²8 • C³a (Doubled 0, Bar Ear) (189) I-2 R-3
  Obverse III²8 – 0 is doubled slightly at bottom right outside. Closed 9. Diagonal die gouge in lower part of ear opening.

21 III²5 • C³a (Far Date) (181) I-2 R-3

22 III² • C³c (High O) (181) I-2 R-3
  Reverse C³c – III O set high.

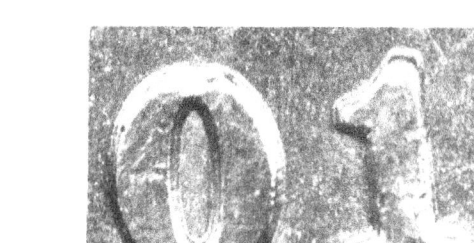
7 O Doubled 0

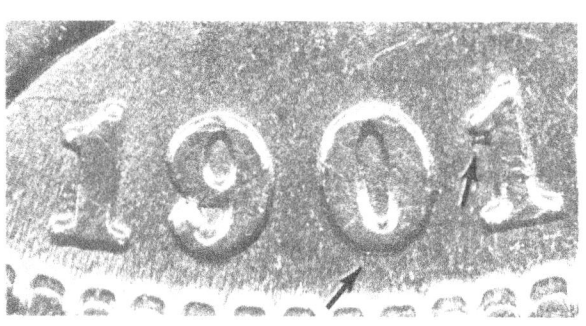
8 O Doubled 1-01

1901-O

11 O Slanted Date

12 R C⁴/C³

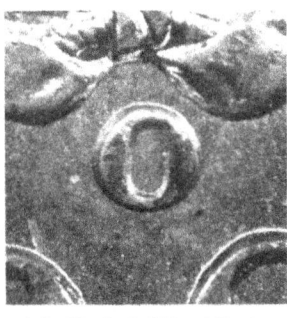

9 R High O Tilted Right

13 R C⁴/C³

14 R C⁴/C³

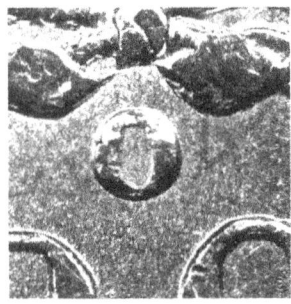

10 R O Set High

15 R C⁴/C³

16 R C⁴/C³

17 R C⁴/C³

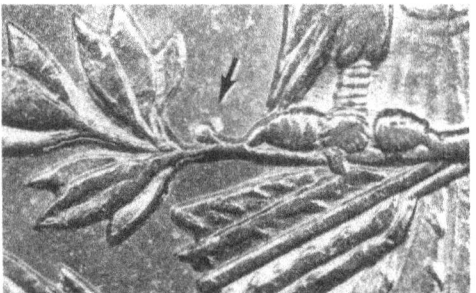

18 R C⁴/C³

20 O Die Gouge in Ear

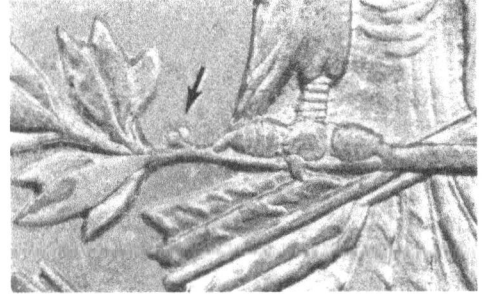

19 R C⁴/C³

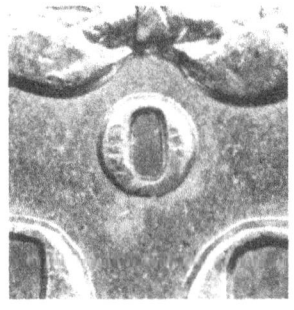

22 R High O

20 O Doubled 0

1901-O

23   III²1 • C⁴/C³i (2 Olive Reverse)   (181)   I-3   R-3
      Obverse III²1 – Vertical polishing lines in Liberty head nose and mouth.
      Reverse C⁴/C³i – Extra olive to right of olive connected to olive branch. Doubling at base of left and lower olive leaf cluster, top of upper arrow feather, back of lower arrow head, upper middle feathers of eagle's left wing, and right side of eagle's nostril and eye. III O mint mark centered and upright with slight shift to right.

24   III²8 • C³c (Low Date, High O)   (181)   I-2   R-3
      Obverse III²8 – Date set low close to rim.

25   III²6 • C³a (Slanted Date)   (181)   I-2   R-3

26   III²9 • C³a (Doubled Profile)   (181)   I-2   R-3
      Obverse III²9 – Liberty head profile is doubled all along forehead, nose, lips and chin.

27   III²10 • C⁴/C³k (Doubled 01, 2 Olive Reverse)   (181)   I-3   R-4
      Obverse III²10 – Doubled 01 in date. 0 doubled strongly at bottom outside. 1 doubled at top right corner of vertical shaft. Date set at left side of normal position. Slightly doubled Liberty head profile.
      Reverse C⁴/C³k – Extra olive to right of olive connected to olive branch. Doubling at base of left olive leaf cluster, back of lower arrow head, upper part of eagle's left wing, and right side of eagle's nostril and eye. Centered and upright III O mint mark.

28   III²11 • C⁴/C³g (Doubled Ear, 2 Olive Reverse)   (181)   I-3   R-3
      Obverse III²11 – Ear slightly doubled at very top below hairline and below inner ear fill. Date set in normal position and slanted with first 1 closest to rim.

29   III²5 • C³c (Far Date, High O)   (181)   I-2   R-3

30   III²1 • C³d (O Set Right)   (181)   I-2   R-3
      Reverse C³d – III O mint mark upright and set slightly to right.

31   III²6 • C³b (Slanted Date, O Tilted Right)   (181)   I-2   R-3

32   III²9 • C³c (Doubled Profile, High O)   (181)   I-2   R-3

23 R C⁴/C³

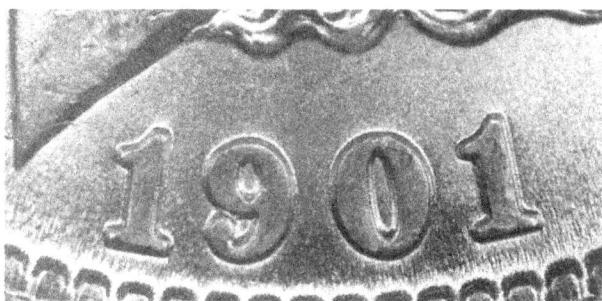
24 O Low Date

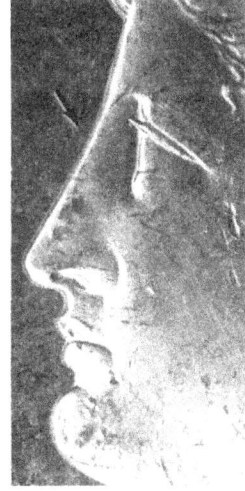
26 O Doubled Profile

27 O Doubled 01

27 R C⁴/C³

28 O Doubled Ear

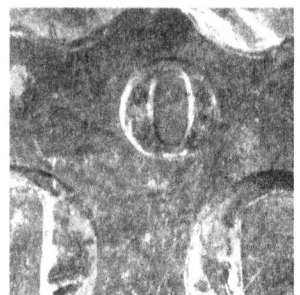
30 R O Set Right

1901-S

Typically the 1901-S is weakly struck although sharply struck specimens exist. Often on weakly struck coins, planchet striations will show in areas not fully struck up against the dies on both obverse and reverse. A few minor die varieties exist but none are significant. Proof-likes are extremely rare and have little contrast.

1   III²1 • C³a (Normal Die)   (189)   I-1   R-2
    Obverse III²1 – Normal die of III² type with closed 9.
    Reverse C³a – Normal die of C³ type with large V S mint mark centered and upright.

2   III²1 • C⁴a (Normal Die)   (189)   I-1   R-2
    Reverse C⁴a – Normal die of C⁴ type with upright V S mint mark.

3   III²1 • C³b (High S Tilted Right)   I-2   R-3
    Reverse C³b – V S mint mark set high and tilted slightly to the right.

4   III²1 • C⁴b (High S)   I-2   R-3
    Reverse C⁴b – V S mint mark set high.

5   III²1 • C⁴/C³a (2 Olive Reverse)   (189)   I-3   R-3
    Reverse C⁴/C³a – Faint shallow extra olive to right of olive connected to olive branch. Doubling at base of top and left olive leaf clusters, right of eagle's nostril, three feathers adjacent to eagle's right leg and back of lower arrow head.

6   III²2 • C⁴/C³b (2 Olive Reverse, Far Date)   (189)   I-3   R-3
    Obverse III²2 – Date set further right than normal.
    Reverse C⁴/C³b – Shallow extra olive to right of olive connected to olive branch. First lower leaf on left wreath doubled at bottom. Reverse overpolished with weak tail feathers and many leaves in wreath disconnected. Gap between the neck and wing appears to be a C³ narrow type but with outline of C⁴ type at edge of wing. A in DOLLAR and right star doubled as in C⁴ type.

7   III²1 • C⁴/C³c (2 Olive Reverse)   (189)   I-3   R-3
    Reverse C⁴/C³c – Extra olive to right of olive connected to olive branch. Doubling at base of middle olive cluster, top of second arrow feather from top, feathers of upper middle part of eagle's left wing, right side of eagle's nostril and back of lower arrow head. Large V S mint mark set high and upright.

8   III²1 • C⁴/C³b (2 Olive Reverse)   (189)   I-3   R-3

9   III²1 • C⁴/C³d (2 Olive Reverse)   (189)   I-3   R-3
    Reverse C⁴/C³d – Shallow extra olive to right of olive connected to olive branch. Doubling on top of olive branch at right of olives, at base of middle and lower olive leaf clusters, at bottom of lower arrow feathers, at bottom of bow ends, back of lower arrowhead, right side of eagle's nostril and top feathers of eagle's left wing. Large V S mint mark set slightly high and upright.

1901-S / 1902-P

3 R High S Tilted Right

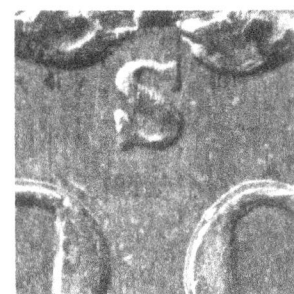
4 R High S

5 R C⁴/C³

6 R C⁴/C³

7 R C⁴/C³

9 R C⁴/C³

1902-P

The strike is usually good for this issue. Luster is usually some what subdued and can be satiny and brilliant, again probably due to the introduction of gas annealing furnaces at that mint in 1901. A few minor die varieties exist but none are significant. Proof-likes are fairly scarce and generally have little contrast with brilliant surfaces. Proofs also have little contrast.

1   III²1 • C⁴a Normal Die)   I-1   R-2
    Obverse III²1 – Normal die of III² type with closed 9.
    Reverse C⁴a – Normal die of C⁴ type.

2   III²2 • C⁴a (Near Date)   I-2   Proof and Regular
    Obverse III²2 – Date set further left than normal. Closed 9.

3   III²3 • C⁴a (Very Near Date)   I-2   R-3
    Obverse III²3 – Date set much further left than normal. Closed 9 variety.

4   III²4 • C⁴a (Doubled Ear)   I-3   R-5
    Obverse III²4 – Ear strongly doubled at right outside and left inside hairline doubled just above ear, and Liberty head profile is doubled along nose, lips and chin.

1902-P

5   III²5 • C⁴a (Doubled Profile)   (189)   I-2   R-3
     Obverse III²5 – Liberty head profile is doubled along forehead, nose, lips and chin.

6   III²2 • C⁴/C³a (Near Date, 2 Olive Reverse)   (189)   I-3   R-3
     Reverse C⁴/C³a – Extra olive to right of olive connected to olive branch. Doubling on top of olive branch at right of olives, at base of top and left olive leaf clusters, tops of arrow feathers, back of lower arrow head, outside of lower leaf on first cluster on right side of wreath, outside of lower large leaf on second cluster on left side of wreath and letters N-TAT-OF towards rim.

7   III²2 • C⁴/C³b (Near Date, 2 Olive Reverse)   (189)   I-3   R-3
     Reverse C⁴/C³b – Shallow extra olive to right of olive connected to olive branch. Doubling at base of top and left olive leaf clusters, faintly on second arrow feather next to olive branch, right of eagle's nostril and eye, and back of lower arrow head.

8   III²1 • C⁴/C³c (2 Olive Reverse)   (189)   I-3   R-3
     Reverse C⁴/C³c – Extra olive to right of olive connected to olive branch. Doubling at base of all three olive leaf clusters, back of lower arrow head, feathers at top of eagle's left wing, and right side of eagle's nostril and eye.

4 O Doubled Ear

4 O Doubled Profile

5 O Doubled Profile

6 R C⁴/C³

7 R C⁴/C³

8 R C⁴/C³

9 O Doubled 1

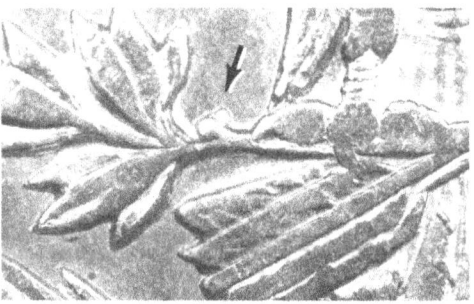

9 R C⁴/C³

1902-P / 1902-O

9   III²5 • C⁴/C³ d (Doubled 1, 2 Olive Reverse)   (189)   I-3   R-3
Obverse III²5 – 1 doubled below crossbar. Date set further left than normal.
Reverse C⁴/C³ d – Extra olive to right of olive connected to olive branch. Doubling on top of olive branch at right of olives, at base of all three olive leaf clusters, on end of second arrow feather next to olive branch, back of lower arrow head, on right of two innermost right wing feathers next to leg, feathers at top of eagle's left wing, right side of eagle's nostril and eye, top leaf of second leaf cluster of left wreath and UNITED STATES OF towards rim.

10   III²1 • C⁴/C³ e (2 Olive Reverse)   (189)   I-3   R-3
Reverse C⁴/C³ e – Shallow extra olive to right of olive connected to olive branch. Doubling on top of olive branch at right of olives, at base of all three olive leaf clusters, on top of upper two leaves in lower olive leaf cluster, at top of all arrow feathers, back of lower arrow head, feathers at top of eagle's left wing and right side of eagle's nostril.

11   III²2 • C⁴/C³ f (2 Olive Reverse)   (186)   I-3   Proof
Reverse C⁴/C³ f – Shallow extra olive to right of olive connected to olive branch. Doubling on top of olive branch at right of olives at base of all three olive leaf clusters, on top of upper leaf in lower olive leaf cluster, at top of lower three arrow feathers, back of lower arrow head, feathers in upper middle of eagle's left wing, and right side of eagle's nostril.

10 R C⁴/C³   Proof 11 R C⁴/C³

1902-O

This issue has a strike that ranges from slightly weak to very flat. Luster is usually good. Fully struck (full hair over ear) pieces that are lustrous with minimal bag marks are difficult to locate for this common "O" mint. Numerous minor die varieties exist but only one is very significant, VAM 3, with small "O". It is very scarce and is known only in low circulated condition. Proof-likes are somewhat scarce but have little contrast. However, proof-likes and semi proof-likes tend to be fully struck quite a bit of the time.

1   III²1 • C⁴ a (Closed 9)   I-1   R-2
Obverse III²1 • Normal die of III² type with closed 9. Some specimens show base of 2 filled in.
Reverse C⁴a – Normal die of C⁴ type with medium III O mint mark, centered and upright.

2   III²2 • C⁴ a (Open 9)   I-1   R-2
Obverse III²2 – Normal die with open 9. Ball of 9 does not touch body of 9.

3   III²1 • C³ a (Small O)   (181)   I-3   R-5
Reverse C³a – Normal die of C³ type with small I O mint mark tilted to the right.

4   III²3 • C⁴ a (Near Date)   (181)   I-2   R-3
Obverse III²3 – Date set further left than normal. Closed 9.

5   III²3 • C⁴ b (Near Date, High O)   (181)   I-2   R-3
Reverse C⁴b – III O mint mark set high and upright.

6   III²1 • C⁴ c (O Tilted Left)   (181)   I-2   R-3
Obverse III²1 – Some specimens show base of 2 filled in. Closed 9.
Reverse C⁴c – III O mint mark set high and tilted to left.

7   III²3 • C⁴ d (Near Date, High O Tilted Left, Bar O)   I-2   R-3
Reverse C⁴d – III O mint mark, set high to right and tilted slightly left. Some specimens show die break at top inside showing as a horizontal bar.

1902-O

8 III²3 • C⁴/C³k (2 Olive Reverse, O/O Down) (181) I-3 R-4
Reverse C⁴/C³k – III O mint mark repunched with original showing as a thin curved line at lower left outside and as a thin vertical line with a curve at top on right inside. Extra olive to right of olive connected to olive branch. Doubling on top of olive branch at right of olives, at base of olive leaf clusters, on end of second arrow feather next to olive branch, middle talon on eagle's right leg, on right side of two innermost right wing feathers next to leg, right of eagle's nostril and eye, and back of lower arrow head. UNI-ED TAT OF doubled faintly towards rim.

9 III²4 • C⁴g (Doubled 1) I-2 R-3
Obverse III²4 – 1 in date doubled just below upper crossbar as a thin horizontal line. Profile of Liberty head doubled on forward hair line, forehead, nose, lips and chin. E PLU and all of left stars doubled slightly towards rim.
Reverse C⁴g – Legend and motto letters doubled towards rim

10 III²5 • C⁴f (Doubled 1) I-2 R-3
Obverse III²5 – 1 in date doubled slightly at bottom of lower crossbar. Closed 9:
Reverse C⁴f – III O mint mark set slightly to right.

11 III²1 • C⁴h (Doubled Reverse) I-3 R-3
Reverse C⁴h – Outer portion doubled with letters doubled outward in radial direction for all legend letters, stars, tops of motto letters and outside edge of right wreath.

12 III²6 • C⁴/C³a (Doubled Profile, 2 Olive Reverse) (181) I-3 R-3
Obverse III²6 – Double nose, lips, chin and neck on Liberty head profile. All stars on left doubled slightly near rim. E-PLURIBUS UNUM doubled slightly on lower portions of letters towards rim. Date set low and further left than normal.
Reverse C⁴/C³a – III O mint mark doubled slightly at top right inside. Shallow extra olive to right of olive connected to olive branch. Doubling on top of arrow feathers, base of left olive leaf cluster, on top of olive branch at right of olives, and back of lower arrow head. OD WE TRUS doubled at top.

1 O Filled 2

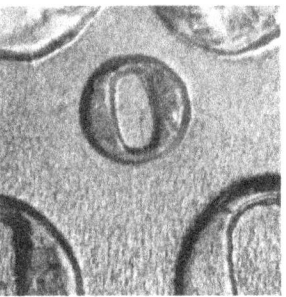
5 R High O

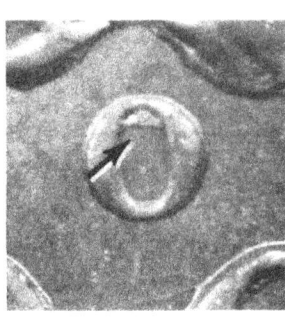
6 R O Tilted Left

7 R Bar O

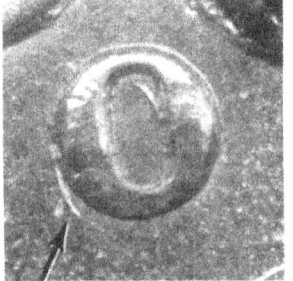
8 R O/O Down

8 R C⁴/C³

9 O Doubled 1

10 O Doubled 1

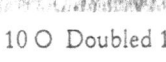
10 R O Set Right

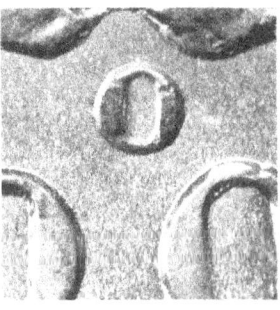

11 R Doubled Reverse

1902-O

12 O Low Date

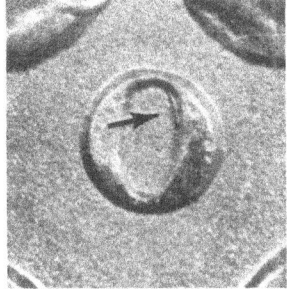

12 R O/O

12 R C⁴/C³

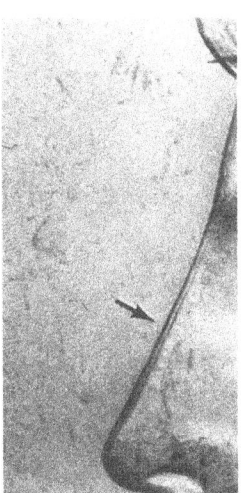

12 O Doubled Profile

13   III²7 • C⁴a (Doubled 1-02)   (181)   I-2   R-3
   Obverse III²7 – Doubled 1-02 in date. 1 doubled strongly at bottom of lower crossbar at mid height. 02 doubled at very bottom as a line on the field. Date set further left than normal.

14   III²8 • C⁴i (Doubled Profile and Reverse Lettering)   (181)   I-2   R-3
   Obverse III²8 – Doubled nose, lips, chin and neck on Liberty head profile.
   Reverse C⁴i – Slightly doubled UNITED STATES OF AMERICA and right star in a radial direction.

15   III²8 • C⁴/C³b (Doubled Profile, 2 Olive Reverse)   (181)   I-3   R-3
   Reverse C⁴/C³b – Extra olive to right of olive connected to branch. Doubled tops of arrow feathers, olive leaves, olive branch to right of olives, eagle's right leg and middle talon, top arrow shaft, and on right of two innermost right wing feathers next to leg. Slightly doubled lower inside of GOD W-U.

16   III²9 • C⁴/C³c (Doubled Ear, 2 Olive Reverse)   (181)   I-3   R-3
   Obverse III²9 – Ear doubled slightly at lower outside. Date set further left than normal with base of 2 filled in. Closed 9.
   Reverse C⁴/C³c – III O mint mark set high and slightly to right. Extra olive to right of olive connected to olive branch. Doubling on top of olive branch at right of olives, at base of left olive leaf cluster, faintly on end of second arrow feather next to olive branch, back of lower arrow head, back of eagle's nostril and right two innermost right wing feathers next to leg. W in WE doubled on right side.

17   III²10 • C⁴/C³d (Doubled Ear, 2 Olive Reverse)   (181)   I-3   R-3
   Obverse III²10 – Ear doubled slightly at very bottom outside. Date set further left than normal. Closed 9.
   Reverse C⁴/C³d – III O mint mark set high, upright and centered. Extra olive to right of olive connected to olive branch. Doubled tops of arrow feathers, top of olive branch at right of olives, at base of left olive leaf clusters, and back of lower arrow head. IN GOD WE TRUST doubled at top. UNITED STATES OF doubled towards rim.

18   III²3 • C⁴/C³e (Near Date, 2 Olive Reverse)   (181)   I-3   R-3
   Reverse C⁴/C³e – Extra olive to right of olive connected to olive branch. Doubling at base of left olive leaf cluster and back of lower arrow head. Pitting in D of DOLLAR and below second leaf cluster of left wreath.

19   III²11 • C⁴/C³f (Doubled Profile, 2 Olive Reverse)   (181)   I-3   R-3
   Obverse III²11 – Doubled front hairline, forehead, nose, lips, and chin on Liberty head. Date set much further left than normal. Closed 9.
   Reverse C⁴/C³f – Extra olive to right of olive connected to olive branch. Doubling at base of top and left olive leaf clusters, top of lower leaf in top olive leaf cluster, top of middle leaf in left olive leaf cluster, top of olive branch at right of olives, middle claw of eagle's right leg, at end of second arrow feather next to olive branch, at top of second leaf cluster of left wreath, next to designer's initial M in bow and right two innermost right wing feathers next to leg.

1902-O

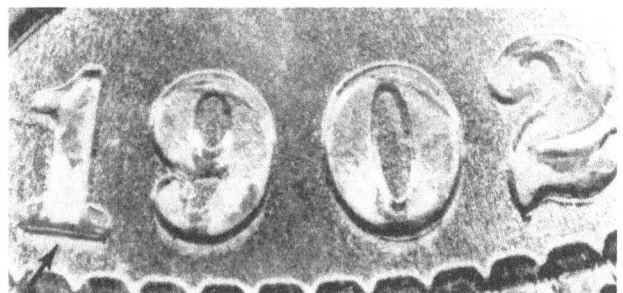

13 O Doubled 1-02

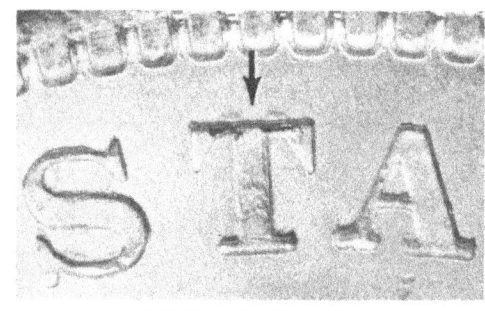

14 R Doubled Lettering

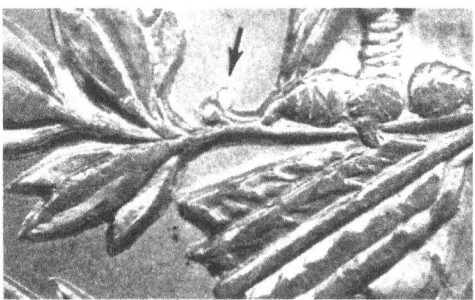

15 R C⁴/C³

16 O Doubled Ear

16 R O Set High and Right

16 R C⁴/C³

17 O Doubled Ear

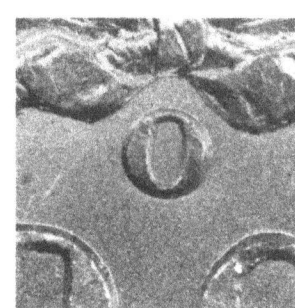

17 R O Set High

17 R C⁴/C³

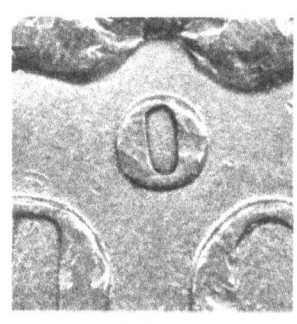

20 R O Tilted Left

19 R C⁴/C³

18 R C⁴/C³

373

1902-O

20	III² 8 • C⁴/C³ g (Doubled Profile, 2 Olive Reverse)	(181)		I-3	R-3

Reverse C⁴/C³ g – III O mint mark set slightly high, to right, and tilted to left. Extra olive to right of olive connected to olive branch. Doubling at base of top and left olive leaf clusters, top of lower leaf in top olive leaf cluster, top of middle leaf in left olive leaf cluster, top of top leaf in lower olive leaf cluster, top of olive branch at right of olives, tops of arrow feathers, back of lower arrow head, faintly on right side of two innermost right wing feathers next to leg, and right of eagle's nostril and eye. IN GOD WE TRUST and NITED STATES OF doubled towards rim.

21	III² 12 • C⁴/C³ h (Tripled Profile, 2 Olive Reverse)	(181)		I-3	R-3

Obverse III² 12 – Tripled front hairline, tip of nose, chin and cap back of Liberty head plus E PLUR lower portions towards rim. Doubled nose, lips, neck, cap top of Liberty head plus left stars and S-UNUM towards rim.

Reverse C⁴/C³ h – Extra olive to right of olive connected to olive branch. Doubling at base of top and left leaf clusters, tops of bottom leaf in top clusters and top leaf in bottom cluster, top of upper 3 arrow feathers, right side of middle talon on eagle's right leg, top of upper arrow head and shaft, and back of lower arrow head.

22	III² 3 • C⁴ j (Near Date, O Tilted Left)	(181)		I-2	R-3

Obverse III² 3 – Base of 2 filled in.

Reverse C⁴ j – III O mint mark tilted to left at normal height.

23	III² 13 • C⁴/C³ i (Doubled Ear, 2 Olive Reverse)	(181)		I-3	R-3

Obverse III² 13 – Ear doubled on inner right side. Date set further left than normal.

Reverse C⁴/C³ i – III O mint mark set slightly high, centered and upright. Extra olive to right of olive connected to olive branch. Doubling on top of olive branch at right of olives, at base of top and left olive leaf clusters, top of middle leaf in left olive leaf cluster, top of top leaf in lower olive leaf cluster, tops of arrow feathers, back of lower arrow head, middle top of eagle's left wing, and back of eagle's nostril and eye. NI-E TATE O doubled faintly towards rim.

24	III² 1 • C⁴ k (O Set High and Right)	(181)		I-2	R-3

Reverse C⁴ k – III O mint mark set high, upright, and slightly to right.

25	III² 14 • C⁴/C³ j (Doubled Obverse, 2 Olive Reverse)	(181)		I-3	R-3

Obverse III² 14 – Outside of ear doubled on right, hairline above ear doubled at bottom and eyelid doubled underneath. Date at left edge of normal position.

Reverse C⁴/C³ j – III O mint mark set slightly high and to right with slight tilt to left. Extra olive to right of olive connected to olive branch. Doubling on top of olive branch at right of olives, at base of top and left olive leaf clusters, on end of second arrow feather next to olive branch, middle talon on eagle's right leg, right of eagle's nostril and eye and back of lower arrow head. UNI-ED TAT OF doubled faintly toward rim.

26	III² 15 • C⁴ l (Doubled Profile and Reverse Lettering)	(181)		I-3	R-3

Obverse III² 15 – Doubled nose, lips, and chin on Liberty head profile. Date set further left than normal.

Reverse C⁴ l – Slightly doubled UNITED STATES OF ER-C in a radial direction, doubled upper right and left wreath towards rim, and IN GOD WE RUST doubled at top. III O mint mark set slightly high and tilted left.

27	III² 1 • C⁴/C³ l (2 Olive Reverse)	(181)		I-3	R-3

Reverse C⁴/C³ l – III O mint mark set slightly high and set slightly to right with slight tilt to right. Extra olive to right of olive connected to olive branch. Doubling on top of olive branch at right of olives, at base of olive leaf clusters, at top of middle leaf in olive leaf clusters, at top of upper leaves in lower olive leaf cluster, top of arrow feathers and sheaves, top of eagle's right claw on right talon, back of lower arrow head, and top feathers in eagle's left wing.

28	III² 15 • C⁴/C³ m (Doubled Profile, 2 Olive Reverse)	(181)		I-3	R-3

Reverse C⁴/C³ m – III O mint mark set slightly high with slight tilt to left. Extra olive to right of olive connected to olive branch. Doubling on top of olive branch at right of olives, at base of olive leaf clusters, at top of upper leaf in lower olive leaf cluster, back of lower arrow head, middle feathers in eagle's left wing, and eagle's nostril. Polishing lines between olive branch and arrow feather and around eagle's legs.

20 R C⁴/C³   21 R C⁴/C³

1902-O

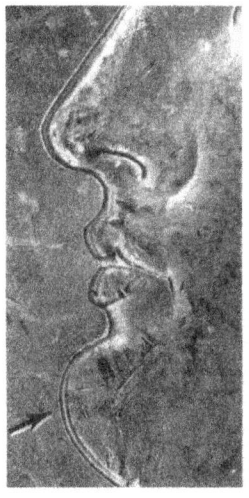
21 O Tripled Profile

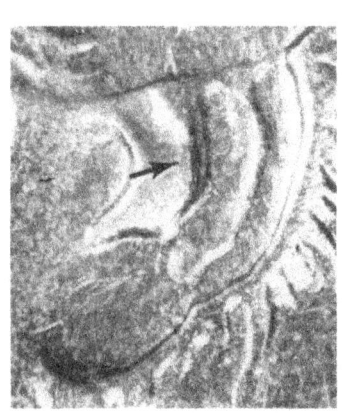
23 O Doubled Ear

25 O Doubled Ear

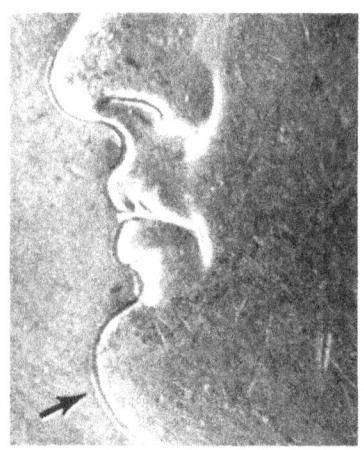
26 O Doubled Profile

23 R C⁴/C³

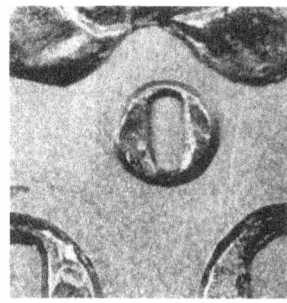
24 R O Set High and Right

25 R C⁴/C³

26 R Doubled Letters

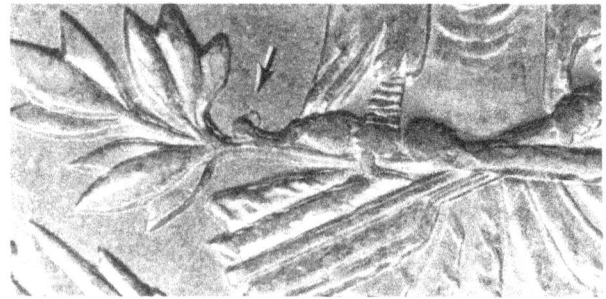
27 R C⁴/C³

28 R C⁴/C³

29 R C⁴/C³

1902-O

29   III² 16 • C⁴/C³ n (Doubled Ear, 2 Olive Reverse)   (181)   I-3   R-3
Obverse III² 16 – Ear doubled slightly at middle outside. Liberty head profile slightly doubled on nose, lips, chin and neck. First U in PLURIBUS has horizontal die gouge on right side.
Reverse C⁴/C³ n – III O mint mark set slightly high, upright and tilted slightly to right. Extra olive to right of olive connected to olive branch. Doubling on very top of olive branch at right of olives, at base of left and bottom olive leaf clusters, around tops of leaves in top olive leaf cluster, back of lower arrow head, upper middle feathers of eagle's left wing, right side of eagle's nostril and eye, and eagle's beak.

30   III² 15 • C⁴/C³ o (Doubled Profile, 2 Olive Reverse)   (181)   I-3   R-3
Reverse C⁴/C³ o – III O mint mark set slightly high, upright and slightly to right. Extra olive to right of olive connected to olive branch. Doubling on top of olive branch at right of olives, at base of olive leaf clusters, around upper leaf in top olive leaf cluster, at top of upper leaf in lower olive leaf cluster, on end of second arrow feather next to olive branch, back lower arrow head, faintly on right two innermost right wing feathers next to leg, upper middle feathers of eagle's left wing, right side of eagle's nostril and eye, eagle's beak, and top of eagle's right wing. Slight doubling of NT-ED STA-E towards rim and D, W-T in motto on right side.

31   III² 3 • C⁴/C³ p (Near Date, 2 Olive Reverse)   (181)   I-3   R-3
Obverse III² 3 – Some specimens show base of 2 filled in.
Reverse C⁴/C³ p – III O mint mark set slightly high and set slightly to right. Extra olive to right of olive connected to olive branch. Doubling on top of olive branch at right of olives, at base of left olive leaf cluster, on end of second arrow feather next to olive branch, back of lower arrow head, right of eagle's nostril and eye, and top middle feathers of eagle's left wing.

32   III² 1 • C⁴/C³ q (2 Olive Reverse)   (181)   I-3   R-3
Obverse III² 1 – Base of 2 filled in.
Reverse C⁴/C³ q – III O mint mark set slightly high, centered, and tilted slightly to left. Extra olive to right of olive connected to olive branch. Doubling at back of lower arrow head, right of eagle's nostril and eye and top feathers of eagle's left wing. UNITED STATE OF doubled faintly toward rim.

33   III² 8 • C⁴ b (Doubled Profile, High O)   I-2   R-3

34   III² 3 • C⁴/C³ r (Near Date, 2 Olive Reverse)   (181)   I-3   R-3
Reverse C⁴/C³ r – III O mint mark set high and tilted left. Extra olive to right of olive connected to olive branch. Doubling on top of olive branch at right of olives, at base of olive leaf clusters, top of upper leaf in bottom olive leaf cluster, tops of arrow feathers, back of lower arrow head, middle feathers of eagle's left wing and right of eagle's nostril and eye.

35   III² 6 • C⁴ j (Doubled Profile, O Tilted Left)   (181)   I-2   R-3
36   III² 9 • C⁴ b (Doubled Ear, High O)   (181)   I-2   R-3
37   III² 1 • C⁴ b (High O)   (181)   I-2   R-3
38   III² 8 • C⁴/C³ s (Doubled Profile, 2 Olive Reverse)   (181)   I-3   R-3
Reverse C⁴/C³ s – III O mint mark centered and upright with slight shift to right. Extra olive to right of olive connected to olive branch. Doubling on top of olive branch at right of olives, at base of olive leaf clusters, top of upper two leaves in bottom olive leaf cluster, tops of arrow feathers and middle of shafts, back of lower arrow head, middle feathers of eagle's left wing and right of eagle's nostril and eye.

39   III² 1 • C⁴/C³ t (2 Olive Reverse)   (181)   I-2   R-3
Reverse C⁴/C³ t – III O mint mark set slightly high, centered and upright. Extra olive to right of olive connected to olive branch. Doubling on top of olive branch at right of olives, at base of all olive leaf clusters, edge of top olive leaf clusters, top leaf of lower olive lead cluster, tops of arrow feathers, back of lower arrow head, middle top of eagle's left wing, right side of two innermost wing feathers next to leg and right of eagle's nostril and eye.

29 O Doubled Ear

30 R C⁴/C³

31 R C⁴/C³

1902-O / 1902-S

40	III²15 • C⁴a (Doubled Profile, Near Date)	(181)	I-2	R-3
41	III²17 • C⁴a (Doubled 1, Near Date)	(181)	I-2	R-3

Obverse III²17 – 1 in date doubled slightly below upper crossbar. Date set further left than normal.

32 R C⁴/C³

34 R C⁴/C³

38 R C⁴/C³

39 R C⁴/C³

41 O Doubled 1

1902-S

Very weakly struck is the norm for this issue with heavy planchet striations across the head, eagle and parts of the fields showing quite often. Full strikes are occasionally seen however. Luster is usually good. A few minor die varieties exist but none are significant. Proof-likes are quite rare and have little contrast.

1	III²1 • C⁴a (Normal Die)		I-1	R-2

Obverse III²1 – Normal die of III² type with closed 9. Some specimens show base of 2 filled in.
Reverse C⁴a – Normal die of C⁴ type with large V S mint mark centered and upright.

2	III²2 • C⁴a (Near Date)	(189)	I-2	R-3

Obverse III²2 – Date set further left than normal.

3	III²3 • C⁴/C³a (Doubled 02, 2 Olive Reverse)	(189)	I-3	R-3

Obverse III²3 – Doubled 02 in date. 0 doubled slightly on top right outside. 2 tripled at top outside.
Reverse C⁴/C³a – Extra olive to right of olive connected to olive branch. Doubling at base of left olive leaf cluster, top of olive branch at right of olives and back of lower arrow head. Slight doubling of E STAT-F towards rim.

4	III²1 • C⁴b (S Tilted Left)		I-2	R-3

Reverse C⁴b – V S mint mark centered tilted left.

5	III²4 • C⁴/C³b (Doubled 19, 2 Olive Reverse)	(189)	I-3	R-3

Obverse III²4 – Doubled 19 in date. 1 doubled below upper crossbar on field surface and at top left and right of lower crossbar on surface of digit. 9 doubled slightly at lower left inside of lower loop. Date set further left than normal.
Reverse C⁴/C³b – Extra olive to right of olive connected to olive branch. Doubling at base of top and left olive leaf cluster, below bottom leaf in left and lower leaf cluster, top of olive branch at right of olives, slightly on top of arrow feathers, back of lower arrow head, and faintly on right of two innermost right wing feathers next to leg. STATES OF doubled faintly towards rim.

1902-S

6 III²5 • C⁴/C³ c (Doubled Profile, 2 Olive Reverse)   (189)   I-3   R-3
Obverse III²5 – Slightly doubled nose, lips, and chin of Liberty head profile.
Reverse C⁴/C³ c – V S mint mark tilted left. Extra olive to right of olive connected to olive branch. Doubling on top of olive branch at right of olives, at base of top and left olive leaf clusters, at top of top leaf in lower olive leaf cluster, on end of second arrow feather next to olive branch, right of eagle's nostril and eye, and back of lower arrow head.

7 III²6 • C⁴/C³ d (Doubled Profile, 2 Olive Reverse)   (189)   I-3   R-3
Obverse III²6 – Slightly doubled nose, lips and chin on Liberty head profile. Date set further left than normal with base of 2 filled in.
Reverse C⁴/C³ d – Extra olive to right of olive connected to olive branch. Doubling at top of olive branch at right of olives, base of left olive leaf cluster, slightly on top of arrow feathers, back of lower arrow head, upper feathers of eagle's left wing, right of eagle's nostril and faintly on right of two innermost right wing feathers next to leg. UNITED STATES OF doubled faintly towards rim.

8 III²5 • C⁴/C³ b (Doubled Profile, 2 Olive Reverse)   (189)   I-3   R-3

1 O Filled 2

3 O Doubled 02

4 R S Tilted Left

5 O Doubled 19

3 R C⁴/C³

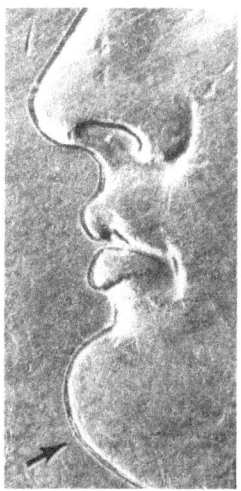
6 O Doubled Profile

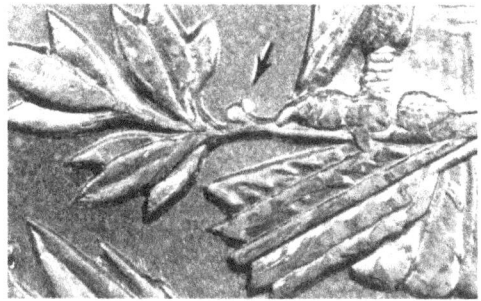
5 R C⁴/C³

6 R C⁴/C³

7 R C⁴/C³

1903-P

Full strike is the general rule for this issue. Luster is seldom very flashy, but tends to be brilliant and subdued. This gives it a sameness look over the devices and field. In terms of full strike and minimal bag marks, the 1903-P is the most generally available in nice condition for the later P mints. A surprisingly few number of minor die varieties exist and none are significant. Proof-likes are fairly scarce and have little contrast. Some proof-likes have numerous fine die polishing lines in the fields. Sliders of this issue are often hard to differentiate from uncirculated specimens because of the brilliant and subdued luster. Proofs have little contrast.

1   III²1 • C⁴a (Closed 9)   I-1   R-2
     Obverse III²1 – Normal die of III² type with closed 9.
     Reverse C⁴a – Normal die of C⁴ type.

2   III²2 • C⁴a (Open 9)   I-1   R-2
     Obverse III²2 – Normal die with open 9.

3   III²3 • C⁴a (Doubled 3)   (189)   I-2   R-3
     Obverse III²3 – 3 in date doubled slightly at top inside of upper loop. Closed 9.

4   III²4 • C⁴a • (Near Date)   I-2   R-3
     Obverse III²4 – Date set further left than normal.

5   III²5 • C⁴a (Doubled Profile, Near Date)   (189)   I-2   R-3
     Obverse III²5 – Slightly doubled lower front hairline, nose, lips, and chin on Liberty head profile. Date set further left than normal.

3 O Doubled 3

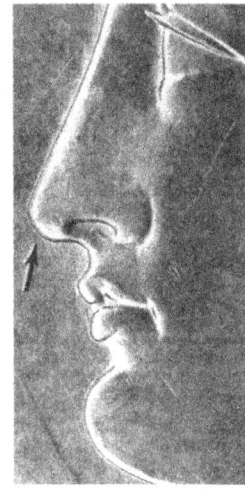

5 O Doubled Profile

1903-O

This issue usually has a good strike and good luster. Only a few minor die varieties exist and none are significant. Proof-likes are very scarce and have little to some light contrast. Semi proof-like are more available but should not be mistaken for full proof-likes.

1   III²1 • C⁴a (Normal Die)   I-1   R-2
     Obverse III²1 – Normal die of III² type with open 9.
     Reverse C⁴a – Normal die of C⁴ type with medium III O mint mark, centered and upright.

2   III²1 • C⁴b (O Tilted Left)   (181)   I-2   R-3
     Reverse C⁴b – Centered III O mint mark tilted slightly to left and set slightly high.

3   III²2 • C⁴c (O Set Right, Tilted Left)   I-2   R-3
     Obverse III²2 – Normal die of III² type with closed 9.
     Reverse C⁴c – III O set right and tilted left.

1903-O / 1903-S

4	III²3 • C⁴c (Doubled 3, O Set Right, Tilted Left) (181)		I-2	R-4
	Obverse III²3 – 3 in date doubled at top outside as thin curved arc. Closed 9. Slight doubling of Liberty head profile including nose, lips and chin.			
5	III²3 • C⁴a (Doubled 3) (189)		I-2	R-4
6	III²1 • C⁴d (High O) (181)		I-2	R-3
	Reverse C⁴d – III O mint mark set high, centered and upright			
7	III²4 • C⁴d (Near Date, High O) (181)		I-2	R-3
	Obverse III²4 – Date set further left than normal.			
8	III²1 • C⁴e (High O Set Right) (181)		I-2	R-3
	Reverse C⁴e – III O mint mark set high and to right with slight tilt to left.			
9	III²5 • C⁴b (Doubled 1, O Tilted Left) (181)		I-2	R-3
	Obverse III²5 – 1 in date doubled slightly at lower right outside of base as a thin line. Liberty head profile slightly doubled along forehead, nose, lips and chin.			
10	III²1 • C⁴f (O Tilted Right) (181)		I-2	R-3
	Reverse C⁴f – III O mint mark centered and tilted slightly to right.			
11	III²2 • C³a (High O) (181)		I-2	R-5
	Reverse C³a – Normal die of C³ type with medium O mint mark, set slightly high, centered and upright.			

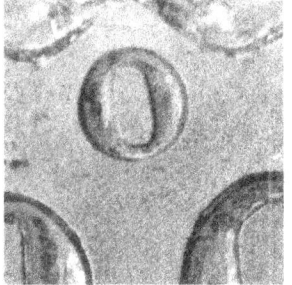 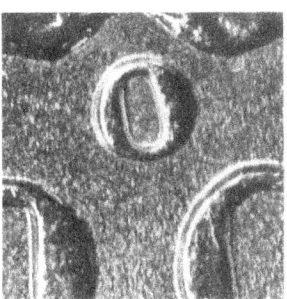 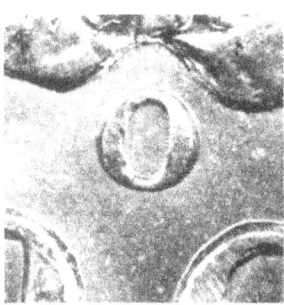 

2 R O Tilted Left   3 R O Set Right, Tilted Left   6 R High O   8 R High O Set Right

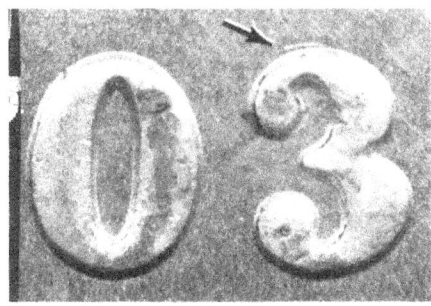  

4 O Doubled 3   9 O Doubled 1   10 R O Tilted Right

1903-S

The strike on this issue is full and the luster very good. Although scarce in mint state, the quality is generally high. A few minor die varieties exist. However, a significant and scarce variety is VAM 2 with a small "S" mint mark of the size used on Barber quarters. The highest grade for this small "S" variety is a slider AU and it is rare above EF grades. Proof-likes are extremely rare and when encountered, have little contrast.

1	III²1 • C⁴a (Normal Die)	I-1	R-2
	Obverse III²1 – Normal die of III² type with open 9.		
	Reverse C⁴a – Normal die of C⁴ type with large V S mint mark centered and upright.		

1903-S

2	III²1 • C⁴b (Small S)	(189)		I-4	R-4

Reverse C⁴b – Normal die with small II S mint mark centered and upright.

3	III²1 • C⁴c (S Tilted Left)	(189)		I-2	R-3

Reverse C⁴c – Centered V S mint mark tilted to the left.

4	III²1 • C⁴/C³a (2 Olive Reverse)	(189)		I-3	R-3

Reverse C⁴/C³a – Extra olive to right of olive connected to olive branch. Doubling at base of left olive leaf cluster, top of top leaf in lower leaf cluster, top of olive branch at right of olives, tops of arrow feathers, top feathers of eagle's left wing, right of eagle's nostril and back of lower arrow head. Centered V S mint mark tilted to left.

5	III²2 • C⁴/C³b (Slanted Date, 2 Olive Reverse)	(189)		I-3	R-3

Obverse III²2 – Slight slant to date with 1 closest to rim.
Reverse C⁴/C³b – Faint shallow extra olive to right of olive connected to olive branch. Doubling at base of top and left olive leaf clusters, right of eagle's nostril and eye, and back of lower arrow head. V S mint mark set upright and slightly high.

6	III²1 • C⁴/C³c (2 Olive Reverse)	(189)		I-3	R-3

Reverse C⁴/C³c – Faint shallow extra olive to right of olive connected to olive branch. Doubling at back of lower arrow head. V S mint mark is centered and upright.

7	III²2 • C⁴c (Slanted Date, S Tilted Left)	(189)		I-2	R-3
8	III²1 • C⁴/C³d (2 Olive Reverse)	(189)		I-3	R-3

Reverse C⁴/C³d – Faint shallow extra olive to right of olive connected to olive branch. Doubling at base of top and left olive leaf cluster, back of lower arrow head, upper part of eagle's left wing, and right side of eagle's nostril and eye. Centered V S mint mark with slight tilt to right.

9	III²1 • C⁴d (S Set Right)	(189)		I-2	R-3

Reverse C⁴d – V S mint mark set slightly to right and upright.

3 R S Tilted Left

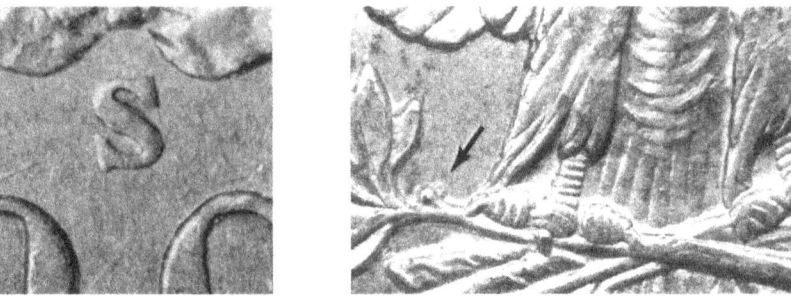

4 R C⁴/C³

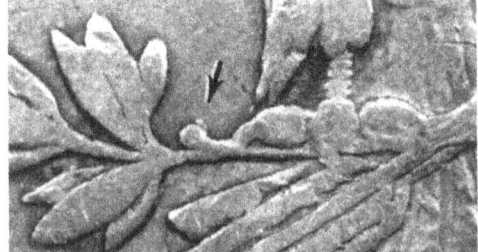

5 R C⁴/C³

5 O Slanted Date

6 R C⁴/C³

8 R C⁴/C³

1904-P

Generally the strike has a touch of weakness although full strikes are available. Luster is generally dull and subdued. A few minor die varieties exist but none are significant. Full proof-likes with deep mirrors are very rare and the few known specimens exhibited little contrast. Proofs have little contrast like the two previous issues and most are marred by hairlines and dull luster.

1	III²1 • C⁴a (Normal Die)		I-1	R-2

Obverse III²1 – Normal die of III² type with closed 9.
Reverse C⁴a – Normal die of C⁴ type.

1A	III²1 • C⁴a (Pitted Reverse)		I-2	R-3

Reverse C⁴a – Reverse pitted around D in DOLLAR.

2	III²2 • C⁴a (Doubled 1-4)		I-2	R-3

Obverse III²2 – 1 and 4 in date doubled slightly above the bottom crossbars.

3	III²3 • C⁴a (Spiked 1, Doubled 4)		I-2	R-3

Obverse III²3 – 1 in date has short vertical spike above bottom crossbar on right side. 4 is doubled at bottom of both crossbars. Liberty head profile slightly doubled.

4	III²4 • C⁴a (Doubled 9-4)	(181)	I-2	R-3

Obverse III²4 – Doubled 9-4 in date. 1 has a spike of metal projecting up from right side of base. 9 is doubled strongly at bottom outside of both loops. 4 is doubled slightly at left bottom of crossbar. Liberty head profile slightly doubled.

5	III²5 • C⁴a (Doubled Profile)	(189)	I-2	R-3

Obverse III²5 – Slightly doubled profile of Liberty head including forehead, nose, lips and chin.

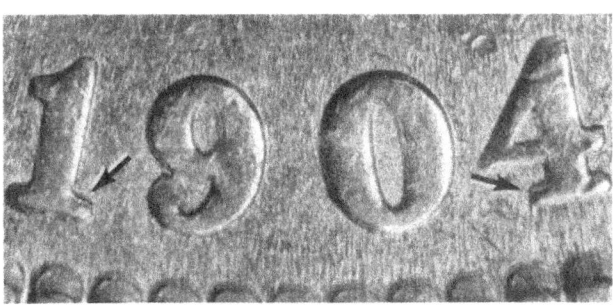

2 O Doubled 1-4

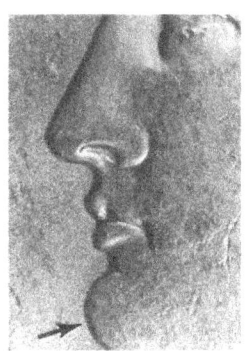

5 O Doubled Profile

3 O Spiked 1, Doubled 4

4 O Doubled 9-4

1904-O

The strike is usually slightly weak although quantities of fully struck as well as flat strikes can be encountered because of the large mintage. Luster is generally good. Many hundreds of original mint bags were released by the Treasury in 1962-64 making the 1904-O the most available BU O mint after the 1885-O. Quite a few minor die varieties exist but none are particularly significant. Proof-likes are fairly available but generally have little contrast. A few deep mirrors with some light contrast are known.

1     $III^2 1 \cdot C^4 a$ (Normal Die)   I-1   R-2
Obverse $III^2 1$ – Normal die of III^2 type with closed 9.
Reverse $C^4 a$ – Normal die of C^4 type with medium III O mint mark centered and upright.

1A $III^2 1 \cdot C^4 a$ (Polishing Lines on Reverse)   (181)   I-2   R-3
Reverse $C^4 a$ – Heavy vertical polishing lines in eagle's wings and horizontal polishing lines in eagle's tail feathers and arrow feathers.

2     $III^2 1 \cdot C^4 b \cdot$ (O Tilted Left)   I-2   R-3
Reverse $C^4 b$ – Normal die with III 0 mint mark tilted to the left.

3     $III^2 2 \cdot C^4 a$ (Doubled 19)   I-2   R-3
Obverse $III^2 2$ – Doubled 19 in date. 1 doubled below upper crossbar and slightly at bottom. 9 doubled strongly at bottom. Closed 9 variety.

4     $III^2 3 \cdot C^4 a$ (Doubled Date)   I-2   R-3
Obverse $III^2 3$ – Entire date is doubled. 1 doubled at top right of bottom crossbar as vertical line with hooks on end. Doubled 9 in date on lower left outside and top inside of upper loop. 0 doubled slightly at bottom outside and 4 at top left outside. Closed 9. Some specimens have a filled 4.

4A $III^2 3 \cdot C^4 a$ (Doubled Date)   I-2   R-3
Reverse $C^4 a$ – Pitted reverse and polishing marks as in 5A reverse.

5     $III^2 4 \cdot C^4 a$ (Doubled 1-4)   I-2   R-3
Obverse $III^2 4$ – Doubled 1-4 in date. 1 doubled at bottom of top crossbar. Lower crossbar of 4 doubled at top right. Closed 9. Profile of Liberty head is slightly doubled.

5A $III^2 4 \cdot C^4 a$ (Doubled 1-4)   I-2   R-3
Reverse $C^4 a$ – Reverse pitted around OL in DOLLAR. Heavy polishing marks in eagle's wings and tail feathers plus wreath bow.

6     $III^2 4 \cdot C^4 b$ (Doubled 1-4)   (181)   I-2   R-3
Obverse $III^2 4$ – Some have a filled 4.
Reverse $C^4 b$ – Heavy polishing marks on eagle and in wreath bow.

7     $III^2 1 \cdot C^4 c$ (O Set Right)   I-2   R-3
Reverse $C^4 c$ – III O mint mark set high and slightly to right.

8     $III^2 5 \cdot C^4 a$ (Far Date)   I-2   R-3
Obverse $III^2 5$ – Date set further right than normal. Closed 9.

9     $III^2 6 \cdot C^4 d$ (Low Date)   I-2   R-3
Obverse $III^2 6$ – Date set lower than normal. Closed 9.
Reverse $C^4 d$ – III O mint mark set right and tilted left.

10     $III^2 1 - C^4 e$ (O/O)   I-2   R-3
Reverse $C^4 e$ – III O mint mark set high and tilted to left with short curved segment at bottom right outside. Polishing lines in wreath center, olive branch leaves, eagle's tail feathers and wings.

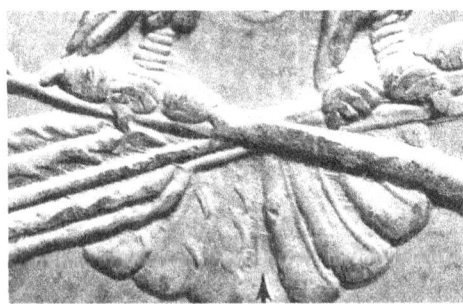  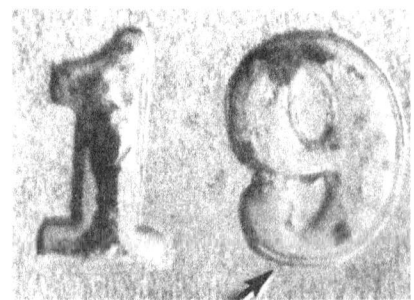

1A R Polishing Lines in TF   2 R O Tilted Left   3 O Doubled 19

1904-O

4 O Doubled Date

4 O Filled 4

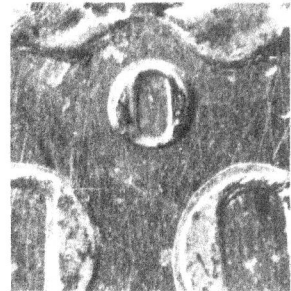
7 R O Set Right

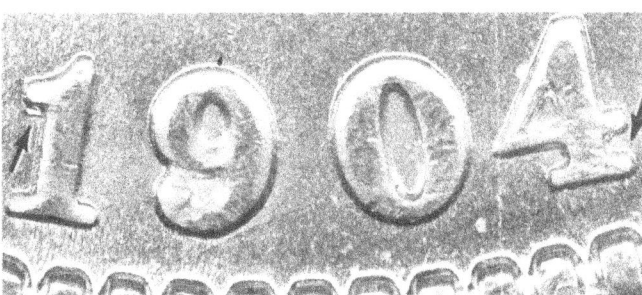
5 O Doubled 1-4

5A R Pitted Reverse

9 O Low Date

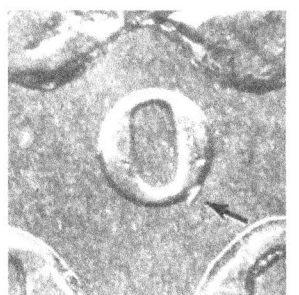
10 R O/O

11 O Doubled Profile

11 III²7 • C⁴a (Doubled Profile) (189) I-2 R-3
   Obverse III²7 – Profile of Liberty head is doubled in forward hairline, forehead, nose, lips and chin.

12 III²8 • C⁴b (Doubled 9-4) (189) I-2 R-3
   Obverse III²8 – Doubled 9-4 in date. 9 doubled on bottom outside of both loops. 4 doubled slightly on left side of lower half of vertical shaft.

13 III²1 • C⁴f (High O) (181) I-2 R-3
   Reverse C⁴f – III O mint mark set high, centered and upright. Some show heavy polishing lines in eagle's wings, neck and tail feathers plus wreath center and right side.

14 III²2 • C⁴f (Double 19, High O) (181) I-2 R-3

15 III²1 • C⁴g (High O Tilted Left) (189) I-2 R-3
   Reverse C⁴g – III O mint mark set high and slightly to right with slant to left. Fine polishing lines in eagle's tail feathers and wings.

16 III²9 • C⁴a (Slanted Date) (181) I-2 R-3
   Obverse III²9 – Slight slant to date with 1 closest to rim.

17 III²4 • C⁴b (Doubled 1-4) (181) I-2 R-3
   Reverse C⁴b – Heavy polishing marks on eagle and in wreath bow on some specimens.

1904-O

18	III²7 • C⁴f (Doubled Profile, High O)	(181)	I-2	R-3

Reverse C⁴f – Not all specimens have polishing lines in eagle.

19	III²10 • C⁴f (Doubled 9, High O)	(189)	I-2	R-3

Obverse III²10 – 9 doubled at lower left outside of upper and lower loops.
Reverse C⁴f – Polishing lines in eagle and wreath like VAM 13.

20	III²1 • C⁴h (High O Tilted Left)	(189)	I-2	R-3

Reverse C⁴h – III O mint mark set high and slightly to left with slant to left.

21	III²11 • C⁴f (Doubled O, High O)	(189)	I-2	R-3

Obverse III²11 – III O mint mark doubled at top outside.

22	III²7 • C⁴b (Doubled Profile, O Tilted Left)	(189)	I-2	R-3
23	III²5 • C⁴f (Far Date, High O)	(181)	I-2	R-3
24	III²12 • C⁴a (Doubled 9-4)	(181)	I-2	R-4

Obverse III²12 – Doubled 9-4 in date. 9 doubled at top right inside of lower loop as short spike. 4 doubled at very top as short horizontal line.

12 O Doubled 9-4

13 R Polishing Lines

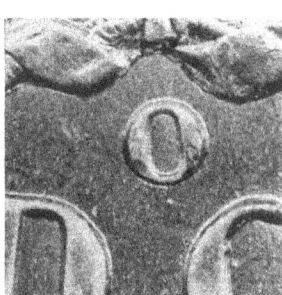
15 R High O, Tilted Left

16 O Slanted Date

19 O Doubled 9

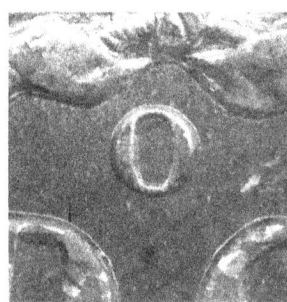
20 R High O, Tilted Left

21 O Doubled 0

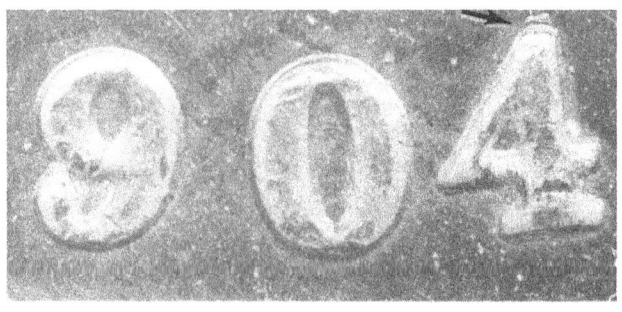
24 O Doubled 9-4

1904-O / 1904-S

25   III² 13 • C⁴ b (Doubled Profile and 9, O Tilted Left)   (181)   I-2   R-3
   Obverse III² 13 – Profile of Liberty head is doubled in nose, lips and chin. 9 doubled slightly on lower left outside of bottom loop. Date set on left side of normal position.

26   III² 14 • C⁴ h (Doubled 19 and Profile, High O Tilted Left)   (181)   I-2   R-3
   Obverse III² 14 – 1 doubled slightly below upper crossbar. 9 doubled slightly at lower left outside of upper loop. Profile of Liberty head doubled from hair down to neck. Date set further right than normal.

27   III² 1 • C⁴ i (Doubled AR)   (181)   I-2   R-3
   Reverse C⁴ i – AR in DOLLAR doubled slightly at very bottom. III O mint mark tilted slightly left.

28   III² 1 • C⁴ j (Doubled Reverse Legend)   (189)   I-2   R-3
   Reverse C⁴ j – UNITED STATES OF AMERICA and IN GOD WE TRUST doubled and tripled slightly towards rim.

25 O Doubled 9

26 O Doubled 19

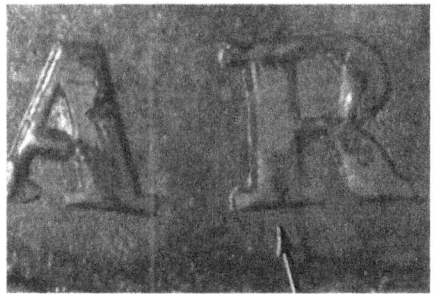
27 R Doubled AR

28 R Doubled Legend

1904-S

Most specimens of this issue have a touch of weakness in the strike although full strikes can be located. Luster is good. A few minor die varieties exist but none are very significant. Proof-likes are extremely rare and are seldom encountered in the market. Those known have little contrast.

1   III² 1 • C⁴ a (Normal Die)   I-1   R-2
   Obverse III² 1 – Normal die of III² type with closed 9.
   Reverse C⁴ a – Normal die of C⁴ type with large V S mint mark centered and upright.

1A   III² 1 – C⁴ a (Die Gouge in STATES)   (189)   I-2   R-3
   Reverse C⁴ a – Diagonal die gouge through A in STATES.

1B   III² 1 • C⁴ a (Filled 4)   (189)   I-2   R-4
   Obverse III² 1 – Die chips in 4 to almost fill upper part.

2   III² 2 • C⁴ a (Doubled Profile)   (189)   I-2   R-3
   Obverse III² 2 – Profile of Liberty head is doubled on forward hairline, forehead, nose, lips and chin. E PLURI U-UM doubled slightly on lower portions of letters towards rim. Date set further right than normal.

1904-S

3   III²3 • C⁴/C³ a (Slanted Date, 2 Olive Reverse)   (189)   I-3   R-3
    Obverse III²3 – Slight slant to date with 2 closest to rim.
    Reverse C⁴/C³ a – Extra Olive to right of olive connected to olive branch. Doubling at base of top and left olive leaf clusters, right of eagle's nostril and eye, and back of lower arrow head. GOD WE doubled on right side.

4   III²1 • C⁴/C³ b (2 Olive Reverse)   (189)   I-3   R-3
    Reverse C⁴/C³ b – Shallow extra olive to right olive connected to olive branch. Doubling at base of all three olive clusters, back of lower arrow head, feathers at top of eagle's left wing, right side of eagle's nostril and eye, and lower right of OD WE TR. V S mint mark centered and tilted right.

5   III²4 • C⁴ b (Doubled 4, High S)   (189)   I-2   R-3
    Obverse III²4 – 4 doubled slightly below crossbar and base.
    Reverse C⁴ b – Large V S mint mark set high and upright.

6   III²5 • C⁴ a (Doubled 4)   (189)   I-2   R-3
    Obverse III²5 – 4 doubled slightly at bottom inside of opening and at top right of bottom crossbar.

1A R Die Gouge in A
(Photo courtesy of Goldfreed)

3 R C⁴/C³

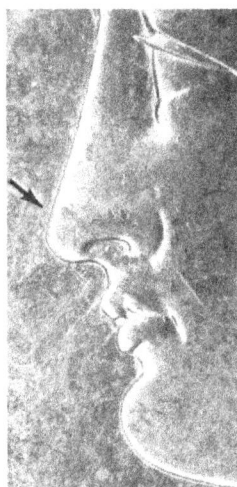

2 O Doubled Profile

1B O Filled 4

4 R C⁴/C³

6 O Doubled 4

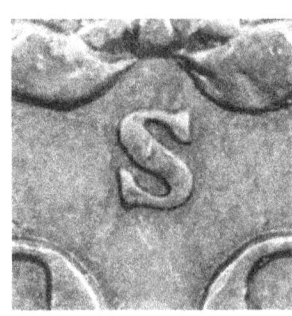

5 R High S

5 O Doubled 4

1921-P

A slight touch of weakness is usually evident in the lower wreath leaves on the reverse. Fully struck coins with all wreath leaves detailed are somewhat difficult to locate. Luster is usually average but many are dull due to long use of dies with metal flow evident on die extremities. Occasionally some specimens show exceptional luster with quite a bit of frosting on the devices. The design of the 1921 Morgan is slightly different than the previous issues. In 1910 all master dies and hubs were destroyed at the Philadelphia mint except for those in current production. Thus, new master dies had a slightly flatter and coarser look. The central relief is lower, the hair details and eagle's wing feathers are coarser and more deeply outlined. The eagle's breast is flat and the feathers have little detail. Aesthetically, the 1921 design is not as pleasing to most people.

Because of the large mintage, a number of minor die varieties exist. Two minor design types are known for the 1921-P. The initial design had 17 berries in the right reverse wreath and shallow middle part of the olive branch. The later design which was also used on all 1921-S and D had 16 berries in the right wreath and full olive branches. Both design types are common for the 1921-P. Some of the first design type had edge reeding with a very low count of 157 (instead of normal 189) and are known as VAM 2 "infrequent reeding". Seven different obverse/reverse die combinations are known so this edge variety is not particularly scarce. One of the infrequent reeding varieties, VAM 4, has N of IN on the reverse repunched with strong doubling. VAM 1B has the heaviest die polishing lines known for the Morgan series.

A curious phenomena shows up on some of the second design 1921-P, D and S coins. Small circular dots show on various portions of the obverse and reverse dies. These may have been used to identify some of the first dies of the second 1921 design and some may also be marks from Rockwell hardness tests on dies. The most prominent dots visible to the naked eye are VAM's 8 and 9 which have a small circular raised dot on the field below eagle's right wing and on field between eagle's left wing and top arrow head point respectively. Smaller dots are on a number of other dies but most are not significant and were probably caused by gas bubbles trapped in the die steel melts.

Proof-likes are fairly scarce and only have little to light contrast. Proof-likes exist for both design types as well as for all seven die varieties with infrequent reeding edge. A fair number of the proof-likes exhibit cloudy spots due to storage contamination. It is very difficult to find nice proof-likes with deep mirrors, fully struck, spot free, some contrast and with minimal bag marks. Because of a large mintage and high survival rate, proof-likes should ordinarily be fairly available. Apparently at some point in 1921, all three mints discarded the practice of basining working dies. Since 1916, silver coins had designs not intended to be basined. With all three mints working to capacity in 1921 to replace the dollars melted in 1918-20, short cuts were probably taken in production. Without the basining step the design was not usually struck up completely in the wreath area.

Two types of proofs exist. A regular proof issue of 12 pieces was produced, known as Chapman proofs, because Henry Chapman of Philadelphia persuaded the Philadelphia mint to strike them. They have very deep mirrors and light contrast similar to the 1902-1904 proofs. They are the rarest of the Morgan proofs. A second 1921 proof type is the so-called Zerbe proof. These lack the depth of mirror and contrast of the Chapman proofs and are more correctly termed presentation pieces. It is estimated that 20-200 pieces were produced to appease Farran Zerbe because of the delay in the production of the new Peace dollars. Zerbe proofs can be identified by a small die scratch from the second U in UNUM to the denticles.

1	IV • D¹a (17 Berries)		I-2	R-3

Obverse IV 1 – Normal die of IV type with open 9. Both 1's in date are doubled at top left side. Some specimens show a small dot after first 1.

Reverse D¹a – Extra berry inside of the right wreath opposite top berry to give a total of 17 berries rather than normal 16 for type D² reverse. TED of UNITED, ST-T-S of STATES are slightly doubled to three o'clock.

1A	IV 1 • D¹a (Pitted Reverse)		I-3	R-4

Reverse D¹a – 17 berry reverse with pitted die around eagle's tail feathers and center of wreath and many hundreds of fine polishing marks on lower part of die.

1B	IV 1 • D¹a (Polished Reverse)	(189)	I-3	R-3

Reverse D¹a – Die excessively polished with heavy raised lines all over field of coins.

1C	IV 1 • D¹a (Wreath Die Gouge)	(189)	I-2	R-4

Reverse D¹a – Thin vertical die gouge from eagle's tail feathers down through wreath bow.

2	IV 1 • D¹a (Infrequent Reeding)	(157)	I-5	R-3

Edge – This edge is infrequently reeded having about 34 reeds per linear inch.

2A	IV 1 – D¹a (Infrequent Reeding, Reverse Die Gouges)	(157)	I-5	R-3

Reverse D¹a – Two short vertical die gouges down from denticles above S and T in STATES. Edge Infrequent Reeding.

1921-P

1 O Doubled 1-1

1 O Dot Date

1 R Extra Berry

1A R Pitted Reverse

1C R Die Gouge

1B R Die Polishing Lines

1 R Doubled Letters

3	IV 1 • D²a (16 Berries)		I-1	R-1

Reverse D²a – Normal die of D² type with 16 berries in wreath. There is a spike gouge above the bottom crossbar on right side of F in OF for all die varieties.

3A	IV 1 • D²a (Spike Tail Feathers)		I-2	R-5

Reverse D²a – Horizontal die gouge extending to right from number 3 tail feather.

3B	IV 1 • D²a (Pitted Reverse)		I-2	R-4

Reverse D²a – 16 berries reverse with pitted die to right of wreath bow above and inside D of DOLLAR.

3C	IV 1 • D²a (Pitted Reverse)	(189)	I-2	R-4

Reverse D²a – Pitted die around LL of DOLLAR.

3D	IV 1 • D²a (Overpolished Wing)	(189)	I-2	R-3

Reverse D²a – Eagle's left wing overpolished near body as are tail feathers next to eagle's right leg with many fine polishing lines present.

3E	IV 1 • D²a (Pitted Reverse)	(189)	I-2	R-4

Reverse D²a – Pitted die around arrow feathers.

3F	IV 1 • D²a (Pitted Reverse)	(189)	I-2	R-4

Reverse D²a – Pitted die around lower right wreath and AR in DOLLAR.

1921-P

2A R Die Gouges

3A R Spiked Tail Feathers

Infrequent Edge Reeding

3B R Pitted

3C R Pitted Reverse

3E R Pitted Reverse

3F R Pitted Reverse

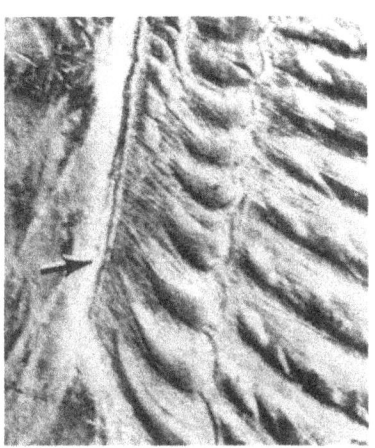
3D R Overpolished Wing

3G R Pitted Reverse

3H R Die Gouge in Olive Leaves

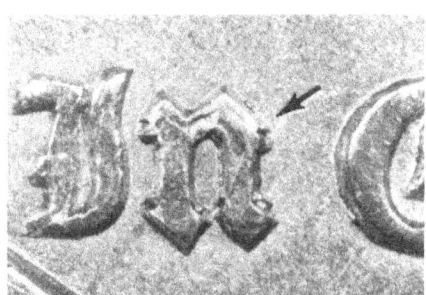
4 R Doubled N

1921-P

3G	**IV 1 • D²a (Pitted Reverse)**	(189)	I-2	R-4

Reverse D²a – Pitted die around UN of UNITED.

3H	**IV 1 • D²a (Die Gouge Olive Leaves)**	(189)	I-2	R-4

Reverse D²a – Long thick horizontal die gouge through upper olive leaf cluster.

4	**IV 1 – D¹b (Infrequent Reeding, Doubled N)**	(157)	I-5	R-3

Reverse D¹b – N of IN set low and doubled above serifs and at very top. Edge is infrequently reeded.

5	**IV 2 • D²a (Doubled Date, Tripled Stars)**	(189)	I-2	R-3

Obverse IV 2 – Entire date is doubled with tops of all digits doubled and left side of diagonal shaft of 2 also doubled. All left and right stars plus E-PL slightly tripled towards rim, with 4-7 stars on the left tripled the strongest.
Reverse D²a – Eagle's left wing is overpolished near body.

6	**IV 3 – D²a (Doubled Date and Stars)**	(189)	I-2	R-3

Obverse IV 3 – Outline of all date digits are doubled towards rim as are first three stars on left, all stars on right and tops of NUM.

7	**IV 1 • D¹c (Tripled Reverse)**	(189)	I-2	R-3

Reverse D¹c – Tripled ITED-T on left side, doubled U-E at bottom inside and doubled L-R at bottom outside.

8	**IV 4 • D²b (Dot Next to Wing)**	(189)	I-4	R-3

Obverse VI 4 – Very small circular raised dot to left of M in UNUM.
Reverse D²b – Small circular raised dot on field next to eagle's right wing. Possibly used to identify first dies of D² reverse.

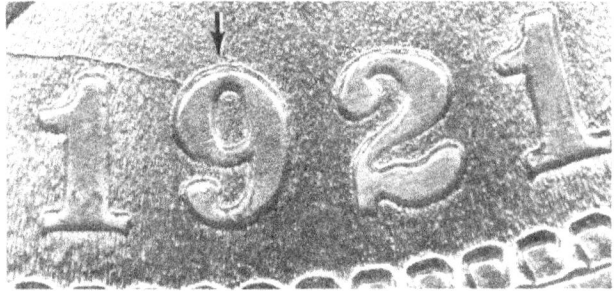
5 O Doubled Date

6 O Doubled Date

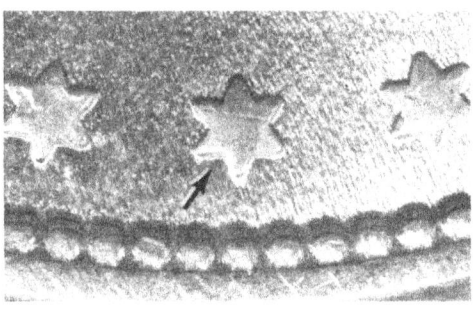
5 O Tripled Stars

5 R Tripled ITED

8 O Dot

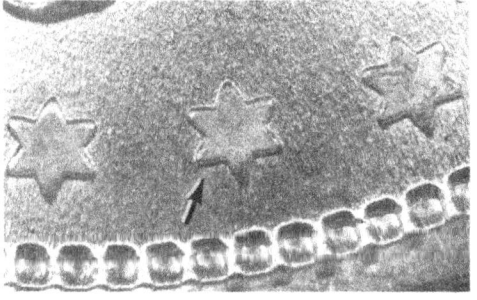
6 O Doubled Stars

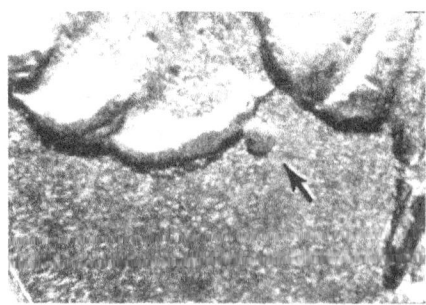
8 R Dot

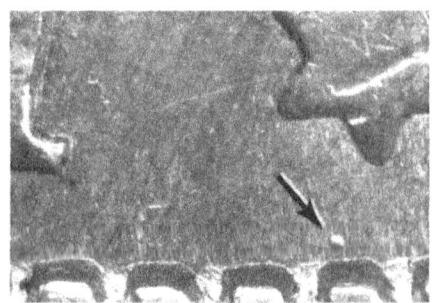
9 O Dot

1921-P

9   IV 5 • D²c (Dot Below Wing)   (189)   I-4   R-3
Obverse IV 5 – Small circular raised dot above B in PLURIBUS, and below first star on right.
Reverse D²c – Small circular raised dot on field between eagle's left wing and top arrow head point, between two top arrow feathers, and above S in TRUST.

10   IV 6 • D²a (Doubled Date and Stars)   (189)   I-3   R-3
Obverse IV 6 – Outline of all date digits are doubled towards rim as are all right and left stars.

11   IV 3 • D²d (Doubled Date and Stars, Doubled Reverse)   (189)   I-2   R-3
Reverse D²d – Doubled right star and U-TED STATES OF A-ERICA and LL-R towards center, bottom right of G of GOD, and bottom of eagle's lower beak.

12   IV 7 • D¹a (Tripled Stars)   (189)   I-2   R-3
Obverse IV 7 – All stars on right and 4 to 7 stars on left are tripled towards rim with first three left stars slightly doubled.
Reverse D¹a – Horizontal polishing lines in all tail feathers.

13   IV 8 • D¹a (Doubled Stars and Date)   (189)   I-2   R-3
Obverse IV 8 – All left and right stars, date digits and E PLURIBUS UNUM doubled slightly towards rim.
Edge – Infrequent reeding variety.

14   IV 9 • D²a (Tripled Stars)   (189)   I-2   R-3
Obverse IV 9 – Left stars and E-PL tripled towards rim with date digits and right stars very slightly doubled towards rim.

NOTE: In the 1921-P series there appear numerous raised dots on various locations on both the obverse and reverse sides. It was first thought that these raised dots were put there by the mint workmen for some presently unknown reason. Current thought however is that these dots are the result of imperfect die steel and not the result of being deliberately put there. Therefore, these are not listed as die varieties at this time.

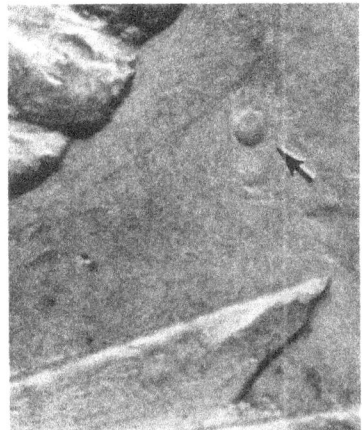

9 R Dot

11 O Doubled Stars and Letters

12 O Tripled Stars

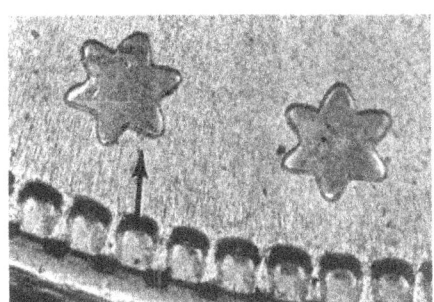

13 O Doubled Stars

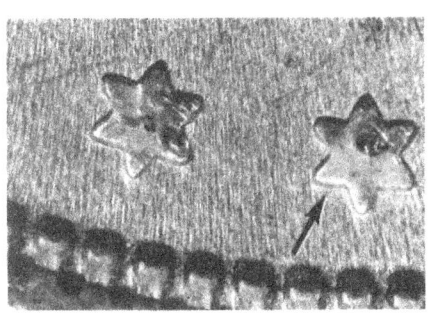

14 O Doubled Stars

1921-D

The strike on this issue is invariably slightly weak to quite weak on the wreath leaves. Fully struck specimens with all wreath leaves full are very difficult to locate. Luster is usually average but varies from fairly frosty to dull because of the high mintage and long use of the dies. A few die varieties exist. VAM 3 is significant with a dot just below eagle's right wing that can be seen with the naked eye. Full proof-likes are very scarce and have only a little contrast. A number of semi proof-like pieces exist with frosty devices but these should not be mistaken for full proof-likes.

1   IV 1 • D²a (Normal Die)   I-1   R-1
Obverse IV 1 – Normal die of IV type.
Reverse D²a – Normal die of D² type with small centered I D mint mark There is a spike above the bottom crossbar on the right side of F in OF for all die varieties. Both 1's in date are doubled at top left.

1A   IV 1 • D²a (TRUT)   I-2   R-4
Reverse D²a – Die fill in S of TRUST to form TRUT.

1B   IV 1 • D²a (Capped R Die Chip)   (189)   I-3   R-5
Reverse D²a – Heavily die cracked with die chip above R in AMERICA.

2   IV 2 • D²a (Doubled Date)   I-2   R-3
Obverse IV 2 – Entire date doubled. The doubling is to the upper left of all numbers.
Reverse D²a – Some specimens show diagonal die gouge through upper part of D in DOLLAR.

2A   IV 2 • D²a (Doubled Date, Die Gouge in O)   (189)   I-2   R-3
Reverse D²a – Die gouge at top right inside of O in DOLLAR.

3   IV 3 • D²b (Dot Next to Wing)   (189)   I-4   R-3
Obverse IV 3 – Small circular raised dot below eye and two in hair between ear and date.
Reverse D²b – Small circular raised dot on field next to eagle's right wing, in middle of eagle's left wing next to body, in upper loop of S in STAT, in middle of sixth tail feather, and above and below stem to right of first berry in left wreath.

4   IV 1 • D²c (Dots on Reverse)   (189)   I-3   R-3
Reverse D²c – Small circular raised dot on field above left olive leaf cluster with smaller dot just to left of it. Additional very small dots at junction of eagle's right wing and neck, on lower middle of eagle's right wing, in middle of eagle's sixth tail feather, and to left of arrow feather ends on field.

5   IV 4 • D²a (Tripled Date and Stars)   (189)   I-2   R-3
Obverse IV 4 – Date tripled with doubling at very top outside and below serifs and loops towards rim. Left stars tripled and right stars doubled towards rim.

NOTE: As in the 1921-P series, in the D series there appear numerous raised dots on various locations on both the obverse and reverse sides. It was first thought that these raised dots were put there by the mint workmen for some presently unknown reason. Current thought however is that these dots are the result of imperfect die steel and not the result of being deliberately put there. Therefore, these are not listed as die varieties at this time.

1B R Die Chip Above R

1A R
TRUT

2 O Doubled Date

1921-D / 1921-S

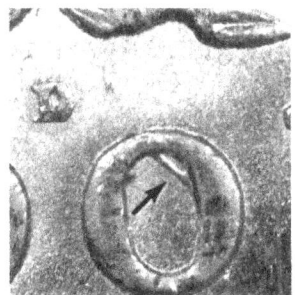

2A R Die Gouge in O

3 O Dot

3 R Die Crack in Wing

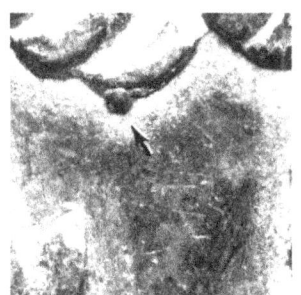

3 R Dot

4 R Dot

5 O Tripled Date

5 O Tripled Stars

1921-S

Most specimens of this issue were not fully struck. They show weakness in the wreath leaves and a mushy appearance on the cheek, hair and eagle's breast due the planchet roughness not being smoothed out by the dies. Luster is generally dull, either because of strike weakness on cheek and eagle's breast and/or die wear in fields. A fully struck piece with good luster is very rare. Only a few die varieties exist. VAM 4 has a dot below the eagle's left wing and although not as large as the largest dots for the 1921-P and D, it is still barely visible to the naked eye. VAM 1B has two prominent diagonal die gouges at the top of the Liberty head.

Full proof-likes are extremely rare and the few known specimen have little contrast. Even semi proof-like coins are very scarce. Apparently the working dies were not basined and polished at this mint except in a couple isolated cases to repair the dies.

Twenty-four branch mint proofs were reported struck for Farren Zerbe supposedly to compliment the Philadelphia proofs also struck for him. Less than half a dozen specimens are known and the one piece Wayne Miller has examined had little contrast.

1921-S

1	IV 1 • D²a (Normal Die)		I-1	R-1

Obverse IV 1 – Normal die of IV type.
Reverse D²a – Normal die of D² type with small centered I S mint mark. There is a spike above the bottom crossbar on the right side of F in OF for all die varieties. Both 1's in date are doubled at top left.

1A	IV 1 • D²a (Die Scratch)		I-2	R-3

Obverse IV 1 – Diagonal die scratch connecting B and U in PLURIBUS.

1B	IV 1 • D²a (Thorn Head)	(189)	I-3	R-4

Obverse IV 1 – Two large horizontal die gouges at top of head with upper one appearing as a thorn from the top wheat leaf and the lower one as a band on the right of the top cotton leaf.

1C	IV 1 • D²a (Pitted Reverse)	(189)	I-2	R-3

Reverse D²a – Pitted die around arrow heads.

2	IV 1 • D²b (S Shifted Left)		I-2	R-3

Reverse D²b – Small I S mint mark shifted left.

3	IV 2 • D²a (Doubled Date and Stars)	(189)	I-2	R-3

Obverse IV 2 – Outline of all date digits is doubled towards rim as are all left and right stars. Some specimens show a die chip in lower loop of 2.

4	IV 2 • D²c (Dot Below Wing)	(189)	I-3	R-3

Reverse D²c – Very small circular raised dot on field between eagle's left wing and arrow shafts and under eagle's jaw.

NOTE: As in the 1921-P series, in the S series there appear numerous raised dots on various locations on both the obverse and reverse sides. It was first thought that these raised dots were put there by the mint workmen for some presently unknown reason. Current thought however is that these dots are the result of imperfect die steel and not the result of being deliberately put there. Therefore, these are not listed as die varieties at this time.

1A O Die Scratch

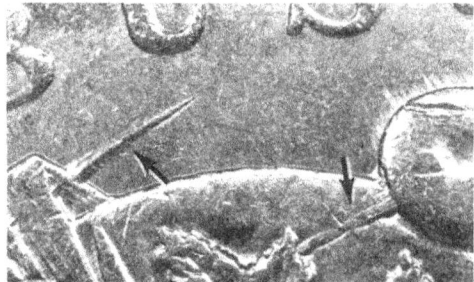

1B O Die Gouges

2 R S Shifted Left

1C R Pitted Reverse

3 O Doubled Date

1921-S

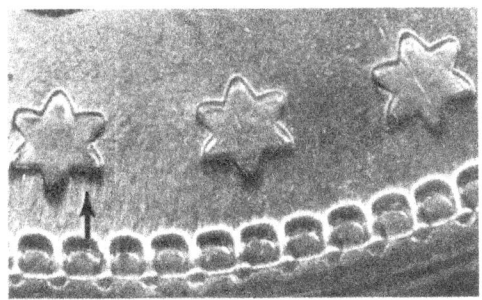

3 O Doubled Stars

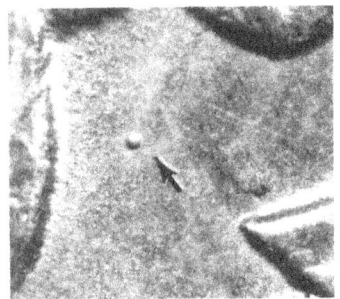

4 R Dot

Chapter 9
GSA Sale of Carson City Dollars

During late 1972 through 1974 and again in 1980 the General Services Administration of the U. S. Government conducted seven mail order sales of some three million Morgan Carson City silver dollars. With total gross sales of $107 million, this was the largest sale of a U. S. coin series in numismatic history.

BACKGROUND OF THE SALES

Ever since the Morgan dollars were first struck, the Treasury, mints and the Federal Reserve banks held huge stocks of Morgan and Peace dollars. The silver dollar was not widely accepted for public use which caused millions of these dollars to be stored for many years in uncirculated condition. Then the release of previously scarce New Orleans mint Morgans (1898, 1902, 1903, and 1904) during 1962 and 1963 from the Federal Reserve Banks stimulated collector and speculator interest.

The Treasury holdings of silver dollars in Washington, D.C.. dwindled from 180 million in January 1960 to 28 million on January 1, 1964. As the Treasury stocks of these dollars became low, word circulated that the older Morgan dollars were also being passed out in addition to the common Peace dollars. A run on the Treasury resulted in March 1964 as collectors, dealers and speculators scrambled to get these remaining silver dollars at face value.

Before the Treasury completely ran out of these dollars, the General Accounting Office made an audit of the Treasury's remaining silver dollars. Nearly three million were discovered to be uncirculated Carson City silver dollars of special numismatic value. These three million silver dollars were set aside and were withheld from public distribution when the silver dollar sales were halted by the Treasury on March 26, 1964.

The problem of how to equitably dispose of these scarce Carson City dollars was turned over to the Joint Committee on the Coinage. In its report to Congress, the Commission recommended the mail bid procedure for disposing of the coins with pre-established minimum prices.

Section 205(a) of the Bank Holding Company Act Amendments (Public Law 91-607) of December 1970 authorized the General Services Administration to sell these dollars. In July 1971, Congress provided an appropriation of $10 million for the GSA to develop and implement the dollar disposal program. A small group of GSA staff was assembled in Washington, D.C. on November 1971, to arrange for the coin inspecting, sorting, ordering, packaging and mailing details.

More than thirty forms, cards and letters and labels were designed and produced. Millions of brochures and 100,000 posters were printed and distributed to the 40,000 U. S. Post Offices and nearly 60,000 banks, savings and loans and credit unions in a massive advertising campaign.[1] Several special documentary movies were produced and shown on television. Three hundred and ninety two special coin displays of one each of ten different Carson City dollar years for sale were fabricated. They were sent to various banks on a rotational basis and were used at important coin shows for the GSA display.

TRANSFER OF DOLLARS

On December 6, 1971, the GSA took possession of the dollars from the Treasury Department. The 2.9 million dollars weighing 77 tons were transferred from the Treasury vaults in Washington, D.C. to the U. S. Bullion Depository at West Point, New York, where the various inspection and packaging operations were to be carried out. Seven heavily-guarded semi-trailer trucks were used to haul the valuable cargo and by January 1972, all of the dollars were at West Point.[2]

The bag count of silver dollars was verified by Treasury and GSA representatives and the bags of dollars were placed in ten bins in one vault of the Depository. There were separate bins for each of those years with substantial quantities of Carson City dollars, namely, 1878 and 1880 through 1885. Another bin held the years with only a few thousand Carson City dollars; 1879, 1890 and 1891. The last two bins were for the mixed circulated late non-Carson City dollars and the mixed circulated dollars. All bins had a wooden plank flooring above the concrete floor so the canvas bags would not pick up any moisture from the floor.

INITIAL SORTING

Late in March 1972, a special team of noted numismatists examined a separate group of fifty coins with varying degree of toning and tarnish to establish grading standards for the silver dollars. Members of this team were John J. Pittman, President of the American Numismatic Association, Rochester, New York; Amon Carter, Jr. a member of the Joint Commission on the Coinage, Fort Worth, Texas; Henry Grunthal, curator of European and Modern Coins for the American Numismatic Society, New York, New York; Clifford Mishler, editor of *Coins* and *Numismatic News Weekly*, Iola, Wisconsin; and Margo Russell, editor of *Coin World*, Sidney, Ohio.[3] The fifty coins were divided into two groups; twenty two that fell below acceptable standards and twenty eight that were acceptable. These coins were permanently mounted in two clear plastic cases to be used as standards in the sorting process.

Then began the long process of sorting the coins. Initially an automatic scanning machine was considered for use for sorting. This machine could automatically scan both the obverse and reverse sides of the coin and determine the date and mint mark by comparison with standard designs. However, use of this machine was rejected because it was apt to add more scratches and nicks. Furthermore, it could not discriminate the more subtle grading requirements such as tarnish, scratches and errors. In the end, reliance had to be made on the eyes of the trained inspectors.

Hand sorting of the 2.9 million coins was performed by six white gloved women with four to five supervisors. Each coin was first segregate by date and mint mark. Then within this group the coins were further sorted into one of three categories: (1) uncirculated that met the grading standards, (2) Tarnished or slightly scratched, and (3) errors (such as off center strikes, laminations and filled dies) or rejects (gouged or badly scratched).

The Bank Holding Company Act Amendments which were signed by President Nixon on December 31, 1970, authorizing the sale of the dollars by GSA did not permit error or variety coins to be sold separately from the normal coins. Thus, they were mixed in at random with the two categories of coins sold; those that met the grading standards and those that fell below the grading standard to be sold at a reduced cost. Also at the suggestion of various coin collectors, the GSA rejected the idea of cleaning the tarnished coins. It was felt that this would introduce controversy on the condition of the coins.

As the coins were sorted they were packed into special wooden boxes with sliding masonite tops. Tolerances of the boxes were such that not one coin more than fifty stacks of twenty coins could fit into a box. Each box of a thousand had a seal and was recorded in the log book. This sorting operation took most of the remainder of 1972.

GSA HOLDINGS OF SILVER DOLLARS

As a result of the sorting operations, the GSA had five categories of silver dollars: (1) uncirculated CC, (2) mixed CC, (3) mixed uncirculated (of other mints), (4) mixed circulated, and (5) unsalable (due to severe gouge or badly worn). *Table 9-1* shows the quantities of coins in each category.[4] Note that the mixed CC category included uncirculated CC dollars that were tarnished and scratched and were therefore to be sold at reduced prices. Also note that this mixed CC category also included one each of the uncirculated 1889-CC, 1892-CC and the 1893-CC. These were put in this category since there was not enough to include as separate bid categories of the uncirculated CC.

Since the uncirculated 1878-CC were sold at the same price ($15), the culled (tarnished/scratched) 1878-CC had to be sold at a lower price. All 13,426 culled 1878-CC were put in the mixed circulated category and sold for $3 each.

Table 9-2 shows a further breakdown of the GSA sorting categories for the CC dollars. The rejects/errors consisted of 2 to 5 percent of the total coins of each year. The scratched/tarnished consisted of 10 to 30 percent of the total coins with the years 1878, 1882, 1883, and 1884 particularly high. The initial sorting culled out 72,000 1882-CC, 78,000 1883-CC, and 77,000 1884-CC as scratched/tarnished. Later, additional coins were added to this category for these three years.

1880-CC Storage Bin

Storage Box for 1000 Coins

Table 9-1 ORIGINAL GSA HOLDINGS FOR SALE

Year	Uncirc. CC	Mixed CC	Mixed Uncirc.	Mixed Circ.	Unsalable	Total
1878 CC	47,567			13,426 (culled)		60,993
1879 CC	3,633	490				4,123
1880 CC	114,942	16,587				131,529
1881 CC	122,709	24,776				147,485
1882 CC	382,913	222,116				605,029
1883 CC	523,853	231,665				755,518
1884 CC	788,630	174,008				962,638
1885 CC	130,823	17,462				148,285
1889 CC		1				1
1890 CC	3,610	339				3,949
1891 CC	5,177	510				5,687
1892 CC		1				1
1893 CC		1				1
Various P,O,S			27,980			27,980
Various				84,165	311	84,476
Totals	2,123,857	687,956	27,980	97,591	311	2,937,695

Table 9-2 GSA CARSON CITY SILVER DOLLAR CATEGORIES

CC Year	Unc.	Scratched/ Tarnished	Combined	Rejects/ Errors	Unc. Overdates	Tarnished Overdates	% Mixed CC	% Mixed Circ.	% Total Minted
1878	47,567		— 13,426 —					14	2.7
1879	3,633		— 490 —				.07		.5
1880	114,942	12,087		4,500	(45,000)	(5,000)	2.41		22.1
1881	122,709	16,776		8,000			3.60		49.6
1882	382,913	216,116		6,000			32.29		44.6
1883	523,853	221,665		10,000			33.67		62.7
1884	788,630	159,008		15,000			25.29		84.6
1885	130,823	11,462		6,000			2.54		64.9
1890	3,610	325		14			.05		.1
1891	5,177	423		87			.08		.3

Early in 1973 it was noted that some of the 1880-CC dollars in the GSA displays were of the strong overdates. At the request of members of the numismatic hobby, the GSA further segregated the 1880-CC strong overdates into separate boxes in the spring of 1973. These were examined by numismatists (Van Allen and Mallis) for varieties early in May 1973. Sampling of the various dates of Carson City dollars revealed numerous minor varieties for each date such as doubled dates and mint marks. Of special importance were the strong overdates of the 1880-CC; VAM 4 (80/79), VAM 5 (8/7 High), and VAM 6 (8/7 Low). From the sampling it was estimated that 15,000 VAM 4, 13,000 VAM 5, and 10,000 VAM 6 were in the uncirculated category, while 1,600 VAM 4, 1,900 VAM 5 and 1,000 VAM 6 were in the mixed category. Totals of these overdates sold by the GSA were about 16,000 VAM 4, 15,000 VAM 5 and 11,000 VAM 6.

There were 27,980 mixed non-CC uncirculated coins. Anywhere from one to five bags existed for 1879-S, 1880-S, 1881-S, 1882-S, 1883-P, 1883-O, 1884-O, 1885-P, 1885-O, and 1887-O. The remaining were common date 1922 and 1923-P Peace dollars.

Some 84,000 mixed circulated coins also were for sale. They consisted of many different dates from all mints. Their condition was mostly VF to AU with a few F. The culls of damaged and mutilated coins were removed by the GSA.

For the mixed CC category the 1882, 1883 and 1884 years constituted 81 percent of the total amount. The 1880, 1881, and 1885 each constituted 2 to 4 percent with 1879, 1890 and 1891 comprising much less than a percent each. The 1878-CC comprised 14 percent of the

Table 9-3 GSA DOLLAR SALES

Year	1972-1974 Min. Bid ($)	Oct. '72 Mar. '73	June '73 July '73	Oct. '73	Feb. '74	April '74 June '74	February 1980 Prices ($)	February 1980 Quantity	July 1980 Min Bid $180	Mixed CC 2nd, 5th & 6th Sales
1878 CC	15		47,556							
1879 CC	300				3,608					512
1880 CC	60			73,856		36,794			4,281	16,588
1881 CC	60			70,865		32,826			18,975	24,814
1882 CC	30	291,494	55,597			35,689				222,261
1883 CC	30	257,391	40,391			30,320	60	195,745		231,780
1884 CC	30	267,733	64,384			28,349	65	428,152		174,068
1885 CC	60			67,782		31,470			31,564	17,463
1889 CC										1
1890 CC	30		3,589							357
1891 CC	30		5,157							525
1892 CC										1
1893 CC										1
Mixed CC	15		170,299			218,666	45	299,390		
Mixed Unc.	5		27,949							
Mixed Circ.*	3		97,563							
Totals	3	816,618	512,585	212,503	3,608	414,114		923,290	54,820	688,371

* Includes 13,426 tarnished/scratched/error 1878-CC.

total mixed circulated category.

For some of the years the GSA holdings were a sizeable percentage of the total amounts minted. About 85 percent of 1884 mintage was held while approximately 60 percent for 1883 and 1885 and 50 percent for 1881 and 1882 were held. The dumping of such large quantities of coins of a given year on the market would naturally have a depressing effect on prices. To minimize such an effect, the GSA established minimum bid prices for each category and year CC based on the current market values. It was only natural that some categories would not be sold out at these minimum bid prices as the free market prices dropped.

PACKAGING THE COINS

All the uncirculated CC and other mint silver dollars were packaged into plastic holders for single coins. The CC dollars were then placed in a special velvet lined presentation case. Circulated Morgan and Peace silver dollars were placed individually in a mylar display packet and enclosed in a carrying envelope.

Packaging of the silver dollars commenced in mid-fall of 1972 at the West Point Depository and was completed in mid-summer 1973. Two complete assembly lines for packaging the coins were installed there. Each line employed 22 women plus several supervisors and helpers. Their salaries were a major cost of the sale of the silver dollars.

During the packaging operations the women workers all wore cotton gloves and handling of the coins was at a minimum. The coin was placed in a hole in the black plastic insert. The inscription on this insert stated Carson City Uncirculated Silver Dollar, Carson City Silver Dollar, or Silver Dollar depending on the category of the coin.

Next, the plastic insert with coin was placed into a two-piece, clear plastic holder. These two halves were fused together by a sonic sealer. All CC dollars were placed in a special presentation case along with a card describing the background of the Carson City dollars. A special card was added to the 1880-CC boxes to alert the recipient of possible overdates. The box was then placed in a mailing carton with the coin date or category stamped on the outside.

GSA SALES

The GSA conducted a total of seven sales; five between 1972 and 19774 and two in 1980. The first five sales generated net revenues of about $55.3 million with expenses of $7.8 million. Net revenues from the last two 1980 sales were $52 million with expenses close to $2 million.

Terms of the first five sales were those recommended by the Joint Commission on Coinage. Coins were sold by public mail bid with pre-established minimum prices. They were to be sold to the highest bidder with a limit of one coin per category per bidder. If there were less bidders than coins then the coins were to be awarded to all bidders at the minimum price. Only U.S. citizens could bid on the coins.

From October 1972 to March 1973 the first sales were conducted for the 1882-CC, 1883-CC and 1884-CC categories at a minimum bid of $30 each. This was somewhat below the then current market price of $35 to $40 a

GSA Presentation Case

coin for these dates. As shown in *Table 9*-3 only 250,000 to 290,000 of each date were sold. Since none of the dates were sold out they all went for $30 each.

The second sale from June to July 1973 featured 1878-CC, 1882-CC, 1883-CC, 1884-CC, 1890-CC 1891-CC, mixed CC, mixed uncirculated, and mixed circulated. All but the 1882-CC, 1883-CC, 1884-CC and mixed CC were sold out with an average price of $16.55 for the 1878-CC, $58.22 for the 1890-CC, $53.85 for the 1891-CC and $5.55 for the mixed uncirculated.

In the third sale of October 1973 the 1880-CC, 1881-CC, and 1885-CC were offered at $60 each. With a 1973 market price of around $65 to $70 each, response to this sale was slow with only one-half to two-thirds of the coins selling at the minimum bid price.

The fourth sale in February 1974 featured the 1879-CC with only 3,608 coins available at $300 each minimum bid. All were sold at an average of $478.39 per coin.

All of the dates not previously sold were again offered in the fifth sale, April to June 1974. Only the 1882-CC sold out at an average price of $33.08 each. By this time the market was pretty well saturated and sales had fallen off. There still remained 195,724 1883-CC, 428,128 1884-CC, 4,261 1880-CC, 18,960 1881-CC, 31,548 1882-CC and 298,968 mixed CC. The Carson City dollar sales had stimulated the overall silver dollar market but predictably the market value of the dates with substantial offerings had dropped.

After the fifth sale the GSA determined it was not feasible to offer the remaining 978,000 coins under the same terms and conditions because of the saturated market. Public Law 96-2, enacted on March 7, 1979, amended the Bank Holding Company Act of 1970 and authorized selling the remaining coins at such prices and terms and conditions deemed proper by the Administration.

On November 13, 1979 the GSA announced the sale plan for the remaining coins. There were to be two sales. The first running February 8, 1980 through April 8, 1980 would offer the 1883-CC at $42 each, 1884-CC at $40 each and the mixed CC at $20 each. There would be no limit per order but orders per category would initially be filled with 500 coins. A second sale was to be held in July 1980 and would offer the 1880-CC, 1881-CC and 1885-CC in a sealed-bid auction with the minimum prices of $180 per coin. Orders were limited to five coins of each category.

When these two last sales were announced on November 13, 1979 the spot price for silver was $16 per ounce. As the date for the first sale approached the price of silver was rapidly increasing. By January 4, 1980 it had reached $36 an ounce. On January 7, 1980 the GSA suspended the prices announced in November since at that point the mixed CC category coins each contained $28 worth of silver compared to the $20 selling price. The GSA decided to announce prices on the date the sale opened, February 8, 1980. Because of this, 17 million brochures, 60,000 posters and 750,000 mail order folders with the old prices worth $341,000 had to be scrapped. Prices on the day of the sale would be available via toll-free telephone and notices in 55 major daily newspapers and weekly numismatic publications.

Prices set on the day of the sale on February 8, 1980 were 1883-CC at $65 each, 1884-CC at $60 each and mixed CC at $45 each. By that time silver prices had dropped from a high of $50 per ounce to about $38 per ounce. Uncirculated 1883-CC and 1884-CC dollars were trading around $70-$75 in the open market and the coin market was at the height of the bull market frenzy. As a result, the public interest in the sale was far greater than envisioned by the GSA. During the first 10 days 350,000 orders were received and an additional 150,000 during the remainder of the sale.

The GSA chose a limit of 10 coins per order for the 1883-CC, 20 for the 1884-CC, and five for the mixed CC. It had reserved the right to reduce the limits in the terms and conditions of the sale. Only orders received during the first ten days would be selected since it was projected that no more than 350,000 orders could be processed within its budget. However, only 181,814 orders actually received any coins-roughly one-third of the total orders. There were many customer complaints about not receiving any coins, the lengthy time for status notification and the lengthy time it took to receive the returned orders, refund checks and finally the coins. A lower coin limit per order could have been set to provide a greater percentage of orders with at least some coins.

The last sale held on July 1980 for the 1880-CC, 1881-CC and 1885-CC was also sold out with approximately 18,000 bids received. This last sale was conducted without any major problems, unlike the previous sales.

Overall, the sales of the Carson City silver dollars was financially successful to the Government with net receipts of close to $100 million for about 3 million coins. But it took a lengthy time from the date the CC dollars were first put aside in 1964 until they were first offered for sale in 1972. And it was 16 years by the time the final sale was conducted. The sixth sale left many customers bitter because of not receiving any coins and long delays in processing their orders and receiving their coins.

It helped stimulate the silver dollar market in the mid-1970's and again in 1980. Although the market for many of the Carson City dollars dropped somewhat in value after the 1972 to 1974 sales, their prices rebounded a few years later. By 1984 the CC dollars were selling from two to over ten times the 1972-74 GSA selling prices in grades MS 60 to MS 65. They are still a very popular numismatic item because of the magic of the CC mint mark.

Footnotes

[1] U.S. General Services Administration, News Release #5954, October 31, 1972.

[2] Ibid.

[3] GSA News Release #5952, October 31, 1972.

[4] All dollar quantities given in this Chapter were obtained directly from GSA in Washington, D.C.

Chapter 10
Redfield Hoard and Continental-Illinois Bank Hoard

REDFIELD HOARD

Certainly no other private hoard of United States coins in recent history has received so much publicity or created such interest as the so-called Redfield hoard. It was of prime interest to silver dollar collectors and investors since the hoard contained over 400,000 Morgan and Peace silver dollars. Although not nearly as large a quantity as the General Services Administration sales that had almost three million Carson City silver dollars or the Continental-Illinois Bank hoard of about one and one-half million Morgan dollars, it still had a major impact on the dollar market.

Other hoards of hundreds of bags of silver dollars existed (and may still exist) after nearly all of the hundred of thousands of silver bags were finally released to the public in the mid-1960's. Many gambling casinos in Nevada, for example, had large stocks of silver dollars on hand for a while. But none of these hoards had the publicity, so many scarcer dates, or were sold in such a large single transaction of $7.3 million up until the mid-1970's.

Much of the details of the Redfield hoard are clothed in secrecy. Little is known of the life of the man who accumulated the hoard, LaVere Redfield. The quantities of dates and mint marks of the coins were never publicly released and were open to much speculation. Many court cases resulted from the intrigue surrounding the disbursements of the Redfield fortune. This chapter attempts to unravel some of the mystery of the Redfield hoard.

Accumulation Of The Hoard

Born on October 29, 1897, in Ogden, Utah, LaVere Redfield grew up in poverty. When he was twenty four years old he married a woman named Nell who was then twenty eight years old.

LaVere Redfield began to accumulate his fortune as a young man when he moved with his wife to Los Angeles. During the depression he speculated in land and oil stocks. He bought land at tax sales and stocks at deflated prices. He always practiced thrift as a result of a childhood of poverty.

At the age of thirty seven, after making many millions of dollars, he moved to Nevada in 1935. There he bought a large farm and lived the life of a farmer. He continued to invest in real estate in Nevada and at one time

LaVere Redfield
(Photo Courtesy Paramount Coin Corp.)

owned over eighty square miles in Washaw County where Reno is located. Many of the people farming the land that Redfield owned were eventually given the land with just a promise without any formal deeds. Later he bought a three story stone chateau in Reno from an unsuccessful gubernatorial candidate where he lived for the rest of his life with his wife, Nell.

Redfield never gave the appearance of being a multi-millionaire. He would walk around Reno in old denims and shirts like any other farmer. To save money he would buy cases of bent unlabeled cans of food because they were cheaper. His car was an old pick-up truck which he would roll down the hill from his house in the morning to save the battery. But on the other hand he carried large amounts of cash on his person. At one real estate auction in Reno after being the successful bidder at fifty thousand dollars, he paid off the amount in cash from a shopping bag he had with him.

Redfield distrusted the government and the banks and preferred hard currency. For several decades he accumulated silver coins in his basement. Most of these were silver dollars. Employee friends at the bank would alert him whenever unusual bags of silver dollars were in the banks and Redfield would trade paper money for silver dollars at face

Paramount Redfield Dollar

Redfield Mansion
(Photo Courtesy Paramount Coin Corp.)

value. These he would dump down a coal chute to the basement of his house, where they sat for many years. He was not a collector in the usual sense, but more an accumulator of hard assets.

As a hoarder and accumulator, Redfield did not go through the coins and pick out the best ones. So the bags of silver dollars were the usual mixture of various grades including uncirculated. But he learned which dates commanded some premiums and would obtain these from the banks in favor of the more common date dollars. Thus his accumulation was mostly S mint Morgan and Peace dollars with some Carson City and Philadelphia Mints. Apparently Redfield did some limited trading and selling of silver dollars when to his advantage. But primarily he just preferred to put his extra money into hard assets that some day would bring premium prices.

Not very much is known of Redfield's personal life. He occasionally went on gambling sprees and played blackjack at the Reno casinos for very high stakes. He did not smoke and drank only sparingly with dinner. His world travelling was done in a modest fashion in keeping with his character around Reno.

Redfield received national publicity when his house was robbed in 1952. Burglars removed a four hundred pound safe in a robbery involving jewels, negotiable securities and about one and one half million dollars in cash. A female friend masterminded the burglary and Redfield was reluctantly forced to testify in the case after fleeing to California to avoid it.

In 1963 another burglary took place in which about one hundred thousand silver dollars were taken. That case has never been solved.

Because of his attempts to conceal his wealth, he came under increasing surveillance by the Internal Revenue Service. In 1960, acting as his own lawyer, he was convicted of a $350,000 income tax evasion charge. He was sentenced to serve five years at Terminal Island, but in 1962 was paroled after serving eighteen months. While in jail, he received a free gall bladder operation.

Redfield died on September 6, 1974 in Reno at the age of seventy six. His wife died later in April of 1981. Labeled an eccentric multimillionaire by the press, this frugal and wise investor amassed a fortune estimated between seventy million to two hundred million dollars. At the time of his death, authorities in charge of the estate, and the Internal Revenue Service found 680 bags of precious metals, mostly silver and gold coins, hidden in the basement of his home. Behind false walls constructed of cardboard boxes and concrete under enormous piles of trash were 407,283 Morgan and Peace silver dollars, 351,259 of which were uncirculated. A note found with the hoard to the beneficiary of Redfield's will read "The government can't tax wealth that can't be located. Burn this and tell no one. Carry on as though no coin or currency was left." Ironically, it was the Internal Revenue Authorities who found this note.

Also left by Redfield were uncashed dividend checks dating back to 1959, three containers of stamps, nineteen thousand sets of bronze coins, paper money and huge land holdings. The silver dollars were just a small portion of his huge estate.

Aquisistion Of The Dollars From The Estate

Court battles began immediately after Redfield's death. There were two wills found. The first dated October 10, 1972 was a hand written document leaving half of his estate to his widow and half to a niece in Idaho Falls. A second will dated May 1974, also hand written, left most of the estate to the University of Nevada, The City of Reno, Nevada, Nevada State Prison and Reno's Veteran's Hospital. However, a handwriting expert's testimony proved the second will to be a forgery, so the estate went to his widow and niece.

From October 1974 through April 1975, Stack's of New York, was retained to undertake an appraisal of the numismatic items of the estate. It is doubtful if every item in the estate was examined and listed because of the time and effort it would have taken to physically examine over four hundred thousand coins. Samples were probably taken of the circulated coins and an estimated

Bags of Silver Dollars from Redfield Hoard
(Photo Courtesy Paramount Coin Corp.)

value given. Also samples were probably only taken of the various uncirculated bags to verify the dates and mint marks. Many silver dollars were found loose in the basement of the Redfield house and these were shoveled into bags (to the chagrin of numismatists) prior to inventoried. This mixed up some of the dates and as a result probably precluded a completely accurate inventory by Stacks. This was borne out later by some silver rolls from the Redfield estate containing a few odd dates.

Stack's appraised the portion of the Redfield collection that was later sold to A-Mark for five million, two hundred thousand dollars. They advised the three executrices that disclosure of the coin inventory might depress the market price.

A suit for seven hundred and thirty thousand dollars plus damages was filed by Stack's later in 1976 against the executrices of the estate and their attorney, Gerald C. Smith for their appraisal fee. Stack's alleged that a one thousand dollars per day appraisal services fee had been agreed upon even though it was not in writing and that this appraisal fee would be waived in lieu of a ten percent commission of the gross sales amount of the collection, if the estate utilized the advice and assistance it received from Stack's. Also, the fee would be waived if Stack's handled the liquidation, but as it later turned out, Stack's did not handle the liquidation.

Early in 1975, Steve Markoff, Chairman, and Gary Gordon, President of A-Mark Coins Company of Beverly Hills, California, heard a rumor of a large coin collection in an estate in Reno, Nevada. Contact with the court house in Reno revealed it was the LaVere Redfield estate and the name of the attorney handling the estate. It took six months of talking and interviews with attorneys, judges of court, bankers and accountants before the estate thought A-Mark was serious. Finally after signing a non-disclosure agreement that the nature of the collection could not be revealed under severe financial penalties, A-Mark examined the collection.

On November 4, 1975, the probate court entered an order authorizing the executrices to sell the coins at private sale. A-Mark signed an agreement on December 17, 1975 to purchase a portion of the Redfield collection for approximately five million, nine hundred thousand dollars, to be consummated on January 19, 1976.

Meanwhile, Joel Rettew, a fifty percent owner of Rare Coin Galleries learned of the existence of the Redfield hoard in September 1975 from a Reno physician who was also a coin collector. Rettew contracted one of the executrices, Luana Miles, who advised him to employ Nevada counsel and seek an opportunity to bid on the coins. Rare Coin Galleries did not have sufficient funds to purchase the Redfield coin hoard so they formed a joint venture agreement with Bowers and Ruddy on December 23, 1975. Bowers and Ruddy was a majority owned subsidiary of General Mills who would provide the actual funds for the purchase of the hoard. Although the joint venture contacted the estate they could not obtain any information on the Redfield hoard.

On December 22, 1975 Rettew contracted Stack's and although he did not obtain any information on the hoard, he did learn of a dispute between Stack's and the estate of the two hundred and fifty thousand dollar appraisal fee claimed by Stack's. On December 31, 1975 the joint venture provided a letter agreement to Stack's stating they would pay Stack's a consulting fee of two hundred and fifty thousand dollars for providing an opinion of the value and method of evaluation of the Redfield coins if they ended up buying the estate coins. Stack's then provided Rare Coin Galleries Bowers and Ruddy information on the hoard which they had not provided to anyone else. Bowers and Ruddy used this information to authorize a funding bid for the Redfield hoard from General Mills.

On January 9, 1976 the joint venture filed a bid in the amount of $6,501,156 accompanied by a bank check in that amount. General Mills had authorized Bowers and Ruddy to commit up to seven million dollars of General Mills funds to purchase the Redfield coins. Because of this bid, the probate court found that the November 4, 1975 order for a private sale was erroneously entered because it would result in the sale of the estate assets at less than the best possible price obtainable. Since the coins and title had not yet passed to A-Mark nor had the coins been paid for, the court declared the December 17, 1975 purchase agreement between A-Mark and the estate to be void. The probate court then ordered a public sale to be held on January 27, 1976. A-Mark naturally appealed the probate court's order but the Supreme Court of Nevada affirmed the order.

This public sale of the Redfield hoard took place in the probate court on January 27, 1976. Besides A-Mark and the joint venture of Rare Coin Galleries and Bowers and Merena, other coin dealers present with intention of bidding for the hoard included Leon Hendrickson of Indiana, Jules Karp of New York, John Love of Montana and Carl White. However, the court refused to disclose the official inventory so only A-Mark knew the exact hoard contents and Rare Coin Galleries and Bowers and Ruddy joint venture only had an opinion of the hoard value and a method of evaluation provided by Stack's.

Bidding began at $6.7 million dollars and progressed at one hundred thousand dollar increments between A-Mark and the joint venture. A-Mark won with a bid of seven million, three hundred thousand dollars, the largest single transaction by far for coins up to that time. At the next raise A-Mark would have had to recess and discuss it.

A-Marks primary financing was supplied by Girard Trust Bank of Philadelphia. However, Jules Karp and Leon Hendrickson each advanced A-Mark three hundred and fifty thousand dollars for a total of seven hundred thousand dollars in a joint agreement which was also used to purchase the Redfield hoard. A dispute arose between A-Mark and Karp and Hendrickson. A-Mark contended that the advance was in the nature of a sixty day loan, while Karp and Hendrickson contended that it was for the purchase of a proportionate interest in the Redfield collection. A compromise settlement was reached in which Karp and Hendrickson received seven hundred thousand dollars plus one hundred and fifty 1879-CC MS-60 silver dollars, fourteen thousand common uncirculated silver dollars dated prior to 1904 and seven thousand circulated silver dollars. They also agreed not to disclose any information concerning the value of the coins of the Redfield collection.

A-Mark brought suit against the Redfield estate seeking a reduction in the price of the coins of one million four hundred thousand dollars, the difference between the original agreement and the later bid price. They alleged they already had contractual rights to the property. However, the Supreme Court of Nevada affirmed the probate court's power to annul its order for a private sale and direct, instead, a public sale. A probate court has jurisdiction to vacate a prior order upon learning that it was entered into through mistake.

A suit was also brought by A-Mark against General Mills, Bowers & Ruddy, Rare Coin Galleries, James Ruddy, David Bowers and Joel Rettew, alleging intentional interference with a contractual relationship with an advantageous business relationship. However, the trial court concluded in the case, which dragged on until 1983, that A-Mark never had a valid contract with the Redfield estate for the purchase of the Redfield collection with which the defendants could have interfered and that the conduct of the defendants in seeking to bid on the coins was not a wrong act against A-Mark.

Dispersion Of The Hoard

A-Mark took physical possession of the coins in Reno, Nevada. Transporting 407,596 silver dollars in 441 bags weighing twelve and one half tons and worth at least $7.3 million was not a simple task. A Brinks semi-trailer truck, lined with sixteen inches of foam rubber was used to transport the coins over a secret route escorted by the State Highway patrol. While the bags of coins were being loaded into the truck at Reno in a very secret operation, someone driving by saw a man holding a shot gun and thought the bank was being robbed. Shortly after the police, newspaper and television people showed up. The coins had to be locked up again until the circus died down.

The large loan A-Mark had used to purchase the coins had to be repaid as quickly as possible to minimize the interest charges. But such a large quantity of silver dollars, with supposedly 351,259 grading uncirculated, could not be dumped onto the market all at one time without depressing their prices. A-Mark enacted a three year marketing plan for most of the dollars with planned distribution well into the 1980's.

Three coin firms consisting of Paramount International Coin, Robert L Hughes and John Love were designated as primary distributors and each received major portions of the Redfield hoard from A-Mark. They had to sign agreements which stipulated the dispersal plan and that the contents of the hoard would not be disclosed. Paramount and Hughes did aggressive marketing with full page ads in numismatic newspapers and magazines plus flyers. Paramount packaged the dollars in sonically sealed plastic holders identifying each coin's grade and that it was from the Redfield collection. Hughes placed the dollars in a custom holder with a certificate identifying it as a Redfield dollar plus a photo of the front page of the *Coin World* article on the Redfield hoard sale. All of the dollars were heavily promoted as being part of the Redfield hoard.

Although the exact quantity of dates and mints of the Redfield dollars has not been disclosed, Redfield dates are known through the extensive advertising. The Redfield dates are listed in *Table 10-1* (with estimated quantities of bags indicated taken from John Highfill's book *The Comprehensive U.S. Silver Dollar Encyclopedia*).

The hoard contained virtually no scarcer date O Mints and relatively few P Mints, being heavy in S Mints. As expected in a hoard of this size, many of the dollars were of very high quality while many were also dirty or spotted and heavily bagmarked.

Through clever promotion strategy, the market reacted positively to the availability of the Redfield dollars. Overall, the market was stimulated by new collectors of dollars being added because of their availability. Specific Redfield dates did not have any uniform pattern of price changes in the late 1970s when they were heavily marketed. Some dates were up in grade MS-65 but down in grade MS-60, such as the 1886-S, 1888-S, 1889-S and 1895-S. Overall the Redfield Peace dollar dates moved up with the market. The later date Morgan S Mints carried the stigma of a Redfield date for many years with relatively slow price appreciation except for the 1901-S which was

Table 10-1 REDFIELD HOARD DATES

Estimated Quantities of Bags					
1878-S	Dozens	1889-S	3-5	1898-S	Under 1
1879-CC	½	1890-P	Many	1899-S	Under 1
1879-S	Dozens	1890-S	Many	1900-S	Few
1879-S Rev. '78	3	1891-CC	3-5	1902-S	1
		1891-S	Many	1903-P	Under 1
1880-S	Dozens	1892-P	1-2	1921-S	Under 1
1881-S	Dozens (Most common)	1892-CC	2-4	1922-S	Few
		1893-P	1-3	1923-S	Few
1882-S	Dozens	1893-CC	Few	1924-S	Under 1
1883-S	¼	1895-S	¼	1925-S	3-4
1885-CC	1	1896-P	Couple Dozen	1926-S	Many
1886-S	Several	1896-S	Under 1	1927-S	3-5
1887-S	Many	1897-P	Couple Dozen	1928-S	Several
1888-S	2	1897-S	Couple Dozen	1935-S	Under 1
1889-P	Many	1898-P	Couple Dozen		

not a Redfield date. It was not until 1982 and 1983 that the 1890-S and 1891-S had the Redfield stigma lifted and made exceptionally rapid advances in price. The common date early S mints followed the general market advances of 1979 through 1984 because the Redfield quantities of those dates were rather small with little market impact compared to the thousands of bags of these dates widely available throughout the country.

The Redfield hoard had the greatest market impact on the scarcer S Mint dates because of the significant quantities of uncirculated specimens suddenly available. In general, it had a slightly depressing effect on their price advances over the years coupled later with a slow market on the more expensive coins in the early and mid-1980s. But within ten years of the Redfield hoard making its first splash on the dollar market, the stimulus or stigma of these dollars had all but faded away.

CONTINENTAL-ILLINOIS BANK HOARD

This hoard of Morgan silver dollars was clothed in secrecy until the publishing of some details about it in John Highfill's book, *The Comprehensive U.S. Silver Dollar Encyclopedia*. It was the largest single, private hoard of U.S. silver dollars to be released into the coin market since the final dispersal of silver dollars by the Treasury Department in the early 1960's.

During the final rush for silver dollars from the Treasury Department in 1962 and 1963, many millions of Morgan and Peace silver dollars were purchased at face value. These were resold in the open market in the mid-60's at slightly over face value. Many private individuals accumulated hoards of these cartwheels from tens to hundreds of bags. The Redfield hoard was probably the largest hoard of a single individual that was held for many years. A number of coin dealers handled hundreds of bags of silver dollars but these generally were turned over and resold as quickly as possible so they really weren't considered hoards. The casinos in Nevada kept considerable stocks of silver for use in gambling. But these disappeared when the price of silver rose above $1.29 per ounce in 1967 and the bullion content of a silver dollar became worth more than one dollar.

Some banks accumulated hoards of silver dollars as collateral for loans. Most of the bank hoards were probably bags of coins left over from the early 1960s when silver dollars traded freely in commerce and most banks had some stock of silver dollars as well as other coins. The banks ceased to give silver dollars out shortly after the Treasury Department exhausted their supply in 1964 and they traded at over face value on the open market.

The Continental-Illinois Bank of Chicago released the largest known hoard of about 1,500 bags of Morgan silver dollars to the coin market in 1982-84. Because of financial problems, the bank was forced to sell its hoard of silver dollars at that time. Ed Milas of RARCOA, in Chicago, purchased all of the bags of silver dollars sold by the bank. The purchase price or details of the transaction have never been made public. But estimates have put the value of the transaction at around fifty million dollars.

The recession of 1982-83 and tumble of bullion prices from the 1980 peak had depressed the coin market. Coin prices had fallen severely and activity was slow. With these economic conditions, RARCOA and two other firms, SilverTowne of Winchester, Indiana, and Colonial Coins of Houston, Texas, were selected to help disperse the hoard of silver dollars. The coins were marketed in a quiet and controlled way. The deal was kept in secrecy and over a year was taken to disperse the silver dollars. Most of the employees of these three firms were not aware of the size or details of the hoard. This was done to not adversely affect the coin market.

Exact quantities of the silver dollars by date and mint in this hoard have not been released. What has been published to date reveals that there were about 1,000 bags of a thousand coins each of uncirculated coins and about 500 bags of circulated coins. The Brilliant Uncirculated coins dated from 1878-1904 with most of them being 1878-1888 with a lot of common S Mint coins. The quality of these BU coins were very high, since most of them came from the bank in the original mint canvas bags. Because of the long-term storage in canvas bags, many of the coins had beautiful toning on them. The AU coins were 1878-1885 with most of them being 1879-1882 O-Mint coins.

Of the known primary hoard distribution, SilverTowne handled at least 350 BU bags and 500 AU bags. Colonial Coins handled about 500 BU bags which were primarily 1879-1882 S-Mint coins, 1883-1885 O-Mint coins, and 1885-1887 P-Mint coins. The exceptional quality of these common date coins was, in general, far superior to those of the Redfield hoard. They were stored in the original mint bags and carefully handled by the distributors. In contrast, the Redfield bags of coins were thrown down a chute to his basement. Some of these bags broke open and the coins were later shoveled up. Some were supposedly contaminated with peach juice from ruptured cans that were stored in his basement.

During the release of the Continental-Illinois Bank hoard, late in 1982 through 1984, the coin market picked up again. The demand for nice silver dollars was high and their availability actually fueled the increased activity. Through careful marketing and an overall rising coin market, this large hoard of silver dollars was readily absorbed and prices actually increased substantially for quality coins.

FURTHER REFERENCES

Please check Amazon Kindle for Michael S. Fey, Ph.D., and Leroy Van Allen & A. George Mall is publications. For hard copy print of books, please contact Dr. Fey at RCI, P.O. Box C, Ironia, N J 07845 or eMail: Feyms@aol.com.

Hard copy books are also available at *The Institute for Silver Dollar Education and Research*, at website: *Ilovesilverdollars.org* or by contacting Executive Director John Baumgart at John.Baumgart@comcast.net

Amazon Kindle

Fey, Michael S. 2019. *The Complete Virtual Guide to Pricing Your Morgan Silver Dollars*. 286 pp. RCI

Van Allen, Leroy, & A. George Mallis. 2023. *Part I or II or III of Three. Comprehensive Catalog and Encyclopedia or Morgan & Peace Dollars*. RCI Total 520 pp.

Leroy Van Allen. 2011. *Wonders of Morgan Dollars*. 139 pp. RCI

Leroy Van Allen. 2013. *Wonders of Peace Dollars*. 273 pp. RCI

Leroy Van Allen. 2006. *Morgan Dollars 8 & 7 Over 8 Tail Feather Story*. 52 pp. RCI

Leroy Van Allen. 2010. *1878 P 7 Tail Feather Morgan Dollar Attribution Guide*. 130 pp. RCI

Leroy Van Allen. 2006. *1878 S Morgan Dollar Attribution Guide*. 139 pp. RCI

Fey, Michael S. 2009 The Top 100 Morgan Dollar Varieties: The VAM Keys

FURTHER REFERENCES

Hard Copy Books

Fey, Michael S. 2019. The Top 100 Morgan Dollar Varieties: The VAM Keys. 286 pp. RCI

Fey, Michael S. 2008. *A Decade of Top 100 Insights*. RCI 174 pp.

Van Allen, Leroy. 1991. *RotaFlip Die Rotation Booklet and Guide*. 1991. RCI

Kimpton, M.D., Mark. 2005. *Elite Clashed Morgan Dollars*. RCI 160 pp

Van Allen, Leroy, & A. George Mallis. 2023. *Comprehensive Catalog and Encyclopedia or Morgan & Peace Dollars*. RCI Total 520 pp.

Van Allen, Leroy 2011. *Wonders of Morgan Dollars*. 139 pp. RCI

Van Allen, Leroy 2013. *Wonders of Peace Dollars*. 273 pp. RCI

Van Allen, Leroy 2006. *Morgan Dollars 8 & 7 Over 8 Tail Feather Story*. 52 pp. RCI

Van Allen, Leroy 2010. *1878 P 7 Tail Feather Morgan Dollar Attribution Guide*. 130 pp. RCI

Van Allen, Leroy 2006. *1878 S Morgan Dollar Attribution Guide*. 139 pp. RCI

Van Allen, Leroy 2013. *Die Gouges and Scratches Peace Dollar Attribution Guide. 109 pp* RCI

Van Allen, Leroy 2008. *1921 Scribbles Morgan Dollar Attribution Guide*. 234 pp. RCI

Van Allen, Leroy. 2013. *Misplaced Date Digits Morgan Dollar Attribution Guide. 57 pp* RCI

Van Allen, Leroy. 2017. *Dashed Under 8 Morgan Dollar Attribution Guide*. 53 pp. RCI

Van Allen, Leroy. 2009. *Overdates and Over Mint Marks of Morgan Dollar Attribution Guide*. 53 pp. RCI

Van Allen, Leroy. 2015. *Denticle & Die Impressions Morgan Dollar Attribution Guide*. 109 pp. RCI

Van Allen, Leroy. 2009. *1921 P Infrequently Reeded or Wide Reeding Morgan Dollar Attribution Guide*. 31 pp. RCI

Van Allen, Leroy. 2011 *Amazing Changing 1921 S VAM 1B Thorn Head Morgan Dollar*. 2011. 22 pp. RCI

Van Allen, Leroy. 2009. *1889 P Doubled Ear Morgan Dollar Attribution Guide*. 32 pp. RCI

Van Allen, Leroy. 2016. *Micro o and Other Counterfeit Morgan and Peace Dollars. 191 pp* RCI

Van Allen, Leroy. 2005. *Micro o Mint Mark on Morgan Dollars*. 32 pp. RCI

Van Allen, Leroy. 2005. *Die Markers for 1921 Morgan and Peace Proof Dollars*. 9 pp. RCI

Van Allen, Leroy and Baumgart, John. 1992-Date Various VAM Book Yearly Supplements. RCI

www.ingramcontent.com/pod-product-compliance
Lightning Source LLC
Chambersburg PA
CBHW061810290426

44110CB00026B/2841